70

NEW

10

The Bible for Students
of Literature and Art

G. B. HARRISON was born in 1894 and educated at the University of Cambridge. He was for many years on the faculty of the University of London, whence (after a period in Canada) he came to the University of Michigan in 1949. He has written many books on Shakespeare and the Elizabethan period, of which the most important are the five volumes of *Elizabethan* and *Jacobean Journals, Elizabethan Plays and Players,* and *Shakespeare at Work.* In 1962 he set forth his notions on the teaching of English literature in *Profession of English.* He has also edited *Shakespeare: the Complete Works.*

The Bible for Students of Literature and Art

Selected,

with an Introduction by

G. B. HARRISON

Anchor Books
Doubleday & Company, Inc.
Garden City, New York

The Biblical passages included in this volume are taken from *The Reader's Bible*, published in 1951 by Oxford University Press, and reprinted by permission of Oxford University Press.

The Bible for Students of Literature and Art was published simultaneously in a hardbound edition by Doubleday & Company, Inc.

Anchor Books edition: 1964

PREFACE

From the fall of Rome to the end of the nineteenth century, educated readers shared certain literary experiences, of which familiarity with the Bible was the most common. Today most students of literature lack this kind of education and have only the haziest knowledge of the book or of its contents, with the result that they inevitably miss much of the meaning and significance of many works of past generations. Similarly, students of art will miss some of the meaning of the pictures and sculptures of the past unless they know at firsthand the stories by which artists were first inspired.

There are many ways of reading the Bible. Christian theologians regard the Old Testament as a forecast of events which culminated in the Incarnation of Jesus Christ. A Jewish scholar, to whom Christianity is but one of several divergences from Judaism, takes an entirely different view of the Bible and of the Messianic prophecies; to him there is no "old" testament, and he rejects the "new." But because the biblical passages included in this volume have been selected for their literary and artistic significance, the emphasis and framework of this book must in some degree be Christian, since English writers from the beginning to the present century were brought up in the Christian tradition.

In making this selection from the Bible I have chosen those stories and passages to which a student is most likely to find reference in his reading. In selecting passages from the synoptic gospels, I have preferred to give extracts from each rather than to attempt any kind of continuous narrative compiled from all three, though for the events in the last week of Jesus' life on earth I have included Luke's account entire, with a few details from Matthew and Mark. I have deliberately refrained from discussion of those textual and doctrinal matters which concern students of scripture and theology—evolution, the composition of the narratives in Genesis, the synoptic problems, and the rest. A student of literature to whom the Bible is a new experience should first encounter the book as literature.

The translation chosen is the King James version, which for three hundred and fifty years has been the most familiar to English-speaking writers and readers of all kinds. The present text is based on *The Reader's Bible* and set out in a modern format. I would express my thanks to the Oxford University Press for permission to use this handsome volume. I would also thank those colleagues and friends who read this work in manuscript and made many valuable suggestions, especially Dr. A. K. Stevens, Rt. Rev. John F. Bradley, Dr. David Granskou, and Dr. David Sidorsky.

G. B. Harrison

CONTENTS

THE NEW TESTAMENT

INTRODUCTION

1. The Books of the Bible: the Old Testament

The Bible—the word is a latinized form of a Greek word meaning The Book—is not a book but a collection of many books, written and compiled over a period of fifteen hundred years and more. It is in two parts, called the Old Testament and the New Testament. The Old Testament is a selection of the religious books of the Jews who are descended from the twelve tribes founded by the sons of the Patriarch Jacob (or Israel). These books are very varied in subject, content, and date of writing.

The first five books of the Old Testament are known as the Pentateuch: Genesis (or the beginning), Exodus (the way out, or the departure from Egypt), Leviticus (the laws given by Moses in the desert to his followers), Numbers (mainly genealogies and itineraries), and Deuteronomy (which repeats much of Leviticus in the form of discourses by Moses before he died). These are followed by Joshua (how the Israelites conquered and occupied Palestine), Judges (the turbulent period after the death of Joshua), two books called Samuel (the story of the Israelites from the time they united into a kingdom to the long reign of David), two books of Kings (which tell of the death of David and the split into the two kingdoms of Israel and Judah until both kingdoms were destroyed and the Jews carried away into Babylon), Ezra and Nehemiah (the return of the captives from Babylonia and the re-establishment in Palestine). Two subsidiary books, called

Chronicles, contain parts omitted from Kings. The period from the return to Palestine (c. 538 B.C.) to the birth of Jesus in 8–6 B.C.[1] is partly filled by the two books of Maccabees, which carry the narrative down to 135 B.C.

These books are all more or less historical, but the writers and compilers were not so much concerned with recording the history of the descendants of Abraham as with the story of their relationship with God.

In addition, there are eighteen books of the Prophets, of whom the most important are Isaiah, Jeremiah, Ezekiel and Daniel—political, moral, and religious exhortations, for the most part, in times of crisis, but regarded as especially important both by Jews and by Christians alike for their prophecies concerning the Messiah—the Saviour who was to appear to restore his People. The Prophets wrote during the later generations of the two kingdoms and during and after the captivity in Babylon.

As well there is a collection of religious poetry—the Psalms of David, though not all are his composing; some stories, Ruth, Judith, Esther, and Tobit; a long philosophical dialogue in verse, which is almost a drama—the Book of Job; several books of wise sayings—Proverbs, Ecclesiastes, The Wisdom of Solomon and Ecclesiasticus; and what is on the surface a collection of passionate love poems, called variously The Canticle of Canticles, The Song of Songs, and The Song of Solomon.

Some of the books are very ancient. Traditionally, the Pentateuch was written by Moses and though modern experts agree that in its present form it is much later, at least some parts may be as early. There is thus great variety in the Old Testament. Most of the books were written in Hebrew, the ancient language of the Jews, but not all the original Hebrew versions survive. Some exist only in the Greek translation known as the Septuagint, made in Alexandria about 250 B.C.

[1] See Appendix 1.

The books which survive only in the Septuagint version are Tobit, Judith, The Wisdom of Solomon, Ecclesiasticus, I and II Esdras, I and II Maccabees, as well as some portions of Daniel and Esther. These are not regarded as part of the inspired scriptures by Protestants (or by Jews) and are therefore usually omitted from their Bibles, or, if printed, are called the Apocrypha. They were, however, accepted by the Council of Trent and are thus considered by Catholics to be "canonical." "Canonical" means "according to the rule," that is, judged to be in a special way inspired and of greater significance than other books. The Jewish canon of the scriptures—the books of the Old Testament—was generally accepted by about A.D. 100.

Most European writers of the past were educated in the Christian tradition, and a detailed knowledge of the Bible was an essential part of their schooling. To Christians as to Jews the Old Testament is far more than a collection of ancient religious books; it is a record of the past and future relationship between man and God.

2. The Old Testament: the Narratives

The pattern of the relationship between God and man begins with the creation of the world in six stages, culminating with the first man, Adam, and Eve, his mate. Man and woman are set in a paradise—the Garden of Eden—but they are forbidden to eat the fruit of the Tree of the Knowledge of Good and Evil. The Serpent persuades Eve to disobey the command; she eats and gives some of the fruit to Adam. This, in Christian theology, is the first or Original Sin. Thereafter mankind is under a curse for Adam's disobedience. Adam and Eve are cast out of the garden and their life becomes hard and full of sorrows. Two sons are born to them: Cain, who is a tiller of the ground, and Abel, who is a shepherd. Cain grows jealous of his brother and kills him, thereby committing the first murder; and he becomes "a fugitive and a vagabond in the earth."

In time the human race multiplies and grows so evil that God determines to destroy his own creation, except for the one righteous man, Noah, and his family. Noah is warned that a great flood will overwhelm the world, and he is commanded to build an ark (or boat) into which his wife, his three sons and their wives, and a selection of the beasts are collected and thereby saved. Thereafter mankind again multiplies.

The historical record of the Jewish people begins at the twelfth chapter of Genesis with the call of Abram. Abram lived in Ur of the Chaldees[2] in Babylonia. He was commanded to leave his country and go to the land of Canaan. Abram obeyed the call and God appeared to him and said, "I am the Almighty God; walk before me, and be thou perfect. And I will make my covenant between me and thee, and will multiply thee exceedingly." This was the original covenant (or Old Testament), and marked the separation of Abraham (as he was thenceforward called) and his descendants from the rest of mankind. As a sign of the separation, Abraham was commanded that he and all the male members of his race should be circumcised. But as yet Abraham had no legitimate son and Sarah his wife was an old woman; she laughed at the prophecy. Nevertheless in her age she conceived a son who was called Isaac.

When the boy grew up, Abraham sent his servant to his own country to find Isaac a wife from his own kin. The man returned with Rebekah, who bore Isaac twin sons, Esau and Jacob. Isaac loved Esau, who was a hunter; but Jacob was his mother's favorite. At length Isaac grew old and blind, and knowing that he was soon to die, he wished to bless his elder son Esau. Rebekah heard his words, and while Esau was away hunting, she dressed Jacob in Esau's

[2] The ruins of Ur of the Chaldees are still conspicuous in the desert a few miles from Nasiriya on the Euphrates.

clothing and sent him in to the old man. Thus Jacob cheated his brother of his blessing, and then, fearing Esau's wrath, he fled away to Laban, his mother's brother.

Laban had two daughters, Leah and Rachel. Jacob loved Rachel and agreed to serve Laban for seven years that he might marry her, but at the marriage Laban substituted Leah. So Jacob served Laban for another seven years for Rachel. He became very prosperous until Laban grew jealous. Jacob then determined to go back to Canaan with his four wives and their eleven sons, of whom Joseph, Rachel's son, was his favorite. Jacob was afraid of Esau and to appease him he sent his family and flocks ahead; and that night "there wrestled a man with him until the breaking of the day." When morning came, Jacob would not let the man go until he had blessed him. "And he said, 'Let me go, for the day breaketh.' And he said, 'I will not let thee go, except thou bless me.' And he said unto him, 'What is thy name?' And he said, 'Jacob.' And he said, 'Thy name shall be called no more Jacob, but Israel: for as a prince hast thou power with God and with men, and hast prevailed.'" The brothers met and parted without strife. So Jacob and his sons settled in Canaan, but on the way there Rachel had died in giving birth to Benjamin.

Because he was their father's favorite, Joseph was hated by his brothers, especially when he told them of his dreams which signified that he would become their ruler. At first they were for killing him, but they traded him to some Ishmeelites who sold him as a slave to Potiphar, captain of the soldiers of Pharaoh, king of Egypt. Joseph was so trusted by his master that he was set in charge of the household, but Potiphar's wife fell in love with him, and when Joseph would not yield to her love, she accused him falsely and he was put in prison where he was so highly regarded that he was made overseer of the prisoners. Among the prisoners were Pharaoh's chief butler and chief baker; both had prophetic dreams which Joseph interpreted truly.

Two years later Pharaoh himself was disturbed by dreams which none of his wise men could interpret. The chief butler remembered Joseph, who was sent for. He interpreted Pharaoh's dreams as forewarnings of great plenty to be followed by great scarcity, and Pharaoh was so much impressed by Joseph's wisdom that Joseph was made overseer of the land of Egypt, and married an Egyptian wife.

In due course the famine spread, and Jacob and his sons were in need of corn. He sent his sons down to Egypt to buy corn but he kept Benjamin at home. Joseph recognized his brethren, but they did not recognize him. He treated them roughly and demanded that they bring Benjamin. On the second journey to Egypt they brought Benjamin. Then Joseph revealed himself and sent for his old father and all his tribe to come and live in Egypt, where they settled in Goshen.

Eventually Joseph and all his generation died, and the Israelites multiplied. The new Pharaoh oppressed them first by forced labor, and then by the command that all male children should be killed at birth; but the infant Moses was concealed by his mother who set him adrift on the river in a basket which was taken up by Pharaoh's daughter, who adopted the child as her own. When Moses grew up, he visited his own people and slew an Egyptian who was beating a Hebrew. He was obliged to flee and took refuge with Jethro in Midian. Here God called him and commanded him to go back to Egypt to gather his people together and lead them out of Egypt to the land of Canaan. Pharaoh was very unwilling to listen even when Moses and Aaron his brother showed many signs of their mission in the form of plagues which afflicted the Egyptians until the final visitation when all the first-born in Egypt were slain in one night.

Moses led the Israelites across the Red Sea and into the desert. When they reached Mount Sinai, Moses withdrew to the mountain to commune with God. Here he was given the Ten Commandments and the laws by which the Israelites were to be bound; above all that they should preserve their pure worship of the one God. When Moses came down from the mountain he found that the people had already fallen into idolatry and were dancing round a golden calf.

For the next forty years Moses tried to mold his followers, always mutinous and discontented, into a people. To give form to their worship, a movable shrine—the tabernacle[8]—was built which housed in its inner sanctuary the ark of the covenant—a chest covered with gold and surmounted by two golden cherubim which remained the most sacred emblem until the Babylonian captivity.

Moses died within sight of the Promised Land and Joshua took over the leadership. He led the people to the capture of Jericho; and finally most of the land of Canaan was subdued and divided among the twelve tribes. After Joshua's death the Israelites continually lapsed into idolatry and were oppressed by their neighbors until they were rescued by local leaders or "judges." Of these the most important were the prophetess Deborah, Gideon, Jephthah, and Samson the strong man.

The last of the judges was Samuel the prophet. In his old age the people demanded that he should give them a king, like their neighbors. Very reluctantly Samuel anointed Saul, who became the first of the kings of Israel. In the beginning of his reign Saul was victorious over his enemies, especially the Philistines, but he disobeyed the divine command and Samuel was sent to anoint David, then a young man, to succeed Saul. David was famous first for slaying the Philistine giant Goliath with a sling stone. He was also a singer and musician; and when Saul fell into fits of madness David would play to him. David became so great a leader that Saul grew to hate him and tried to kill him.

[8] See Appendix 3.

So David fled and became an exile until Saul and his son Jonathan were killed in battle by the Philistines.

David now became king of the tribe of Judah, but the other tribes remained faithful to the descendants of Saul. Eventually David subdued them and was anointed king of all Israel. He captured Jerusalem from the original inhabitants and made it his capital. In his old age David had to face the rebellion of his son Absalom. When David died as a very old man the kingdom was more firmly established than at any time before or since. David and Moses are thus regarded as the two great figures of ancient Jewish history.

David was succeeded by his son Solomon, who was renowned for his wisdom, his wealth, and his buildings, above all the great Temple at Jerusalem which thereafter became the Holy City. In later life Solomon degenerated; he "loved many strange women" from the Canaanite tribes, by whom he was turned away to worship the gods of the heathen. Solomon had oppressed his people and made many enemies, among them Jeroboam. When Solomon died and was succeeded by his son Rehoboam, Jeroboam led the people against Rehoboam, demanding that their burdens should be lifted. Rehoboam refused. Jeroboam and his following revolted and founded a new kingdom of Israel, leaving only the tribes of Judah and Benjamin faithful to the house of David.

Jeroboam set up a rival center of worship at Bethel lest his people should be encouraged to go up to Jerusalem to worship and so be led back to the house of David. As a result the Israelites lapsed into the paganism of their neighbors. For the next two hundred years the two kingdoms of Israel and Judah existed side by side, sometimes warring against each other, sometimes in alliance against their neighbors.

Of the kings of Israel, the most powerful was Ahab, who married the Zidonian princess Jezebel; both worshiped the local god Baal and persecuted the true worshipers of Yahweh.[4] Naturally both were detested by the sacred writers. Ahab fortified and adorned Samaria, his capital, and he allied with Jehoshaphat, king of Judah. He was killed in battle in 853 B.C. Nevertheless, in spite of the falling away of the kings, this was the great age of the prophets in both kingdoms.

In 721 B.C. Shalmaneser, king of Assyria, captured Samaria and took away the surviving people. The little kingdom of Judah lasted until 587 B.C. when Nebuchadnezzar, king of Babylon, took Jerusalem, and sacked and burned the Temple. He then carried away the leading Jews to Babylonia, leaving only the poorest of the inhabitants in Palestine.

Fifty years later, after Cyrus, king of Persia, conquered the Babylonians and decreed that the Jews might return to Palestine, a party went back to resettle Jerusalem. In spite of the bitter hostility of the people of the land, the Temple at Jerusalem was rebuilt by 515 B.C., and gradually Jewish life was restored. There had been a great change in the spirit of the Jews during the captivity. All temptation to fall away into idolatry had gone, and instead they developed that rigid faith and exclusive nationalism which ever since has been a notable characteristic of the Jewish people.

But the troubles continued. The Persians were in turn conquered by Alexander the Great; and after his death Palestine became the battleground of the warring generals who succeeded to his kingdom. Some of the events of those years are related in the two books of the Maccabees, which record the heroic leadership of the sons of Mattathiah.

The religious history of the Jews, as told in the Old Testament, ends with the Second Book of the Maccabees. Historically the date was about 135 B.C.

A century later (30 B.C.) Palestine had become part of the Roman Empire, administered by a Roman procurator,

[4] See Appendix 2.

although the Jews were nominally subjects of their King Herod. They were allowed to follow their own national customs and religion, and the Temple sacrifices and services were maintained. In all their difficulties, devout Jews still hoped for ultimate delivery through the divine Messiah (or Christ), whose coming was so often foreshadowed in the words of the Prophets.

At this point Jews and Christians part company. Jews deny the belief of Christians that the promised Messiah did indeed come in the person of Jesus Christ, son of Mary the Virgin, and that he revealed his divinity through his life, his teaching, his miracles, and above all his resurrection after he had died on the cross. During his lifetime Jesus gathered a band of disciples from whom he chose twelve and whom he trained to establish his spiritual kingdom on earth—the Christian Church. These things are the theme of the New Testament. The "Old Testament" was the original covenant made between Yahweh and Abraham and renewed with Moses, which was superseded in the "New Testament" offered by Jesus to his followers (p. 434).

3. The New Testament

The New Testament is a collection of what scholars call "original sources" for the origin and doctrine of the Christian Church. It begins with four Gospels—"gospel" means good news—Matthew, Mark, Luke, and John, which tell of the birth, life, teaching, miracles, death, and resurrection of Jesus. The first three Gospels are called "synoptic" (literally, having the same view) for the writers have much in common and their narratives are founded on the same sources; the fourth—John—tells far more of the higher teachings of Jesus and is less concerned with the details of his life. Then comes the Acts of the Apostles which relates the ascension of Jesus forty days after his resurrection, the descent of the Holy Spirit on the Apostles ten days later, the first preachings of his followers, and the spread of the Christian Faith first at Jerusalem and then, after the conversion of Paul, throughout the Roman world. There is also a collection of nine Epistles (or letters) written by Paul to the congregations which he had founded and four personal Epistles; the Epistle to the Hebrews; an Epistle written by James; two by Peter; three by John; and one by Jude. Finally, a book of allegorical and mystical visions called the Apocalypse or Revelation of John.

All these come down in the Greek which was the universal second language at the beginning of the first century A.D. The books of the New Testament were written between A.D. 55 and 100. These books are but a small selection of early Christian writings which still survive. Apart from the many works of the early Fathers of the Church (that is, writers of the first five centuries), there is a considerable collection of early Gospels, Epistles, Visions, and Sayings. Some were fictions, either composed by pious enthusiasts or invented to support one or another of the early heresies. By A.D. 360 the books of the New Testament as now known were accepted by the Church as authentic, and in 397 at the Council of Carthage they were formally declared to be the Canon of the Christian Scriptures.

The earliest documents of Christianity are the Epistles of Paul; it was some time before there was any gospel or other written account of the Founder. Teaching in early times was not from text books, but in the form of oral instructions which were memorized and repeated to the teacher. This was the Jewish method of instruction, and Jewish teachers and pupils developed large and accurate memories. At first the Christian Faith was handed along by word of mouth. The first evangelists ("evangel" has the same meaning as "gospel") were the Apostles chosen by Jesus himself and others of his disciples appointed to teach converts.

This kind of oral teaching was called *catechesis* (literally "echoing"); and an evangelist was one who echoed the teaching which he had himself received. As Christianity spread, oral teaching was no longer adequate and written testimony was needed. The Gospels are thus written records of the *catecheses* of different Apostles. Before long a number of these records were in circulation, but four only —the four Gospels included in the New Testament—were generally accepted and are often quoted by the early Fathers. The Church had been in existence for more than a quarter of a century before the first Gospel was written.

Several early traditions are preserved in *The Ecclesiastical History* of Bishop Eusebius Pamphili of Cæsarea (A.D. c. 264–c. 349), the first historian of the Church. His history takes the story down to 328, and was compiled largely from earlier sources. Eusebius quotes from Irenaeus (c. 120–202): "Matthew published among the Hebrews a written Gospel in their own dialect, while Peter and Paul were preaching in Rome and establishing the Church. And after their deaths, Mark, the disciple and interpreter of Peter, also handed down in writing what was preached by Peter; and Luke, the follower of Paul, put in a book the Gospel as preached by him. Then John, the disciple of the Lord (who also leaned on his breast) also gave out his Gospel while living at Ephesus in Asia" (V, viii, 1).

Of Mark's Gospel, Eusebius quotes from the lost work of Papias: "Mark, having become Peter's interpreter, wrote down accurately, although not in order, what he remembered of the sayings and doings of the Lord; for he was neither a hearer nor a follower of the Lord, but later, as I have said, of Peter, who taught to suit the occasion, but without making any arrangement of the Lord's sayings. So Mark did not err in thus writing down some things as he remembered them; for he gave attention to one thing: to leave out nothing that he had heard, and to make no false statement" (III, xxxix, 15).

Of Luke, Eusebius records that he was born at Antioch and was by training a physician. He had long been a com-

panion of Paul and was on familiar terms with the rest of
the Apostles, from whom he gathered materials for his
Gospel, which was based on the traditions of those who
had been witnesses from the beginning. The Acts of the
Apostles he compiled not from hearsay but from the evidence of his own eyes. (III, iv, 6.)

According to Eusebius and to other ancient authorities
John wrote his Gospel at the request of his disciples while
living at Ephesus in Asia Minor; but this was long after
the other three when John was a very old man.

These traditions were generally accepted until the rise
of the "higher criticism" in the early nineteenth century.
Since then, biblical scholars of differing schools have questioned the traditions and put forth a variety of conflicting
views, which, however, are rather the concern of students
of the Bible than of students of literature and art.

4. Translations of the Bible

Early Christians of the Roman world read their Bibles
—both Old Testament and New—in Greek; but by the
fourth century Latin was taking the place of Greek as the
second language of the civilized world as today English is
replacing French. Several Latin versions of the Bible were
made. About 383, Jerome, then living in Rome, was
asked by Pope Damasus to revise the current Latin version
of the New Testament. On the death of the Pope, Jerome
left Rome and went to live in a monastery in Bethlehem.
Jerome was a great scholar and linguist; he learned Hebrew from a rabbi; and in Palestine between 390 and 405
he translated the Old Testament into Latin. Jerome's Latin
Bible is known as the Vulgate; it was a skillful translation,
a task which in the words of their preface to the King
James Bible the translators note "he performed with that
evidence of great learning, judgement, industry, and faithfulness, that he hath for ever bound the Church unto him
in a debt of special remembrance and thankfulness." The

xxii   INTRODUCTION

Vulgate has remained the authorized version of the scriptures for the Catholic Church, and was indeed the Bible for most Europeans till the translations into the vernacular of the sixteenth and seventeenth centuries. Since Latin was the universal language for educated persons in the Middle Ages and until the end of the eighteenth century, Jerome's Vulgate was sufficient for most purposes. Translation into English might have been made earlier than it was had not the Bible become a matter of bitter religious and political controversy.

The first popular translation into English was that known as "Wycliffe's Bible." John Wycliffe was a contemporary of Chaucer. Wycliffe became a heretic. He began by attacking the abuses of the Church, especially its wealth, but he went on to deny its authority and the validity of much of the dogma. Like other reformers, he appealed to the Bible as the sole rule of faith. As a natural result English versions of the Bible (translated from the Vulgate) were circulating in England by the end of the fourteenth century; and they had the popularity of all forbidden books. Since Wycliffe and his views were mixed up with the revolutionary tenets of the Lollards, it followed that his Bible was officially regarded as "subversive."

Wycliffe died in 1384. His version gives a good specimen of popular English prose at the end of the fourteenth century, but it is not of great importance for an understanding of the Bible. No great advance could be made until the original Greek text was once more available. In 1516 the great Catholic humanist Erasmus published his *Novum Instrumentum*—the Greek text with a Latin version in parallel columns. Henceforward the New Testament could again be translated from its original.

The next English translator, and by far the greatest, was William Tyndale (or Hitchins). He was born about 1484. He took his B.A. at Oxford in 1512 and his M.A. in 1515. Then he went to Cambridge to study, and after being ordained priest he became tutor and chaplain in the household of a gentleman in Gloucestershire. Tyndale was a good theologian and preacher at a time when preaching was at a low ebb in the English church. By this time Luther's doctrines were being much talked about and when Tyndale argued with his seniors at table—and came off best in the argument—he was snubbed and called a heretic. So he became a man with a grievance and conceived the desire to translate the scriptures into English. His inspiration was Erasmus, who in the introduction to his Greek Testament had vigorously urged that the sacred scriptures should be translated into every language.

In 1523—seven years after Luther had made his first protest—Tyndale went up to London to find support for his proposed translation and he sought the patronage of Cuthbert Tunstall, Bishop of London. The interview was unsuccessful, which was not surprising, for Tyndale was an unattractive man; he was, in his own words, "evil favored in this world, and without grace in the sight of men, speechless, rude, dull, and slow-witted." When the bishop was confronted with this somewhat uncouth priest whose main recommendation was a grievance, he could hardly be expected to entrust him with such an inflammable task as the translation of the Bible at a time when Bible reading was associated with Lutheranism.

Tyndale was angry and his sense of frustration increased. Nine months later he left England to join the Lutherans. He conferred with Luther and took up residence at Cologne. Here, with the assistance of William Roy, an ex-friar, he set about getting his translation into print. The work had hardly begun when his enemies heard of it and Tyndale fled. Tyndale's first incomplete version was published with a long preface, mostly taken direct from Luther, which branded it as anti-Catholic. Tyndale and Roy then set up at Worms and there the whole of the New Testament was printed. Many copies of this edition were smuggled into England. In his version Tyndale used

Erasmus' Greek text, the Vulgate, and Luther's German translation.

Tyndale was now the most conspicuous English Lutheran and he turned to anti-Catholic propaganda. In 1528 he published *The Obedience of a Christian Man,* which drew from Sir Thomas More an answering *Dialogue.* These two books are clear statements from two masters of plain (and abusive) English in the early sixteenth century of the fundamental differences between Protestants and Catholics. Tyndale followed up his New Testament with translations of the Pentateuch in 1530 and of Jonah in 1531. His New Testament was revised in 1534–35.

As a very vocal leader of Protestants abroad, Tyndale was naturally in great danger, and in 1535 he was betrayed to the officers of the Emperor Charles V. After a long period in prison he was brought before the Inquisition and condemned for heresy. He was degraded from his priesthood and handed over to the secular power. In October 1536 he was strangled and burned. Tyndale had shown great courage and patience throughout. He was not, however, put to death solely for translating the Bible. Once he became a Lutheran, his attacks on the Church and the sacraments were increasingly bitter and violent.

Tyndale's incomplete translations were revised and finished by Miles Coverdale, another Protestant refugee. As translators Tyndale and Coverdale were superb. All other English versions of the Bible until modern times were not so much new translations as revisions of their work.

Between Tyndale and the publication of the King James Bible in 1611, there were several English versions, such as "Matthew's Bible," published in 1537, which was sanctioned by Archbishop Cranmer for use in English churches. Another new edition, also published with the approval of Cranmer, in 1539, was known as the "Great Bible" or "Cranmer's Bible." From this version the Psalms as translated by Coverdale from the Vulgate are still sung in the Anglican Church.

During the brief reign of the Catholic Mary (1553–58) Protestant versions of the Bible were discouraged. As a result the English Protestant exiles in Geneva prepared their own version, with Calvinistic notes, often very abusive. This was known as the Geneva or "Breeches" Bible; it was the most popular English Bible for fifty years. The New Testament of the Geneva version appeared in 1557, and the whole Bible in 1560. In the reign of Queen Elizabeth I (1558–1603), another version was published in 1568, called the "Bishops' Bible" because it was revised by a party of bishops and issued for church reading. Like its predecessors, it was a conservative revision of its predecessors. Indeed sample comparisons of all these versions, especially in the New Testament, show that there were few changes from Tyndale's original.

Between Tyndale-Coverdale and the King James version, the Catholic exiles on the Continent translated the Bible afresh from the Vulgate, keeping as close as possible to the Latin original. This is known as the Douay Bible. Of this version the New Testament appeared at Rheims in 1582, and the Old Testament at Douay in 1609. It was of considerable value to the translators of the King James Bible. Between 1749 and 1763 the original Douay Bible was revised by Bishop Richard Challoner who considerably modernized its archaic and latinized language, at times using the wording of the King James version. Until quite recently this version of the Douay Bible was the standard translation for English-speaking Catholics.

The King James (or "Authorized Version" as it is known in England) arose out of the Hampton Court Conference in January 1604. Early in his reign, King James, newly come from Scotland, summoned a conference to see whether any reconciliation could be made between the central party of the Anglicans and the extremer and Calvinistically inclined party. This purpose was not successful, but during the conference Dr. John Rainolds (or Reynolds), president of Corpus Christi College in Oxford, proposed that there might be a new translation of the Bible because those which were allowed in the reigns of Henry VIII and Edward VI were corrupt and not answerable to the truth of the original.

The king, but not his bishops, was enthusiastic. The new translation was well organized. A team of fifty-four scholars was appointed and the bishops were instructed to inform all scholars in Hebrew or Greek to send in their suggestions. Committees met at Oxford, Cambridge, and London. Rules were drawn up: the Bishops' Bible was to be the standard and as little altered as possible, but certain much disputed words were to be rendered in the traditionally accepted way—such as *ecclesia,* which was to be translated "church" and not "congregation." And there were to be no marginal notes—the sorest objection to the Geneva version—except such as were needed to make clearer the literal meaning of the original or for cross reference.

The committees were subdivided into companies, in which each man was to take the same chapters and when all had done their work of revision the team was to meet and agree on the final draft. Work on the revision was started about 1607. Seeing that so many were involved and that the work was so considerable, it is a tribute to the zeal of the translators that the King James Bible was in print in 1611—only seven years after the plan had first been proposed.

Moreover, it is also a tribute to the good sense and tact of the translators that they were content to revise rather than rewrite the previous versions, for English prose writers in 1610 were not usually addicted to good plain English. They might so easily have preferred fine writing of the kind admired in such men as John Lyly, or Philip Sidney, or Robert Burton, or Thomas Browne, or even the heavy erudition of their own "Epistle Dedicatory" to King James or "The Translators to the Reader."

On the other hand, the King James Bible was not "the Bible in modern English"; it was Tyndale revised, and Tyndale had been dead for more than seventy years during which there had been great change in the English language. Ordinary Englishmen were ceasing to address each other as "thou" and "ye," or to talk like the heroes of the Pentateuch. By thus preserving the earlier style, the translators perpetuated a kind of "sanctified English" whereby the Bible became a book set apart from all other reading, so that there is a sense of impropriety, almost of profanity, in any modern rendering of the sacred text.

5. The Bible and English Literature

Intimate knowledge of the Bible did not begin with its translation into the vernacular. Long before Luther, Tyndale, or the Reformation, in the Middle Ages and earlier, English men and women were far more familiar with the great stories and sayings of the Old Testament and the New than are most modern writers. They went to church and they saw pictures on the walls and in the windows; they watched or acted in the miracle plays; and they listened to Bible stories. Even so earthy a lady as the Wife of Bath could justify her peculiar theories of life by an appeal to the New Testament. But before the Reformation, the ordinary Christian regarded the Church as the sole teacher of faith and the custodian of morals. Since the Church guaranteed the Bible, he was satisfied to leave its interpretation to others more expert than himself. Thus to the generation of Chaucer, the Bible was but one book of many, even as the source of knowledge of the faith.

After the Reformation, those who broke away from the Church and rejected her as their teacher, based their whole faith on the Bible alone, which was now regarded as the only guarantee of salvation. It became the daily reading, often the only reading, of many pious souls. The sixteenth and seventeenth century translations were thus made at a time when the Bible had suddenly become the most important of all books.

As a work of art, the English Bible was (and still is) incomparably the finest collection of writings in English prose. Of this excellence, one of the most important causes was the Latin of Jerome's Vulgate in which Tyndale and his generation first came to know the Bible. The vigor of the early translations into English was carried over from the strength of Jerome's Latin, behind which lies the original Hebrew of the Old Testament. For readers who knew their Vulgate, a translation into English must necessarily have been exact; they would have been repelled by paraphrase or any kind of literary device, no matter how clever or ornate.

Writers of the books of the New Testament were Jews who from boyhood had learned their scriptures by heart. Jesus himself was a constant reader of the Old Testament. When he was asked to speak in the synagogue in Capernaum (p. 400), he turned immediately to the passage in Isaiah which foretold his mission. His words again and again quote or echo the Law and the Prophets; and some of the parables, especially those directed against the Pharisees, were based on passages in the Old Testament which his hearers immediately recognized, as in the parable of the vineyard (p. 429) which was an echo of Isaiah's words (p. 299). The New Testament thus continues the literary tradition of the Old.

There are three main reasons for the abiding greatness of the Bible as literature. The first is the stories themselves, especially of the Old Testament: Adam and Eve, Cain and Abel, Noah and the Flood, the Sacrifice of Isaac, Jacob and Esau, Joseph and his Brethren, Moses and Pharaoh, Jephthah, Samson, David and Goliath, David's lament for Absalom, Ahab and Jezebel, Jonah and the Great Fish, Daniel, Judith. . . . The authors of these stories lack the minute analyses and tortuous subtleties of modern writers, but they were used to telling tales to eager and exacting listeners, and they had an instinct for vivid detail, movement, and dramatic incident, and for drawing character, scenery, and event.

The appeal of the New Testament is different, for it is concerned with the one central figure who altered history more drastically than any other man who ever lived. Whether he accepts or rejects the claims of Christianity, the reader of the Gospels is inevitably involved in their message. Yet the writers of the New Testament had special difficulties; they were Jews writing in Greek, which was not their native tongue; but the urgency of their message transcended language.

A second reason is that both Old and New Testaments are full of the stark problems which concern every man—with the nature and existence of God, with man and his ultimate destiny, with the moral laws on which his happiness depends, with man's hopes and fears, joys, and sorrows, with the questions which have been asked since man first began to wonder.

And, thirdly, these are expressed in such memorable language—concrete, vivid, tangible. The writers of the Old Testament—psalmists and prophets—had not learned to smother thought in abstract words or soporific paraphrase. Everything is visualized in hard metaphors and living similes. In ecstasy, the Psalmist cries out:

O God, thou art my God; early will I seek thee:
My soul thirsteth for thee,
My flesh longeth for thee
In a dry and thirsty land, where no water is.

And in penitent agony he pleads:

Purge me with hyssop, and I shall be clean:
Wash me, and I shall be whiter than snow.
Make me to hear joy and gladness;
That the bones which thou hast broken may rejoice.

And the wise old men with their proverbs so perfectly and tersely express universal truths:

> A soft answer turneth away wrath:
> But grievous words stir up anger.
> The tongue of the wise useth knowledge aright:
> But the mouth of fools poureth out foolishness.

Nevertheless, though the Bible was for three centuries after the Reformation the most read book in the English language, few writers in English have used the Bible as a direct source for great drama or narrative poems. Milton's *Paradise Lost* is a conspicuous exception. Dryden's *Absalom and Achitophel* is hardly a religious work, while Byron's *Cain* and Browning's *Saul* are not so much Bible-inspired as sophistications of simpler themes. Short poems, however, in the form of meditation and comment are common, especially in the work of poets of the first half of the seventeenth century—Herbert, Vaughan, Crashaw, and at times Donne.

Artists, naturally, have found their subjects in the Bible, especially in the life of Jesus and of his Mother, and above all in the incidents of the Passion which are portrayed again and again in every style from the Byzantine to the Baroque. Few artists in earlier times refrained from attempting an Annunciation, a Holy Family, and a Crucifixion.

In literature, however, the real influence of the Bible is less obvious but more pervasive, in direct or oblique reference to the great stories, in echoes, quotations, proverbial sayings, rhythms, and memories. To all of these, readers once responded instinctively and in the right way, for they knew their Bibles by heart; its phrases were always on their lips and in their hearts.

Few modern readers or writers hear or recognize these echoes. It may be that Everyman now needs a *Bible for*

Students of Literature and Art; and if the content of this book is unfamiliar to him, he will soon realize how often he unconsciously uses its language. He may even be brought to seek a fuller familiarity with the whole work.

The Old Testament

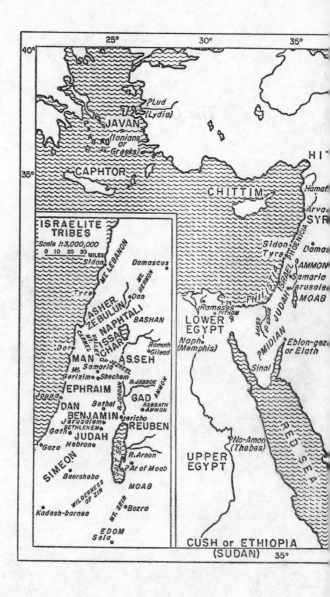

OLD TESTAMENT

Scale 1:10,000,000

0   100   200   300 miles

From GENESIS

Creation. In the beginning God created the heaven and the earth. And the earth was without form, and void; and darkness was upon the face of the deep. And the spirit of God moved upon the face of the waters. And God said, "Let there be light": and there was light. And God saw the light, that it was good: and God divided the light from the darkness. And God called the light Day, and the darkness he called Night. And the evening and the morning were the first day.

And God said, "Let there be a firmament in the midst of the waters, and let it divide the waters from the waters". And God made the firmament, and divided the waters which were under the firmament from the waters which were above the firmament: and it was so. And God called the firmament Heaven. And the evening and the morning were the second day.

And God said, "Let the waters under the heaven be gathered together unto one place, and let the dry land appear": and it was so. And God called the dry land Earth; and the gathering together of the waters called he Seas: and God saw that it was good. And God said, "Let the earth bring forth grass, the herb yielding seed, and the fruit tree yielding fruit after his kind, whose seed is in itself, upon the earth": and it was so. And the earth brought forth grass, and herb yielding seed after his kind, and the tree yielding fruit, whose seed was in itself, after his kind: and God saw that it was good. And the evening and the morning were the third day.

And God said, "Let there be lights in the firmament of the heaven to divide the day from the night; and let them be for signs, and for seasons, and for days, and years: and let them be for lights in the firmament of the heaven to give light upon the earth": and it was so. And God made two great lights; the greater light to rule the day, and the lesser light to rule the night: he made the stars also. And God set them in the firmament of the heaven to give light upon the earth, and to rule over the day and over the night, and to divide the light from the darkness: and God saw that it was good. And the evening and the morning were the fourth day.

And God said, "Let the waters bring forth abundantly the moving creature that hath life, and fowl that may fly above the earth in the open firmament of heaven". And God created great whales, and every living creature that moveth, which the waters brought forth abundantly, after their kind, and every winged fowl after his kind: and God saw that it was good. And God blessed them, saying, "Be fruitful, and multiply, and fill the waters in the seas, and let fowl multiply in the earth". And the evening and the morning were the fifth day.

And God said, "Let the earth bring forth the living creature after his kind, cattle, and creeping thing, and beast of the earth after his kind": and it was so. And God made the beast of the earth after his kind, and cattle after their kind, and every thing that creepeth upon the earth after his kind: and God saw that it was good. And God said, "Let us make man in our image, after our likeness: and let them have dominion over the fish of the sea, and over the fowl of the air, and over the cattle, and over all the earth, and over every creeping thing that creepeth upon the earth". So God created man in his own image, in the image of God created he him; male and female created he them. And God blessed them, and God said unto them, "Be fruitful, and multiply, and replenish the earth, and subdue it: and have dominion over the fish of the sea, and over the fowl of the air, and over every living thing that moveth upon the earth". And God said, "Behold, I have given you every herb bearing seed, which is upon the face of all the earth, and every tree, in the which is the fruit of a tree yielding seed; to you it shall be for meat. And to every beast of the earth, and to every fowl of the air, and to every thing that creepeth upon the earth, wherein there is life, I have given every green herb for meat:" and it was so. And God saw every thing that he had made, and, behold, it was very good. And the evening and the morning were the sixth day.

Thus the heavens and the earth were finished, and all the host of them. And on the seventh day God ended his work which he had made; and he rested on the seventh day from all his work which he had made. And God blessed the seventh day, and sanctified it: because that in it he had rested from all his work which God created and made.

[1:1–31; 2:1–3]

The Creation of Man. These are the generations of the heavens and of the earth when they were created, in the day that the LORD God made the earth and the heavens, and every plant of the field before it was in the earth, and every herb of the field before it grew: for the LORD God had not caused it to rain upon the earth, and there was not a man to till the ground. But there went up a mist from the earth, and watered the whole face of the ground. And the LORD God formed man of the dust of the ground, and breathed into his nostrils the breath of life; and man became a living soul. [2:4–7]

The Garden of Eden. And the LORD God planted a garden eastward in Eden; and there he put the man whom he had formed. And out of the ground made the LORD God to grow every tree that is pleasant to the sight, and good for food; the tree of life also in the midst of the garden, and the tree of knowledge of good and evil. And a river went out of Eden to water the garden; and from thence it was parted, and became into four heads. The name of the first is Pison: that is it which compasseth the whole land of Havilah, where there is gold; and the gold of that land is good: there is bdellium and the onyx stone. And the name of the second river is Gihon: the same is it that compasseth the whole land of Ethiopia. And the name of the third river is Hiddekel: that is it which goeth toward the east of Assyria. And the fourth river is Euphrates. And the LORD God took the man, and put him into the garden of Eden to dress it and to keep it. And the LORD God commanded the man, saying, "Of every tree of the garden thou mayest freely eat: but of the tree of the knowledge of good and evil, thou shalt not eat of it: for in the day that thou eatest thereof thou shalt surely die".

[2:8–17]

The Creation of Eve. And the LORD God said, "It is not good that the man should be alone; I will make him an help meet for him". And out of the ground the LORD God formed every beast of the field, and every fowl of the air; and brought them unto Adam to see what he would call them: and whatsoever Adam called every living creature, that was the name thereof. And Adam gave names to all cattle, and to the fowl of the air, and to every beast of the field; but for Adam there was not found an help meet for him. And the LORD God caused a deep sleep to fall upon Adam, and he slept: and he took one of his ribs, and closed up the flesh instead thereof; and the rib, which the LORD God had taken from man, made he a woman, and brought her unto the man. And Adam said, "This is now bone of my bones, and flesh of my flesh: she shall be called Woman, because she was taken out of Man". Therefore shall a man leave his father and his mother, and shall cleave unto his wife: and they shall be one flesh. And they were both naked, the man and his wife, and were not ashamed.

[2:18–25]

The Temptation. Now the serpent was more subtil than any beast of the field which the LORD God had made. And he said unto the woman, "Yea, hath God said, 'Ye

shall not eat of every tree of the garden'?" And the
woman said unto the serpent, "We may eat of the fruit of
the trees of the garden: but of the fruit of the tree which
is in the midst of the garden, God hath said, 'Ye shall not
eat of it, neither shall ye touch it, lest ye die'". And the
serpent said unto the woman, "Ye shall not surely die:
for God doth know that in the day ye eat thereof, then your
eyes shall be opened, and ye shall be as gods, knowing
good and evil". And when the woman saw that the tree was
good for food, and that it was pleasant to the eyes, and a
tree to be desired to make one wise, she took of the fruit
thereof, and did eat, and gave also unto her husband with
her; and he did eat. And the eyes of them both were
opened, and they knew that they were naked; and they
sewed fig leaves together, and made themselves aprons.
And they heard the voice of the LORD God walking in the
garden in the cool of the day: and Adam and his wife hid
themselves from the presence of the LORD God amongst
the trees of the garden. And the LORD God called unto
Adam, and said unto him, "Where art thou?" And he
said, "I heard thy voice in the garden, and I was afraid,
because I was naked; and I hid myself". And he said,
"Who told thee that thou wast naked? Hast thou eaten of
the tree, whereof I commanded thee that thou shouldest
not eat?" And the man said, "The woman whom thou
gavest to be with me, she gave me of the tree, and I did
eat". And the LORD God said unto the woman, "What is
this that thou hast done?" And the woman said, "The
serpent beguiled me, and I did eat". And the LORD God
said unto the serpent, "Because thou hast done this, thou
art cursed above all cattle, and above every beast of the
field; upon thy belly shalt thou go, and dust shalt thou eat
all the days of thy life: and I will put enmity between thee
and the woman, and between thy seed and her seed; it
shall bruise thy head, and thou shalt bruise his heel". Unto
the woman he said, "I will greatly multiply thy sorrow
and thy conception; in sorrow thou shalt bring forth chil-

dren; and thy desire shall be to thy husband, and he shall rule over thee". And unto Adam he said, "Because thou hast hearkened unto the voice of thy wife, and hast eaten of the tree, of which I commanded thee, saying, Thou shalt not eat of it: cursed is the ground for thy sake; in sorrow shalt thou eat of it all the days of thy life; thorns also and thistles shall it bring forth to thee; and thou shalt eat the herb of the field; in the sweat of thy face shalt thou eat bread, till thou return unto the ground; for out of it wast thou taken: for dust thou art, and unto dust shalt thou return". And Adam called his wife's name Eve; because she was the mother of all living. Unto Adam also and to his wife did the LORD God make coats of skins, and clothed them. [3:1-21]

Adam Cast out of Eden. And the LORD God said, "Behold, the man is become as one of us, to know good and evil: and now, lest he put forth his hand, and take also of the tree of life, and eat, and live for ever": therefore the LORD God sent him forth from the garden of Eden, to till the ground from whence he was taken. So he drove out the man; and he placed at the east of the garden of Eden Cherubims, and a flaming sword which turned every way, to keep the way of the tree of life. [3:22-24]

Cain and Abel. And Adam knew Eve his wife; and she conceived, and bare Cain, and said, "I have gotten a man from the LORD". And she again bare his brother Abel. And Abel was a keeper of sheep, but Cain was a tiller of the ground. And in process of time it came to pass, that Cain brought of the fruit of the ground an offering unto the LORD. And Abel, he also brought of the firstlings of his flock and of the fat thereof. And the LORD had respect unto Abel and to his offering: but unto Cain and to his offering he had not respect. And Cain was very wroth, and his countenance fell. And the LORD said unto Cain, "Why art thou wroth? and why is thy countenance fallen? If thou doest well, shalt thou not be accepted? and if thou doest not well, sin lieth at the door. And unto thee shall be his desire, and thou shalt rule over him." And Cain talked with Abel his brother: and it came to pass, when they were in the field, that Cain rose up against Abel his brother, and slew him. And the LORD said unto Cain, "Where is Abel thy brother?" And he said, "I know not: Am I my brother's keeper?" And he said, "What hast thou done? the voice of thy brother's blood crieth unto me from the ground. And now art thou cursed from the earth, which hath opened her mouth to receive thy brother's blood from thy hand; when thou tillest the ground, it shall not henceforth yield unto thee her strength; a fugitive and a vagabond shalt thou be in the earth." And Cain said unto the LORD, "My punishment is greater than I can bear. Behold, thou hast driven me out this day from the face of the earth; and from thy face shall I be hid; and I shall be a fugitive and a vagabond in the earth; and it shall come to pass, that every one that findeth me shall slay me." And the LORD said unto him, "Therefore whosoever slayeth Cain, vengeance shall be taken on him sevenfold". And the LORD set a mark upon Cain, lest any finding him should kill him. [4:1–15]

Noah. And it came to pass, when men began to multiply on the face of the earth, and daughters were born unto them, that the sons of God saw the daughters of men that they were fair; and they took them wives of all which they chose. And the LORD said, "My spirit shall not always strive with man, for that he also is flesh: yet his days shall be an hundred and twenty years". There were giants in the earth in those days; and also after that, when the sons of God came in unto the daughters of men, and they bare children to them, the same became mighty men which were of old, men of renown. And GOD saw that the wickedness of man was great in the earth, and that every imagination of the thoughts of his heart was only evil continually. And it repented the LORD that he had made man on the earth, and it grieved him at his heart. And the LORD said, "I will destroy man whom I have created from the face of the earth; both man, and beast, and the creeping thing, and the fowls of the air; for it repenteth me that I have made them". But Noah found grace in the eyes of the LORD.

These are the generations of Noah: Noah was a just man and perfect in his generations, and Noah walked with God. And Noah begat three sons, Shem, Ham, and Japheth. The earth also was corrupt before God, and the earth was filled with violence. And God looked upon the earth, and, behold, it was corrupt; for all flesh had corrupted his way upon the earth.   [6:1–12]

Noah's Ark. And God said unto Noah, "The end of all flesh is come before me; for the earth is filled with violence through them; and, behold, I will destroy them with the earth. Make thee an ark of gopher wood; rooms shalt thou make in the ark, and shalt pitch it within and without with pitch. And this is the fashion which thou shalt make it of: The length of the ark shall be three hundred cubits, the breadth of it fifty cubits, and the height of it thirty cubits. A window shalt thou make to the ark, and in a cubit shalt thou finish it above; and the door of the ark shalt thou set in the side thereof; with lower, second, and third stories shalt thou make it. And, behold, I, even I, do bring a flood of waters upon the earth, to destroy all flesh, wherein is the breath of life, from under heaven; and every thing that is in the earth shall die. But with thee will I establish my covenant; and thou shalt come into the ark, thou, and thy sons, and thy wife, and thy sons' wives with thee. And of every living thing of all flesh, two of every sort shalt thou bring into the ark, to keep them alive with thee; they shall be male and female. Of fowls after their kind, and of cattle after their kind, of every creeping thing of the earth after his kind, two of every sort shall come unto thee, to keep them alive. And take thou unto thee of all food that is eaten, and thou shalt gather it to thee; and it shall be for food for thee, and for them." Thus did Noah; according to all that God commanded him, so did he.
          [6:13–22]

Noah Enters the Ark. And the LORD said unto Noah, "Come thou and all thy house into the ark; for thee have I seen righteous before me in this generation. Of every clean beast thou shalt take to thee by sevens, the male and his female: and of beasts that are not clean by two, the male and his female. Of fowls also of the air by sevens, the male and the female; to keep seed alive upon the face of all the earth. For yet seven days, and I will cause it to rain upon the earth forty days and forty nights; and every living substance that I have made will I destroy from off the face of the earth." And Noah did according unto all that the LORD commanded him.

And Noah was six hundred years old when the flood of waters was upon the earth. And Noah went in, and his sons, and his wife, and his sons' wives with him, into the ark, because of the waters of the flood. Of clean beasts, and of beasts that are not clean, and of fowls, and of every thing that creepeth upon the earth, there went in two and two unto Noah into the ark, the male and the female, as God had commanded Noah. [7:1–9]

The Great Flood. And it came to pass after seven days, that the waters of the flood were upon the earth. In the six hundredth year of Noah's life, in the second month, the seventeenth day of the month, the same day were all the fountains of the great deep broken up, and the windows of heaven were opened. And the rain was upon the earth forty days and forty nights. In the selfsame day entered Noah, and Shem, and Ham, and Japheth, the sons of Noah, and Noah's wife, and the three wives of his sons with them, into the ark; they, and every beast after his kind, and all the cattle after their kind, and every creeping thing that creepeth upon the earth after his kind, and every fowl after his kind, every bird of every sort. And they went in unto Noah into the ark, two and two of all flesh, wherein is the breath of life. And they that went in, went in male and female of all flesh, as God had commanded him: and the LORD shut him in. And the flood was forty days upon the earth; and the waters increased, and bare up the ark, and it was lift up above the earth. And the waters prevailed, and were increased greatly upon the earth; and the ark went upon the face of the waters. And the waters prevailed exceedingly upon the earth; and all the high hills, that were under the whole heaven, were covered. Fifteen cubits upward did the waters prevail; and the mountains were covered. And all flesh died that moved upon the earth, both of fowl, and of cattle, and of beast, and of every creeping thing that creepeth upon the earth, and every man: all in whose nostrils was the breath of life, of all that was in the dry land, died. And every living substance was destroyed which was upon the face of the ground, both man, and cattle, and the creeping things, and the fowl of the heaven; and they were destroyed from the earth: and Noah only remained alive, and they that were with him in the ark. And the waters prevailed upon the earth an hundred and fifty days.   [7:10–24]

The Waters Subside. And God remembered Noah, and every living thing, and all the cattle that was with him in the ark: and God made a wind to pass over the earth, and the waters asswaged; the fountains also of the deep and the windows of heaven were stopped, and the rain from heaven was restrained; and the waters returned from off the earth continually: and after the end of the hundred and fifty days the waters were abated. And the ark rested in the seventh month, on the seventeenth day of the month, upon the mountains of Ararat. And the waters decreased continually until the tenth month: in the tenth month, on the first day of the month, were the tops of the mountains seen. And it came to pass at the end of forty days, that Noah opened the window of the ark which he had made: and he sent forth a raven, which went forth to and fro, until the waters were dried up from off the earth. Also he sent forth a dove from him, to see if the waters were abated from off the face of the ground; but the dove found no rest for the sole of her foot, and she returned unto him into the ark, for the waters were on the face of the whole earth: then he put forth his hand, and took her, and pulled her in unto him into the ark. And he stayed yet other seven days; and again he sent forth the dove out of the ark; and the dove came in to him in the evening; and, lo, in her mouth was an olive leaf pluckt off: so Noah knew that the waters were abated from off the earth. And he stayed yet other seven days; and sent forth the dove; which returned not again unto him any more. And it came to pass in the six hundredth and first year, in the first month, the first day of the month, the waters were dried up from off the earth: and Noah removed the covering of the ark, and looked, and, behold, the face of the ground was dry. And in the second month, on the seven and twentieth day of the month, was the earth dried. [8:1–14]

Noah Leaves the Ark. And God spake unto Noah, saying, "Go forth of the ark, thou, and thy wife, and thy sons, and thy sons' wives with thee. Bring forth with thee every living thing that is with thee, of all flesh, both of fowl, and of cattle, and of every creeping thing that creepeth upon the earth; that they may breed abundantly in the earth, and be fruitful, and multiply upon the earth." And Noah went forth, and his sons, and his wife, and his sons' wives with him: every beast, every creeping thing, and every fowl, and whatsoever creepeth upon the earth, after their kinds, went forth out of the ark. And Noah builded an altar unto the LORD; and took of every clean beast, and of every clean fowl, and offered burnt offerings on the altar. And the LORD smelled a sweet savour; and the LORD said in his heart, "I will not again curse the ground any more for man's sake; for the imagination of man's heart is evil from his youth; neither will I again smite any more every thing living, as I have done. While the earth remaineth, seedtime and harvest, and cold and heat, and summer and winter, and day and night shall not cease". [8:15–22]

Noah Blessed. And God blessed Noah and his sons,

and said unto them, "Be fruitful, and multiply, and replenish the earth. And the fear of you and the dread of you shall be upon every beast of the earth, and upon every fowl of the air, upon all that moveth upon the earth, and upon all the fishes of the sea; into your hand are they delivered. Every moving thing that liveth shall be meat for you; even as the green herb have I given you all things. But flesh with the life thereof, which is the blood thereof, shall ye not eat. And surely your blood of your lives will I require; at the hand of every beast will I require it, and at the hand of man; at the hand of every man's brother will I require the life of man. Whoso sheddeth man's blood, by man shall his blood be shed: for in the image of God made he man. And you, be ye fruitful, and multiply; bring forth abundantly in the earth, and multiply therein."

And God spake unto Noah, and to his sons with him, saying, "And I, behold, I establish my covenant with you, and with your seed after you; and with every living creature that is with you, of the fowl, of the cattle, and of every beast of the earth with you; from all that go out of the ark, to every beast of the earth. And I will establish my covenant with you; neither shall all flesh be cut off any more by the waters of a flood; neither shall there any more be a flood to destroy the earth." [9:1–11]

The Sign of the Rainbow. And God said, "This is the token of the covenant which I make between me and you and every living creature that is with you, for perpetual generations: I do set my bow in the cloud, and it shall be for a token of a covenant between me and the earth. And it shall come to pass, when I bring a cloud over the earth, that the bow shall be seen in the cloud: and I will remember my covenant, which is between me and you and every living creature of all flesh; and the waters shall no more become a flood to destroy all flesh. And the bow shall be in the cloud; and I will look upon it, that I may remember the everlasting covenant between God and every living creature of all flesh that is upon the earth." And God said

unto Noah, "This is the token of the covenant, which I
have established between me and all flesh that is upon the
earth".

And the sons of Noah, that went forth of the ark, were
Shem, and Ham, and Japheth: and Ham is the father of
Canaan. These are the three sons of Noah: and of them
was the whole earth overspread.   [9:12–19]

The Tower of Babel. And the whole earth was of one
language, and of one speech. And it came to pass, as they
journeyed from the east, that they found a plain in the
land of Shinar; and they dwelt there. And they said one to
another, "Go to, let us make brick, and burn them
throughly". And they had brick for stone, and slime had
they for morter. And they said, "Go to, let us build us a
city and a tower, whose top may reach unto heaven; and
let us make us a name, lest we be scattered abroad upon
the face of the whole earth". And the LORD came down
to see the city and the tower, which the children of men
builded. And the LORD said, "Behold, the people is one,
and they have all one language; and this they begin to do:
and now nothing will be restrained from them, which they
have imagined to do. Go to, let us go down, and there
confound their language, that they may not understand one
another's speech." So the LORD scattered them abroad
from thence upon the face of all the earth: and they left off
to build the city. Therefore is the name of it called Babel;
because the LORD did there confound the language of all
the earth: and from thence did the LORD scatter them
abroad upon the face of all the earth.   [11:1–9]

The Call of Abraham. [The religious history of the
Jews begins with the call of Abraham (Genesis 12). Terah,
the father of Abraham (as yet called Abram), dwelt in
Ur of the Chaldees; he had three sons, Abram, Nahor,
and Haran. Haran died before his father, leaving a grand-
son called Lot. "And Terah took Abram his son, and Lot
the son of Haran his son's son, and Sarai his daughter in
law, his son Abram's wife; and they went forth with them

from Ur of the Chaldees, to go into the land of Canaan; and they came unto Haran, and dwelt there." (11:31)]

Now the LORD had said unto Abram, "Get thee out of thy country, and from thy kindred, and from thy father's house, unto a land that I will shew thee: and I will make of thee a great nation, and I will bless thee, and make thy name great; and thou shalt be a blessing: and I will bless them that bless thee, and curse him that curseth thee: and in thee shall all families of the earth be blessed". So Abram departed, as the LORD had spoken unto him; and Lot went with him: and Abram was seventy and five years old when he departed out of Haran. And Abram took Sarai his wife, and Lot his brother's son, and all their substance that they had gathered, and the souls that they had gotten in Haran; and they went forth to go into the land of Canaan; and into the land of Canaan they came. And Abram passed through the land unto the place of Sichem, unto the plain of Moreh. And the Canaanite was then in the land. And the LORD appeared unto Abram, and said, "Unto thy seed will I give this land": and there builded he an altar unto the LORD, who appeared unto him. And he removed from thence unto a mountain on the east of Beth-el, and pitched his tent, having Beth-el on the west, and Hai on the east: and there he builded an altar unto the LORD, and called upon the name of the LORD. And Abram journeyed, going on still toward the south.

[12:1-9]

Sarah and Hagar. Now Sarai Abram's wife bare him no children: and she had an handmaid, an Egyptian, whose name was Hagar. And Sarai said unto Abram, "Behold now, the LORD hath restrained me from bearing: I pray thee, go in unto my maid; it may be that I may obtain children by her". And Abram hearkened to the voice of Sarai. And Sarai Abram's wife took Hagar her maid the Egyptian, after Abram had dwelt ten years in the land of Canaan, and gave her to her husband Abram to be his wife. And he went in unto Hagar, and she conceived: and when she saw that she had conceived, her mistress was despised in her eyes. And Sarai said unto Abram, "My wrong be upon thee: I have given my maid into thy bosom; and when she saw that she had conceived, I was despised in her eyes: the LORD judge between me and thee". But Abram said unto Sarai, "Behold, thy maid is in thy hand; do to her as it pleaseth thee". And when Sarai dealt hardly with her, she fled from her face. And the angel of the LORD found her by a fountain of water in the wilderness, by the fountain in the way to Shur. And he said, "Hagar, Sarai's maid, whence camest thou? and whither wilt thou go?" And she said, "I flee from the face of my mistress Sarai". And the angel of the LORD said unto her, "Return to thy mistress, and submit thyself under her hands". And the angel of the LORD said unto her, "I will multiply thy seed exceedingly, that it shall not be numbered for multitude". And the angel of the LORD said unto her, "Behold, thou art with child, and shalt bear a son, and shalt call his name Ishmael; because the LORD hath heard thy affliction. And he will be a wild man; his hand will be against every man, and every man's hand against him; and he shall dwell in the presence of all his brethren." And she called the name of the LORD that spake unto her, "Thou God seest me": for she said, "Have I also here looked after him that seeth me?" Wherefore the well was called Beer-lahai-roi; behold, it is between Kadesh and Bered. And Hagar bare Abram a son: and Abram called his son's name, which Hagar bare, Ishmael. And Abram was fourscore and six years old, when Hagar bare Ishmael to Abram.   [16:1–16]

God's Covenant with Abraham.   And when Abram was ninety years old and nine, the LORD appeared to Abram, and said unto him, "I am the Almighty God; walk before me, and be thou perfect. And I will make my covenant between me and thee, and will multiply thee exceedingly." And Abram fell on his face: and God talked with him, saying, "As for me, behold, my covenant is with thee, and thou shalt be a father of many nations. Neither shall thy name any more be called Abram, but thy name shall be Abraham; for a father of many nations have I made thee. And I will make thee exceeding fruitful, and I will make nations of thee, and kings shall come out of thee. And I will establish my covenant between me and thee and thy seed after thee in their generations for an everlasting covenant, to be a God unto thee, and to thy seed after thee. And I will give unto thee, and to thy seed after thee, the land wherein thou art a stranger, all the land of Canaan, for an everlasting possession; and I will be their God." And God said unto Abraham, "Thou shalt keep my covenant therefore, thou, and thy seed after thee in their generations. This is my covenant, which ye shall keep, between me and you and thy seed after thee; Every man child among you shall be circumcised. And ye shall circumcise the flesh of your foreskin; and it shall be a token of the covenant betwixt me and you. And he that is eight days old shall be circumcised among you, every man child in your generations, he that is born in the house, or bought with money of any stranger, which is not of thy seed. He that is born in thy house, and he that is bought with thy money, must needs be circumcised: and my covenant shall be in your flesh for an everlasting covenant. And the uncircumcised man child whose flesh of his foreskin is not circumcised, that soul shall be cut off from his people; he hath broken my covenant."

And God said unto Abraham, "As for Sarai thy wife, thou shalt not call her name Sarai, but Sarah shall her name be. And I will bless her, and give thee a son also of her: yea, I will bless her, and she shall be a mother of nations; kings of people shall be of her." Then Abraham fell upon his face, and laughed, and said in his heart, "Shall a child be born unto him that is an hundred years old? and shall Sarah, that is ninety years old, bear?" And Abraham said unto God, "O that Ishmael might live before thee!" And God said, "Sarah thy wife shall bear thee a son indeed; and thou shalt call his name Isaac: and I will establish my covenant with him for an everlasting covenant, and with his seed after him. And as for Ishmael, I have heard thee: Behold, I have blessed him, and will make him fruitful, and will multiply him exceedingly; twelve princes shall he beget, and I will make him a great nation. But my covenant will I establish with Isaac, which Sarah shall bear unto thee at this set time in the next year." And he left off talking with him, and God went up from Abraham. And Abraham took Ishmael his son, and all that were born in his house, and all that were bought with his money, every male among the men of Abraham's house; and circumcised the flesh of their foreskin in the selfsame day, as God had said unto him. And Abraham was ninety years old and nine, when he was circumcised in the flesh of his foreskin. And Ishmael his son was thirteen years old, when he was circumcised in the flesh of his foreskin. In the selfsame day was Abraham circumcised, and Ishmael his son. And all the men of his house, born in the house, and bought with money of the stranger, were circumcised with him.   [17:1–27]

A Son Promised to Sarah. And the LORD appeared unto him in the plains of Mamre: and he sat in the tent door in the heat of the day; and he lift up his eyes and looked, and, lo, three men stood by him: and when he saw them, he ran to meet them from the tent door, and bowed himself toward the ground, and said, "My Lord, if now I have found favour in thy sight, pass not away, I pray thee, from thy servant: let a little water, I pray you, be fetched, and wash your feet, and rest yourselves under the tree: and I will fetch a morsel of bread, and comfort ye your hearts; after that ye shall pass on: for therefore are ye come to your servant". And they said, "So do, as thou hast said". And Abraham hastened into the tent unto Sarah, and said, "Make ready quickly three measures of fine meal, knead it, and make cakes upon the hearth". And Abraham ran unto the herd, and fetcht a calf tender and good, and gave it unto a young man; and he hasted to dress it. And he took butter, and milk, and the calf which he had dressed, and set it before them; and he stood by them under the tree, and they did eat. And they said unto him, "Where is Sarah thy wife?" And he said, "Behold, in the tent". And he said, "I will certainly return unto thee according to the time of life; and, lo, Sarah thy wife shall have a son". And Sarah heard it in the tent door, which was behind him. Now Abraham and Sarah were old and well stricken in age; and it ceased to be with Sarah after the manner of women. Therefore Sarah laughed within herself, saying, "After I am waxed old shall I have pleasure, my lord being old also?" And the LORD said unto Abraham, "Wherefore did Sarah laugh, saying, 'Shall I of a surety bear a child, which am old?' Is any thing too hard for the LORD? At the time appointed I will return unto thee, according to the time of life, and Sarah shall have a son." Then Sarah denied, saying, "I laughed not"; for she was afraid. And he said, "Nay; but thou didst laugh".

[18:1–15]

Abraham Pleads for Sodom. And the men rose up from thence, and looked toward Sodom: and Abraham went with them to bring them on the way. And the LORD said, "Shall I hide from Abraham that thing which I do; seeing that Abraham shall surely become a great and mighty nation, and all the nations of the earth shall be blessed in him? For I know him, that he will command his children and his household after him, and they shall keep the way of the LORD, to do justice and judgment; that the LORD may bring upon Abraham that which he hath spoken of him." And the LORD said, "Because the cry of Sodom and Gomorrah is great, and because their sin is very grievous; I will go down now, and see whether they have done altogether according to the cry of it, which is come unto me; and if not, I will know". And the men turned their faces from thence, and went toward Sodom: but Abraham stood yet before the LORD.

And Abraham drew near, and said, "Wilt thou also destroy the righteous with the wicked? Peradventure there be fifty righteous within the city: wilt thou also destroy and not spare the place for the fifty righteous that are therein? That be far from thee to do after this manner, to slay the righteous with the wicked: and that the righteous should be as the wicked, that be far from thee: Shall not the Judge of all the earth do right?" And the LORD said, "If I find in Sodom fifty righteous within the city, then I will spare all the place for their sakes". And Abraham answered and said, "Behold now, I have taken upon me to speak unto the Lord, which am but dust and ashes: Peradventure there shall lack five of the fifty righteous: wilt thou destroy all the city for lack of five?" And he said, "If I find there forty and five, I will not destroy it". And he spake unto him yet again, and said, "Peradventure there shall be forty found there". And he said, "I will not do it for forty's sake". And he said unto him, "Oh let not the Lord be angry, and I will speak: Peradventure there shall thirty be found there". And he said, "I will not do it, if I find thirty there". And he said, "Behold now, I have taken upon me to speak unto the Lord: Peradventure there shall be twenty found there". And he said, "I will not destroy it for twenty's sake". And he said, "Oh let not the Lord be angry, and I will speak yet but this once: Peradventure ten shall be found there". And he said, "I will not destroy it for ten's sake". And the LORD went his way, as soon as he had left communing with Abraham: and Abraham returned unto his place.   [18:16–33]

The Wickedness of Sodom. And there came two angels to Sodom at even; and Lot sat in the gate of Sodom: and Lot seeing them rose up to meet them; and he bowed himself with his face toward the ground; and he said, "Behold now, my lords, turn in, I pray you, into your servant's house, and tarry all night, and wash your feet, and ye shall rise up early, and go on your ways". And they said, "Nay; but we will abide in the street all night". And he pressed upon them greatly; and they turned in unto him, and entered into his house; and he made them a feast, and did bake unleavened bread, and they did eat. But before they lay down, the men of the city, even the men of Sodom, compassed the house round, both old and young, all the people from every quarter: and they called unto Lot, and said unto him, "Where are the men which came in to thee this night? bring them out unto us, that we may know them". And Lot went out at the door unto them, and shut the door after him, and said, "I pray you, brethren, do not so wickedly. Behold now, I have two daughters which have not known man; let me, I pray you, bring them out unto you, and do ye to them as is good in your eyes: only unto these men do nothing; for therefore came they under the shadow of my roof." And they said, "Stand back". And they said again, "This one fellow came in to sojourn, and he will needs be a judge: now will we deal worse with thee, than with them". And they pressed sore upon the man, even Lot, and came near to break the door. But the men put forth their hand, and pulled Lot into the house to them, and shut to the door. And they smote the men that were at the door of the house with blindness, both small and great: so that they wearied themselves to find the door. And the men said unto Lot, "Hast thou here any besides? son in law, and thy sons, and thy daughters, and whatsoever thou hast in the city, bring them out of this place: for we will destroy this place, because the cry of them is waxen great before the face of the LORD; and the LORD hath sent us to destroy it". And Lot went out, and spake unto his sons in law, which married his daughters, and said, "Up, get you out of this place; for the LORD will destroy this city". But he seemed as one that mocked unto his sons in law.   [19:1–14]

Sodom Destroyed. And when the morning arose, then the angels hastened Lot, saying, "Arise, take thy wife, and thy two daughters, which are here; lest thou be consumed in the iniquity of the city". And while he lingered, the men laid hold upon his hand, and upon the hand of his wife, and upon the hand of his two daughters; the LORD being merciful unto him: and they brought him forth, and set him without the city. And it came to pass, when they had brought them forth abroad, that he said, "Escape for thy life; look not behind thee, neither stay thou in all the plain; escape to the mountain, lest thou be consumed". And Lot said unto them, "Oh, not so, my Lord: behold now, thy servant hath found grace in thy sight, and thou hast magnified thy mercy, which thou hast shewed unto me in saving my life; and I cannot escape to the mountain, lest some evil take me, and I die: behold now, this city is near to flee unto, and it is a little one: Oh, let me escape thither, (is it not a little one?) and my soul shall live". And he said unto him, "See, I have accepted thee concerning this thing also, that I will not overthrow this city, for the which thou hast spoken. Haste thee, escape thither; for I cannot do any thing till thou be come thither." Therefore the name of the city was called Zoar. The sun was risen upon the earth when Lot entered into Zoar. Then the LORD rained upon Sodom and upon Gomorrah brimstone and fire from the LORD out of heaven; and he overthrew those cities, and all the plain, and all the inhabitants of the cities, and that which grew upon the ground. But his wife looked back from behind him, and she became a pillar of salt. And Abraham gat up early in the morning to the place where he stood before the LORD: and he looked toward Sodom and Gomorrah, and toward all the land of the plain, and beheld, and, lo, the smoke of the country went up as the smoke of a furnace.   [19:15–28]

Isaac Born. And the LORD visited Sarah as he had said, and the LORD did unto Sarah as he had spoken. For Sarah conceived, and bare Abraham a son in his old age, at the set time of which God had spoken to him. And Abraham called the name of his son that was born unto him, whom Sarah bare to him, Isaac. And Abraham circumcised his son Isaac being eight days old, as God had commanded him. And Abraham was an hundred years old, when his son Isaac was born unto him. And Sarah said, "God hath made me to laugh, so that all that hear will laugh with me". And she said, "Who would have said unto Abraham, that Sarah should have given children suck? for I have borne him a son in his old age".   [21:1–7]

Hagar Cast Out.   And the child grew, and was weaned: and Abraham made a great feast the same day that Isaac was weaned. And Sarah saw the son of Hagar the Egyptian, which she had borne unto Abraham, mocking. Wherefore she said unto Abraham, "Cast out this bondwoman and her son: for the son of this bondwoman shall not be heir with my son, even with Isaac". And the thing was very grievous in Abraham's sight because of his son. And God said unto Abraham, "Let it not be grievous in thy sight because of the lad, and because of thy bondwoman; in all that Sarah hath said unto thee, hearken unto her voice; for in Isaac shall thy seed be called. And also of the son of the bondwoman will I make a nation, because he is thy seed." And Abraham rose up early in the morning, and took bread, and a bottle of water, and gave it unto Hagar, putting it on her shoulder, and the child, and sent her away: and she departed, and wandered in the wilderness of Beer-sheba. And the water was spent in the bottle, and she cast the child under one of the shrubs. And she went, and sat her down over against him a good way off, as it were a bowshot: for she said, "Let me not see the death of the child". And she sat over against him, and lift up her voice, and wept. And God heard the voice of the lad; and the angel of God called to Hagar out of heaven, and said unto her, "What aileth thee, Hagar? fear not; for God hath heard the voice of the lad where he is. Arise, lift up the lad, and hold him in thine hand; for I will make him a great nation." And God opened her eyes, and she saw a well of water; and she went, and filled the bottle with water, and gave the lad drink. And God was with the lad; and he grew, and dwelt in the wilderness, and became an archer. And he dwelt in the wilderness of Paran: and his mother took him a wife out of the land of Egypt.

[21:8–21]

The Sacrifice of Isaac. And it came to pass after these things, that God did tempt Abraham, and said unto him, "Abraham": and he said, "Behold, here I am". And he said, "Take now thy son, thine only son Isaac, whom thou lovest, and get thee into the land of Moriah; and offer him there for a burnt offering upon one of the mountains which I will tell thee of". And Abraham rose up early in the morning, and saddled his ass, and took two of his young men with him, and Isaac his son, and clave the wood for the burnt offering, and rose up, and went unto the place of which God had told him. Then on the third day Abraham lifted up his eyes, and saw the place afar off. And Abraham said unto his young men, "Abide ye here with the ass; and I and the lad will go yonder and worship, and come again to you". And Abraham took the wood of the burnt offering, and laid it upon Isaac his son; and he took the fire in his hand, and a knife; and they went both of them together. And Isaac spake unto Abraham his father, and said, "My father": and he said, "Here am I, my son". And he said, "Behold the fire and the wood: but where is the lamb for a burnt offering?" And Abraham said, "My son, God will provide himself a lamb for a burnt offering": so they went both of them together. And they came to the place which God had told him of; and Abraham built an altar there, and laid the wood in order, and bound Isaac his son, and laid him on the altar upon the wood. And Abraham stretched forth his hand, and took the knife to slay his son. And the angel of the LORD called unto him out of heaven, and said, "Abraham, Abraham": and he said, "Here am I". And he said, "Lay not thine hand upon the lad, neither do thou any thing unto him: for now I know that thou fearest God, seeing thou hast not withheld thy son, thine only son from me". And Abraham lifted up his eyes, and looked, and behold behind him a ram caught in a thicket by his horns: and Abraham went and took the ram, and offered him up for a burnt offering in the stead of his son. And Abraham called the name of that place Jehovah-jireh: as it is said to this day, "In the mount of the LORD it shall be seen". And the angel of the LORD called unto Abraham out of heaven the second time, and said, "By myself have I sworn, saith the LORD, for because thou hast done this thing, and hast not withheld thy son, thine only son: that in blessing I will bless thee, and in multiplying I will multiply thy seed as the stars of the heaven, and as the sand which is upon the sea shore; and thy seed shall possess the gate of his enemies; and in thy seed shall all the nations of the earth be blessed; because thou hast obeyed my voice". So Abraham returned unto his young men, and they rose up and went together to Beer-sheba; and Abraham dwelt at Beer-sheba. [22:1–19]

Isaac Marries Rebekah. [When Isaac grew up, Abraham was unwilling that he should marry one of the Canaanites. He therefore sent his servant to his own kindred in Mesopotamia to find a wife for Isaac. The servant came to the city of Nahor, Abraham's brother, and there encountered Rebekah, Nahor's daughter, and he asked whether Rebekah would go back with him.]

And they said, "We will call the damsel, and enquire at her mouth". And they called Rebekah, and said unto her, "Wilt thou go with this man?" And she said, "I will go". And they sent away Rebekah their sister, and her nurse, and Abraham's servant, and his men. And they blessed Rebekah, and said unto her, "Thou art our sister, be thou the mother of thousands of millions, and let thy seed possess the gate of those which hate them". And Rebekah arose, and her damsels, and they rode upon the camels, and followed the man: and the servant took Rebekah, and went his way. And Isaac came from the way of the well Lahai-roi; for he dwelt in the south country. And Isaac went out to meditate in the field at the eventide: and he lifted up his eyes, and saw, and, behold, the camels were coming. And Rebekah lifted up her eyes, and when she saw Isaac, she lighted off the camel. For she had said unto the servant, "What man is this that walketh in the field to meet us?" And the servant had said, "It is my master": therefore she took a veil, and covered herself. And the servant told Isaac all things that he had done. And Isaac brought her into his mother Sarah's tent, and took Rebekah, and she became his wife; and he loved her: and Isaac was comforted after his mother's death.   [24:57–67]

Esau and Jacob Born. And these are the generations of Isaac, Abraham's son: Abraham begat Isaac: and Isaac was forty years old when he took Rebekah to wife, the daughter of Bethuel the Syrian of Padan-aram, the sister to Laban the Syrian. And Isaac intreated the LORD for his wife, because she was barren: and the LORD was intreated of him, and Rebekah his wife conceived. And the children struggled together within her; and she said, "If it be so, why am I thus?" And she went to enquire of the LORD. And the LORD said unto her,

> "Two nations are in thy womb,
> And two manner of people shall be separated from
>   thy bowels;
> And the one people shall be stronger than the other
>   people;
> And the elder shall serve the younger".

And when her days to be delivered were fulfilled, behold, there were twins in her womb. And the first came out red, all over like an hairy garment; and they called his name Esau. And after that came his brother out, and his hand took hold on Esau's heel; and his name was called Jacob: and Isaac was threescore years old when she bare them. And the boys grew: and Esau was a cunning hunter, a man of the field; and Jacob was a plain man, dwelling in

tents. And Isaac loved Esau, because he did eat of his
venison: but Rebekah loved Jacob.   [25:19–28]

Esau Sells His Birthright. And Jacob sod pottage: and
Esau came from the field, and he was faint: and Esau said
to Jacob, "Feed me, I pray thee, with that same red pottage; for I am faint": therefore was his name called
Edom: And Jacob said, "Sell me this day thy birthright".
And Esau said, "Behold, I am at the point to die: and
what profit shall this birthright do to me?" And Jacob
said, "Swear to me this day"; and he sware unto him:
and he sold his birthright unto Jacob. Then Jacob gave
Esau bread and pottage of lentiles; and he did eat and
drink, and rose up, and went his way: thus Esau despised
his birthright.   [25:29–34]

Jacob Cheats Esau of His Blessing. And it came to
pass, that when Isaac was old, and his eyes were dim,
so that he could not see, he called Esau his eldest son,
and said unto him, "My son": and he said unto him,
"Behold, here am I". And he said, "Behold now, I am
old, I know not the day of my death: now therefore take,
I pray thee, thy weapons, thy quiver and thy bow, and go
out to the field, and take me some venison; and make
me savoury meat, such as I love, and bring it to me, that
I may eat; that my soul may bless thee before I die".
And Rebekah heard when Isaac spake to Esau his son.
And Esau went to the field to hunt for venison, and to
bring it. And Rebekah spake unto Jacob her son, saying,
"Behold, I heard thy father speak unto Esau thy brother,
saying, 'Bring me venison, and make me savoury meat, that
I may eat, and bless thee before the LORD before my death'.
Now therefore, my son, obey my voice according to that
which I command thee. Go now to the flock, and fetch
me from thence two good kids of the goats; and I will
make them savoury meat for thy father, such as he loveth:
and thou shalt bring it to thy father, that he may eat, and
that he may bless thee before his death." And Jacob said to

Rebekah his mother, "Behold, Esau my brother is a hairy man, and I am a smooth man: my father peradventure will feel me, and I shall seem to him as a deceiver; and I shall bring a curse upon me, and not a blessing". And his mother said unto him, "Upon me be thy curse, my son: only obey my voice, and go fetch me them". And he went, and fetched, and brought them to his mother: and his mother made savoury meat, such as his father loved. And Rebekah took goodly raiment of her eldest son Esau, which were with her in the house, and put them upon Jacob her younger son: and she put the skins of the kids of the goats upon his hands, and upon the smooth of his neck: and she gave the savoury meat and the bread, which she had prepared, into the hand of her son Jacob. And he came unto his father, and said, "My father": and he said, "Here am I; who art thou, my son?" And Jacob said unto his father, "I am Esau thy firstborn; I have done according as thou badest me: arise, I pray thee, sit and eat of my venison, that thy soul may bless me". And Isaac said unto his son, "How is it that thou hast found it so quickly, my son?" And he said, "Because the LORD thy God brought it to me". And Isaac said unto Jacob, "Come near, I pray thee, that I may feel thee, my son, whether thou be my very son Esau or not". And Jacob went near unto Isaac his father; and he felt him, and said, "The voice is Jacob's voice, but the hands are the hands of Esau". And he discerned him not, because his hands were hairy, as his brother Esau's hands: so he blessed him. And he said, "Art thou my very son Esau?" And he said, "I am". And he said, "Bring it near to me, and I will eat of my son's venison, that my soul may bless thee". And he brought it near to him, and he did eat: and he brought him wine, and he drank. And his father Isaac said unto him, "Come near now, and kiss me, my son". And he came near, and kissed him: and he smelled the smell of his raiment, and blessed him, and said,

"See, the smell of my son is as the smell of a field
    which the LORD hath blessed:
Therefore God give thee of the dew of heaven,
And the fatness of the earth,
And plenty of corn and wine:
Let people serve thee,
And nations bow down to thee:
Be lord over thy brethren,
And let thy mother's sons bow down to thee:
Cursed be every one that curseth thee,
And blessed be he that blesseth thee".

And it came to pass, as soon as Isaac had made an end of
blessing Jacob, and Jacob was yet scarce gone out from the
presence of Isaac his father, that Esau his brother came in
from his hunting. And he also had made savoury meat,
and brought it unto his father, and said unto his father,
"Let my father arise, and eat of his son's venison, that thy
soul may bless me". And Isaac his father said unto him,
"Who art thou?" And he said, "I am thy son, thy firstborn Esau". And Isaac trembled very exceedingly, and
said, "Who? where is he that hath taken venison, and
brought it me, and I have eaten of all before thou camest,
and have blessed him? yea, and he shall be blessed". And
when Esau heard the words of his father, he cried with a
great and exceeding bitter cry, and said unto his father,
"Bless me, even me also, O my father". And he said, "Thy
brother came with subtilty, and hath taken away thy
blessing". And he said, "Is not he rightly named Jacob?
for he hath supplanted me these two times: he took away
my birthright; and, behold, now he hath taken away my
blessing". And he said, "Hast thou not reserved a blessing for me?" And Isaac answered and said unto Esau, "Behold, I have made him thy lord, and all his brethren have
I given to him for servants; and with corn and wine have
I sustained him: and what shall I do now unto thee, my
son?" And Esau said unto his father, "Hast thou but one

blessing, my father? bless me, even me also, O my father".
And Esau lifted up his voice, and wept. And Isaac his
father answered and said unto him,

> "Behold, thy dwelling shall be the fatness of the earth,
> And of the dew of heaven from above;
> And by thy sword shalt thou live,
> And shalt serve thy brother;
> And it shall come to pass when thou shalt have the
> dominion,
> That thou shalt break his yoke from off thy neck".

And Esau hated Jacob because of the blessing wherewith
his father blessed him: and Esau said in his heart, "The
days of mourning for my father are at hand; then will I
slay my brother Jacob". And these words of Esau her
elder son were told to Rebekah: and she sent and called
Jacob her younger son, and said unto him, "Behold, thy
brother Esau, as touching thee, doth comfort himself, pur-
posing to kill thee. Now therefore, my son, obey my voice;
and arise, flee thou to Laban my brother to Haran; and
tarry with him a few days, until thy brother's fury turn
away; until thy brother's anger turn away from thee, and
he forget that which thou hast done to him: then I will
send, and fetch thee from thence: why should I be deprived
also of you both in one day?"

And Rebekah said to Isaac, "I am weary of my life because of the daughters of Heth: if Jacob take a wife of the
daughters of Heth, such as these which are of the daughters of the land, what good shall my life do me?"

[27:1–46]

Jacob Goes to Laban. And Isaac called Jacob, and
blessed him, and charged him, and said unto him, "Thou
shalt not take a wife of the daughters of Canaan. Arise,
go to Padan-aram, to the house of Bethuel thy mother's
father; and take thee a wife from thence of the daughters
of Laban thy mother's brother. And God Almighty bless
thee, and make thee fruitful, and multiply thee, that thou

mayest be a multitude of people; and give thee the blessing of Abraham, to thee, and to thy seed with thee; that thou mayest inherit the land wherein thou art a stranger, which God gave unto Abraham." [28:1–4]

[So Jacob journeyed to his uncle Laban and came to a well, and there Rachel, Laban's younger daughter, came to water her father's sheep. And Jacob loved Rachel, and he agreed with Laban that he would serve with him for seven years for Rachel]

. . . and they seemed unto him but a few days, for the love he had to her. And Jacob said unto Laban, "Give me my wife, for my days are fulfilled, that I may go in unto her". And Laban gathered together all the men of the place, and made a feast. And it came to pass in the evening, that he took Leah his daughter, and brought her to him; and he went in unto her. And Laban gave unto his daughter Leah Zilpah his maid for an handmaid. And it came to pass, that in the morning, behold, it was Leah: and he said to Laban, "What is this thou hast done unto me? did not I serve with thee for Rachel? wherefore then hast thou beguiled me?" And Laban said, "It must not be so done in our country, to give the younger before the firstborn. Fulfil her week, and we will give thee this also for the service which thou shalt serve with me yet seven other years." And Jacob did so, and fulfilled her week: and he gave him Rachel his daughter to wife also. And Laban gave to Rachel his daughter Bilhah his handmaid to be her maid. And he went in also unto Rachel, and he loved also Rachel more than Leah, and served with him yet seven other years. [29:20–30]

[Jacob had children by Leah and by Bilhah and Zilpah, but for a long time Rachel was barren. At last]

. . . God hearkened to her, and opened her womb. And she conceived, and bare a son; and said, "God hath taken away my reproach": and she called his name Joseph; and said, "The LORD shall add to me another son".

And it came to pass, when Rachel had borne Joseph,

that Jacob said unto Laban, "Send me away, that I may go unto mine own place, and to my country. Give me my wives and my children, for whom I have served thee, and let me go: for thou knowest my service which I have done thee." And Laban said unto him, "I pray thee, if I have found favour in thine eyes, tarry: for I have learned by experience that the LORD hath blessed me for thy sake". And he said, "Appoint me thy wages, and I will give it". And he said unto him, "Thou knowest how I have served thee, and how thy cattle was with me. For it was little which thou hadst before I came, and it is now increased unto a multitude; and the LORD hath blessed thee since my coming: and now when shall I provide for mine own house also?" [30:22–30]

Jacob and the Speckled Cattle. And he said, "What shall I give thee?" And Jacob said, "Thou shalt not give me any thing: if thou wilt do this thing for me, I will again feed and keep thy flock: I will pass through all thy flock to day, removing from thence all the speckled and spotted cattle, and all the brown cattle among the sheep, and the spotted and speckled among the goats: and of such shall be my hire. So shall my righteousness answer for me in time to come, when it shall come for my hire before thy face: every one that is not speckled and spotted among the goats, and brown among the sheep, that shall be counted stolen with me." And Laban said, "Behold, I would it might be according to thy word". And he removed that day the he goats that were ringstraked and spotted, and all the she goats that were speckled and spotted, and every one that had some white in it, and all the brown among the sheep, and gave them into the hand of his sons. And he set three days' journey betwixt himself and Jacob: and Jacob fed the rest of Laban's flocks. And Jacob took him rods of green poplar, and of the hazel and chesnut tree; and pilled white strakes in them, and made the white appear which was in the rods. And he set the rods which he had pilled before the flocks in the gutters in the watering troughs when the flocks came to drink, that they should conceive when they came to drink. And the flocks conceived before the rods, and brought forth cattle ringstraked, speckled, and spotted. And Jacob did separate the lambs, and set the faces of the flocks toward the ringstraked, and all the brown in the flock of Laban; and he put his own flocks by themselves, and put them not unto Laban's cattle. And it came to pass, whensoever the stronger cattle did conceive, that Jacob laid the rods before the eyes of the cattle in the gutters, that they might conceive among the rods. But when the cattle were feeble, he put them not in: so the feebler were Laban's, and the stronger Jacob's. And the man increased exceedingly, and had much cattle, and maidservants, and menservants, and camels, and asses. [30:31–43]

Jacob Returns to Canaan. [Jacob's wealth grew and Laban's sons became jealous. So while Laban was shearing his sheep, Jacob took his wives, children, flocks, and herds, and fled away by night to return to the land of Canaan. Laban was angry and pursued after Jacob but they were reconciled; and Laban went back while Jacob continued his journey. Then he sent messengers and a great gift of his flocks and cattle to his brother Esau for he was greatly afraid.]

And he rose up that night, and took his two wives, and his two womenservants, and his eleven sons, and passed over the ford Jabbok. And he took them, and sent them over the brook, and sent over that he had. And Jacob was left alone; and there wrestled a man with him until the breaking of the day. And when he saw that he prevailed not against him, he touched the hollow of his thigh; and the hollow of Jacob's thigh was out of joint, as he wrestled with him. And he said, "Let me go, for the day breaketh". And he said, "I will not let thee go, except thou bless me". And he said unto him, "What is thy name?" And he said, "Jacob". And he said, "Thy name shall be called no more Jacob, but Israel: for as a prince hast thou power

with God and with men, and hast prevailed". And Jacob
asked him, and said, "Tell me, I pray thee, thy name".
And he said, "Wherefore is it that thou dost ask after my
name?" And he blessed him there. And Jacob called the
name of the place Peniel: "for I have seen God face to
face, and my life is preserved". And as he passed over
Penuel the sun rose upon him, and he halted upon his
thigh. Therefore the children of Israel eat not of the sinew
which shrank, which is upon the hollow of the thigh, unto
this day: because he touched the hollow of Jacob's thigh
in the sinew that shrank.   [32:22–32]

[The next day Jacob and Esau met and parted without
strife. Then Rachel conceived again but she died in giving
birth to a son whom Jacob named Benjamin.]

Joseph's Dreams.   And Jacob dwelt in the land wherein
his father was a stranger, in the land of Canaan. These are
the generations of Jacob. Joseph, being seventeen years
old, was feeding the flock with his brethren; and the lad
was with the sons of Bilhah, and with the sons of Zilpah,
his father's wives: and Joseph brought unto his father their
evil report. Now Israel loved Joseph more than all his children, because he was the son of his old age: and he made
him a coat of many colours. And when his brethren saw
that their father loved him more than all his brethren, they
hated him, and could not speak peaceably unto him. And
Joseph dreamed a dream, and he told it his brethren: and
they hated him yet the more. And he said unto them,
"Hear, I pray you, this dream which I have dreamed: For,
behold, we were binding sheaves in the field, and, lo, my
sheaf arose, and also stood upright; and, behold, your
sheaves stood round about, and made obeisance to my
sheaf". And his brethren said to him, "Shalt thou indeed
reign over us? or shalt thou indeed have dominion over
us?" And they hated him yet the more for his dreams, and
for his words. And he dreamed yet another dream, and
told it his brethren, and said, "Behold, I have dreamed a
dream more; and, behold, the sun and the moon and the

eleven stars made obeisance to me". And he told it to his father, and to his brethren: and his father rebuked him, and said unto him, "What is this dream that thou hast dreamed? Shall I and thy mother and thy brethren indeed come to bow down ourselves to thee to the earth?" And his brethren envied him; but his father observed the saying. And his brethren went to feed their father's flock in Shechem. And Israel said unto Joseph, "Do not thy brethren feed the flock in Shechem? come, and I will send thee unto them". And he said to him, "Here am I". And he said to him, "Go, I pray thee, see whether it be well with thy brethren, and well with the flocks; and bring me word again". So he sent him out of the vale of Hebron, and he came to Shechem. And a certain man found him, and, behold, he was wandering in the field: and the man asked him, saying, "What seekest thou?" And he said, "I seek my brethren: tell me, I pray thee, where they feed their flocks". And the man said, "They are departed hence; for I heard them say, 'Let us go to Dothan'". And Joseph went after his brethren, and found them in Dothan.

[37:1–17]

Joseph Hated by His Brethren. And when they saw him afar off, even before he came near unto them, they conspired against him to slay him. And they said one to another, "Behold, this dreamer cometh. Come now therefore, and let us slay him, and cast him into some pit, and we will say, Some evil beast hath devoured him: and we shall see what will become of his dreams." And Reuben heard it, and he delivered him out of their hands; and said, "Let us not kill him". And Reuben said unto them, "Shed no blood, but cast him into this pit that is in the wilderness, and lay no hand upon him"; that he might rid him out of their hands, to deliver him to his father again. And it came to pass, when Joseph was come unto his brethren, that they stript Joseph out of his coat, his coat of many colours that was on him; and they took him, and cast him into a pit: and the pit was empty, there was no water in it. And

they sat down to eat bread: and they lifted up their eyes
and looked, and, behold, a company of Ishmeelites came
from Gilead with their camels bearing spicery and balm
and myrrh, going to carry it down to Egypt. And Judah
said unto his brethren, "What profit is it if we slay our
brother, and conceal his blood? Come, and let us sell him
to the Ishmeelites, and let not our hand be upon him; for
he is our brother and our flesh." And his brethren were
content.   [37:18–27]

Joseph Sold into Egypt.   Then there passed by Midianites merchantmen; and they drew and lifted up Joseph
out of the pit, and sold Joseph to the Ishmeelites for twenty
pieces of silver: and they brought Joseph into Egypt. And
Reuben returned unto the pit; and, behold, Joseph was
not in the pit; and he rent his clothes. And he returned
unto his brethren, and said, "The child is not; and I,
whither shall I go?" And they took Joseph's coat, and
killed a kid of the goats, and dipped the coat in the blood;
and they sent the coat of many colours, and they brought
it to their father; and said, "This have we found: know
now whether it be thy son's coat or no". And he knew it,
and said, "It is my son's coat; an evil beast hath devoured
him; Joseph is without doubt rent in pieces". And Jacob
rent his clothes, and put sackcloth upon his loins, and
mourned for his son many days. And all his sons and all
his daughters rose up to comfort him; but he refused to be
comforted; and he said, "For I will go down into the grave
unto my son mourning". Thus his father wept for him. And
the Midianites sold him into Egypt unto Potiphar, an
officer of Pharaoh's, and captain of the guard. [37:28–36]

Potiphar's Wife Tempts Joseph.   And Joseph was
brought down to Egypt; and Potiphar, an officer of
Pharaoh, captain of the guard, an Egyptian, bought him
of the hands of the Ishmeelites, which had brought him
down thither. And the LORD was with Joseph, and he was
a prosperous man; and he was in the house of his master
the Egyptian. And his master saw that the LORD was with

him, and that the LORD made all that he did to prosper in his hand. And Joseph found grace in his sight, and he served him: and he made him overseer over his house, and all that he had he put into his hand. And it came to pass from the time that he had made him overseer in his house, and over all that he had, that the LORD blessed the Egyptian's house for Joseph's sake; and the blessing of the LORD was upon all that he had in the house, and in the field. And he left all that he had in Joseph's hand; and he knew not aught he had, save the bread which he did eat. And Joseph was a goodly person, and well favoured.

And it came to pass after these things, that his master's wife cast her eyes upon Joseph; and she said, "Lie with me". But he refused, and said unto his master's wife, "Behold, my master wotteth not what is with me in the house, and he hath committed all that he hath to my hand; there is none greater in this house than I; neither hath he kept back any thing from me but thee, because thou art his wife: how then can I do this great wickedness, and sin against God?" And it came to pass, as she spake to Joseph day by day, that he hearkened not unto her, to lie by her, or to be with her. And it came to pass about this time, that Joseph went into the house to do his business; and there was none of the men of the house there within. And she caught him by his garment, saying, "Lie with me": and he left his garment in her hand, and fled, and got him out. And it came to pass, when she saw that he had left his garment in her hand, and was fled forth, that she called unto the men of her house, and spake unto them, saying, "See, he hath brought in an Hebrew unto us to mock us; he came in unto me to lie with me, and I cried with a loud voice: and it came to pass, when he heard that I lifted up my voice and cried, that he left his garment with me, and fled, and got him out". And she laid up his garment by her, until his lord came home. And she spake unto him according to these words, saying, "The Hebrew servant, which thou hast brought unto us, came in unto me to mock me: and it came to pass, as I lifted up my voice and cried, that he left his garment with me, and fled out". And it came to pass, when his master heard the words of his wife, which she spake unto him, saying, "After this manner did thy servant to me"; that his wrath was kindled. And Joseph's master took him, and put him into the prison, a place where the king's prisoners were bound: and he was there in the prison. But the LORD was with Joseph, and shewed him mercy, and gave him favour in the sight of the keeper of the prison. And the keeper of the prison committed to Joseph's hand all the prisoners that were in the prison; and whatsoever they did there, he was the doer of it. The keeper of the prison looked not to any thing that was under his hand; because the LORD was with him, and that which he did, the LORD made it to prosper.   [39:1–23]

[In prison, Joseph interpreted the dreams of two of Pharaoh's servants, the chief of the bakers and the chief of the butlers.]

Pharaoh's Dreams.   And it came to pass at the end of two full years, that Pharaoh dreamed: and, behold, he stood by the river. And, behold, there came up out of the river seven well favoured kine and fatfleshed; and they fed in a meadow. And, behold, seven other kine came up after them out of the river, ill favoured and leanfleshed; and stood by the other kine upon the brink of the river. And the ill favoured and leanfleshed kine did eat up the seven well favoured and fat kine. So Pharaoh awoke. And he slept and dreamed the second time: and, behold, seven ears of corn came up upon one stalk, rank and good. And, behold, seven thin ears and blasted with the east wind sprung up after them. And the seven thin ears devoured the seven rank and full ears. And Pharaoh awoke, and, behold, it was a dream. And it came to pass in the morning that his spirit was troubled; and he sent and called for all the magicians of Egypt, and all the wise men thereof: and Pharaoh told them his dream; but there was none that could interpret them unto Pharaoh. Then spake the chief butler unto Pharaoh, saying, "I do remember my faults this day: Pharaoh was wroth with his servants, and put me in ward in the captain of the guard's house, both me and the chief baker: and we dreamed a dream in one night, I and he; we dreamed each man according to the interpretation of his dream. And there was there with us a young man, an Hebrew, servant to the captain of the guard; and we told him, and he interpreted to us our dreams; to each man according to his dream he did interpret. And it came to pass, as he interpreted to us, so it was; me he restored unto mine office, and him he hanged." [41:1–13]

Joseph Summoned. Then Pharaoh sent and called Joseph, and they brought him hastily out of the dungeon: and he shaved himself, and changed his raiment, and came in unto Pharaoh. And Pharaoh said unto Joseph, "I have dreamed a dream, and there is none that can interpret it: and I have heard say of thee, that thou canst understand a dream to interpret it". And Joseph answered Pharaoh, saying, "It is not in me: God shall give Pharaoh an answer of peace". And Pharaoh said unto Joseph, "In my dream, behold, I stood upon the bank of the river: and, behold, there came up out of the river seven kine, fatfleshed and well favoured; and they fed in a meadow: and, behold, seven other kine came up after them, poor and very ill favoured and leanfleshed, such as I never saw in all the land of Egypt for badness: and the lean and the ill favoured kine did eat up the first seven fat kine: and when they had eaten them up, it could not be known that they had eaten them; but they were still ill favoured, as at the beginning. So I awoke. And I saw in my dream, and, behold, seven ears came up in one stalk, full and good: and, behold, seven ears, withered, thin, and blasted with the east wind, sprung up after them: and the thin ears devoured the seven good ears: and I told this unto the magicians; but there was none that could declare it to me."

[41:14–24]

Joseph Interprets the Dreams. And Joseph said unto Pharaoh, "The dream of Pharaoh is one: God hath shewed Pharaoh what he is about to do. The seven good kine are seven years; and the seven good ears are seven years: the dream is one. And the seven thin and ill favoured kine that came up after them are seven years; and the seven empty ears blasted with the east wind shall be seven years of famine. This is the thing which I have spoken unto Pharaoh: What God is about to do he sheweth unto Pharaoh. Behold, there come seven years of great plenty throughout all the land of Egypt: and there shall arise after them seven years of famine; and all the plenty shall be forgotten in the land of Egypt; and the famine shall consume the land; and the plenty shall not be known in the land by reason of that famine following; for it shall be very grievous. And for that the dream was doubled unto Pharaoh twice; it is because the thing is established by God, and God will shortly bring it to pass. Now therefore let Pharaoh look out a man discreet and wise, and set him over the land of Egypt. Let Pharaoh do this, and let him appoint officers over the land, and take up the fifth part of the land of Egypt in the seven plenteous years. And let them gather all the food of those good years that come, and lay up corn under the hand of Pharaoh, and let them keep food in the cities. And that food shall be for store to the land against the seven years of famine, which shall be in the land of Egypt; that the land perish not through the famine." And the thing was good in the eyes of Pharaoh, and in the eyes of all his servants. [41:25-37]

Joseph Promoted. And Pharaoh said unto his servants, "Can we find such a one as this is, a man in whom the spirit of God is?" And Pharaoh said unto Joseph, "Forasmuch as God hath shewed thee all this, there is none so discreet and wise as thou art: thou shalt be over my house, and according unto thy word shall all my people be ruled: only in the throne will I be greater than thou". And Pharaoh said unto Joseph, "See, I have set thee over all the land of Egypt". And Pharaoh took off his ring from his hand, and put it upon Joseph's hand, and arrayed him in vestures of fine linen, and put a gold chain about his neck; and he made him to ride in the second chariot which he had; and they cried before him, "Bow the knee": and he made him ruler over all the land of Egypt. And Pharaoh said unto Joseph, "I am Pharaoh, and without thee shall no man lift up his hand or foot in all the land of Egypt". And Pharaoh called Joseph's name Zaphnath-paaneah; and he gave him to wife Asenath the daughter of Potipherah priest of On. And Joseph went out over all the land of Egypt. And Joseph was thirty years old when he stood before Pharaoh king of Egypt. And Joseph went out from the presence of Pharaoh, and went throughout all the land of Egypt. And in the seven plenteous years the earth brought forth by handfuls. And he gathered up all the food of the seven years, which were in the land of Egypt, and laid up the food in the cities: the food of the field, which was round about every city, laid he up in the same. And Joseph gathered corn as the sand of the sea, very much, until he left numbering; for it was without number. And unto Joseph were born two sons before the years of famine came, which Asenath the daughter of Potipherah priest of On bare unto him. And Joseph called the name of the firstborn Manasseh: "For God", said he, "hath made me forget all my toil, and all my father's house". And the name of the second called he Ephraim: "For God hath caused me to be fruitful in the land of my affliction". And the seven years of plenteousness, that was in the land of Egypt, were ended. And the seven years of dearth began to come, according as Joseph had said: and the dearth was in all lands; but in all the land of Egypt there was bread. And when all the land of Egypt was famished, the people cried to Pharaoh for bread: and Pharaoh said unto all the Egyptians, "Go unto Joseph; what he saith to you, do". And the famine was over all the face of the earth: and Joseph opened all the storehouses, and sold unto the

Egyptians; and the famine waxed sore in the land of
Egypt. And all countries came into Egypt to Joseph for
to buy corn; because that the famine was so sore in all
lands. [41:38–57]

Joseph's Brethren Come Down to Egypt. Now when
Jacob saw that there was corn in Egypt, Jacob said unto
his sons, "Why do ye look one upon another?" And he
said, "Behold, I have heard that there is corn in Egypt:
get you down thither, and buy for us from thence; that we
may live, and not die". And Joseph's ten brethren went
down to buy corn in Egypt. But Benjamin, Joseph's
brother, Jacob sent not with his brethren; for he said,
"Lest peradventure mischief befall him". And the sons of
Israel came to buy corn among those that came: for the
famine was in the land of Canaan. And Joseph was the
governor over the land, and he it was that sold to all the
people of the land: and Joseph's brethren came, and
bowed down themselves before him with their faces to the
earth. And Joseph saw his brethren, and he knew them,
but made himself strange unto them, and spake roughly
unto them; and he said unto them, "Whence come ye?"
And they said, "From the land of Canaan to buy food".
And Joseph knew his brethren, but they knew not him.
And Joseph remembered the dreams which he dreamed of
them, and said unto them, "Ye are spies; to see the nakedness of the land ye are come". And they said unto him,
"Nay, my lord, but to buy food are thy servants come.
We are all one man's sons; we are true men, thy servants
are no spies." And he said unto them, "Nay, but to see
the nakedness of the land ye are come". And they said,
"Thy servants are twelve brethren, the sons of one man in
the land of Canaan; and, behold, the youngest is this day
with our father, and one is not". And Joseph said unto
them, "That is it that I spake unto you, saying, Ye are
spies: hereby ye shall be proved: By the life of Pharaoh ye
shall not go forth hence, except your youngest brother
come hither. Send one of you, and let him fetch your

brother, and ye shall be kept in prison, that your words may be proved, whether there be any truth in you: or else by the life of Pharaoh surely ye are spies." And he put them all together into ward three days. And Joseph said unto them the third day, "This do, and live; for I fear God: if ye be true men, let one of your brethren be bound in the house of your prison: go ye, carry corn for the famine of your houses: but bring your youngest brother unto me; so shall your words be verified, and ye shall not die". And they did so. And they said one to another, "We are verily guilty concerning our brother, in that we saw the anguish of his soul, when he besought us, and we would not hear; therefore is this distress come upon us". And Reuben answered them, saying, "Spake I not unto you, saying, Do not sin against the child; and ye would not hear? therefore, behold, also his blood is required". And they knew not that Joseph understood them; for he spake unto them by an interpreter. And he turned himself about from them, and wept; and returned to them again, and communed with them, and took from them Simeon, and bound him before their eyes.   [42:1–24]

Joseph's Brethren Return to Canaan. Then Joseph commanded to fill their sacks with corn, and to restore every man's money into his sack, and to give them provision for the way: and thus did he unto them. And they laded their asses with the corn, and departed thence. And as one of them opened his sack to give his ass provender in the inn, he espied his money; for, behold, it was in his sack's mouth. And he said unto his brethren, "My money is restored; and, lo, it is even in my sack": and their heart failed them, and they were afraid, saying one to another, "What is this that God hath done unto us?" And they came unto Jacob their father unto the land of Canaan, and told him all that befell unto them; saying, "The man, who is the lord of the land, spake roughly to us, and took us for spies of the country. And we said unto him, We are true men; we are no spies: we be twelve brethren, sons of our father; one is not, and the youngest is this day with our father in the land of Canaan. And the man, the lord of the country, said unto us, 'Hereby shall I know that ye are true men; leave one of your brethren here with me, and take food for the famine of your households, and be gone: and bring your youngest brother unto me: then shall I know that ye are no spies, but that ye are true men: so will I deliver you your brother, and ye shall traffick in the land'." And it came to pass as they emptied their sacks, that, behold, every man's bundle of money was in his sack: and when both they and their father saw the bundles of money, they were afraid. And Jacob their father said unto them, "Me have ye bereaved of my children: Joseph is not, and Simeon is not, and ye will take Benjamin away: all these things are against me". And Reuben spake unto his father, saying, "Slay my two sons, if I bring him not to thee: deliver him into my hand, and I will bring him to thee again". And he said, "My son shall not go down with you; for his brother is dead, and he is left alone: if mischief befall him by the way in the which ye go, then shall ye bring down my gray hairs with sorrow to the grave".

[42:25-38]

Joseph's Brethren Come Again to Egypt. And the famine was sore in the land. And it came to pass, when they had eaten up the corn which they had brought out of Egypt, their father said unto them, "Go again, buy us a little food". And Judah spake unto him, saying, "The man did solemnly protest unto us, saying, 'Ye shall not see my face, except your brother be with you'. If thou wilt send our brother with us, we will go down and buy thee food: but if thou wilt not send him, we will not go down: for the man said unto us, 'Ye shall not see my face, except your brother be with you'." And Israel said, "Wherefore dealt ye so ill with me, as to tell the man whether ye had yet a brother?" And they said, "The man asked us straitly of our state, and of our kindred, saying, 'Is your father yet alive? have ye another brother?' and we told him according to the tenor of these words: could we certainly know that he would say, 'Bring your brother down'?" And Judah said unto Israel his father, "Send the lad with me, and we will arise and go; that we may live, and not die, both we, and thou, and also our little ones. I will be surety for him; of my hand shalt thou require him: if I bring him not unto thee, and set him before thee, then let me bear the blame for ever: for except we had lingered, surely now we had returned this second time." And their father Israel said unto them, "If it must be so now, do this; take of the best fruits in the land in your vessels, and carry down the man a present, a little balm, and a little honey, spices, and myrrh, nuts, and almonds: and take double money in your hand; and the money that was brought again in the mouth of your sacks, carry it again in your hand; peradventure it was an oversight: take also your brother, and arise, go again unto the man: and God Almighty give you mercy before the man, that he may send away your other brother, and Benjamin. If I be bereaved of my children, I am bereaved." [43:1–14]

Joseph and His Brethren. And the men took that present, and they took double money in their hand, and Benjamin; and rose up, and went down to Egypt, and stood before Joseph. And when Joseph saw Benjamin with them, he said to the ruler of his house, "Bring these men home, and slay, and make ready; for these men shall dine with me at noon". And the man did as Joseph bade; and the man brought the men into Joseph's house. And the men were afraid, because they were brought into Joseph's house; and they said, "Because of the money that was returned in our sacks at the first time are we brought in; that he may seek occasion against us, and fall upon us, and take us for bondmen, and our asses". And they came near to the steward of Joseph's house, and they communed with him at the door of the house, and said, "O sir, we came indeed down at the first time to buy food: and it came to pass, when we came to the inn, that we opened our sacks, and, behold, every man's money was in the mouth of his sack, our money in full weight: and we have brought it again in our hand. And other money have we brought down in our hands to buy food: we cannot tell who put our money in our sacks." And he said, "Peace be to you, fear not: your God, and the God of your father, hath given you treasure in your sacks: I had your money". And he brought Simeon out unto them. And the man brought the men into Joseph's house, and gave them water, and they washed their feet; and he gave their asses provender. And they made ready the present against Joseph came at noon: for they heard that they should eat bread there.

[43:15–25]

Joseph Entertains His Brethren. And when Joseph came home, they brought him the present which was in their hand into the house, and bowed themselves to him to the earth. And he asked them of their welfare, and said, "Is your father well, the old man of whom ye spake? Is he yet alive?" And they answered, "Thy servant our father is in good health, he is yet alive". And they bowed down their heads, and made obeisance. And he lifted up his eyes, and saw his brother Benjamin, his mother's son, and said, "Is this your younger brother, of whom ye spake unto me?" And he said, "God be gracious unto thee, my son". And Joseph made haste; for his bowels did yearn upon his brother: and he sought where to weep; and he entered into his chamber, and wept there. And he washed his face, and went out, and refrained himself, and said, "Set on bread". And they set on for him by himself, and for them by themselves, and for the Egyptians, which did eat with him, by themselves: because the Egyptians might not eat bread with the Hebrews; for that is an abomination unto the Egyptians. And they sat before him, the firstborn according to his birthright, and the youngest according to his youth: and the men marvelled one at another. And he took and sent messes unto them from before him: but Benjamin's mess was five times so much as any of theirs.

And they drank, and were merry with him.   [43:26–34]

Joseph's Brethren Leave Egypt. And he commanded
the steward of his house, saying, "Fill the men's sacks
with food, as much as they can carry, and put every
man's money in his sack's mouth. And put my cup, the
silver cup, in the sack's mouth of the youngest, and his corn
money." And he did according to the word that Joseph
had spoken. As soon as the morning was light, the men
were sent away, they and their asses. And when they were
gone out of the city, and not yet far off, Joseph said unto
his steward, "Up, follow after the men; and when thou dost
overtake them, say unto them, 'Wherefore have ye rewarded evil for good? Is not this it in which my lord
drinketh, and whereby indeed he divineth? ye have done
evil in so doing.'" And he overtook them, and he spake
unto them these same words. And they said unto him,
"Wherefore saith my lord these words? God forbid that
thy servants should do according to this thing: behold,
the money, which we found in our sacks' mouths, we
brought again unto thee out of the land of Canaan: how
then should we steal out of thy lord's house silver or gold?
With whomsoever of thy servants it be found, both let him
die, and we also will be my lord's bondmen." And he said,
"Now also let it be according unto your words: he with
whom it is found shall be my servant; and ye shall be
blameless". Then they speedily took down every man his
sack to the ground, and opened every man his sack. And
he searched, and began at the eldest, and left at the
youngest: and the cup was found in Benjamin's sack.
Then they rent their clothes, and laded every man his ass,
and returned to the city. And Judah and his brethren
came to Joseph's house; for he was yet there: and they
fell before him on the ground. And Joseph said unto them,
"What deed is this that ye have done? wot ye not that such
a man as I can certainly divine?" And Judah said, "What
shall we say unto my lord? what shall we speak? or how
shall we clear ourselves? God hath found out the iniquity

of thy servants: behold, we are my lord's servants, both we, and he also with whom the cup is found." And he said, "God forbid that I should do so: but the man in whose hand the cup is found, he shall be my servant; and as for you, get you up in peace unto your father".   [44:1-17]

Judah Pleads for Benjamin. Then Judah came near unto him, and said, "Oh my lord, let thy servant, I pray thee, speak a word in my lord's ears, and let not thine anger burn against thy servant: for thou art even as Pharaoh. My lord asked his servants, saying, 'Have ye a father, or a brother?' And we said unto my lord, We have a father, an old man, and a child of his old age, a little one; and his brother is dead, and he alone is left of his mother, and his father loveth him. And thou saidst unto thy servants, 'Bring him down unto me, that I may set mine eyes upon him'. And we said unto my lord, The lad cannot leave his father: for if he should leave his father, his father would die. And thou saidst unto thy servants, 'Except your youngest brother come down with you, ye shall see my face no more'. And it came to pass when we came up unto thy servant my father, we told him the words of my lord. And our father said, 'Go again, and buy us a little food'. And we said, We cannot go down: if our youngest brother be with us, then will we go down: for we may not see the man's face, except our youngest brother be with us. And thy servant my father said unto us, 'Ye know that my wife bare me two sons: and the one went out from me, and I said, Surely he is torn in pieces; and I saw him not since: and if ye take this also from me, and mischief befall him, ye shall bring down my gray hairs with sorrow to the grave'. Now therefore when I come to thy servant my father, and the lad be not with us; seeing that his life is bound up in the lad's life; it shall come to pass, when he seeth that the lad is not with us, that he will die: and thy servants shall bring down the gray hairs of thy servant our father with sorrow to the grave. For thy servant became surety for the lad unto my father, saying, If I

bring him not unto thee, then I shall bear the blame to my
father for ever. Now therefore, I pray thee, let thy servant
abide instead of the lad a bondman to my lord; and let the
lad go up with his brethren. For how shall I go up to my
father, and the lad be not with me? lest peradventure I
see the evil that shall come on my father." [44:18–34]

Joseph Reveals Himself to His Brethren. Then Joseph
could not refrain himself before all them that stood by
him; and he cried, "Cause every man to go out from me".
And there stood no man with him, while Joseph made
himself known unto his brethren. And he wept aloud: and
the Egyptians and the house of Pharaoh heard. And Joseph
said unto his brethren, "I am Joseph; doth my father yet
live?" And his brethren could not answer him; for they
were troubled at his presence. And Joseph said unto his
brethren, "Come near to me, I pray you". And they came
near. And he said, "I am Joseph your brother, whom ye
sold into Egypt. Now therefore be not grieved, nor angry
with yourselves, that ye sold me hither: for God did send
me before you to preserve life. For these two years hath
the famine been in the land: and yet there are five years, in
the which there shall neither be earing nor harvest. And
God sent me before you to preserve you a posterity in the
earth, and to save your lives by a great deliverance. So now
it was not you that sent me hither, but God: and he hath
made me a father to Pharaoh, and lord of all his house,
and a ruler throughout all the land of Egypt. Haste ye,
and go up to my father, and say unto him, 'Thus saith thy
son Joseph, God hath made me lord of all Egypt: come
down unto me, tarry not: and thou shalt dwell in the
land of Goshen, and thou shalt be near unto me, thou,
and thy children, and thy children's children, and thy
flocks, and thy herds, and all that thou hast: and there
will I nourish thee; for yet there are five years of famine;
lest thou, and thy household, and all that thou hast, come
to poverty'. And, behold, your eyes see, and the eyes of
my brother Benjamin, that it is my mouth that speaketh

unto you. And ye shall tell my father of all my glory in
Egypt, and of all that ye have seen; and ye shall haste and
bring down my father hither." And he fell upon his brother
Benjamin's neck, and wept; and Benjamin wept upon his
neck. Moreover he kissed all his brethren, and wept upon
them: and after that his brethren talked with him.

[45:1–15]

Joseph Sends for His Father. And the fame thereof
was heard in Pharaoh's house, saying, "Joseph's brethren
are come": and it pleased Pharaoh well, and his servants.
And Pharaoh said unto Joseph, "Say unto thy brethren,
'This do ye; lade your beasts, and go, get you unto the land
of Canaan; and take your father and your households,
and come unto me: and I will give you the good of the land
of Egypt, and ye shall eat the fat of the land. Now thou art
commanded, this do ye; take you wagons out of the land of
Egypt for your little ones, and for your wives, and bring
your father, and come. Also regard not your stuff; for the
good of all the land of Egypt is yours.'" And the children
of Israel did so: and Joseph gave them wagons, according
to the commandment of Pharaoh, and gave them provision
for the way. To all of them he gave each man changes of
raiment; but to Benjamin he gave three hundred pieces of
silver, and five changes of raiment. And to his father he
sent after this manner; ten asses laden with the good things
of Egypt, and ten she asses laden with corn and bread and
meat for his father by the way. So he sent his brethren
away, and they departed: and he said unto them, "See that
ye fall not out by the way". And they went up out of Egypt,
and came into the land of Canaan unto Jacob their father,
and told him, saying, "Joseph is yet alive, and he is governor over all the land of Egypt". And Jacob's heart
fainted, for he believed them not. And they told him all
the words of Joseph, which he had said unto them: and
when he saw the wagons which Joseph had sent to carry
him, the spirit of Jacob their father revived: and Israel

said, "It is enough; Joseph my son is yet alive: I will go
and see him before I die".   [45:16-28]

The Death of Jacob. [So Jacob and all his family
came down to Egypt and Pharaoh gave them a place to
live in the land of Goshen. And here, Jacob, knowing
that he was soon to die, blessed his sons.]

And he charged them, and said unto them, "I am to be
gathered unto my people: bury me with my fathers in the
cave that is in the field of Ephron the Hittite, in the cave
that is in the field of Machpelah, which is before Mamre, in
the land of Canaan, which Abraham bought with the field
of Ephron the Hittite for a possession of a buryingplace.
There they buried Abraham and Sarah his wife; there they
buried Isaac and Rebekah his wife; and there I buried
Leah. The purchase of the field and of the cave that is
therein was from the children of Heth." And when Jacob
had made an end of commanding his sons, he gathered up
his feet into the bed, and yielded up the ghost, and was
gathered unto his people.   [49:29-33]

[In time Joseph also died, having first made his brethren
promise that they would carry his bones with them when
they returned into Canaan.]

From EXODUS

The Israelites Oppressed. Now there arose up a new king over Egypt, which knew not Joseph. And he said unto his people, "Behold, the people of the children of Israel are more and mightier than we: come on, let us deal wisely with them; lest they multiply, and it come to pass, that, when there falleth out any war, they join also unto our enemies, and fight against us, and so get them up out of the land". Therefore they did set over them taskmasters to afflict them with their burdens. And they built for Pharaoh treasure cities, Pithom and Raamses. But the more they afflicted them, the more they multiplied and grew. And they were grieved because of the children of Israel. And the Egyptians made the children of Israel to serve with rigour: and they made their lives bitter with hard bondage, in morter, and in brick, and in all manner of service in the field: all their service, wherein they made them serve, was with rigour.

And the king of Egypt spake to the Hebrew midwives, of which the name of the one was Shiphrah, and the name of the other Puah: and he said, "When ye do the office of a midwife to the Hebrew women, and see them upon the stools; if it be a son, then ye shall kill him: but if it be a daughter, then she shall live". But the midwives feared God, and did not as the king of Egypt commanded them, but saved the menchildren alive. And the king of Egypt called for the midwives, and said unto them, "Why have ye done this thing, and have saved the menchildren alive?" And the midwives said unto Pharaoh, "Because the

Hebrew women are not as the Egyptian women; for they are lively, and are delivered ere the midwives come in unto them". Therefore God dealt well with the midwives: and the people multiplied, and waxed very mighty. And it came to pass, because the midwives feared God, that he made them houses. And Pharaoh charged all his people, saying, "Every son that is born ye shall cast into the river, and every daughter ye shall save alive".   [1:8–22]

The Birth of Moses. And there went a man of the house of Levi, and took to wife a daughter of Levi. And the woman conceived, and bare a son: and when she saw him that he was a goodly child, she hid him three months. And when she could not longer hide him, she took for him an ark of bulrushes, and daubed it with slime and with pitch, and put the child therein; and she laid it in the flags by the river's brink. And his sister stood afar off, to wit what would be done to him. And the daughter of Pharaoh came down to wash herself at the river; and her maidens walked along by the river's side; and when she saw the ark among the flags, she sent her maid to fetch it. And when she had opened it, she saw the child: and, behold, the babe wept. And she had compassion on him, and said, "This is one of the Hebrews' children".   [2:1–6]

Moses Adopted by Pharaoh's Daughter. Then said his sister to Pharaoh's daughter, "Shall I go and call to thee a nurse of the Hebrew women, that she may nurse the child for thee?" And Pharaoh's daughter said to her, "Go". And the maid went and called the child's mother. And Pharaoh's daughter said unto her, "Take this child away, and nurse it for me, and I will give thee thy wages". And the woman took the child, and nursed it. And the child grew, and she brought him unto Pharaoh's daughter, and he became her son. And she called his name Moses: and she said, "Because I drew him out of the water".   [2:7–10]

Moses Flees from Egypt. And it came to pass in those days, when Moses was grown, that he went out unto his brethren, and looked on their burdens: and he spied an

Egyptian smiting an Hebrew, one of his brethren. And he looked this way and that way, and when he saw that there was no man, he slew the Egyptian, and hid him in the sand. And when he went out the second day, behold, two men of the Hebrews strove together: and he said to him that did the wrong, "Wherefore smitest thou thy fellow?" And he said, "Who made thee a prince and a judge over us? intendest thou to kill me, as thou killedst the Egyptian?" And Moses feared, and said, "Surely this thing is known". Now when Pharaoh heard this thing, he sought to slay Moses. But Moses fled from the face of Pharaoh, and dwelt in the land of Midian: and he sat down by a well. Now the priest of Midian had seven daughters: and they came and drew water, and filled the troughs to water their father's flock. And the shepherds came and drove them away: but Moses stood up and helped them, and watered their flock. And when they came to Reuel their father, he said, "How is it that ye are come so soon to day?" And they said, "An Egyptian delivered us out of the hand of the shepherds, and also drew water enough for us, and watered the flock". And he said unto his daughters, "And where is he? why is it that ye have left the man? call him, that he may eat bread". And Moses was content to dwell with the man: and he gave Moses Zipporah his daughter. And she bare him a son, and he called his name Gershom: for he said, "I have been a stranger in a strange land".

[2:11–22]

The Burning Bush. Now Moses kept the flock of Jethro his father in law, the priest of Midian: and he led the flock to the backside of the desert, and came to the mountain of God, even to Horeb. And the angel of the LORD appeared unto him in a flame of fire out of the midst of a bush: and he looked, and, behold, the bush burned with fire, and the bush was not consumed. And Moses said, "I will now turn aside, and see this great sight, why the bush is not burnt". And when the LORD saw that he turned aside to see, God called unto him out of the midst of the bush, and said, "Moses, Moses". And he said, "Here am I". And he said, "Draw not nigh hither: put off thy shoes from off thy feet, for the place whereon thou standest is holy ground". Moreover he said, "I am the God of thy father, the God of Abraham, the God of Isaac, and the God of Jacob". And Moses hid his face; for he was afraid to look upon God.   [3:1-6]

Moses Sent to Deliver His People. And the LORD said, "I have surely seen the affliction of my people which are in Egypt, and have heard their cry by reason of their taskmasters; for I know their sorrows; and I am come down to deliver them out of the hand of the Egyptians, and to bring them up out of that land unto a good land and a large, unto a land flowing with milk and honey; unto the place of the Canaanites, and the Hittites, and the Amorites, and the Perizzites, and the Hivites, and the Jebusites. Now therefore, behold, the cry of the children of Israel is come unto me: and I have also seen the oppression wherewith the Egyptians oppress them. Come now therefore, and I will send thee unto Pharaoh, that thou mayest bring forth my people the children of Israel out of Egypt." And Moses said unto God, "Who am I, that I should go unto Pharaoh, and that I should bring forth the children of Israel out of Egypt?" And he said, "Certainly I will be with thee; and this shall be a token unto thee, that I have sent thee: When thou hast brought forth the people out of Egypt, ye shall serve God upon this mountain".   [3:7-12]

The Revelation of God's Name. And Moses said unto God, "Behold, when I come unto the children of Israel, and shall say unto them, The God of your fathers hath sent me unto you; and they shall say to me, 'What is his name?' what shall I say unto them?" And God said unto Moses, I AM THAT I AM:[1] and he said, "Thus shalt thou say unto the children of Israel, 'I AM hath sent me unto you'". And God said moreover unto Moses, "Thus shalt thou

---

[1] See Appendix 2.

say unto the children of Israel, 'The LORD God of your
fathers, the God of Abraham, the God of Isaac, and the
God of Jacob, hath sent me unto you: this is my name for
ever, and this is my memorial unto all generations'. Go,
and gather the elders of Israel together, and say unto
them, 'The LORD God of your fathers, the God of Abraham, of Isaac, and of Jacob, appeared unto me, saying, I
have surely visited you, and seen that which is done to you
in Egypt: and I have said, I will bring you up out of the
affliction of Egypt unto the land of the Canaanites, and the
Hittites, and the Amorites, and the Perizzites, and the
Hivites, and the Jebusites, unto a land flowing with milk
and honey'. And they shall hearken to thy voice: and thou
shalt come, thou and the elders of Israel, unto the king
of Egypt, and ye shall say unto him, 'The LORD God of
the Hebrews hath met with us: and now let us go, we beseech thee, three days' journey into the wilderness, that
we may sacrifice to the LORD our God'. And I am sure that
the king of Egypt will not let you go, no, not by a mighty
hand. And I will stretch out my hand, and smite Egypt
with all my wonders which I will do in the midst thereof:
and after that he will let you go. And I will give this people
favour in the sight of the Egyptians: and it shall come to
pass, that, when ye go, ye shall not go empty: but every
woman shall borrow of her neighbour, and of her that
sojourneth in her house, jewels of silver, and jewels of
gold, and raiment: and ye shall put them upon your sons,
and upon your daughters; and ye shall spoil the Egyptians."
[3:13–22]

Moses' Reluctance. And Moses answered and said,
"But, behold, they will not believe me, nor hearken unto
my voice: for they will say, 'The LORD hath not appeared
unto thee'". And the LORD said unto him, "What is that
in thine hand?" And he said, "A rod". And he said, "Cast
it on the ground". And he cast it on the ground, and it
became a serpent; and Moses fled from before it. And the
LORD said unto Moses, "Put forth thine hand, and take it

by the tail". And he put forth his hand, and caught it, and it became a rod in his hand: "That they may believe that the LORD God of their fathers, the God of Abraham, the God of Isaac, and the God of Jacob, hath appeared unto thee". And the LORD said furthermore unto him, "Put now thine hand into thy bosom". And he put his hand into his bosom: and when he took it out, behold, his hand was leprous as snow. And he said, "Put thine hand into thy bosom again". And he put his hand into his bosom again; and plucked it out of his bosom, and, behold, it was turned again as his other flesh. "And it shall come to pass, if they will not believe thee, neither hearken to the voice of the first sign, that they will believe the voice of the latter sign. And it shall come to pass, if they will not believe also these two signs, neither hearken unto thy voice, that thou shalt take of the water of the river, and pour it upon the dry land: and the water which thou takest out of the river shall become blood upon the dry land."

And Moses said unto the LORD, "O my Lord, I am not eloquent, neither heretofore, nor since thou hast spoken unto thy servant: but I am slow of speech, and of a slow tongue". And the LORD said unto him, "Who hath made man's mouth? or who maketh the dumb, or deaf, or the seeing, or the blind? have not I the LORD? Now therefore go, and I will be with thy mouth, and teach thee what thou shalt say." And he said, "O my Lord, send, I pray thee, by the hand of him whom thou wilt send". And the anger of the LORD was kindled against Moses, and he said, "Is not Aaron the Levite thy brother? I know that he can speak well. And also, behold, he cometh forth to meet thee: and when he seeth thee, he will be glad in his heart. And thou shalt speak unto him, and put words in his mouth: and I will be with thy mouth, and with his mouth, and will teach you what ye shall do. And he shall be thy spokesman unto the people: and he shall be, even he shall be to thee instead of a mouth, and thou shalt be to him

instead of God. And thou shalt take this rod in thine
hand, wherewith thou shalt do signs." [4:1–17]

[So Moses went back to the Israelites and spoke to the
elders of the people.]

The Burdens of the Israelites Increased. And afterward Moses and Aaron went in, and told Pharaoh, "Thus
saith the LORD God of Israel, 'Let my people go, that they
may hold a feast unto me in the wilderness'". And Pharaoh said, "Who is the LORD, that I should obey his voice
to let Israel go? I know not the LORD, neither will I let
Israel go." And they said, "The God of the Hebrews hath
met with us: let us go, we pray thee, three days' journey
into the desert, and sacrifice unto the LORD our God; lest
he fall upon us with pestilence, or with the sword". And
the king of Egypt said unto them, "Wherefore do ye,
Moses and Aaron, let the people from their works? get
you unto your burdens". And Pharaoh said, "Behold, the
people of the land now are many, and ye make them rest
from their burdens". And Pharaoh commanded the same
day the taskmasters of the people, and their officers, saying, "Ye shall no more give the people straw to make brick,
as heretofore: let them go and gather straw for themselves.
And the tale of the bricks, which they did make heretofore,
ye shall lay upon them; ye shall not diminish aught thereof:
for they be idle; therefore they cry, saying, 'Let us go and
sacrifice to our God'. Let there more work be laid upon
the men, that they may labour therein; and let them not
regard vain words." And the taskmasters of the people
went out, and their officers, and they spake to the people,
saying, "Thus saith Pharaoh, 'I will not give you straw.
Go ye, get you straw where ye can find it: yet not aught
of your work shall be diminished.'"

So the people were scattered abroad throughout all the
land of Egypt to gather stubble instead of straw. And the
taskmasters hasted them, saying, "Fulfil your works, your
daily tasks, as when there was straw". And the officers of
the children of Israel, which Pharaoh's taskmasters had

set over them, were beaten, and demanded, "Wherefore
have ye not fulfilled your task in making brick both yesterday and to day, as heretofore?" Then the officers of the
children of Israel came and cried unto Pharaoh, saying,
"Wherefore dealest thou thus with thy servants? There is
no straw given unto thy servants, and they say to us,
'Make brick': and, behold, thy servants are beaten; but the
fault is in thine own people." But he said, "Ye are idle, ye
are idle: therefore ye say, 'Let us go and do sacrifice to the
LORD'. Go therefore now, and work; for there shall no
straw be given you, yet shall ye deliver the tale of bricks."

[5:1–18]

The People Complain. And the officers of the children
of Israel did see that they were in evil case, after it was
said, "Ye shall not minish aught from your bricks of your
daily task". And they met Moses and Aaron, who stood in
the way, as they came forth from Pharaoh: and they said
unto them, "The LORD look upon you, and judge; because
ye have made our savour to be abhorred in the eyes of
Pharaoh, and in the eyes of his servants, to put a sword in
their hand to slay us". And Moses returned unto the LORD,
and said, "Lord, wherefore hast thou so evil entreated this
people? why is it that thou hast sent me? For since I came
to Pharaoh to speak in thy name, he hath done evil to this
people; neither hast thou delivered thy people at all."

Then the LORD said unto Moses, "Now shalt thou see
what I will do to Pharaoh: for with a strong hand shall he
let them go, and with a strong hand shall he drive them
out of his land".

And God spake unto Moses, and said unto him, "I am
the LORD: and I appeared unto Abraham, unto Isaac, and
unto Jacob, by the name of God Almighty, but by my
name JEHOVAH[2] was I not known to them. And I have
also established my covenant with them, to give them the

[2] See Appendix 2.

land of Canaan, the land of their pilgrimage, wherein they were strangers. And I have also heard the groaning of the children of Israel, whom the Egyptians keep in bondage; and I have remembered my covenant. Wherefore say unto the children of Israel, 'I am the LORD, and I will bring you out from under the burdens of the Egyptians, and I will rid you out of their bondage, and I will redeem you with a stretched out arm, and with great judgments: and I will take you to me for a people, and I will be to you a God: and ye shall know that I am the LORD your God, which bringeth you out from under the burdens of the Egyptians. And I will bring you in unto the land, concerning the which I did swear to give it to Abraham, to Isaac, and to Jacob; and I will give it you for an heritage: I am the LORD.'" And Moses spake so unto the children of Israel: but they hearkened not unto Moses for anguish of spirit, and for cruel bondage. [5:19–23; 6:1–9]

[Moses and Aaron again appeared before Pharaoh but he hardened his heart and would not let the people go. Then Egypt was afflicted by plagues. The river turned to blood and the fish died and the river stank. And out of the river came forth a plague of frogs; and after the frogs, a plague of lice on man and beast; and after the lice, came swarms of flies; and after the flies, boils breaking out on man and beast; and after the boils, thunder and hail which destroyed the flax and barley; and after the hail, swarms of locusts which ate up what the hail had left; and after the locusts, there was darkness over the land of Egypt for three days. At each plague Pharaoh sent for Moses and besought him to take away the plague and he would let the people go; but as soon as the plague had gone, Pharaoh again hardened his heart.]

The Last Plague. And the LORD said unto Moses, "Yet will I bring one plague more upon Pharaoh, and upon Egypt; afterwards he will let you go hence: when he shall let you go, he shall surely thrust you out hence altogether. Speak now in the ears of the people, and let every man borrow of his neighbour, and every woman of her neighbour, jewels of silver, and jewels of gold." And the LORD gave the people favour in the sight of the Egyptians. Moreover the man Moses was very great in the land of Egypt, in the sight of Pharaoh's servants, and in the sight of the people.

And Moses said, "Thus saith the LORD, 'About midnight will I go out into the midst of Egypt: and all the firstborn in the land of Egypt shall die, from the firstborn of Pharaoh that sitteth upon his throne, even unto the firstborn of the maidservant that is behind the mill; and all the firstborn of beasts. And there shall be a great cry throughout all the land of Egypt, such as there was none like it, nor shall be like it any more.' But against any of the children of Israel shall not a dog move his tongue, against man or beast: that ye may know how that the LORD doth put a difference between the Egyptians and Israel. And all these thy servants shall come down unto me, and bow down themselves unto me, saying, 'Get thee out, and all the people that follow thee': and after that I will go out." And he went out from Pharaoh in a great anger.

And the LORD said unto Moses, "Pharaoh shall not hearken unto you; that my wonders may be multiplied in the land of Egypt". And Moses and Aaron did all these wonders before Pharaoh: and the LORD hardened Pharaoh's heart, so that he would not let the children of Israel go out of his land. [11:1–10]

Preparations for Departure. And the LORD spake unto Moses and Aaron in the land of Egypt, saying, "This month shall be unto you the beginning of months: it shall be the first month of the year to you. Speak ye unto all the congregation of Israel, saying, 'In the tenth day of this month they shall take to them every man a lamb, according to the house of their fathers, a lamb for an house: and if the household be too little for the lamb, let him and his neighbour next unto his house take it according to the number of the souls; every man according to his eating

shall make your count for the lamb. Your lamb shall be
without blemish, a male of the first year: ye shall take it
out from the sheep, or from the goats: and ye shall keep
it up until the fourteenth day of the same month: and the
whole assembly of the congregation of Israel shall kill it
in the evening. And they shall take of the blood, and strike
it on the two side posts and on the upper door post of the
houses, wherein they shall eat it. And they shall eat the
flesh in that night, roast with fire, and unleavened bread;
and with bitter herbs they shall eat it. Eat not of it raw,
nor sodden at all with water, but roast with fire; his head
with his legs, and with the purtenance thereof. And ye
shall let nothing of it remain until the morning; and that
which remaineth of it until the morning ye shall burn
with fire. And thus shall ye eat it; with your loins girded,
your shoes on your feet, and your staff in your hand; and
ye shall eat it in haste: it is the LORD's passover. For I will
pass through the land of Egypt this night, and will smite
all the firstborn in the land of Egypt, both man and beast;
and against all the gods of Egypt I will execute judgment:
I am the LORD. And the blood shall be to you for a token
upon the houses where ye are: and when I see the blood,
I will pass over you, and the plague shall not be upon you
to destroy you, when I smite the land of Egypt. And this
day shall be unto you for a memorial; and ye shall keep it
a feast to the LORD throughout your generations; ye shall
keep it a feast by an ordinance for ever. Seven days shall
ye eat unleavened bread; even the first day ye shall put
away leaven out of your houses: for whosoever eateth
leavened bread from the first day until the seventh day,
that soul shall be cut off from Israel. And in the first day
there shall be an holy convocation, and in the seventh day
there shall be an holy convocation to you; no manner of
work shall be done in them, save that which every man
must eat, that only may be done of you. And ye shall observe the feast of unleavened bread; for in this selfsame
day have I brought your armies out of the land of Egypt:

therefore shall ye observe this day in your generations by an ordinance for ever. In the first month, on the fourteenth day of the month at even, ye shall eat unleavened bread, until the one and twentieth day of the month at even. Seven days shall there be no leaven found in your houses: for whosoever eateth that which is leavened, even that soul shall be cut off from the congregation of Israel, whether he be a stranger, or born in the land. Ye shall eat nothing leavened; in all your habitations shall ye eat unleavened bread.'"   [12:1–20]

The Firstborn in Egypt Slain.   And it came to pass, that at midnight the LORD smote all the firstborn in the land of Egypt, from the firstborn of Pharaoh that sat on his throne unto the firstborn of the captive that was in the dungeon; and all the firstborn of cattle. And Pharaoh rose up in the night, he, and all his servants, and all the Egyptians; and there was a great cry in Egypt; for there was not a house where there was not one dead. And he called for Moses and Aaron by night, and said, "Rise up, and get you forth from among my people, both ye and the children of Israel; and go, serve the LORD, as ye have said. Also take your flocks and your herds, as ye have said, and be gone; and bless me also." And the Egyptians were urgent upon the people, that they might send them out of the land in haste; for they said, "We be all dead men". And the people took their dough before it was leavened, their kneadingtroughs being bound up in their clothes upon their shoulders. And the children of Israel did according to the word of Moses; and they borrowed of the Egyptians jewels of silver, and jewels of gold, and raiment: and the LORD gave the people favour in the sight of the Egyptians, so that they lent unto them such things as they required. And they spoiled the Egyptians.   [12:29–36]

The Passover Established.   And the LORD spake unto Moses, saying, "Sanctify unto me all the firstborn, whatsoever openeth the womb among the children of Israel, both of man and of beast: it is mine".

And Moses said unto the people, "Remember this day, in which ye came out from Egypt, out of the house of bondage; for by strength of hand the LORD brought you out from this place: there shall no leavened bread be eaten. This day came ye out in the month Abib. And it shall be when the LORD shall bring thee into the land of the Canaanites, and the Hittites, and the Amorites, and the Hivites, and the Jebusites, which he sware unto thy fathers to give thee, a land flowing with milk and honey, that thou shalt keep this service in this month. Seven days thou shalt eat unleavened bread, and in the seventh day shall be a feast to the LORD. Unleavened bread shall be eaten seven days; and there shall no leavened bread be seen with thee, neither shall there be leaven seen with thee in all thy quarters. And thou shalt shew thy son in that day, saying, 'This is done because of that which the LORD did unto me when I came forth out of Egypt'. And it shall be for a sign unto thee upon thine hand, and for a memorial between thine eyes, that the LORD's law may be in thy mouth: for with a strong hand hath the LORD brought thee out of Egypt. Thou shalt therefore keep this ordinance in his season from year to year. [13:1–10]

Pharaoh Pursues the Israelites. And the LORD spake unto Moses, saying, "Speak unto the children of Israel, that they turn and encamp before Pi-hahiroth, between Migdol and the sea, over against Baal-zephon: before it shall ye encamp by the sea. For Pharaoh will say of the children of Israel, 'They are entangled in the land, the wilderness hath shut them in'. And I will harden Pharaoh's heart, that he shall follow after them; and I will be honoured upon Pharaoh, and upon all his host; that the Egyptians may know that I am the LORD." And they did so. And it was told the king of Egypt that the people fled: and the heart of Pharaoh and of his servants was turned against the people, and they said, "Why have we done this, that we have let Israel go from serving us?" And he made ready his chariot, and took his people with him:

and he took six hundred chosen chariots, and all the chariots of Egypt, and captains over every one of them. And the LORD hardened the heart of Pharaoh king of Egypt, and he pursued after the children of Israel: and the children of Israel went out with an high hand. But the Egyptians pursued after them, all the horses and chariots of Pharaoh, and his horsemen, and his army, and overtook them encamping by the sea, beside Pi-hahiroth, before Baal-zephon. And when Pharaoh drew nigh, the children of Israel lifted up their eyes, and, behold, the Egyptians marched after them; and they were sore afraid: and the children of Israel cried out unto the LORD. And they said unto Moses, "Because there were no graves in Egypt, hast thou taken us away to die in the wilderness? wherefore hast thou dealt thus with us, to carry us forth out of Egypt? Is not this the word that we did tell thee in Egypt, saying, Let us alone, that we may serve the Egyptians? For it had been better for us to serve the Egyptians, than that we should die in the wilderness." And Moses said unto the people, "Fear ye not, stand still, and see the salvation of the LORD, which he will shew to you to day: for the Egyptians whom ye have seen to day, ye shall see them again no more for ever. The LORD shall fight for you, and ye shall hold your peace."

And the LORD said unto Moses, "Wherefore criest thou unto me? speak unto the children of Israel, that they go forward: but lift thou up thy rod, and stretch out thine hand over the sea, and divide it: and the children of Israel shall go on dry ground through the midst of the sea. And I, behold, I will harden the hearts of the Egyptians, and they shall follow them: and I will get me honour upon Pharaoh, and upon all his host, upon his chariots, and upon his horsemen. And the Egyptians shall know that I am the LORD, when I have gotten me honour upon Pharaoh, upon his chariots, and upon his horsemen." And the angel of God, which went before the camp of Israel, removed and went behind them; and the pillar of the cloud went from before their face, and stood behind them: and it came between the camp of the Egyptians and the camp of Israel; and it was a cloud and darkness to them, but it gave light by night to these: so that the one came not near the other all the night. [14:1–20]

The Crossing of the Red Sea. And Moses stretched out his hand over the sea; and the LORD caused the sea to go back by a strong east wind all that night, and made the sea dry land, and the waters were divided. And the children of Israel went into the midst of the sea upon the dry ground: and the waters were a wall unto them on their right hand, and on their left. And the Egyptians pursued, and went in after them to the midst of the sea, even all Pharaoh's horses, his chariots, and his horsemen. And it came to pass, that in the morning watch the LORD looked unto the host of the Egyptians through the pillar of fire and of the cloud, and troubled the host of the Egyptians, and took off their chariot wheels, that they drave them heavily: so that the Egyptians said, "Let us flee from the face of Israel; for the LORD fighteth for them against the Egyptians". [14:21–25]

The Egyptians Drowned. And the LORD said unto Moses, "Stretch out thine hand over the sea, that the waters may come again upon the Egyptians, upon their chariots, and upon their horsemen". And Moses stretched forth his hand over the sea, and the sea returned to his strength when the morning appeared; and the Egyptians fled against it; and the LORD overthrew the Egyptians in the midst of the sea. And the waters returned, and covered the chariots, and the horsemen, and all the host of Pharaoh that came into the sea after them; there remained not so much as one of them. But the children of Israel walked upon dry land in the midst of the sea; and the waters were a wall unto them on their right hand, and on their left. Thus the LORD saved Israel that day out of the hand of the Egyptians; and Israel saw the Egyptians dead upon the sea shore. And Israel saw that great work which the LORD did upon the Egyptians: and the people feared the LORD, and believed the LORD, and his servant Moses.   [14:26–31]

The People Murmur. ⸺And they took their journey from Elim, and all the congregation of the children of Israel came unto the wilderness of Sin, which is between Elim and Sinai, on the fifteenth day of the second month after their departing out of the land of Egypt. And the whole congregation of the children of Israel murmured against Moses and Aaron in the wilderness: and the children of Israel said unto them, "Would to God we had died by the hand of the LORD in the land of Egypt, when we sat by the flesh pots, and when we did eat bread to the full; for ye have brought us forth into this wilderness, to kill this whole assembly with hunger". Then said the LORD unto Moses, "Behold, I will rain bread from heaven for you; and the people shall go out and gather a certain rate every day, that I may prove them, whether they will walk in my law, or no. And it shall come to pass, that on the sixth day they shall prepare that which they bring in; and it shall be twice as much as they gather daily." And Moses and Aaron said unto all the children of Israel, "At even, then ye shall know that the LORD hath brought you out from the land of Egypt: and in the morning, then ye shall see the glory of the LORD; for that he heareth your murmurings against the LORD: and what are we, that ye murmur against us?" And Moses said, "This shall be, when the LORD shall give you in the evening flesh to eat, and in the morning bread to the full; for that the LORD heareth your murmurings which ye murmur against him: and what are we? your murmurings are not against us, but against the LORD". And Moses spake unto Aaron, "Say unto all the congregation of the children of Israel, 'Come near before the LORD: for he hath heard your murmurings'". And it came to pass, as Aaron spake unto the whole congregation of the children of Israel, that they looked toward the wilderness, and, behold, the glory of the LORD appeared in the cloud. And the LORD spake unto Moses, saying, "I have heard the murmurings of the children of Israel: speak unto them, saying, 'At even ye shall eat flesh, and in the morning ye shall be filled with bread; and ye shall know that I am the LORD your God'". [16:1–12]

Manna Sent. And it came to pass, that at even the quails came up, and covered the camp: and in the morning the dew lay round about the host. And when the dew that lay was gone up, behold, upon the face of the wilderness there lay a small round thing, as small as the hoar frost on the ground. And when the children of Israel saw it, they said one to another, "It is manna": for they wist not what it was. And Moses said unto them, "This is the bread which the LORD hath given you to eat. This is the thing which the LORD hath commanded, 'Gather of it every man according to his eating, an omer for every man, according to the number of your persons; take ye every man for them which are in his tents'." And the children of Israel did so, and gathered, some more, some less. And when they did mete it with an omer, he that gathered much had nothing over, and he that gathered little had no lack; they gathered every man according to his eating. And Moses said, "Let no man leave of it till the morning". Notwithstanding they hearkened not unto Moses; but some of them left of it until the morning, and it bred worms, and stank: and Moses was wroth with them. And they gathered it every morning, every man according to his eating: and when the sun waxed hot, it melted. And it came to pass, that on the sixth day they gathered twice as much bread, two omers for one man: and all the rulers of the congregation came and told Moses. [16:13–22]

The Sabbath Rest to Be Observed. And he said unto them, "This is that which the LORD hath said, 'To morrow is the rest of the holy sabbath unto the LORD: bake that which ye will bake to day, and seethe that ye will seethe; and that which remaineth over lay up for you to be kept until the morning'". And they laid it up till the morning, as Moses bade: and it did not stink, neither was there any worm therein. And Moses said, "Eat that to day; for to day is a sabbath unto the LORD: to day ye shall not find it in the field. Six days ye shall gather it; but on the seventh day, which is the sabbath, in it there shall be none." And it came to pass, that there went out some of the people on the seventh day for to gather, and they found none. And the LORD said unto Moses, "How long refuse ye to keep my commandments and my laws? See, for that the LORD hath given you the sabbath, therefore he giveth you on the sixth day the bread of two days; abide ye every man in his place, let no man go out of his place on the seventh day." So the people rested on the seventh day. And the house of Israel called the name thereof Manna: and it was like coriander seed, white; and the taste of it was like wafers made with honey. And Moses said, "This is the thing which the LORD commandeth, 'Fill an omer of it to be kept for your generations; that they may see the bread wherewith I have fed you in the wilderness, when I brought you forth from the land of Egypt'". And Moses said unto Aaron, "Take a pot, and put an omer full of manna therein, and lay it up before the LORD, to be kept for your generations". As the LORD commanded Moses, so Aaron laid it up before the Testimony, to be kept. And the children of Israel did eat manna forty years, until they came to a land inhabited; they did eat manna, until they came unto the borders of the land of Canaan. Now an omer is the tenth part of an ephah.   [16:23–36]

Moses Strikes the Rock for Water. And all the congregation of the children of Israel journeyed from the wilderness of Sin, after their journeys, according to the commandment of the LORD, and pitched in Rephidim: and there was no water for the people to drink. Wherefore the people did chide with Moses, and said, "Give us water that we may drink". And Moses said unto them, "Why chide ye with me? wherefore do ye tempt the LORD?" And the people thirsted there for water; and the people murmured against Moses, and said, "Wherefore is this that thou hast brought us up out of Egypt, to kill us and our children and our cattle with thirst?" And Moses cried unto the LORD, saying, "What shall I do unto this people? they be almost ready to stone me". And the LORD said unto Moses, "Go on before the people, and take with thee of the elders of Israel; and thy rod, wherewith thou smotest the river, take in thine hand, and go. Behold, I will stand before thee there upon the rock in Horeb; and thou shalt smite the rock, and there shall come water out of it, that the people may drink." And Moses did so in the sight of the elders of Israel. And he called the name of the place Massah, and Meribah, because of the chiding of the children of Israel, and because they tempted the LORD, saying, "Is the LORD among us, or not?" [17:1-7]

Amalek Defeated. Then came Amalek, and fought with Israel in Rephidim. And Moses said unto Joshua, "Choose us out men, and go out, fight with Amalek: to morrow I will stand on the top of the hill with the rod of God in mine hand". So Joshua did as Moses had said to him, and fought with Amalek: and Moses, Aaron, and Hur went up to the top of the hill. And it came to pass, when Moses held up his hand, that Israel prevailed: and when he let down his hand, Amalek prevailed. But Moses' hands were heavy; and they took a stone, and put it under him, and he sat thereon; and Aaron and Hur stayed up his hands, the one on the one side, and the other on the other side; and his hands were steady until the going down of the sun. And Joshua discomfited Amalek and his people with the edge of the sword. And the LORD said unto Moses, "Write this for a memorial in a book, and rehearse it in the ears of Joshua: for I will utterly put out the remembrance of Amalek from under heaven". And Moses built an altar, and called the name of it Jehovah-nissi: for he said, "Because the LORD hath sworn that the LORD will have war with Amalek from generation to generation". [17:8-16]

Moses Prepares to Commune with God. In the third month, when the children of Israel were gone forth out of the land of Egypt, the same day came they into the wilderness of Sinai. For they were departed from Rephidim, and were come to the desert of Sinai, and had pitched in the wilderness; and there Israel camped before the mount. And Moses went up unto God, and the LORD called unto him out of the mountain, saying, "Thus shalt thou say to the house of Jacob, and tell the children of Israel; 'Ye have seen what I did unto the Egyptians, and how I bare you on eagles' wings, and brought you unto myself. Now therefore, if ye will obey my voice indeed, and keep my covenant, then ye shall be a peculiar treasure unto me above all people: for all the earth is mine: and ye shall be unto me a kingdom of priests, and an holy nation.' These are the words which thou shalt speak unto the children of Israel." And Moses came and called for the elders of the people, and laid before their faces all these words which the LORD commanded him. And all the people answered together, and said, "All that the LORD hath spoken we will do". And Moses returned the words of the people unto the LORD. And the LORD said unto Moses, "Lo, I come unto thee in a thick cloud, that the people may hear when I speak with thee, and believe thee for ever". And Moses told the words of the people unto the LORD. And the LORD said unto Moses, "Go unto the people, and sanctify them to day and to morrow, and let them wash their clothes, and be ready against the third day: for the third day the LORD will come down in the sight of all the people upon mount Sinai. And thou shalt set bounds unto the people round about, saying, 'Take heed to yourselves, that ye go not up into the mount, or touch the border of it: whosoever toucheth the mount shall be surely put to death: there shall not an hand touch it, but he shall surely be stoned, or shot through; whether it be beast or man, it shall not live: when the trumpet soundeth long, they shall come up to the mount'." And Moses went down from the mount unto the people, and sanctified the people; and they washed their clothes. And he said unto the people, "Be ready against the third day: come not at your wives".

[19:1–15]

God Appears on Mount Sinai. And it came to pass on the third day in the morning, that there were thunders and lightnings, and a thick cloud upon the mount, and the voice of the trumpet exceeding loud; so that all the people that was in the camp trembled. And Moses brought forth the people out of the camp to meet with God; and they stood at the nether part of the mount. And mount Sinai was altogether on a smoke, because the LORD descended upon it in fire: and the smoke thereof ascended as the smoke of a furnace, and the whole mount quaked greatly. And when the voice of the trumpet sounded long, and waxed louder and louder, Moses spake, and God answered him by a voice. And the LORD came down upon mount Sinai, on the top of the mount: and the LORD called Moses up to the top of the mount; and Moses went up. And the LORD said unto Moses, "Go down, charge the people, lest they break through unto the LORD to gaze, and many of them perish. And let the priests also, which come near to the LORD, sanctify themselves, lest the LORD break forth upon them." And Moses said unto the LORD, "The people cannot come up to mount Sinai: for thou chargedst us, saying, 'Set bounds about the mount, and sanctify it'". And the LORD said unto him, "Away, get thee down, and thou shalt come up, thou, and Aaron with thee: but let not the priests and the people break through to come up unto the LORD, lest he break forth upon them". So Moses went down unto the people, and spake unto them.

[19:16–25]

The Ten Commandments. And God spake all these words, saying,

"I am the LORD thy God, which have brought thee out of the land of Egypt, out of the house of bondage.

"Thou shalt have no other gods before me.

"Thou shalt not make unto thee any graven image, or any likeness of any thing that is in heaven above, or that is in the earth beneath, or that is in the water under the earth: thou shalt not bow down thyself to them, nor serve them: for I the LORD thy God am a jealous God, visiting the iniquity of the fathers upon the children unto the third and fourth generation of them that hate me; and shewing mercy unto thousands of them that love me, and keep my commandments.

"Thou shalt not take the name of the LORD thy God in vain; for the LORD will not hold him guiltless that taketh his name in vain.

"Remember the sabbath day, to keep it holy. Six days shalt thou labour, and do all thy work: but the seventh day is the sabbath of the LORD thy God: in it thou shalt not do any work, thou, nor thy son, nor thy daughter, thy manservant, nor thy maidservant, nor thy cattle, nor thy stranger that is within thy gates: for in six days the LORD made heaven and earth, the sea, and all that in them is, and rested the seventh day: wherefore the LORD blessed the sabbath day, and hallowed it.

"Honour thy father and thy mother: that thy days may be long upon the land which the LORD thy God giveth thee.

"Thou shalt not kill.

"Thou shalt not commit adultery.

"Thou shalt not steal.

"Thou shalt not bear false witness against thy neighbour.

"Thou shalt not covet thy neighbour's house, thou shalt not covet thy neighbour's wife, nor his manservant, nor his maidservant, nor his ox, nor his ass, nor any thing that is thy neighbour's."

And all the people saw the thunderings, and the lightnings, and the noise of the trumpet, and the mountain smoking: and when the people saw it, they removed, and stood afar off. And they said unto Moses, "Speak thou with us, and we will hear: but let not God speak with us, lest we die". And Moses said unto the people, "Fear not:

for God is come to prove you, and that his fear may be before your faces, that ye sin not". And the people stood afar off, and Moses drew near unto the thick darkness where God was.

And the LORD said unto Moses, "Thus thou shalt say unto the children of Israel, 'Ye have seen that I have talked with you from heaven. Ye shall not make with me gods of silver, neither shall ye make unto you gods of gold. An altar of earth thou shalt make unto me, and shalt sacrifice thereon thy burnt offerings, and thy peace offerings, thy sheep, and thine oxen: in all places where I record my name I will come unto thee, and I will bless thee. And if thou wilt make me an altar of stone, thou shalt not build it of hewn stone: for if thou lift up thy tool upon it, thou hast polluted it. Neither shalt thou go up by steps unto mine altar, that thy nakedness be not discovered thereon.'"

[20:1–26]

The Golden Calf. And when the people saw that Moses delayed to come down out of the mount, the people gathered themselves together unto Aaron, and said unto him, "Up, make us gods, which shall go before us; for as for this Moses, the man that brought us up out of the land of Egypt, we wot not what is become of him". And Aaron said unto them, "Break off the golden earrings, which are in the ears of your wives, of your sons, and of your daughters, and bring them unto me". And all the people brake off the golden earrings which were in their ears, and brought them unto Aaron. And he received them at their hand, and fashioned it with a graving tool, after he had made it a molten calf: and they said, "These be thy gods, O Israel, which brought thee up out of the land of Egypt". And when Aaron saw it, he built an altar before it; and Aaron made proclamation, and said, "To morrow is a feast to the LORD". And they rose up early on the morrow, and offered burnt offerings, and brought peace offerings; and the people sat down to eat and to drink, and rose up to play.

And the LORD said unto Moses, "Go, get thee down; for thy people, which thou broughtest out of the land of Egypt, have corrupted themselves: they have turned aside quickly out of the way which I commanded them: they have made them a molten calf, and have worshipped it, and have sacrificed thereunto, and said, 'These be thy gods, O Israel, which have brought thee up out of the land of Egypt'". And the LORD said unto Moses, "I have seen this people, and, behold, it is a stiffnecked people: now therefore let me alone, that my wrath may wax hot against them, and that I may consume them: and I will make of thee a great nation". And Moses besought the LORD his God, and said, "LORD, why doth thy wrath wax hot against thy people, which thou hast brought forth out of the land of Egypt with great power, and with a mighty hand? Wherefore should the Egyptians speak, and say, 'For mischief did he bring them out, to slay them in the mountains, and to consume them from the face of the earth'? Turn from thy fierce wrath, and repent of this evil against thy people. Remember Abraham, Isaac, and Israel, thy servants, to whom thou swarest by thine own self, and saidst unto them, 'I will multiply your seed as the stars of heaven, and all this land that I have spoken of will I give unto your seed, and they shall inherit it for ever'." And the LORD repented of the evil which he thought to do unto his people.

[32:1–14]

Moses Comes Down from Mount Sinai. And Moses turned, and went down from the mount, and the two tables of the testimony were in his hand: the tables were written on both their sides; on the one side and on the other were they written. And the tables were the work of God, and the writing was the writing of God, graven upon the tables. And when Joshua heard the noise of the people as they shouted, he said unto Moses, "There is a noise of war in the camp". And he said, "It is not the voice of them that shout for mastery, neither is it the voice of them that cry for being overcome: but the noise of them that sing do I hear". And it came to pass, as soon as he came nigh unto the camp, that he saw the calf, and the dancing: and Moses' anger waxed hot, and he cast the tables out of his hands, and brake them beneath the mount. And he took the calf which they had made, and burnt it in the fire, and ground it to powder, and strawed it upon the water, and made the children of Israel drink of it. And Moses said unto Aaron, "What did this people unto thee, that thou hast brought so great a sin upon them?" And Aaron said, "Let not the anger of my lord wax hot: thou knowest the people, that they are set on mischief. For they said unto me, 'Make us gods, which shall go before us: for as for this Moses, the man that brought us up out of the land of Egypt, we wot not what is become of him'. And I said unto them, Whosoever hath any gold, let them break it off. So they gave it me: Then I cast it into the fire, and there came out this calf."

[32:15-24]

The Idolaters Punished. And when Moses saw that the people were naked; (for Aaron had made them naked unto their shame among their enemies:) then Moses stood in the gate of the camp, and said, "Who is on the LORD's side? let him come unto me". And all the sons of Levi gathered themselves together unto him. And he said unto them, "Thus saith the LORD God of Israel, 'Put every man his sword by his side, and go in and out from gate to gate throughout the camp, and slay every man his brother, and every man his companion, and every man his neighbour'". And the children of Levi did according to the word of Moses: and there fell of the people that day about three thousand men. For Moses had said, "Consecrate yourselves to day to the LORD, even every man upon his son, and upon his brother; that he may bestow upon you a blessing this day". And it came to pass on the morrow, that Moses said unto the people, "Ye have sinned a great sin: and now I will go up unto the LORD; peradventure I shall make an atonement

for your sin". And Moses returned unto the LORD, and
said, "Oh, this people have sinned a great sin, and have
made them gods of gold. Yet now, if thou wilt forgive
their sin—; and if not, blot me, I pray thee, out of thy book
which thou hast written." And the LORD said unto Moses,
"Whosoever hath sinned against me, him will I blot out of
my book. Therefore now go, lead the people unto the
place of which I have spoken unto thee: behold, mine
Angel shall go before thee: nevertheless in the day when
I visit I will visit their sin upon them." And the LORD
plagued the people, because they made the calf, which
Aaron made.   [32:25–35]

The Tabernacle. [Moses caused the craftsmen to
make a movable shrine, known as the tabernacle, or the
"tent of the congregation," which contained the sacred
vessels and the ark of the covenant. When all had been
made, the tabernacle was erected and the ark set up in its
place in the holy of holies.[8]]

Then a cloud covered the tent of the congregation, and
the glory of the LORD filled the tabernacle. And Moses
was not able to enter into the tent of the congregation,
because the cloud abode thereon, and the glory of the
LORD filled the tabernacle. And when the cloud was taken
up from over the tabernacle, the children of Israel went
onward in all their journeys: but if the cloud were not
taken up, then they journeyed not till the day that it was
taken up. For the cloud of the LORD was upon the tabernacle by day, and fire was on it by night, in the sight of all
the house of Israel, throughout all their journeys.

[40:34–38]

*Moses was also commanded to consecrate his brother
Aaron and his sons to minister in the office of priests;
and the form of the vestments was laid down for Aaron
to wear when he went into the holy place of the tabernacle. The priesthood was to descend through the chil-*

---

[8] See Appendix 3.

dren of Aaron. The Levites, the descendants of the tribe of Levi, also, were to be set apart from the other tribes for the service of the tabernacle and of the priests. (Exodus 28; Numbers 1:47–54.)

From LEVITICUS

Some precepts from the Mosaic Law

Purification of Women. And the LORD spake unto
Moses, saying, "Speak unto the children of Israel, saying,
'If a woman have conceived seed, and borne a man child:
then she shall be unclean seven days; according to the
days of the separation for her infirmity shall she be unclean. And in the eighth day the flesh of his foreskin shall
be circumcised. And she shall then continue in the blood
of her purifying three and thirty days; she shall touch no
hallowed thing, nor come into the sanctuary, until the days
of her purifying be fulfilled. But if she bear a maid child,
then she shall be unclean two weeks, as in her separation:
and she shall continue in the blood of her purifying threescore and six days. And when the days of her purifying
are fulfilled, for a son, or for a daughter, she shall bring a
lamb of the first year for a burnt offering, and a young
pigeon, or a turtledove, for a sin offering, unto the door
of the tabernacle of the congregation, unto the priest: who
shall offer it before the LORD, and make an atonement for
her; and she shall be cleansed from the issue of her blood.
This is the law for her that hath borne a male or a female.
And if she be not able to bring a lamb, then she shall
bring two turtles, or two young pigeons; the one for the
burnt offering, and the other for a sin offering: and the
priest shall make an atonement for her, and she shall be
clean.' "   [12:1–8]

The Laws concerning Leprosy. "When the plague of leprosy is in a man, then he shall be brought unto the priest; and the priest shall see him: and, behold, if the rising be white in the skin, and it have turned the hair white, and there be quick raw flesh in the rising; it is an old leprosy in the skin of his flesh, and the priests shall pronounce him unclean, and shall not shut him up: for he is unclean. And if a leprosy break out abroad in the skin, and the leprosy cover all the skin of him that hath the plague from his head even to his foot, wheresoever the priest looketh; then the priest shall consider: and, behold, if the leprosy have covered all his flesh, he shall pronounce him clean that hath the plague: it is all turned white: he is clean. But when raw flesh appeareth in him, he shall be unclean. And the priest shall see the raw flesh, and pronounce him to be unclean: for the raw flesh is unclean: it is a leprosy. Or if the raw flesh turn again, and be changed unto white, he shall come unto the priest; and the priest shall see him: and, behold, if the plague be turned into white; then the priest shall pronounce him clean that hath the plague: he is clean.

. . . .

"And the leper in whom the plague is, his clothes shall be rent, and his head bare, and he shall put a covering upon his upper lip, and shall cry, 'Unclean, unclean'. All the days wherein the plague shall be in him he shall be defiled; he is unclean: he shall dwell alone; without the camp shall his habitation be." [13:9–17, 45–46]

The Significance of Blood. "And whatsoever man there be of the house of Israel, or of the strangers that sojourn among you, that eateth any manner of blood; I will even set my face against that soul that eateth blood, and will cut him off from among his people. For the life of the flesh is in the blood: and I have given it to you upon the altar to make an atonement for your souls: for it is the blood that maketh an atonement for the soul. Therefore I said unto the children of Israel, No soul of you shall eat blood, neither shall any stranger that sojourneth among you eat blood." [17:10–12]

Sexual Purity. And the LORD spake unto Moses, saying, "Again, thou shalt say to the children of Israel, 'Whosoever he be of the children of Israel, or of the strangers that sojourn in Israel, that giveth any of his seed unto Molech; he shall surely be put to death: the people of the land shall stone him with stones. And I will set my face against that man, and will cut him off from among his people; because he hath given of his seed unto Molech, to defile my sanctuary, and to profane my holy name. And if the people of the land do any ways hide their eyes from the man, when he giveth of his seed unto Molech, and kill him not: then I will set my face against that man, and against his family, and will cut him off, and all that go a whoring after him, to commit whoredom with Molech, from among their people. And the soul that turneth after such as have familiar spirits, and after wizards, to go a whoring after them, I will even set my face against that soul, and will cut him off from among his people.

"'Sanctify yourselves therefore, and be ye holy: for I am the LORD your God. And ye shall keep my statutes, and do them: I am the LORD which sanctify you. For every one that curseth his father or his mother shall be surely put to death: he hath cursed his father or his mother; his blood shall be upon him.

"'And the man that committeth adultery with another man's wife, even he that committeth adultery with his neighbour's wife, the adulterer and the adulteress shall surely be put to death. And the man that lieth with his father's wife hath uncovered his father's nakedness: both of them shall surely be put to death; their blood shall be upon them. And if a man lie with his daughter in law, both of them shall surely be put to death: they have wrought confusion; their blood shall be upon them. If a man also lie with mankind, as he lieth with a woman, both of them

have committed an abomination: they shall surely be put
to death; their blood shall be upon them. And if a man
take a wife and her mother, it is wickedness: they shall
be burnt with fire, both he and they; that there be no
wickedness among you. And if a man lie with a beast, he
shall surely be put to death: and ye shall slay the beast.
And if a woman approach unto any beast, and lie down
thereto, thou shalt kill the woman, and the beast: they
shall surely be put to death; their blood shall be upon
them. And if a man shall take his sister, his father's daughter, or his mother's daughter, and see her nakedness, and
she see his nakedness; it is a wicked thing; and they shall
be cut off in the sight of their people: he hath uncovered
his sister's nakedness; he shall bear his iniquity. And if a
man shall lie with a woman having her sickness, and shall
uncover her nakedness; he hath discovered her fountain,
and she hath uncovered the fountain of her blood: and
both of them shall be cut off from among their people.
And thou shalt not uncover the nakedness of thy mother's
sister, nor of thy father's sister: for he uncovereth his near
kin: they shall bear their iniquity. And if a man shall lie
with his uncle's wife, he hath uncovered his uncle's nakedness: they shall bear their sin; they shall die childless.
And if a man shall take his brother's wife, it is an unclean
thing: he hath uncovered his brother's nakedness; they
shall be childless.' "   [20:1-21]

From THE BOOK OF NUMBERS

The Book of Numbers is concerned with names, genealogies, and details of the journeyings of the Israelites in the desert; but it includes some precepts of the law and a few further incidents.

Spies Sent into Canaan. [Leaders from each tribe were chosen, and]

. . . Moses sent them to spy out the land of Canaan, and said unto them, "Get you up this way southward, and go up into the mountain: and see the land, what it is; and the people that dwelleth therein, whether they be strong or weak, few or many; and what the land is that they dwell in, whether it be good or bad; and what cities they be that they dwell in, whether in tents, or in strong holds; and what the land is, whether it be fat or lean, whether there be wood therein, or not. And be ye of good courage, and bring of the fruit of the land." Now the time was the time of the firstripe grapes. So they went up, and searched the land from the wilderness of Zin unto Rehob, as men come to Hamath. And they ascended by the south, and came unto Hebron; where Ahiman, Sheshai, and Talmai, the children of Anak, were. (Now Hebron was built seven years before Zoan in Egypt.) And they came unto the brook of Eshcol, and cut down from thence a branch with one cluster of grapes, and they bare it between two upon a staff; and they brought of the pomegranates, and of the figs. The place was called the brook Eshcol, because of the cluster of grapes which the children of Israel cut down from thence. And they returned from searching of the land after forty days. [13:17–25]

The Spies' Unfavorable Report. And they went and came to Moses, and to Aaron, and to all the congregation of the children of Israel, unto the wilderness of Paran, to Kadesh; and brought back word unto them, and unto all the congregation, and shewed them the fruit of the land. And they told him, and said, "We came unto the land whither thou sentest us, and surely it floweth with milk and honey; and this is the fruit of it. Nevertheless the people be strong that dwell in the land, and the cities are walled, and very great: and moreover we saw the children of Anak there. The Amalekites dwell in the land of the south: and the Hittites, and the Jebusites, and the Amorites, dwell in the mountains: and the Canaanites dwell by the sea, and by the coast of Jordan." And Caleb stilled the people before Moses, and said, "Let us go up at once, and possess it; for we are well able to overcome it". But the men that went up with him said, "We be not able to go up against the people; for they are stronger than we". And they brought up an evil report of the land which they had searched unto the children of Israel, saying, "The land, through which we have gone to search it, is a land that eateth up the inhabitants thereof; and all the people that we saw in it are men of a great stature. And there we saw the giants, the sons of Anak, which come of the giants: and we were in our own sight as grasshoppers, and so we were in their sight." [13:26–33]

The People Murmur. And all the congregation lifted up their voice, and cried; and the people wept that night. And all the children of Israel murmured against Moses and against Aaron: and the whole congregation said unto them, "Would God that we had died in the land of Egypt! or would God we had died in this wilderness! And wherefore hath the LORD brought us unto this land, to fall by the sword, that our wives and our children should be a prey? were it not better for us to return into Egypt?" And they said one to another, "Let us make a captain, and let us return into Egypt". Then Moses and Aaron fell on their faces before all the assembly of the congregation of the children of Israel. And Joshua the son of Nun, and Caleb the son of Jephunneh, which were of them that searched the land, rent their clothes: and they spake unto all the company of the children of Israel, saying, "The land, which we passed through to search it, is an exceeding good land. If the LORD delight in us, then he will bring us into this land, and give it us; a land which floweth with milk and honey. Only rebel not ye against the LORD, neither fear ye the people of the land; for they are bread for us: their defence is departed from them, and the LORD is with us: fear them not." But all the congregation bade stone them with stones. And the glory of the LORD appeared in the tabernacle of the congregation before all the children of Israel.   [14:1–10]

Murmurers Punished. [The LORD was angry with the people but Moses pleaded for them.]

And the LORD spake unto Moses and unto Aaron, saying, "How long shall I bear with this evil congregation, which murmur against me? I have heard the murmurings of the children of Israel, which they murmur against me. Say unto them, 'As truly as I live, saith the LORD, as ye have spoken in mine ears, so will I do to you: your carcases shall fall in this wilderness; and all that were numbered of you, according to your whole number, from twenty years old and upward, which have murmured against me, doubtless ye shall not come into the land, concerning which I sware to make you dwell therein, save Caleb the son of Jephunneh, and Joshua the son of Nun. But your little ones, which ye said should be a prey, them will I bring in, and they shall know the land which ye have despised. But as for you, your carcases, they shall fall in this wilderness. And your children shall wander in the wilderness forty years, and bear your whoredoms, until your carcases be wasted in the wilderness. After the number of the days in which ye searched the land, even forty days, each day for a year, shall ye bear your iniquities, even forty years, and ye shall know my breach of promise. I the LORD have said, I will surely do it unto all this evil congregation, that are gathered together against me: in this wilderness they shall be consumed, and there they shall die.'" And the men, which Moses sent to search the land, who returned, and made all the congregation to murmur against him, by bringing up a slander upon the land, even those men that did bring up the evil report upon the land, died by the plague before the LORD. But Joshua the son of Nun, and Caleb the son of Jephunneh, which were of the men that went to search the land, lived still. And Moses told these sayings unto all the children of Israel: and the people mourned greatly. And they rose up early in the morning, and gat them up into the top of the mountain, saying, "Lo, we be here, and will go up unto the place which the LORD hath promised: for we have sinned". And Moses said, "Wherefore now do ye transgress the commandment of the LORD? but it shall not prosper. Go not up, for the LORD is not among you; that ye be not smitten before your enemies. For the Amalekites and the Canaanites are there before you, and ye shall fall by the sword: because ye are turned away from the LORD, therefore the LORD will not be with you." But they presumed to go up unto the hill top: nevertheless the ark of the covenant of the LORD, and Moses, departed not out of the camp. Then the Amalekites came down, and the Canaanites which dwelt in that hill, and smote them, and discomfited them, even unto Hormah.   [14:26–45]

Moses Strikes the Rock. Then came the children of Israel, even the whole congregation, into the desert of Zin in the first month: and the people abode in Kadesh; and Miriam died there, and was buried there. And there was no water for the congregation: and they gathered themselves together against Moses and against Aaron. And the people chode with Moses, and spake, saying, "Would God that we had died when our brethren died before the LORD! And why have ye brought up the congregation of the LORD into this wilderness, that we and our cattle should die there? And wherefore have ye made us to come up out of Egypt, to bring us in unto this evil place? it is no place of seed, or of figs, or of vines, or of pomegranates; neither is there any water to drink." And Moses and Aaron went from the presence of the assembly unto the door of the tabernacle of the congregation, and they fell upon their faces: and the glory of the LORD appeared unto them. And the LORD spake unto Moses, saying, "Take the rod, and gather thou the assembly together, thou, and Aaron thy brother, and speak ye unto the rock before their eyes; and it shall give forth his water, and thou shalt bring forth to them water out of the rock: so thou shalt give the congregation and their beasts drink". And Moses took the rod from before the LORD, as he commanded him. And Moses and Aaron gathered the congregation together before the rock, and he said unto them, "Hear now, ye rebels; must we fetch you water out of this rock?" And Moses lifted up his hand, and with his rod he smote the rock twice: and the water came out abundantly, and the congregation drank, and their beasts also. And the LORD spake unto Moses and Aaron, "Because ye believed me not, to sanctify me in the eyes of the children of Israel, therefore ye shall not bring this congregation into the land which I have given them". This is the water of Meribah; because the children of Israel strove with the LORD, and he was sanctified in them.   [20:1–13]

The Fiery Serpents. And they journeyed from mount Hor by the way of the Red sea, to compass the land of Edom: and the soul of the people was much discouraged because of the way. And the people spake against God, and against Moses, "Wherefore have ye brought us up out of Egypt to die in the wilderness? for there is no bread, neither is there any water; and our soul loatheth this light bread". And the LORD sent fiery serpents among the people, and they bit the people; and much people of Israel died. Therefore the people came to Moses, and said, "We have sinned, for we have spoken against the LORD, and against thee; pray unto the LORD, that he take away the serpents from us". And Moses prayed for the people. And the LORD said unto Moses, "Make thee a fiery serpent, and set it upon a pole: and it shall come to pass, that every one that is bitten, when he looketh upon it, shall live". And Moses made a serpent of brass, and put it upon a pole, and it came to pass, that if a serpent had bitten any man, when he beheld the serpent of brass, he lived.

[21:4-9]

Balaam and Balak. [The Israelites pitched in the plain of Moab; and Balak, King of Moab, sent for Balaam to come and curse the Israelites; but Balaam was warned by God not to go. At the second summons]

. . . God came unto Balaam at night, and said unto him, "If the men come to call thee, rise up, and go with them; but yet the word which I shall say unto thee, that shalt thou do". And Balaam rose up in the morning, and saddled his ass, and went with the princes of Moab. And God's anger was kindled because he went: and the angel of the LORD stood in the way for an adversary against him. Now he was riding upon his ass, and his two servants were with him. And the ass saw the angel of the LORD standing in the way, and his sword drawn in his hand: and the ass turned aside out of the way, and went into the field: and Balaam smote the ass, to turn her into the way. But the angel of the LORD stood in a path of the vineyards, a wall being on this side, and a wall on that side. And when the ass saw the angel of the LORD, she thrust herself unto the wall, and crushed Balaam's foot against the wall: and he smote her again. And the angel of the LORD went further, and stood in a narrow place, where was no way to turn either to the right hand or to the left. And when the ass saw the angel of the LORD, she fell down under Balaam: and Balaam's anger was kindled, and he smote the ass with a staff. [22:20–27]

Balaam's Ass Speaks. And the LORD opened the mouth of the ass, and she said unto Balaam, "What have I done unto thee, that thou hast smitten me these three times?" And Balaam said unto the ass, "Because thou hast mocked me: I would there were a sword in mine hand, for now would I kill thee". And the ass said unto Balaam, "Am not I thine ass, upon which thou hast ridden ever since I was thine unto this day? was I ever wont to do so unto thee?" And he said, "Nay". Then the LORD opened the eyes of Balaam, and he saw the angel of the LORD standing in the way, and his sword drawn in his hand: and he bowed down his head, and fell flat on his face. And the angel of the LORD said unto him, "Wherefore hast thou smitten thine ass these three times? behold, I went out to withstand thee, because thy way is perverse before me: and the ass saw me, and turned from me these three times: unless she had turned from me, surely now also I had slain thee, and saved her alive". And Balaam said unto the angel of the LORD, "I have sinned; for I knew not that thou stoodest in the way against me: now therefore, if it displease thee, I will get me back again". And the angel of the LORD said unto Balaam, "Go with the men: but only the word that I shall speak unto thee, that thou shalt speak". So Balaam went with the princes of Balak. And when Balak heard that Balaam was come, he went out to meet him unto a city of Moab, which is in the border of Arnon, which is in the utmost coast. And Balak said unto Balaam, "Did I not earnestly send unto thee to call thee? wherefore camest thou not unto me? am I not able indeed to promote thee to honour?" And Balaam said unto Balak, "Lo, I am come unto thee: have I now any power at all to say any thing? the word that God putteth in my mouth, that shall I speak". And Balaam went with Balak, and they came unto Kirjath-huzoth. And Balak offered oxen and sheep, and sent to Balaam, and to the princes that were with him. And it came to pass on the morrow, that Balak took Balaam, and brought him up into the high places of Baal, that thence he might see the utmost part of the people.

And Balaam said unto Balak, "Build me here seven altars, and prepare me here seven oxen and seven rams". And Balak did as Balaam had spoken; and Balak and Balaam offered on every altar a bullock and a ram. And Balaam said unto Balak, "Stand by thy burnt offering, and I will go: peradventure the LORD will come to meet me: and whatsoever he sheweth me I will tell thee". And he went to an high place. And God met Balaam: and he said unto him, "I have prepared seven altars, and I have offered upon every altar a bullock and a ram".

[22:28–41; 23:1–4]

Balaam's Curse Turned into a Blessing. And the LORD put a word in Balaam's mouth, and said, "Return unto Balak, and thus thou shalt speak". And he returned unto him, and, lo, he stood by his burnt sacrifice, he, and all the princes of Moab. And he took up his parable, and said,

> "Balak the king of Moab hath brought me from Aram,
> Out of the mountains of the east, saying,
> 'Come, curse me Jacob,
> And come, defy Israel'.
> How shall I curse, whom God hath not cursed?
> Or how shall I defy, whom the LORD hath not defied?
> For from the top of the rocks I see him,
> And from the hills I behold him:
> Lo, the people shall dwell alone,
> And shall not be reckoned among the nations.
> Who can count the dust of Jacob,
> And the number of the fourth part of Israel?
> Let me die the death of the righteous,
> And let my last end be like his!"

And Balak said unto Balaam, "What hast thou done unto me? I took thee to curse mine enemies, and, behold, thou hast blessed them altogether." And he answered and said, "Must I not take heed to speak that which the LORD hath put in my mouth?"   [23:5–12] and the stork, and the heron after her kind, and the lap wing, and the bat. And every creeping thing that flieth is unclean unto you: they shall not be eaten. But of all clean fowls ye may eat.

From DEUTERONOMY

Clean and Unclean Beasts. "Thou shalt not eat any abominable thing. These are the beasts which ye shall eat: the ox, the sheep, and the goat, the hart, and the roebuck, and the fallow deer, and the wild goat, and the pygarg,[1] and the wild ox, and the chamois. And every beast that parteth the hoof, and cleaveth the cleft into two claws, and cheweth the cud among the beasts, that ye shall eat. Nevertheless these ye shall not eat of them that chew the cud, or of them that divide the cloven hoof; as the camel, and the hare, and the coney: for they chew the cud, but divide not the hoof; therefore they are unclean unto you. And the swine, because it divideth the hoof, yet cheweth not the cud, it is unclean unto you: ye shall not eat of their flesh, nor touch their dead carcase.

"These ye shall eat of all that are in the waters: all that have fins and scales shall ye eat: and whatsoever hath not fins and scales ye may not eat; it is unclean unto you.

"Of all clean birds ye shall eat. But these are they of which ye shall not eat: the eagle, and the ossifrage,[2] and the ospray, and the glede,[3] and the kite, and the vulture after his kind, and every raven after his kind, and the owl, and the night hawk, and the cuckow, and the hawk after his kind, the little owl, and the great owl, and the swan, and the pelican, and the gier eagle,[2] and the cormorant,

[1] Antelope.

[2] The ossifrage and the gier eagle are birds of the osprey kind—fish hawks.

[3] Buzzard.

and the stork, and the heron after her kind, and the lapwing, and the bat. And every creeping thing that flieth is unclean unto you: they shall not be eaten. But of all clean fowls ye may eat.

"Ye shall not eat of any thing that dieth of itself: thou shalt give it unto the stranger that is in thy gates, that he may eat it; or thou mayest sell it unto an alien: for thou art an holy people unto the Lord thy God. Thou shalt not seethe a kid in his mother's milk." [14:3–21]

Usury. "Thou shalt not lend upon usury to thy brother; usury of money, usury of victuals, usury of any thing that is lent upon usury: unto a stranger thou mayest lend upon usury; but unto thy brother thou shalt not lend upon usury: that the Lord thy God may bless thee in all that thou settest thine hand to in the land whither thou goest to possess it." [23:19–20]

Divorce. "When a man hath taken a wife, and married her, and it come to pass that she find no favour in his eyes, because he hath found some uncleanness in her: then let him write her a bill of divorcement, and give it in her hand, and send her out of his house. And when she is departed out of his house, she may go and be another man's wife. And if the latter husband hate her, and write her a bill of divorcement, and giveth it in her hand, and sendeth her out of his house; or if the latter husband die, which took her to be his wife; her former husband, which sent her away, may not take her again to be his wife, after that she is defiled; for that is abomination before the Lord: and thou shalt not cause the land to sin, which the Lord thy God giveth thee for an inheritance.

"When a man hath taken a new wife, he shall not go out to war, neither shall he be charged with any business: but he shall be free at home one year, and shall cheer up his wife which he hath taken. No man shall take the nether or the upper millstone to pledge: for he taketh a man's life to pledge." [24:1–6]

Beating of Offenders. "If there be a controversy between men, and they come unto judgment, that the judges may judge them; then they shall justify the righteous, and condemn the wicked. And it shall be, if the wicked man be worthy to be beaten, that the judge shall cause him to lie down, and to be beaten before his face, according to his fault, by a certain number. Forty stripes he may give him, and not exceed: lest, if he should exceed, and beat him above these with many stripes, then thy brother should seem vile unto thee.

"Thou shalt not muzzle the ox when he treadeth out the corn." [25:1-4]

Raising up Children for a Dead Brother. "If brethren dwell together, and one of them die, and have no child, the wife of the dead shall not marry without unto a stranger: her husband's brother shall go in unto her, and take her to him to wife, and perform the duty of an husband's brother unto her. And it shall be, that the firstborn which she beareth shall succeed in the name of his brother which is dead, that his name be not put out of Israel. And if the man like not to take his brother's wife, then let his brother's wife go up to the gate unto the elders, and say, 'My husband's brother refuseth to raise up unto his brother a name in Israel, he will not perform the duty of my husband's brother'. Then the elders of his city shall call him, and speak unto him: and if he stand to it, and say, 'I like not to take her'; then shall his brother's wife come unto him in the presence of the elders, and loose his shoe from off his foot, and spit in his face, and shall answer and say, 'So shall it be done unto that man that will not build up his brother's house'. And his name shall be called in Israel, The house of him that hath his shoe loosed." [25:5-10]

The Death of Moses. And Moses went up from the plains of Moab unto the mountain of Nebo, to the top of Pisgah, that is over against Jericho. And the LORD shewed him all the land of Gilead, unto Dan, and all Naphtali, and the land of Ephraim, and Manasseh, and all the land of Judah, unto the utmost sea, and the south, and the plain of the valley of Jericho, the city of palm trees, unto Zoar. And the LORD said unto him, "This is the land which I sware unto Abraham, unto Isaac, and unto Jacob, saying, I will give it unto thy seed: I have caused thee to see it with thine eyes, but thou shalt not go over thither". So Moses the servant of the LORD died there in the land of Moab, according to the word of the LORD. And he buried him in a valley in the land of Moab, over against Beth-peor: but no man knoweth of his sepulchre unto this day. And Moses was an hundred and twenty years old when he died: his eye was not dim, nor his natural force abated. And the children of Israel wept for Moses in the plains of Moab thirty days: so the days of weeping and mourning for Moses were ended. And Joshua the son of Nun was full of the spirit of wisdom; for Moses had laid his hands upon him: and the children of Israel hearkened unto him, and did as the LORD commanded Moses. And there arose not a prophet since in Israel like unto Moses, whom the LORD knew face to face, in all the signs and the wonders, which the LORD sent him to do in the land of Egypt to Pharaoh, and to all his servants, and to all his land, and in all that mighty hand, and in all the great terror which Moses shewed in the sight of all Israel.

[34:1-12]

From JOSHUA

[After the death of Moses, Joshua took command of the people, whom he warned to be ready to cross the river Jordan.]

The Spies Saved by Rahab the Harlot. And Joshua the son of Nun sent out of Shittim two men to spy secretly, saying, "Go view the land, even Jericho". And they went, and came into an harlot's house, named Rahab, and lodged there. And it was told the king of Jericho, saying, "Behold, there came men in hither to night of the children of Israel to search out the country". And the king of Jericho sent unto Rahab, saying, "Bring forth the men that are come to thee, which are entered into thine house: for they be come to search out all the country". And the woman took the two men, and hid them, and said thus, "There came men unto me, but I wist not whence they were: and it came to pass about the time of shutting of the gate, when it was dark, that the men went out: whither the men went I wot not: pursue after them quickly; for ye shall overtake them". But she had brought them up to the roof of the house, and hid them with the stalks of flax, which she had laid in order upon the roof. And the men pursued after them the way to Jordan unto the fords: and as soon as they which pursued after them were gone out, they shut the gate.

And before they were laid down, she came up unto them upon the roof; and she said unto the men, "I know that the LORD hath given you the land, and that your terror is fallen upon us, and that all the inhabitants of the land faint because of you. For we have heard how the LORD dried up the water of the Red sea for you, when ye came out of Egypt; and what ye did unto the two kings of the Amorites, that were on the other side Jordan, Sihon and Og, whom ye utterly destroyed. And as soon as we had heard these things, our hearts did melt, neither did there remain any more courage in any man, because of you: for the LORD your God, he is God in heaven above, and in earth beneath. Now therefore, I pray you, swear unto me by the LORD, since I have shewed you kindness, that ye will also shew kindness unto my father's house, and give me a true token: and that ye will save alive my father, and my mother, and my brethren, and my sisters, and all that they have, and deliver our lives from death". And the men answered her, "Our life for yours, if ye utter not this our business. And it shall be, when the LORD hath given us the land, that we will deal kindly and truly with thee."

Then she let them down by a cord through the window: for her house was upon the town wall, and she dwelt upon the wall. And she said unto them, "Get you to the mountain, lest the pursuers meet you; and hide yourselves there three days, until the pursuers be returned: and afterward may ye go your way". And the men said unto her, "We will be blameless of this thine oath which thou hast made us swear. Behold, when we come into the land, thou shalt bind this line of scarlet thread in the window which thou didst let us down by: and thou shalt bring thy father, and thy mother, and thy brethren, and all thy father's household, home unto thee. And it shall be, that whosoever shall go out of the doors of thy house into the street, his blood shall be upon his head, and we will be guiltless: and whosoever shall be with thee in the house, his blood shall be on our head, if any hand be upon him. And if thou utter this our business, then we will be quit of thine oath which thou hast made us to swear." And she said, "According unto your words, so be it". And she sent them away, and they departed: and she bound the scarlet line in the window. And they went, and came unto the mountain, and abode there three days, until the pursuers were returned: and the pursuers sought them throughout all the way, but found them not. So the two men returned, and descended from the mountain, and passed over, and came to Joshua the son of Nun, and told him all things that befell them: and they said unto Joshua, "Truly the LORD hath delivered into our hands all the land; for even all the inhabitants of the country do faint because of us".

[2:1–24]

The Crossing of the River Jordan. And it came to pass, when the people removed from their tents, to pass over Jordan, and the priests bearing the ark of the covenant before the people; and as they that bare the ark were come unto Jordan, and the feet of the priests that bare the ark were dipped in the brim of the water, (for Jordan overfloweth all his banks all the time of harvest,) that the waters which came down from above stood and rose up upon an heap very far from the city Adam, that is beside Zaretan: and those that came down toward the sea of the plain, even the salt sea, failed, and were cut off: and the people passed over right against Jericho. And the priests that bare the ark of the covenant of the LORD stood firm on dry ground in the midst of Jordan, and all the Israelites passed over on dry ground, until all the people were passed clean over Jordan.

And it came to pass, when all the people were clean passed over Jordan, that the LORD spake unto Joshua, saying, "Take you twelve men out of the people, out of every tribe a man, and command ye them, saying, 'Take you hence out of the midst of Jordan, out of the place where the priests' feet stood firm, twelve stones, and ye shall carry them over with you, and leave them in the lodging place, where ye shall lodge this night'". Then Joshua called the twelve men, whom he had prepared of the children of Israel, out of every tribe a man: and Joshua said unto them, "Pass over before the ark of the LORD your

God into the midst of Jordan, and take ye up every man of you a stone upon his shoulder, according unto the number of the tribes of the children of Israel: that this may be a sign among you, that when your children ask their fathers in time to come, saying, 'What mean ye by these stones?' then ye shall answer them, that the waters of Jordan were cut off before the ark of the covenant of the LORD; when it passed over Jordan, the waters of Jordan were cut off: and these stones shall be for a memorial unto the children of Israel for ever". And the children of Israel did so as Joshua commanded, and took up twelve stones out of the midst of Jordan, as the LORD spake unto Joshua, according to the number of the tribes of the children of Israel, and carried them over with them unto the place where they lodged, and laid them down there.

And Joshua set up twelve stones in the midst of Jordan, in the place where the feet of the priests which bare the ark of the covenant stood: and they are there unto this day. For the priests which bare the ark stood in the midst of Jordan, until every thing was finished that the LORD commanded Joshua to speak unto the people, according to all that Moses commanded Joshua: and the people hasted and passed over. And it came to pass, when all the people were clean passed over, that the ark of the LORD passed over, and the priests, in the presence of the people. And the children of Reuben, and the children of Gad, and half the tribe of Manasseh, passed over armed before the children of Israel, as Moses spake unto them: about forty thousand prepared for war passed over before the LORD unto battle, to the plains of Jericho. On that day the LORD magnified Joshua in the sight of all Israel; and they feared him, as they feared Moses, all the days of his life.

And the LORD spake unto Joshua, saying, "Command the priests that bear the ark of the testimony, that they come up out of Jordan". Joshua therefore commanded the priests, saying, "Come ye up out of Jordan". And it came to pass, when the priests that bare the ark of the

covenant of the LORD were come up out of the midst of
Jordan, and the soles of the priests' feet were lifted up unto
the dry land, that the waters of Jordan returned unto their
place, and flowed over all his banks, as they did before.
And the people came up out of Jordan on the tenth day of
the first month, and encamped in Gilgal, in the east border
of Jericho. And those twelve stones, which they took out
of Jordan, did Joshua pitch in Gilgal. And he spake unto
the children of Israel, saying, "When your children shall
ask their fathers in time to come, saying, 'What mean
these stones?' then ye shall let your children know, saying,
'Israel came over this Jordan on dry land'. For the LORD
your God dried up the waters of Jordan from before you,
until ye were passed over, as the LORD your God did to the
Red sea, which he dried up from before us, until we were
gone over: that all the people of the earth might know the
hand of the LORD, that it is mighty: that ye might fear the
LORD your God for ever." [3:14–17; 4:1–24]

The Attack on Jericho. Now Jericho was straitly shut
up because of the children of Israel: none went out, and
none came in. And the LORD said unto Joshua, "See, I
have given into thine hand Jericho, and the king thereof,
and the mighty men of valour. And ye shall compass the
city, all ye men of war, and go round about the city once.
Thus shalt thou do six days. And seven priests shall bear
before the ark seven trumpets of rams' horns: and the
seventh day ye shall compass the city seven times, and the
priests shall blow with the trumpets. And it shall come to
pass, that when they make a long blast with the ram's
horn, and when ye hear the sound of the trumpet, all the
people shall shout with a great shout; and the wall of the
city shall fall down flat, and the people shall ascend up
every man straight before him." And Joshua the son of
Nun called the priests, and said unto them, "Take up the
ark of the covenant, and let seven priests bear seven trumpets of rams' horns before the ark of the LORD". And he
said unto the people, "Pass on, and compass the city, and

let him that is armed pass on before the ark of the LORD".
And it came to pass, when Joshua had spoken unto the
people, that the seven priests bearing the seven trumpets
of rams' horns passed on before the LORD, and blew with
the trumpets: and the ark of the covenant of the LORD
followed them. And the armed men went before the priests
that blew with the trumpets, and the rearward came after
the ark, the priests going on, and blowing with the trumpets. And Joshua had commanded the people, saying,
"Ye shall not shout, nor make any noise with your voice,
neither shall any word proceed out of your mouth, until
the day I bid you shout; then shall ye shout". So the ark
of the LORD compassed the city, going about it once: and
they came into the camp, and lodged in the camp.

And Joshua rose early in the morning, and the priests
took up the ark of the LORD. And seven priests bearing
seven trumpets of rams' horns before the ark of the LORD
went on continually, and blew with the trumpets: and the
armed men went before them; but the rearward came after
the ark of the LORD, the priests going on, and blowing
with the trumpets. And the second day they compassed the
city once, and returned into the camp: so they did six
days. And it came to pass on the seventh day, that they
rose early about the dawning of the day, and compassed
the city after the same manner seven times: only on that
day they compassed the city seven times. And it came to
pass at the seventh time, when the priests blew with the
trumpets, Joshua said unto the people, "Shout; for the
LORD hath given you the city. And the city shall be accursed, even it, and all that are therein, to the LORD: only
Rahab the harlot shall live, she and all that are with her
in the house, because she hid the messengers that we sent.
And ye, in any wise keep yourselves from the accursed
thing, lest ye make yourselves accursed, when ye take of
the accursed thing, and make the camp of Israel a curse,
and trouble it. But all the silver, and gold, and vessels of
brass and iron, are consecrated unto the LORD: they shall

come into the treasury of the LORD." So the people shouted when the priests blew with the trumpets: and it came to pass, when the people heard the sound of the trumpet, and the people shouted with a great shout, that the wall fell down flat, so that the people went up into the city, every man straight before him, and they took the city.

[6:1–20]

Jericho Taken. And they utterly destroyed all that was in the city, both man and woman, young and old, and ox, and sheep, and ass, with the edge of the sword. But Joshua had said unto the two men that had spied out the country, "Go into the harlot's house, and bring out thence the woman, and all that she hath, as ye sware unto her". And the young men that were spies went in, and brought out Rahab, and her father, and her mother, and her brethren, and all that she had; and they brought out all her kindred, and left them without the camp of Israel. And they burnt the city with fire, and all that was therein: only the silver, and the gold, and the vessels of brass and of iron, they put into the treasury of the house of the LORD. And Joshua saved Rahab the harlot alive, and her father's household, and all that she had; and she dwelleth in Israel even unto this day; because she hid the messengers, which Joshua sent to spy out Jericho. And Joshua adjured them at that time, saying, "Cursed be the man before the LORD, that riseth up and buildeth this city Jericho: he shall lay the foundation thereof in his firstborn, and in his youngest son shall he set up the gates of it". So the LORD was with Joshua; and his fame was noised throughout all the country.

[6:21–27]

The Gibeonites' Trick. And when the inhabitants of Gibeon heard what Joshua had done unto Jericho and to Ai, they did work wilily, and went and made as if they had been ambassadors, and took old sacks upon their asses, and wine bottles, old, and rent, and bound up; and old shoes and clouted upon their feet, and old garments upon them; and all the bread of their provision was dry and mouldy. And they went to Joshua unto the camp at Gilgal, and said unto him, and to the men of Israel, "We be come from a far country: now therefore make ye a league with us". And the men of Israel said unto the Hivites, "Peradventure ye dwell among us; and how shall we make a league with you?" And they said unto Joshua, "We are thy servants". And Joshua said unto them, "Who are ye? and from whence come ye?" And they said unto him, "From a very far country thy servants are come because of the name of the LORD thy God: for we have heard the fame of him, and all that he did in Egypt, and all that he did to the two kings of the Amorites, that were beyond Jordan, to Sihon king of Heshbon, and to Og king of Bashan, which was at Ashtaroth. Wherefore our elders and all the inhabitants of our country spake to us, saying, 'Take victuals with you for the journey, and go to meet them, and say unto them, We are your servants: therefore now make ye a league with us'. This our bread we took hot for our provision out of our houses on the day we came forth to go unto you; but now, behold, it is dry, and it is mouldy: and these bottles of wine, which we filled, were new; and, behold, they be rent: and these our garments and our shoes are become old by reason of the very long journey." And the men took of their victuals, and asked not counsel at the mouth of the LORD.

And Joshua made peace with them, and made a league with them, to let them live: and the princes of the congregation sware unto them. And it came to pass at the end of three days after they had made a league with them, that they heard that they were their neighbours, and that they dwelt among them. And the children of Israel journeyed, and came unto their cities on the third day. Now their cities were Gibeon, and Chephirah, and Beeroth, and Kirjath-jearim. And the children of Israel smote them not, because the princes of the congregation had sworn unto them by the LORD God of Israel. And all the congregation murmured against the princes. But all the princes said

unto all the congregation, "We have sworn unto them by
the LORD God of Israel: now therefore we may not touch
them. This we will do to them; we will even let them live,
lest wrath be upon us, because of the oath which we sware
unto them." And the princes said unto them, "Let them
live; but let them be hewers of wood and drawers of water
unto all the congregation;" as the princes had promised
them. And Joshua called for them, and he spake unto
them, saying, "Wherefore have ye beguiled us, saying,
'We are very far from you'; when ye dwell among us? Now
therefore ye are cursed, and there shall none of you be
freed from being bondmen, and hewers of wood and
drawers of water for the house of my God."

And they answered Joshua, and said, "Because it was
certainly told thy servants, how that the LORD thy God
commanded his servant Moses to give you all the land,
and to destroy all the inhabitants of the land from before
you, therefore we were sore afraid of our lives because of
you, and have done this thing. And now, behold, we are
in thine hand: as it seemeth good and right unto thee to do
unto us, do." And so did he unto them, and delivered
them out of the hand of the children of Israel, that they
slew them not. And Joshua made them that day hewers of
wood and drawers of water for the congregation, and for
the altar of the LORD, even unto this day, in the place
which he should choose.   [9:3–27]

[The five kings of the Amorites attacked the Gibeonites,
who appealed to Joshua. The Israelites came on the kings
by night and put them to flight.]

The Sun Stands Still. Then spake Joshua to the LORD
in the day when the LORD delivered up the Amorites before the children of Israel, and he said in the sight of Israel,

"Sun, stand thou still upon Gibeon;
    And thou, Moon, in the valley of Ajalon".
And the sun stood still, and the moon stayed,

Until the people had avenged themselves upon their
enemies.

Is not this written in the book of Jasher?

"So the sun stood still in the midst of heaven,
And hasted not to go down about a whole day".

And there was no day like that before it or after it, that the
LORD hearkened unto the voice of a man: for the LORD
fought for Israel.   [10:12–14]

[Joshua continued his wars against the inhabitants of
Canaan until most of the land had been captured. The land
was then divided among the tribes of Israel by lot.]

Cities of Refuge Established. The LORD also spake
unto Joshua, saying, "Speak to the children of Israel, saying, 'Appoint out for you cities of refuge, whereof I spake
unto you by the hand of Moses: that the slayer that killeth
any person unawares and unwittingly may flee thither: and
they shall be your refuge from the avenger of blood. And
when he that doth flee unto one of those cities shall stand
at the entering of the gate of the city, and shall declare his
cause in the ears of the elders of that city, they shall take
him into the city unto them, and give him a place, that he
may dwell among them. And if the avenger of blood pursue after him, then they shall not deliver the slayer up
into his hand; because he smote his neighbour unwittingly,
and hated him not beforetime. And he shall dwell in that
city, until he stand before the congregation for judgment,
and until the death of the high priest that shall be in those
days: then shall the slayer return, and come unto his own
city, and unto his own house, unto the city from whence
he fled.' " And they appointed Kedesh in Galilee in mount
Naphtali, and Shechem in mount Ephraim, and Kirjath-
arba, which is Hebron, in the mountain of Judah. And on
the other side Jordan by Jericho eastward, they assigned
Bezer in the wilderness upon the plain out of the tribe of
Reuben, and Ramoth in Gilead out of the tribe of Gad,
and Golan in Bashan out of the tribe of Manasseh. These

were the cities appointed for all the children of Israel, and
for the stranger that sojourneth among them, that whosoever killeth any person at unawares might flee thither, and
not die by the hand of the avenger of blood, until he stood
before the congregation. [20:1–9]

[At last Joshua called the people together and warned
them against idolatry and serving other gods.]

The Death of Joshua. And it came to pass after these
things, that Joshua the son of Nun, the servant of the
LORD, died, being an hundred and ten years old. And they
buried him in the border of his inheritance in Timnath-
serah, which is in mount Ephraim, on the north side of
the hill of Gaash. And Israel served the LORD all the days
of Joshua, and all the days of the elders that overlived
Joshua, and which had known all the works of the LORD,
that he had done for Israel. And the bones of Joseph,
which the children of Israel brought up out of Egypt,
buried they in Shechem, in a parcel of ground which Jacob
bought of the sons of Hamor the father of Shechem for an
hundred pieces of silver: and it became the inheritance of
the children of Joseph. And Eleazar the son of Aaron died;
and they buried him in a hill that pertained to Phinehas
his son, which was given him in mount Ephraim.

[24:29–33]

From JUDGES

[After the death of Joshua there was confusion for several generations.]

The Sins of the Israelites. And the children of Israel did evil in the sight of the LORD, and served Baalim: and they forsook the LORD God of their fathers, which brought them out of the land of Egypt, and followed other gods, of the gods of the people that were round about them, and bowed themselves unto them, and provoked the LORD to anger. And they forsook the LORD, and served Baal and Ashtaroth. And the anger of the LORD was hot against Israel, and he delivered them into the hands of spoilers that spoiled them, and he sold them into the hands of their enemies round about, so that they could not any longer stand before their enemies. Whithersoever they went out, the hand of the LORD was against them for evil, as the LORD had said, and as the LORD had sworn unto them: and they were greatly distressed. Nevertheless the LORD raised up judges, which delivered them out of the hand of those that spoiled them. And yet they would not hearken unto their judges, but they went a whoring after other gods, and bowed themselves unto them: they turned quickly out of the way which their fathers walked in, obeying the commandments of the LORD; but they did not so.

And when the LORD raised them up judges, then the LORD was with the judge, and delivered them out of the hand of their enemies all the days of the judge: for it repented the LORD because of their groanings by reason of them that oppressed them and vexed them. And it came to pass, when the judge was dead, that they returned, and corrupted themselves more than their fathers, in following other gods to serve them, and to bow down unto them; they ceased not from their own doings, nor from their stubborn way. And the anger of the LORD was hot against Israel; and he said, "Because that this people hath transgressed my covenant which I commanded their fathers, and have not hearkened unto my voice; I also will not henceforth drive out any from before them of the nations which Joshua left when he died: that through them I may prove Israel, whether they will keep the way of the LORD to walk therein, as their fathers did keep it, or not". Therefore the LORD left those nations, without driving them out hastily; neither delivered he them into the hand of Joshua. [2:11–23]

Deborah and Barak. And the children of Israel again did evil in the sight of the LORD, when Ehud was dead. And the LORD sold them into the hand of Jabin king of Canaan, that reigned in Hazor; the captain of whose host was Sisera, which dwelt in Harosheth of the Gentiles. And the children of Israel cried unto the LORD: for he had nine hundred chariots of iron; and twenty years he mightily oppressed the children of Israel.

And Deborah, a prophetess, the wife of Lapidoth, she judged Israel at that time. And she dwelt under the palm tree of Deborah between Ramah and Beth-el in mount Ephraim: and the children of Israel came up to her for judgment. And she sent and called Barak the son of Abinoam out of Kedesh-naphtali, and said unto him, "Hath not the LORD God of Israel commanded, saying, 'Go and draw toward mount Tabor, and take with thee ten thousand men of the children of Naphtali and of the children of Zebulun? And I will draw unto thee to the river Kishon Sisera, the captain of Jabin's army, with his chariots and his multitude; and I will deliver him into thine hand.' " And Barak said unto her, "If thou wilt go with me, then I will go: but if thou wilt not go with me, then I will not go". And she said, "I will surely go with thee: notwithstanding the journey that thou takest shall not be for thine honour; for the LORD shall sell Sisera into the hand of a woman". And Deborah arose, and went with Barak to Kedesh. And Barak called Zebulun and Naphtali to Kedesh; and he went up with ten thousand men at his feet: and Deborah went up with him. Now Heber the Kenite, which was of the children of Hobab the father in law of Moses, had severed himself from the Kenites, and pitched his tent unto the plain of Zaanaim, which is by Kedesh. And they shewed Sisera that Barak the son of Abinoam was gone up to mount Tabor. And Sisera gathered together all his chariots, even nine hundred chariots of iron, and all the people that were with him, from Harosheth of the Gentiles unto the river of Kishon. And Deborah said unto Barak, "Up; for this is the day in which the LORD hath delivered Sisera into thine hand: is not the LORD gone out before thee?" So Barak went down from mount Tabor, and ten thousand men after him. And the LORD discomfited Sisera, and all his chariots, and all his host, with the edge of the sword before Barak; so that Sisera lighted down off his chariot, and fled away on his feet. But Barak pursued after the chariots, and after the host, unto Harosheth of the Gentiles: and all the host of Sisera fell upon the edge of the sword; and there was not a man left.   [4:1–16]

Jael Slays Sisera. Howbeit Sisera fled away on his feet to the tent of Jael the wife of Heber the Kenite: for there was peace between Jabin the king of Hazor and the house of Heber the Kenite. And Jael went out to meet Sisera, and said unto him, "Turn in, my lord, turn in to me; fear not". And when he had turned in unto her into the tent, she covered him with a mantle. And he said unto her, "Give me, I pray thee, a little water to drink; for I am thirsty". And she opened a bottle of milk, and gave him drink, and covered him. Again he said unto her, "Stand in the door of the tent, and it shall be, when any man doth come and enquire of thee, and say, 'Is there any man here?' that thou shalt say, 'No'". Then Jael Heber's wife took a nail of the tent, and took an hammer in her hand, and went softly unto him, and smote the nail into his temples, and fastened it into the ground: for he was fast asleep and weary. So he died. And, behold, as Barak pursued Sisera, Jael came out to meet him, and said unto him, "Come, and I will shew thee the man whom thou seekest". And when he came unto her tent, behold, Sisera lay dead, and the nail was in his temples. So God subdued on that day Jabin the king of Canaan before the children of Israel. And the hand of the children of Israel prospered, and prevailed against Jabin the king of Canaan, until they had destroyed Jabin king of Canaan.   [4:17–24]

Gideon. [Now the Midianites oppressed Israel, and Gideon was summoned to lead his people. At first he was reluctant, and asked for a sign.]

And Gideon said unto God, "If thou wilt save Israel by mine hand, as thou hast said, behold, I will put a fleece of wool in the floor; and if the dew be on the fleece only, and it be dry upon all the earth beside, then shall I know that thou wilt save Israel by mine hand, as thou hast said". And it was so: for he rose up early on the morrow, and thrust the fleece together, and wringed the dew out of the fleece, a bowl full of water. And Gideon said unto God, "Let not thine anger be hot against me, and I will speak but this once: let me prove, I pray thee, but this once with the fleece; let it now be dry only upon the fleece, and upon all the ground let there be dew". And God did so that night: for it was dry upon the fleece only, and there was dew on all the ground.

Then Jerubbaal, who is Gideon, and all the people that were with him, rose up early, and pitched beside the well of Harod: so that the host of the Midianites were on the north side of them, by the hill of Moreh, in the valley.

And the LORD said unto Gideon, "The people that are

with thee are too many for me to give the Midianites into their hands, lest Israel vaunt themselves against me, saying, 'Mine own hand hath saved me'. Now therefore go to, proclaim in the ears of the people, saying, 'Whosoever is fearful and afraid, let him return and depart early from mount Gilead'." And there returned of the people twenty and two thousand; and there remained ten thousand.

And the LORD said unto Gideon, "The people are yet too many; bring them down unto the water, and I will try them for thee there: and it shall be, that of whom I say unto thee, This shall go with thee, the same shall go with thee; and of whomsoever I say unto thee, This shall not go with thee, the same shall not go". So he brought down the people unto the water: and the LORD said unto Gideon, "Every one that lappeth of the water with his tongue, as a dog lappeth, him shalt thou set by himself; likewise every one that boweth down upon his knees to drink". And the number of them that lapped, putting their hand to their mouth, were three hundred men: but all the rest of the people bowed down upon their knees to drink water. And the LORD said unto Gideon, "By the three hundred men that lapped will I save you, and deliver the Midianites into thine hand: and let all the other people go every man unto his place". So the people took victuals in their hand, and their trumpets: and he sent all the rest of Israel every man unto his tent, and retained those three hundred men: and the host of Midian was beneath him in the valley.

And it came to pass the same night, that the LORD said unto him, "Arise, get thee down unto the host; for I have delivered it into thine hand. But if thou fear to go down, go thou with Phurah thy servant down to the host: and thou shalt hear what they say; and afterward shall thine hands be strengthened to go down unto the host." Then went he down with Phurah his servant unto the outside of the armed men that were in the host. And the Midianites and the Amalekites and all the children of the east lay along in the valley like grasshoppers for multitude; and their camels were without number, as the sand by the sea side for multitude. And when Gideon was come, behold, there was a man that told a dream unto his fellow, and said, "Behold, I dreamed a dream, and, lo, a cake of barley bread tumbled into the host of Midian, and came unto a tent, and smote it that it fell, and overturned it, that the tent lay along". And his fellow answered and said, "This is nothing else save the sword of Gideon the son of Joash, a man of Israel: for into his hand hath God delivered Midian, and all the host". [6:36–40; 7:1–14]

Gideon's Ruse. And it was so, when Gideon heard the telling of the dream, and the interpretation thereof, that he worshipped, and returned into the host of Israel, and said, "Arise; for the LORD hath delivered into your hand the host of Midian". And he divided the three hundred men into three companies, and he put a trumpet in every man's hand, with empty pitchers, and lamps within the pitchers. And he said unto them, "Look on me, and do likewise: and, behold, when I come to the outside of the camp, it shall be that, as I do, so shall ye do. When I blow with a trumpet, I and all that are with me, then blow ye the trumpets also on every side of all the camp, and say, 'The sword of the LORD, and of Gideon'."

So Gideon, and the hundred men that were with him, came unto the outside of the camp in the beginning of the middle watch; and they had but newly set the watch: and they blew the trumpets, and brake the pitchers that were in their hands. And the three companies blew the trumpets, and brake the pitchers, and held the lamps in their left hands, and the trumpets in their right hands to blow withal: and they cried, "The sword of the LORD, and of Gideon". And they stood every man in his place round about the camp: and all the host ran, and cried, and fled. And the three hundred blew the trumpets, and the LORD set every man's sword against his fellow, even throughout all the host: and the host fled to Beth-shittah in Zererath, and to the border of Abel-meholah, unto Tabbath. And the men of Israel gathered themselves together out of Naphtali, and out of Asher, and out of all Manasseh, and pursued after the Midianites. And Gideon sent messengers throughout all mount Ephraim, saying, "Come down against the Midianites, and take before them the waters unto Beth-barah and Jordan". Then all the men of Ephraim gathered themselves together, and took the waters unto Beth-barah and Jordan. And they took two princes of the Midianites, Oreb and Zeeb; and they slew Oreb upon the rock Oreb, and Zeeb they slew at the winepress of Zeeb, and pursued Midian, and brought the heads of Oreb and Zeeb to Gideon on the other side Jordan.

[7:15–25]

Jephthah. Now Jephthah the Gileadite was a mighty man of valour, and he was the son of an harlot: and Gilead begat Jephthah. And Gilead's wife bare him sons; and his wife's sons grew up, and they thrust out Jephthah, and said unto him, "Thou shalt not inherit in our father's house; for thou art the son of a strange woman". Then Jephthah fled from his brethren, and dwelt in the land of Tob: and there were gathered vain men to Jephthah, and went out with him.

And it came to pass in process of time, that the children of Ammon made war against Israel. And it was so, that when the children of Ammon made war against Israel, the elders of Gilead went to fetch Jephthah out of the land of Tob: and they said unto Jephthah, "Come, and be our captain, that we may fight with the children of Ammon". And Jephthah said unto the elders of Gilead, "Did not ye hate me, and expel me out of my father's house? and why are ye come unto me now when ye are in distress?" And the elders of Gilead said unto Jephthah, "Therefore we turn again to thee now, that thou mayest go with us, and fight against the children of Ammon, and be our head over all the inhabitants of Gilead". And Jephthah said unto the elders of Gilead, "If ye bring me home again to fight against the children of Ammon, and the LORD deliver them before me, shall I be your head?" And the elders of Gilead said unto Jephthah, "The LORD be witness between us, if we do not so according to thy words". Then Jephthah went with the elders of Gilead, and the people made him head and captain over them: and Jephthah uttered all his words before the LORD in Mizpeh. [11:1–11]

Jephthah's Rash Oath. Then the spirit of the LORD came upon Jephthah, and he passed over Gilead, and Manasseh, and passed over Mizpeh of Gilead, and from Mizpeh of Gilead he passed over unto the children of Ammon. And Jephthah vowed a vow unto the LORD, and said, "If thou shalt without fail deliver the children of Ammon into mine hands, then it shall be, that whatsoever cometh forth of the doors of my house to meet me, when I return in peace from the children of Ammon, shall surely be the LORD's, and I will offer it up for a burnt offering". So Jephthah passed over unto the children of Ammon to fight against them; and the LORD delivered them into his hands. And he smote them from Aroer, even till thou come to Minnith, even twenty cities, and unto the plain of the vineyards, with a very great slaughter. Thus the children of Ammon were subdued before the children of Israel. [11:29–33]

Jephthah's Daughter. And Jephthah came to Mizpeh unto his house, and, behold, his daughter came out to meet him with timbrels and with dances: and she was his only child; beside her he had neither son nor daughter. And it came to pass, when he saw her, that he rent his clothes, and said, "Alas, my daughter! thou hast brought me very low, and thou art one of them that trouble me: for I have opened my mouth unto the LORD, and I cannot go back". And she said unto him, "My father, if thou hast opened thy mouth unto the LORD, do to me according to that which hath proceeded out of thy mouth; forasmuch as the LORD hath taken vengeance for thee of thine enemies, even of the children of Ammon". And she said unto her father, "Let this thing be done for me: let me alone two months, that I may go up and down upon the mountains, and bewail my virginity, I and my fellows". And he said, "Go". And he sent her away for two months: and she went with her companions, and bewailed her virginity upon the mountains. And it came to pass at the end of two months, that she returned unto her father, who did with her according to his vow which he had vowed: and she knew no man. And it was a custom in Israel, that the daughters of Israel went yearly to lament the daughter of Jephthah the Gileadite four days in a year. [11:34-40]

"Shibboleth." And the men of Ephraim gathered themselves together, and went northward, and said unto Jephthah, "Wherefore passedst thou over to fight against the children of Ammon, and didst not call us to go with thee? we will burn thine house upon thee with fire". And Jephthah said unto them, "I and my people were at great strife with the children of Ammon; and when I called you, ye delivered me not out of their hands. And when I saw that ye delivered me not, I put my life in my hands, and passed over against the children of Ammon, and the LORD delivered them into my hand: wherefore then are ye come up unto me this day, to fight against me?" Then Jephthah gathered together all the men of Gilead, and fought with Ephraim: and the men of Gilead smote Ephraim, because they said, "Ye Gileadites are fugitives of Ephraim among the Ephraimites, and among the Manassites". And the Gileadites took the passages of Jordan before the Ephraimites: and it was so, that when those Ephraimites which were escaped said, "Let me go over"; that the men of Gilead said unto him, "Art thou an Ephraimite?" If he said, "Nay"; then said they unto him, "Say now Shibboleth": and he said "Sibboleth": for he could not frame to pronounce it right. Then they took him, and slew him at the passages of Jordan: and there fell at that time of the Ephraimites forty and two thousand. [12:1-6]

The Birth of Samson. And the children of Israel did evil again in the sight of the LORD; and the LORD delivered them into the hand of the Philistines forty years.

And there was a certain man of Zorah, of the family of the Danites, whose name was Manoah; and his wife was barren, and bare not. And the angel of the LORD appeared unto the woman, and said unto her, "Behold now, thou art barren, and barest not: but thou shalt conceive, and bare a son. Now therefore beware, I pray thee, and drink not wine nor strong drink, and eat not any unclean thing: for, lo, thou shalt conceive, and bear a son; and no razor shall come on his head: for the child shall be a Nazarite unto God from the womb: and he shall begin to deliver Israel out of the hand of the Philistines."

.   .   .   .

And the woman bare a son, and called his name Samson: and the child grew, and the LORD blessed him. And the spirit of the LORD began to move him at times in the camp of Dan between Zorah and Eshtaol.

[13:1–5, 24–25]

Samson Slays a Lion. And Samson went down to Timnath, and saw a woman in Timnath of the daughters of the Philistines. And he came up, and told his father and his mother, and said, "I have seen a woman in Timnath of the daughters of the Philistines: now therefore get her for me to wife". Then his father and his mother said unto him, "Is there never a woman among the daughters of thy brethren, or among all my people, that thou goest to take a wife of the uncircumcised Philistines?" And Samson said unto his father, "Get her for me; for she pleaseth me well". But his father and his mother knew not that it was of the LORD, that he sought an occasion against the Philistines: for at that time the Philistines had dominion over Israel.

Then went Samson down, and his father and his mother, to Timnath, and came to the vineyards of Timnath: and, behold, a young lion roared against him. And the spirit

of the LORD came mightily upon him, and he rent him as
he would have rent a kid, and he had nothing in his hand:
but he told not his father or his mother what he had done.
And he went down, and talked with the woman; and she
pleased Samson well. And after a time he returned to take
her, and he turned aside to see the carcase of the lion:
and, behold, there was a swarm of bees and honey in the
carcase of the lion. And he took thereof in his hands,
and went on eating, and came to his father and mother,
and he gave them, and they did eat: but he told not them
that he had taken the honey out of the carcase of the lion.
So his father went down unto the woman: and Samson
made there a feast; for so used the young men to do. And
it came to pass, when they saw him, that they brought
thirty companions to be with him.   [14:1–11]

Samson's Riddle. And Samson said unto them, "I will
now put forth a riddle unto you: if ye can certainly
declare it me within the seven days of the feast, and find
it out, then I will give you thirty sheets and thirty change
of garments: but if ye cannot declare it me, then shall ye
give me thirty sheets and thirty change of garments". And
they said unto him, "Put forth thy riddle, that we may hear
it". And he said unto them,

> "Out of the eater came forth meat,
>   And out of the strong came forth sweetness".

And they could not in three days expound the riddle.

And it came to pass on the seventh day, that they said
unto Samson's wife, "Entice thy husband, that he may declare unto us the riddle, lest we burn thee and thy father's
house with fire: have ye called us to take that we have?
is it not so?" And Samson's wife wept before him, and
said, "Thou dost but hate me, and lovest me not: thou
hast put forth a riddle unto the children of my people,
and hast not told it me". And he said unto her, "Behold,
I have not told it my father nor my mother, and shall I tell
it thee?" And she wept before him the seven days, while

their feast lasted: and it came to pass on the seventh day, that he told her, because she lay sore upon him: and she told the riddle to the children of her people. And the men of the city said unto him on the seventh day before the sun went down,

> "What is sweeter than honey?
> And what is stronger than a lion?"

And he said unto them,

> "If ye had not plowed with my heifer,
> Ye had not found out my riddle".

And the spirit of the LORD came upon him, and he went down to Ashkelon, and slew thirty men of them, and took their spoil, and gave change of garments unto them which expounded the riddle. And his anger was kindled, and he went up to his father's house. But Samson's wife was given to his companion, whom he had used as his friend.

[14:12–20]

Samson Burns the Philistines' Corn. But it came to pass within a while after, in the time of wheat harvest, that Samson visited his wife with a kid; and he said, "I will go in to my wife into the chamber". But her father would not suffer him to go in. And her father said, "I verily thought that thou hadst utterly hated her; therefore I gave her to thy companion: is not her younger sister fairer than she? take her, I pray thee, instead of her". And Samson said concerning them, "Now shall I be more blameless than the Philistines, though I do them a displeasure". And Samson went and caught three hundred foxes, and took firebrands, and turned tail to tail, and put a firebrand in the midst between two tails. And when he had set the brands on fire, he let them go into the standing corn of the Philistines, and burnt up both the shocks, and also the standing corn, with the vineyards and olives. Then the Philistines said, "Who hath done this?" And they answered, "Samson, the son in law of the Timnite, because

he had taken his wife, and given her to his companion".
And the Philistines came up, and burnt her and her father
with fire. And Samson said unto them, "Though ye have
done this, yet will I be avenged of you, and after that I will
cease". And he smote them hip and thigh with a great
slaughter: and he went down and dwelt in the top of the
rock Etam.   [15:1–8]

The Jawbone of an Ass. Then the Philistines went up,
and pitched in Judah, and spread themselves in Lehi.
And the men of Judah said, "Why are ye come up against
us?" And they answered, "To bind Samson are we come
up, to do to him as he hath done to us". Then three thousand men of Judah went to the top of the rock Etam, and
said to Samson, "Knowest thou not that the Philistines
are rulers over us? what is this that thou hast done unto
us?" And he said unto them, "As they did unto me, so
have I done unto them". And they said unto him, "We are
come down to bind thee, that we may deliver thee into the
hand of the Philistines". And Samson said unto them,
"Swear unto me, that ye will not fall upon me yourselves".
And they spake unto him, saying, "No; but we will bind
thee fast, and deliver thee into their hand: but surely we
will not kill thee". And they bound him with two new cords,
and brought him up from the rock. And when he came
unto Lehi, the Philistines shouted against him: and the
spirit of the LORD came mightily upon him, and the cords
that were upon his arms became as flax that was burnt
with fire, and his bands loosed from off his hands. And
he found a new jawbone of an ass, and put forth his hand,
and took it, and slew a thousand men therewith. And
Samson said,

"With the jawbone of an ass, heaps upon heaps,
    With the jaw of an ass have I slain a thousand men".

And it came to pass, when he had made an end of speaking, that he cast away the jawbone out of his hand, and
called that place Ramath-lehi. And he was sore athirst,

and called on the LORD, and said, "Thou hast given this great deliverance into the hand of thy servant: and now shall I die for thirst, and fall into the hand of the uncircumcised?" But God clave an hollow place that was in the jaw, and there came water thereout; and when he had drunk, his spirit came again, and he revived: wherefore he called the name thereof En-hakkore, which is in Lehi unto this day. And he judged Israel in the days of the Philistines twenty years. [15:9–20]

Samson and the Gates of Gaza. Then went Samson to Gaza, and saw there an harlot, and went in unto her. And it was told the Gazites, saying, "Samson is come hither". And they compassed him in, and laid wait for him all night in the gate of the city, and were quiet all the night, saying, "In the morning, when it is day, we shall kill him". And Samson lay till midnight, and arose at midnight, and took the doors of the gate of the city, and the two posts, and went away with them, bar and all, and put them upon his shoulders, and carried them up to the top of an hill that is before Hebron. [16:1–3]

Samson and Delilah. And it came to pass afterward, that he loved a woman in the valley of Sorek, whose name was Delilah. And the lords of the Philistines came up unto her, and said unto her, "Entice him, and see wherein his great strength lieth, and by what means we may prevail against him, that we may bind him to afflict him: and we will give thee every one of us eleven hundred pieces of silver". And Delilah said to Samson, "Tell me, I pray thee, wherein thy great strength lieth, and wherewith thou mightest be bound to afflict thee". And Samson said unto her, "If they bind me with seven green withs that were never dried, then shall I be weak, and be as another man". Then the lords of the Philistines brought up to her seven green withs which had not been dried, and she bound him with them. Now there were men lying in wait, abiding with her in the chamber. And she said unto him, "The Philistines be upon thee, Samson". And he brake the withs, as a thread of tow is broken when it toucheth the fire. So his strength was not known. And Delilah said unto Samson, "Behold, thou hast mocked me, and told me lies: now tell me, I pray thee, wherewith thou mightest be bound". And he said unto her, "If they bind me fast with new ropes that never were occupied, then shall I be weak, and be as another man". Delilah therefore took new ropes, and bound him therewith, and said unto him, "The Philistines be upon thee, Samson". And there were liers in wait abiding in the chamber. And he brake them from off his arms like a thread. And Delilah said unto Samson, "Hitherto thou hast mocked me, and told me lies: tell me wherewith thou mightest be bound". And he said unto her, "If thou weavest the seven locks of my head with the web". And she fastened it with the pin, and said unto him, "The Philistines be upon thee, Samson". And he awaked out of his sleep, and went away with the pin of the beam, and with the web. And she said unto him, "How canst thou say, 'I love thee,' when thine heart is not with me? thou hast mocked me these three times, and hast not told me wherein thy great strength lieth".   [16:4–15]

Samson Subdued. And it came to pass, when she pressed him daily with her words, and urged him, so that his soul was vexed unto death; that he told her all his heart, and said unto her, "There hath not come a razor upon mine head; for I have been a Nazarite unto God from my mother's womb: if I be shaven, then my strength will go from me, and I shall become weak, and be like any other man". And when Delilah saw that he had told her all his heart, she sent and called for the lords of the Philistines, saying, "Come up this once, for he hath shewed me all his heart". Then the lords of the Philistines came up unto her, and brought money in their hand. And she made him sleep upon her knees; and she called for a man, and she caused him to shave off the seven locks of his head; and she began to afflict him, and his strength went from him. And she said, "The Philistines be upon

thee, Samson". And he awoke out of his sleep, and said,
"I will go out as at other times before, and shake myself".
And he wist not that the LORD was departed from him.
But the Philistines took him, and put out his eyes, and
brought him down to Gaza, and bound him with fetters
of brass; and he did grind in the prison house. Howbeit
the hair of his head began to grow again after he was
shaven. [16:16–22]

The Death of Samson. Then the lords of the Philistines
gathered them together for to offer a great sacrifice unto
Dagon their god, and to rejoice: for they said, "Our god
hath delivered Samson our enemy into our hand". And
when the people saw him, they praised their god: for they
said, "Our god hath delivered into our hands our enemy,
and the destroyer of our country, which slew many of us".
And it came to pass, when their hearts were merry, that
they said, "Call for Samson, that he may make us sport".
And they called for Samson out of the prison house; and he
made them sport: and they set him between the pillars.
And Samson said unto the lad that held him by the hand,
"Suffer me that I may feel the pillars whereupon the house
standeth, that I may lean upon them". Now the house was
full of men and women; and all the lords of the Philistines
were there; and there were upon the roof about three
thousand men and women, that beheld while Samson made
sport. And Samson called unto the LORD, and said, "O
Lord GOD, remember me, I pray thee, and strengthen me,
I pray thee, only this once, O God, that I may be at once
avenged of the Philistines for my two eyes". And Samson
took hold of the two middle pillars upon which the house
stood, and on which it was borne up, of the one with his
right hand, and of the other with his left. And Samson said,
"Let me die with the Philistines". And he bowed himself
with all his might; and the house fell upon the lords, and
upon all the people that were therein. So the dead which he
slew at his death were more than they which he slew in his

life. Then his brethren and all the house of his father came
down, and took him, and brought him up, and buried him
between Zorah and Eshtaol in the buryingplace of Manoah
his father. And he judged Israel twenty years.

[16:23-31]

THE BOOK OF RUTH

The Sorrows of Naomi. Now it came to pass in the days when the judges ruled, that there was a famine in the land. And a certain man of Beth-lehem-judah went to sojourn in the country of Moab, he, and his wife, and his two sons. And the name of the man was Elimelech, and the name of his wife Naomi, and the name of his two sons Mahlon and Chilion, Ephrathites of Beth-lehem-judah. And they came into the country of Moab, and continued there. And Elimelech Naomi's husband died; and she was left, and her two sons. And they took them wives of the women of Moab; the name of the one was Orpah, and the name of the other Ruth: and they dwelled there about ten years. And Mahlon and Chilion died also both of them; and the woman was left of her two sons and her husband. Then she arose with her daughters in law, that she might return from the country of Moab: for she had heard in the country of Moab how that the LORD had visited his people in giving them bread. Wherefore she went forth out of the place where she was, and her two daughters in law with her; and they went on the way to return unto the land of Judah. And Naomi said unto her two daughters in law, "Go, return each to her mother's house: the LORD deal kindly with you, as ye have dealt with the dead, and with me. The LORD grant you that ye may find rest, each of you in the house of her husband." Then she kissed them; and they lifted up their voice, and wept. And they said unto her, "Surely we will return with thee unto thy people". And Naomi said, "Turn again, my daughters:

why will ye go with me? are there yet any more sons in my
womb, that they may be your husbands? Turn again, my
daughters, go your way; for I am too old to have an husband. If I should say, I have hope, if I should have an husband also to night, and should also bear sons; would ye
tarry for them till they were grown? would ye stay for
them from having husbands? nay, my daughters; for it
grieveth me much for your sakes that the hand of the
LORD is gone out against me." And they lifted up their
voice, and wept again: and Orpah kissed her mother in
law; but Ruth clave unto her. And she said, "Behold, thy
sister in law is gone back unto her people, and unto her
gods: return thou after thy sister in law".   [1:1–15]

Ruth and Naomi. And Ruth said, "Intreat me not to
leave thee, or to return from following after thee: for
whither thou goest, I will go; and where thou lodgest, I
will lodge: thy people shall be my people, and thy God
my God: where thou diest, will I die, and there will I be
buried: the LORD do so to me, and more also, if aught but
death part thee and me". When she saw that she was stedfastly minded to go with her, then she left speaking unto
her. So they two went until they came to Beth-lehem. And
it came to pass, when they were come to Beth-lehem, that
all the city was moved about them, and they said, "Is this
Naomi?" And she said unto them, "Call me not Naomi,
call me Mara: for the Almighty hath dealt very bitterly
with me. I went out full, and the LORD hath brought me
home again empty: why then call ye me Naomi, seeing
the LORD hath testified against me, and the Almighty hath
afflicted me?" So Naomi returned, and Ruth the Moabitess, her daughter in law, with her, which returned out
of the country of Moab: and they came to Beth-lehem in
the beginning of barley harvest.   [1:16–22]

The Kindness of Boaz. And Naomi had a kinsman of
her husband's, a mighty man of wealth, of the family of
Elimelech; and his name was Boaz. And Ruth the Moabitess said unto Naomi, "Let me now go to the field, and

glean ears of corn after him in whose sight I shall find grace". And she said unto her, "Go, my daughter". And she went, and came, and gleaned in the field after the reapers: and her hap was to light on a part of the field belonging unto Boaz, who was of the kindred of Elimelech. And, behold, Boaz came from Beth-lehem, and said unto the reapers, "The LORD be with you". And they answered him, "The LORD bless thee". Then said Boaz unto his servant that was set over the reapers, "Whose damsel is this?" And the servant that was set over the reapers answered and said, "It is the Moabitish damsel that came back with Naomi out of the country of Moab: and she said, 'I pray you, let me glean and gather after the reapers among the sheaves': so she came, and hath continued even from the morning until now, that she tarried a little in the house". Then said Boaz unto Ruth, "Hearest thou not, my daughter? Go not to glean in another field, neither go from hence, but abide here fast by my maidens: let thine eyes be on the field that they do reap, and go thou after them: have I not charged the young men that they shall not touch thee? and when thou art athirst, go unto the vessels, and drink of that which the young men have drawn." Then she fell on her face, and bowed herself to the ground, and said unto him, "Why have I found grace in thine eyes, that thou shouldest take knowledge of me, seeing I am a stranger?" And Boaz answered and said unto her, "It hath fully been shewed me, all that thou hast done unto thy mother in law since the death of thine husband: and how thou hast left thy father and thy mother, and the land of thy nativity, and art come unto a people which thou knewest not heretofore. The LORD recompense thy work, and a full reward be given thee of the LORD God of Israel, under whose wings thou art come to trust." Then she said, "Let me find favour in thy sight, my lord; for that thou hast comforted me, and for that thou hast spoken friendly unto thine handmaid, though I be not like unto one of thine handmaidens". And Boaz said unto her, "At mealtime come thou hither, and eat of the bread, and dip thy morsel in the vinegar". And she sat beside the reapers: and he reached her parched corn, and she did eat, and was sufficed, and left. And when she was risen up to glean, Boaz commanded his young men, saying, "Let her glean even among the sheaves, and reproach her not: and let fall also some of the handfuls of purpose for her, and leave them, that she may glean them, and rebuke her not". So she gleaned in the field until even, and beat out that she had gleaned: and it was about an ephah of barley. And she took it up, and went into the city: and her mother in law saw what she had gleaned: and she brought forth, and gave to her that she had reserved after she was sufficed. And her mother in law said unto her, "Where hast thou gleaned to day? and where wroughtest thou? blessed be he that did take knowledge of thee". And she shewed her mother in law with whom she had wrought, and said, "The man's name with whom I wrought to day is Boaz". And Naomi said unto her daughter in law, "Blessed be he of the LORD, who hath not left off his kindness to the living and to the dead". And Naomi said unto her, "The man is near of kin unto us, one of our next kinsmen". And Ruth the Moabitess said, "He said unto me also, 'Thou shalt keep fast by my young men, until they have ended all my harvest'". And Naomi said unto Ruth her daughter in law, "It is good, my daughter, that thou go out with his maidens, that they meet thee not in any other field". So she kept fast by the maidens of Boaz to glean unto the end of barley harvest and of wheat harvest; and dwelt with her mother in law.   [2:1–23]

The Claim of Kinship.[1]   Then Naomi her mother in law said unto her, "My daughter, shall I not seek rest for thee, that it may be well with thee? And now is not Boaz of our kindred, with whose maidens thou wast? Behold,

[1] For the claim of a childless widow on her husband's kin, see p. 97.

he winnoweth barley to night in the threshingfloor. Wash thyself therefore, and anoint thee, and put thy raiment upon thee, and get thee down to the floor: but make not thyself known unto the man, until he shall have done eating and drinking. And it shall be, when he lieth down, that thou shalt mark the place where he shall lie, and thou shalt go in, and uncover his feet, and lay thee down; and he will tell thee what thou shalt do". And she said unto her, "All that thou sayest unto me I will do". And she went down unto the floor, and did according to all that her mother in law bade her. And when Boaz had eaten and drunk, and his heart was merry, he went to lie down at the end of the heap of corn: and she came softly, and uncovered his feet, and laid her down. And it came to pass at midnight, that the man was afraid, and turned himself: and, behold, a woman lay at his feet. And he said, "Who art thou?" And she answered, "I am Ruth thine handmaid: spread therefore thy skirt over thine handmaid; for thou art a near kinsman". And he said, "Blessed be thou of the LORD, my daughter: for thou hast shewed more kindness in the latter end than at the beginning, inasmuch as thou followedst not young men, whether poor or rich. And now, my daughter, fear not; I will do to thee all that thou requirest: for all the city of my people doth know that thou art a virtuous woman. And now it is true that I am thy near kinsman: howbeit there is a kinsman nearer than I. Tarry this night, and it shall be in the morning, that if he will perform unto thee the part of a kinsman, well; let him do the kinsman's part: but if he will not do the part of a kinsman to thee, then will I do the part of a kinsman to thee, as the LORD liveth: lie down until the morning." And she lay at his feet until the morning: and she rose up before one could know another. And he said, "Let it not be known that a woman came into the floor". Also he said, "Bring the veil that thou hast upon thee, and hold it". And when she held it, he measured six measures of barley, and laid it on her: and she went into

the city. And when she came to her mother in law, she
said, "Who art thou, my daughter?" And she told her all
that the man had done to her. And she said, "These six
measures of barley gave he me; for he said to me, 'Go not
empty unto thy mother in law'". Then said she, "Sit still,
my daughter, until thou know how the matter will fall: for
the man will not be in rest, until he have finished the thing
this day".   [3:1–18]

Boaz Fulfills the Claim of Kinship. Then went Boaz
up to the gate, and sat him down there: and, behold, the
kinsman of whom Boaz spake came by; unto whom he
said, "Ho, such a one! turn aside, sit down here". And he
turned aside, and sat down. And he took ten men of the
elders of the city, and said, "Sit ye down here". And they
sat down. And he said unto the kinsman, "Naomi, that is
come again out of the country of Moab, selleth a parcel
of land, which was our brother Elimelech's: and I thought
to advertise thee, saying, Buy it before the inhabitants, and
before the elders of my people. If thou wilt redeem it,
redeem it: but if thou wilt not redeem it, then tell me, that
I may know: for there is none to redeem it beside thee;
and I am after thee." And he said, "I will redeem it".
Then said Boaz, "What day thou buyest the field of the
hand of Naomi, thou must buy it also of Ruth the Moabitess, the wife of the dead, to raise up the name of the
dead upon his inheritance". And the kinsman said, "I cannot redeem it for myself, lest I mar mine own inheritance:
redeem thou my right to thyself; for I cannot redeem it".
Now this was the manner in former time in Israel concerning redeeming and concerning changing, for to confirm all
things; a man plucked off his shoe, and gave it to his neighbour: and this was a testimony in Israel. Therefore the
kinsman said unto Boaz, "Buy it for thee". So he drew off
his shoe. And Boaz said unto the elders, and unto all the
people, "Ye are witnesses this day, that I have bought all
that was Elimelech's, and all that was Chilion's and
Mahlon's, of the hand of Naomi. Moreover Ruth the Mo-

abitess, the wife of Mahlon, have I purchased to be my wife, to raise up the name of the dead upon his inheritance, that the name of the dead be not cut off from among his brethren, and from the gate of his place: ye are witnesses this day." And all the people that were in the gate, and the elders, said, "We are witnesses. The LORD make the woman that is come into thine house like Rachel and like Leah, which two did build the house of Israel: and do thou worthily in Ephratah, and be famous in Beth-lehem: and let thy house be like the house of Pharez, whom Tamar bare unto Judah, of the seed which the LORD shall give thee of this young woman." So Boaz took Ruth, and she was his wife: and when he went in unto her, the LORD gave her conception, and she bare a son. And the women said unto Naomi, "Blessed be the LORD, which hath not left thee this day without a kinsman, that his name may be famous in Israel. And he shall be unto thee a restorer of thy life, and a nourisher of thine old age: for thy daughter in law, which loveth thee, which is better to thee than seven sons, hath borne him." And Naomi took the child, and laid it in her bosom, and became nurse unto it. And the women her neighbours gave it a name, saying, "There is a son born to Naomi"; and they called his name Obed: he is the father of Jesse, the father of David.

Now these are the generations of Pharez: Pharez begat Hezron, and Hezron begat Ram, and Ram begat Amminadab, and Amminadab begat Nahshon, and Nahshon begat Salmon, and Salmon begat Boaz, and Boaz begat Obed, and Obed begat Jesse, and Jesse begat David.

[4:1–22]

From THE FIRST BOOK OF SAMUEL

[Hannah, the wife of Elkanah an Ephrathite, had no child. They went to the house of the LORD at Shiloh, and Hannah vowed that if she bore a son she would dedicate him to the LORD. Her prayer was answered and the child was named Samuel, who was sent to minister to the LORD before Eli the priest at Shiloh.]

Eli's Evil Sons. Now the sons of Eli were sons of Belial[1]; they knew not the LORD. And the priests' custom with the people was, that, when any man offered sacrifice, the priest's servant came, while the flesh was in seething, with a fleshhook of three teeth in his hand; and he struck it into the pan, or kettle, or caldron, or pot; all that the fleshhook brought up the priest took for himself. So they did in Shiloh unto all the Israelites that came thither. Also before they burnt the fat, the priest's servant came, and said to the man that sacrificed, "Give flesh to roast for the priest; for he will not have sodden flesh of thee, but raw". And if any man said unto him, "Let them not fail to burn the fat presently, and then take as much as thy soul desireth"; then he would answer him, "Nay; but thou shalt give it me now: and if not, I will take it by force". Wherefore the sin of the young men was very great before the LORD: for men abhorred the offering of the LORD.

But Samuel ministered before the LORD, being a child, girded with a linen ephod.[2] Moreover his mother made him a little coat, and brought it to him from year to year,

[1] I.e., of 'worthlessness.'
[2] Priestly garment.

when she came up with her husband to offer the yearly sacrifice. And Eli blessed Elkanah and his wife, and said, "The LORD give thee seed of this woman for the loan which is lent to the LORD". And they went unto their own home. And the LORD visited Hannah, so that she conceived, and bare three sons and two daughters. And the child Samuel grew before the LORD.

Now Eli was very old, and heard all that his sons did unto all Israel; and how they lay with the women that assembled at the door of the tabernacle of the congregation. And he said unto them, "Why do ye such things? for I hear of your evil dealings by all this people. Nay, my sons; for it is no good report that I hear: ye make the LORD's people to transgress. If one man sin against another, the judge shall judge him: but if a man sin against the LORD, who shall intreat for him?" Notwithstanding they hearkened not unto the voice of their father, because the LORD would slay them. And the child Samuel grew on, and was in favour both with the LORD, and also with men.

[2:12–26]

The Call of Samuel. And the child Samuel ministered unto the LORD before Eli. And the word of the LORD was precious in those days; there was no open vision. And it came to pass at that time, when Eli was laid down in his place, and his eyes began to wax dim, that he could not see; and ere the lamp of God went out in the temple of the LORD, where the ark of God was, and Samuel was laid down to sleep; that the LORD called Samuel: and he answered, "Here am I". And he ran unto Eli, and said, "Here am I; for thou calledst me". And he said, "I called not; lie down again". And he went and lay down. And the LORD called yet again, "Samuel". And Samuel arose and went to Eli, and said, "Here am I; for thou didst call me". And he answered, "I called not, my son; lie down again". Now Samuel did not yet know the LORD, neither was the word of the LORD yet revealed unto him. And the LORD called Samuel again the third time. And he arose and went to

Eli, and said, "Here am I; for thou didst call me". And Eli perceived that the LORD had called the child. Therefore Eli said unto Samuel, "Go, lie down: and it shall be, if he call thee, that thou shalt say, 'Speak, LORD; for thy servant heareth'". So Samuel went and lay down in his place.

And the LORD came, and stood, and called as at other times, "Samuel, Samuel". Then Samuel answered, "Speak; for thy servant heareth". And the LORD said to Samuel, "Behold, I will do a thing in Israel, at which both the ears of every one that heareth it shall tingle. In that day I will perform against Eli all things which I have spoken concerning his house: when I begin, I will also make an end. For I have told him that I will judge his house for ever for the iniquity which he knoweth; because his sons made themselves vile, and he restrained them not. And therefore I have sworn unto the house of Eli, that the iniquity of Eli's house shall not be purged with sacrifice nor offering for ever." And Samuel lay until the morning, and opened the doors of the house of the LORD. And Samuel feared to shew Eli the vision. Then Eli called Samuel, and said, "Samuel, my son". And he answered, "Here am I". And he said, "What is the thing that the LORD hath said unto thee? I pray thee hide it not from me: God do so to thee, and more also, if thou hide any thing from me of all the things that he said unto thee." And Samuel told him every whit, and hid nothing from him. And he said, "It is the LORD: let him do what seemeth him good". And Samuel grew, and the LORD was with him, and did let none of his words fall to the ground. And all Israel from Dan even to Beer-sheba knew that Samuel was established to be a prophet of the LORD. And the LORD appeared again in Shiloh: for the LORD revealed himself to Samuel in Shiloh by the word of the LORD.   [3:1–21]

The Israelites Defeated. And the word of Samuel came to all Israel. Now Israel went out against the Philistines to battle, and pitched beside Eben-ezer: and the Philistines pitched in Aphek. And the Philistines put themselves in array against Israel: and when they joined battle, Israel was smitten before the Philistines: and they slew of the army in the field about four thousand men. And when the people were come into the camp, the elders of Israel said, "Wherefore hath the LORD smitten us to day before the Philistines? Let us fetch the ark[3] of the covenant of the LORD out of Shiloh unto us, that, when it cometh among us, it may save us out of the hand of our enemies." So the people sent to Shiloh, that they might bring from thence the ark of the covenant of the LORD of hosts, which dwelleth between the cherubims: and the two sons of Eli, Hophni and Phinehas, were there with the ark of the covenant of God. And when the ark of the covenant of the LORD came into the camp, all Israel shouted with a great shout, so that the earth rang again. And when the Philistines heard the noise of the shout, they said, "What meaneth the noise of this great shout in the camp of the Hebrews?" And they understood that the ark of the LORD was come into the camp. And the Philistines were afraid, for they said, "God is come into the camp". And they said, "Woe unto us! for there hath not been such a thing heretofore. Woe unto us! who shall deliver us out of the hand of these mighty Gods? these are the Gods that smote the Egyptians with all the plagues in the wilderness. Be strong, and quit yourselves like men, O ye Philistines, that ye be not servants unto the Hebrews, as they have been to you: quit yourselves like men, and fight." [4:1–9]

The Ark Taken. And the Philistines fought, and Israel was smitten, and they fled every man into his tent: and there was a very great slaughter; for there fell of Israel thirty thousand footmen. And the ark of God was taken; and the two sons of Eli, Hophni and Phinehas, were slain. And there ran a man of Benjamin out of the army, and came to Shiloh the same day with his clothes rent, and with earth upon his head. And when he came, lo, Eli sat

[3] See Appendix 3.

upon a seat by the wayside watching: for his heart trembled for the ark of God. And when the man came into the
city, and told it, all the city cried out. And when Eli heard
the noise of the crying, he said, "What meaneth the noise
of this tumult?" And the man came in hastily, and told Eli.
[4:10–14]

The Death of Eli. Now Eli was ninety and eight years
old; and his eyes were dim, that he could not see. And the
man said unto Eli, "I am he that came out of the army,
and I fled to day out of the army". And he said, "What is
there done, my son?" And the messenger answered and
said, "Israel is fled before the Philistines, and there hath
been also a great slaughter among the people, and thy two
sons also, Hophni and Phinehas, are dead, and the ark of
God is taken". And it came to pass, when he made mention of the ark of God, that he fell from off the seat backward by the side of the gate, and his neck brake, and he
died: for he was an old man, and heavy. And he had
judged Israel forty years. And his daughter in law,
Phinehas' wife, was with child, near to be delivered: and
when she heard the tidings that the ark of God was taken,
and that her father in law and her husband were dead, she
bowed herself and travailed; for her pains came upon her.
And about the time of her death the women that stood by
her said unto her, "Fear not; for thou hast borne a son".
But she answered not, neither did she regard it. And she
named the child I-chabod, saying, "The glory is departed
from Israel": because the ark of God was taken, and because of her father in law and her husband. And she said,
"The glory is departed from Israel: for the ark of God is
taken".   [4:15–22]

The Ark Among the Philistines. And the Philistines
took the ark of God, and brought it from Eben-ezer unto
Ashdod. When the Philistines took the ark of God, they
brought it into the house of Dagon, and set it by Dagon.
And when they of Ashdod arose early on the morrow, behold, Dagon was fallen upon his face to the earth before

the ark of the LORD. And they took Dagon, and set him in his place again. And when they arose early on the morrow morning, behold, Dagon was fallen upon his face to the ground before the ark of the LORD; and the head of Dagon and both the palms of his hands were cut off upon the threshold; only the stump of Dagon was left to him. Therefore neither the priests of Dagon, nor any that come into Dagon's house, tread on the threshold of Dagon in Ashdod unto this day. [5:1–5]

[Other misfortunes befell the Philistines, who decreed to send the ark back to Israel.]

The People Demand a King. And it came to pass, when Samuel was old, that he made his sons judges over Israel. Now the name of his firstborn was Joel; and the name of his second, Abiah: they were judges in Beersheba. And his sons walked not in his ways, but turned aside after lucre, and took bribes, and perverted judgment.

Then all the elders of Israel gathered themselves together, and came to Samuel unto Ramah, and said unto him, "Behold, thou art old, and thy sons walk not in thy ways: now make us a king to judge us like all the nations". But the thing displeased Samuel, when they said, "Give us a king to judge us". And Samuel prayed unto the LORD. And the LORD said unto Samuel, "Hearken unto the voice of the people in all that they say unto thee: for they have not rejected thee, but they have rejected me, that I should not reign over them. According to all the works which they have done since the day that I brought them up out of Egypt even unto this day, wherewith they have forsaken me, and served other gods, so do they also unto thee. Now therefore hearken unto their voice: howbeit yet protest solemnly unto them, and shew them the manner of the king that shall reign over them."

And Samuel told all the words of the LORD unto the people that asked of him a king. And he said, "This will be the manner of the king that shall reign over you: He will take your sons, and appoint them for himself, for his chariots, and to be his horsemen; and some shall run before his chariots. And he will appoint him captains over thousands, and captains over fifties; and will set them to ear his ground, and to reap his harvest, and to make his instruments of war, and instruments of his chariots. And he will take your daughters to be confectionaries, and to be cooks, and to be bakers. And he will take your fields, and your vineyards, and your oliveyards, even the best of them, and give them to his servants. And he will take the tenth of your seed, and of your vineyards, and give to his officers, and to his servants. And he will take your menservants, and your maidservants, and your goodliest young men, and your asses, and put them to his work. He will take the tenth of your sheep: and ye shall be his servants. And ye shall cry out in that day because of your king which ye shall have chosen you; and the LORD will not hear you in that day." Nevertheless the people refused to obey the voice of Samuel; and they said, "Nay; but we will have a king over us; that we also may be like all the nations; and that our king may judge us, and go out before us, and fight our battles". And Samuel heard all the words of the people, and he rehearsed them in the ears of the LORD. And the LORD said to Samuel, "Hearken unto their voice, and make them a king". And Samuel said unto the men of Israel, "Go ye every man unto his city".

[8:1–22]

Saul and His Father's Asses. Now there was a man of Benjamin, whose name was Kish, the son of Abiel, the son of Zeror, the son of Bechorath, the son of Aphiah, a Benjamite, a mighty man of power. And he had a son, whose name was Saul, a choice young man, and a goodly: and there was not among the children of Israel a goodlier person than he: from his shoulders and upward he was higher than any of the people. And the asses of Kish Saul's father were lost. And Kish said to Saul his son, "Take now one of the servants with thee, and arise, go seek the asses". And he passed through mount Ephraim, and passed through the land of Shalisha, but they found them not: then they passed through the land of Shalim, and there they were not: and he passed through the land of the Benjamites, but they found them not. And when they were come to the land of Zuph, Saul said to his servant that was with him, "Come, and let us return; lest my father leave caring for the asses, and take thought for us". And he said unto him, "Behold now, there is in this city a man of God, and he is an honourable man; all that he saith cometh surely to pass: now let us go thither; peradventure he can shew us our way that we should go". Then said Saul to his servant, "But, behold, if we go, what shall we bring the man? for the bread is spent in our vessels, and there is not a present to bring to the man of God: what have we?" And the servant answered Saul again, and said, "Behold, I have here at hand the fourth part of a shekel of silver: that will I give to the man of God, to tell us our way". (Beforetime in Israel, when a man went to enquire of God, thus he spake, "Come, and let us go to the seer": for he that is now called a Prophet was beforetime called a Seer.)

Then said Saul to his servant, "Well said; come, let us go". So they went unto the city where the man of God was. And as they went up the hill to the city, they found young maidens going out to draw water, and said unto them, "Is the seer here?" And they answered them, and said, "He is; behold, he is before you: make haste now, for he came to day to the city; for there is a sacrifice of the people to day in the high place: as soon as ye be come into the city, ye shall straightway find him, before he go up to the high place to eat: for the people will not eat until he come, because he doth bless the sacrifice; and afterwards they eat that be bidden. Now therefore get you up; for about this time ye shall find him." And they went up into the city: and when they were come into the city, behold, Samuel came out against them, for to go up to the high place. [9:1–14]

Saul Seeks Samuel. Now the LORD had told Samuel in his ear a day before Saul came, saying, "To morrow about this time I will send thee a man out of the land of Benjamin, and thou shalt anoint him to be captain over my people Israel, that he may save my people out of the hand of the Philistines: for I have looked upon my people, because their cry is come unto me". And when Samuel saw Saul, the LORD said unto him, "Behold the man whom I spake to thee of! this same shall reign over my people". Then Saul drew near to Samuel in the gate, and said, "Tell me, I pray thee, where the seer's house is". And Samuel answered Saul, and said, "I am the seer: go up before me unto the high place; for ye shall eat with me to day, and to morrow I will let thee go, and will tell thee all that is in thine heart. And as for thine asses that were lost three days ago, set not thy mind on them; for they are found. And on whom is all the desire of Israel? Is it not on thee, and on all thy father's house?" And Saul answered and said, "Am not I a Benjamite, of the smallest of the tribes of Israel? and my family the least of all the families of the tribe of Benjamin? wherefore then speakest thou so to me?"

And Samuel took Saul and his servant, and brought them into the parlour, and made them sit in the chiefest place among them that were bidden, which were about thirty persons. And Samuel said unto the cook, "Bring the portion which I gave thee, of which I said unto thee, Set it by thee". And the cook took up the shoulder, and that which was upon it, and set it before Saul. And Samuel said, "Behold that which is left! set it before thee, and eat: for unto this time hath it been kept for thee since I said, I have invited the people". So Saul did eat with Samuel that day. And when they were come down from the high place into the city, Samuel communed with Saul upon the top of the house. And they arose early: and it came to pass about the spring of the day, that Samuel called Saul to the top of the house, saying, "Up, that I may send thee away". And Saul arose, and they went out both of them, he and Samuel, abroad. And as they were going down to the end of the city, Samuel said to Saul, "Bid the servant pass on before us," (and he passed on,) "but stand thou still a while, that I may shew thee the word of God".

[9:15–27]

Saul Anointed King. Then Samuel took a vial of oil, and poured it upon his head, and kissed him, and said, "Is it not because the LORD hath anointed thee to be captain over his inheritance? When thou art departed from me to day, then thou shalt find two men by Rachel's sepulchre in the border of Benjamin at Zelzah; and they will say unto thee, 'The asses which thou wentest to seek are found: and, lo, thy father hath left the care of the asses, and sorroweth for you, saying, What shall I do for my son?' Then shalt thou go on forward from thence, and thou shalt come to the plain of Tabor, and there shall meet thee three men going up to God to Beth-el, one carrying three kids, and another carrying three loaves of bread, and another carrying a bottle of wine: and they will salute thee, and give thee two loaves of bread; which thou shalt receive of their hands. After that thou shalt come to the hill of God, where is the garrison of the Philistines: and it shall come to pass, when thou art come thither to the city, that thou shalt meet a company of prophets coming down from the high place with a psaltery, and a tabret, and a pipe, and a harp, before them; and they shall prophesy: and the spirit of the LORD will come upon thee, and thou shalt prophesy with them, and shalt be turned into another man. And let it be, when these signs are come unto thee, that thou do as occasion serve thee; for God is with thee. And thou shalt go down before me to Gilgal; and, behold, I will come down unto thee, to offer burnt offerings, and to sacrifice sacrifices of peace offerings: seven days shalt thou tarry, till I come to thee, and shew thee what thou shalt do." And it was so, that when he had turned his back to go from Samuel, God gave him another heart: and all those signs came to pass that day. [10:1–9]

Saul among the Prophets. And when they came thither to the hill, behold, a company of prophets met him; and the spirit of God came upon him, and he prophesied among them. And it came to pass, when all that knew him beforetime saw that, behold, he prophesied among the prophets, then the people said one to another, "What is this that is come unto the son of Kish? Is Saul also among the prophets?" And one of the same place answered and said, "But who is their father?" Therefore it became a proverb, "Is Saul also among the prophets?" And when he had made an end of prophesying, he came to the high place.

And Saul's uncle said unto him and to his servant, "Whither went ye?" And he said, "To seek the asses: and when we saw that they were no where, we came to Samuel". And Saul's uncle said, "Tell me, I pray thee, what Samuel said unto you". And Saul said unto his uncle, "He told us plainly that the asses were found". But of the matter of the kingdom, whereof Samuel spake, he told him not. [10:10–16]

Saul Presented to the People. And Samuel called the people together unto the LORD to Mizpeh; and said unto the children of Israel, "Thus saith the LORD God of Israel, 'I brought up Israel out of Egypt, and delivered you out of the hand of the Egyptians, and out of the hand of all kingdoms, and of them that oppressed you': and ye have this day rejected your God, who himself saved you out of all your adversities and your tribulations; and ye have said unto him, 'Nay, but set a king over us'. Now therefore present yourselves before the LORD by your tribes, and by your thousands." And when Samuel had caused all the tribes of Israel to come near, the tribe of Benjamin was taken. When he had caused the tribe of Benjamin to come near by their families, the family of Matri was taken, and Saul the son of Kish was taken: and when they sought

him, he could not be found. Therefore they enquired of
the LORD further, if the man should yet come thither. And
the LORD answered, "Behold, he hath hid himself among
the stuff". And they ran and fetched him thence: and
when he stood among the people, he was higher than any
of the people from his shoulders and upward. And Samuel
said to all the people, "See ye him whom the LORD hath
chosen, that there is none like him among all the people?"
And all the people shouted, and said, "God save the king".

Then Samuel told the people the manner of the kingdom, and wrote it in a book, and laid it up before the LORD.
And Samuel sent all the people away, every man to his
house. And Saul also went home to Gibeah; and there
went with him a band of men, whose hearts God had
touched. But the children of Belial said, "How shall this
man save us?" And they despised him, and brought him
no presents. But he held his peace.   [10:17-27]

Saul and the Amalekites. Samuel also said unto Saul,
"The LORD sent me to anoint thee to be king over his
people, over Israel: now therefore hearken thou unto the
voice of the words of the LORD. Thus saith the LORD of
hosts, 'I remember that which Amalek did to Israel, how
he laid wait for him in the way, when he came up from
Egypt. Now go and smite Amalek, and utterly destroy all
that they have, and spare them not; but slay both man
and woman, infant and suckling, ox and sheep, camel and
ass.'"

And Saul gathered the people together, and numbered
them in Telaim, two hundred thousand footmen, and ten
thousand men of Judah. And Saul came to a city of
Amalek, and laid wait in the valley. And Saul said unto
the Kenites, "Go, depart, get you down from among the
Amalekites, lest I destroy you with them: for ye shewed
kindness to all the children of Israel, when they came up
out of Egypt". So the Kenites departed from among the
Amalekites. And Saul smote the Amalekites from Havilah
until thou comest to Shur, that is over against Egypt. And

he took Agag the king of the Amalekites alive, and utterly destroyed all the people with the edge of the sword. But Saul and the people spared Agag, and the best of the sheep, and of the oxen, and of the fatlings, and the lambs, and all that was good, and would not utterly destroy them: but every thing that was vile and refuse, that they destroyed utterly.   [15:1–9]

Samuel Rebukes Saul. Then came the word of the LORD unto Samuel, saying, "It repenteth me that I have set up Saul to be king: for he is turned back from following me, and hath not performed my commandments". And it grieved Samuel; and he cried unto the LORD all night. And when Samuel rose early to meet Saul in the morning, it was told Samuel, saying, "Saul came to Carmel, and, behold, he set him up a place, and is gone about, and passed on, and gone down to Gilgal". And Samuel came to Saul: and Saul said unto him, "Blessed be thou of the LORD: I have performed the commandment of the LORD". And Samuel said, "What meaneth then this bleating of the sheep in mine ears, and the lowing of the oxen which I hear?" And Saul said, "They have brought them from the Amalekites: for the people spared the best of the sheep and of the oxen, to sacrifice unto the LORD thy God; and the rest we have utterly destroyed". Then Samuel said unto Saul, "Stay, and I will tell thee what the LORD hath said to me this night". And he said unto him, "Say on". And Samuel said, "When thou wast little in thine own sight, wast thou not made the head of the tribes of Israel, and the LORD anointed thee king over Israel? And the LORD sent thee on a journey, and said, 'Go and utterly destroy the sinners the Amalekites, and fight against them until they be consumed'. Wherefore then didst thou not obey the voice of the LORD, but didst fly upon the spoil, and didst evil in the sight of the LORD?" And Saul said unto Samuel, "Yea, I have obeyed the voice of the LORD, and have gone the way which the LORD sent me, and have brought Agag the king of Amalek, and have utterly destroyed the

Amalekites. But the people took of the spoil, sheep and oxen, the chief of the things which should have been utterly destroyed, to sacrifice unto the LORD thy God in Gilgal." And Samuel said,

> "Hath the LORD as great delight in burnt offerings and
>   sacrifices,
> As in obeying the voice of the LORD?
> Behold, to obey is better than sacrifice,
> And to hearken than the fat of rams.
> For rebellion is as the sin of witchcraft,
> And stubbornness is as iniquity and idolatry.
> Because thou hast rejected the word of the LORD,
> He hath also rejected thee from being king."

And Saul said unto Samuel, "I have sinned: for I have transgressed the commandment of the LORD, and thy words: because I feared the people, and obeyed their voice. Now therefore, I pray thee, pardon my sin, and turn again with me, that I may worship the LORD." And Samuel said unto Saul, "I will not return with thee: for thou hast rejected the word of the LORD, and the LORD hath rejected thee from being king over Israel". And as Samuel turned about to go away, he laid hold upon the skirt of his mantle, and it rent. And Samuel said unto him, "The LORD hath rent the kingdom of Israel from thee this day, and hath given it to a neighbour of thine, that is better than thou. And also the Strength of Israel will not lie nor repent: for he is not a man, that he should repent." Then he said, "I have sinned: yet honour me now, I pray thee, before the elders of my people, and before Israel, and turn again with me, that I may worship the LORD thy God". So Samuel turned again after Saul; and Saul worshipped the LORD.   [15:10–31]

Agag Slain. Then said Samuel, "Bring ye hither to me Agag the king of the Amalekites". And Agag came unto him delicately. And Agag said, "Surely the bitterness of death is past". And Samuel said, "As thy sword hath made women childless, so shall thy mother be childless among women". And Samuel hewed Agag in pieces before the LORD in Gilgal.

Then Samuel went to Ramah; and Saul went up to his house to Gibeah of Saul. And Samuel came no more to see Saul until the day of his death: nevertheless Samuel mourned for Saul: and the LORD repented that he had made Saul king over Israel.   [15:32–35]

David Anointed King. And the LORD said unto Samuel, "How long wilt thou mourn for Saul, seeing I have rejected him from reigning over Israel? fill thine horn with oil, and go, I will send thee to Jesse the Beth-lehemite: for I have provided me a king among his sons". And Samuel said, "How can I go? if Saul hear it, he will kill me". And the LORD said, "Take an heifer with thee, and say, 'I am come to sacrifice to the LORD'. And call Jesse to the sacrifice, and I will shew thee what thou shalt do: and thou shalt anoint unto me him whom I name unto thee." And Samuel did that which the LORD spake, and came to Beth-lehem. And the elders of the town trembled at his coming, and said, "Comest thou peaceably?" And he said, "Peaceably: I am come to sacrifice unto the LORD: sanctify yourselves, and come with me to the sacrifice". And he sanctified Jesse and his sons, and called them to the sacrifice. And it came to pass, when they were come, that he looked on Eliab, and said, "Surely the LORD's anointed is before him". But the LORD said unto Samuel, "Look not on his countenance, or on the height of his stature; because I have refused him: for the LORD seeth not as man seeth; for man looketh on the outward appearance, but the LORD looketh on the heart". Then Jesse called Abinadab, and made him pass before Samuel. And he said, "Neither hath the LORD chosen this". Then Jesse made Shammah to pass by. And he said, "Neither hath the LORD chosen this". Again, Jesse made seven of his sons to pass before Samuel. And Samuel said unto Jesse, "The LORD hath not chosen these". And Samuel said unto

Jesse, "Are here all thy children?" And he said, "There remaineth yet the youngest, and, behold, he keepeth the sheep". And Samuel said unto Jesse, "Send and fetch him: for we will not sit down till he come hither". And he sent, and brought him in. Now he was ruddy, and withal of a beautiful countenance, and goodly to look to. And the LORD said, "Arise, anoint him: for this is he". Then Samuel took the horn of oil, and anointed him in the midst of his brethren: and the spirit of the LORD came upon David from that day forward. So Samuel rose up, and went to Ramah. [16:1–13]

Saul's Evil Spirit. But the spirit of the LORD departed from Saul, and an evil spirit from the LORD troubled him. And Saul's servants said unto him, "Behold now, an evil spirit from God troubleth thee. Let our lord now command thy servants, which are before thee, to seek out a man, who is a cunning player on an harp: and it shall come to pass, when the evil spirit from God is upon thee, that he shall play with his hand, and thou shalt be well." And Saul said unto his servants, "Provide me now a man that can play well, and bring him to me". Then answered one of the servants, and said, "Behold, I have seen a son of Jesse the Beth-lehemite, that is cunning in playing, and a mighty valiant man, and a man of war, and prudent in matters, and a comely person, and the LORD is with him". Wherefore Saul sent messengers unto Jesse, and said, "Send me David thy son, which is with the sheep". And Jesse took an ass laden with bread, and a bottle of wine, and a kid, and sent them by David his son unto Saul. And David came to Saul, and stood before him: and he loved him greatly; and he became his armourbearer. And Saul sent to Jesse, saying, "Let David, I pray thee, stand before me; for he hath found favour in my sight". And it came to pass, when the evil spirit from God was upon Saul, that David took an harp, and played with his hand: so Saul was refreshed, and was well, and the evil spirit departed from him. [16:14–23]

Goliath the Philistine Giant. Now the Philistines gathered together their armies to battle, and were gathered together at Shochoh, which belongeth to Judah, and pitched between Shochoh and Azekah, in Ephes-dammim. And Saul and the men of Israel were gathered together, and pitched by the valley of Elah, and set the battle in array against the Philistines. And the Philistines stood on a mountain on the one side, and Israel stood on a mountain on the other side: and there was a valley between them. And there went out a champion out of the camp of the Philistines, named Goliath, of Gath, whose height was six cubits and a span. And he had an helmet of brass upon his head, and he was armed with a coat of mail; and the weight of the coat was five thousand shekels of brass. And he had greaves of brass upon his legs, and a target of brass between his shoulders. And the staff of his spear was like a weaver's beam; and his spear's head weighed six hundred shekels of iron: and one bearing a shield went before him. And he stood and cried unto the armies of Israel, and said unto them, "Why are ye come out to set your battle in array? am not I a Philistine, and ye servants to Saul? choose you a man for you, and let him come down to me. If he be able to fight with me, and to kill me, then will we be your servants: but if I prevail against him, and kill him, then shall ye be our servants, and serve us." And the Philistine said, "I defy the armies of Israel this day; give me a man, that we may fight together". When Saul and all Israel heard those words of the Philistine, they were dismayed, and greatly afraid.

Now David was the son of that Ephrathite of Bethlehem-judah, whose name was Jesse; and he had eight sons: and the man went among men for an old man in the days of Saul. And the three eldest sons of Jesse went and followed Saul to the battle: and the names of his three sons that went to the battle were Eliab the firstborn, and next unto him Abinadab, and the third Shammah. And David was the youngest: and the three eldest followed Saul. But

David went and returned from Saul to feed his father's
sheep at Beth-lehem. And the Philistine drew near morning and evening, and presented himself forty days.

[17:1–16]

David Comes to the Camp. And Jesse said unto David
his son, "Take now for thy brethren an ephah of this
parched corn, and these ten loaves, and run to the camp to
thy brethren; and carry these ten cheeses unto the captain
of their thousand, and look how thy brethren fare, and
take their pledge". Now Saul, and they, and all the men of
Israel, were in the valley of Elah, fighting with the Philistines. And David rose up early in the morning, and left the
sheep with a keeper, and took, and went, as Jesse had commanded him; and he came to the trench, as the host was
going forth to the fight, and shouted for the battle. For
Israel and the Philistines had put the battle in array, army
against army. And David left his carriage[4] in the hand of
the keeper of the carriage, and ran into the army, and
came and saluted his brethren. And as he talked with
them, behold, there came up the champion, the Philistine
of Gath, Goliath by name, out of the armies of the Philistines, and spake according to the same words: and David
heard them. And all the men of Israel, when they saw the
man, fled from him, and were sore afraid. And the men of
Israel said, "Have ye seen this man that is come up? surely
to defy Israel is he come up: and it shall be, that the man
who killeth him, the king will enrich him with great riches,
and will give him his daughter, and make his father's
house free in Israel".

And David spake to the men that stood by him, saying,
"What shall be done to the man that killeth this Philistine,
and taketh away the reproach from Israel? for who is this
uncircumcised Philistine, that he should defy the armies of
the living God?" And the people answered him after this
manner, saying, "So shall it be done to the man that killet

[4] I.e., baggage.

him". And Eliab his eldest brother heard when he spake unto the men; and Eliab's anger was kindled against David, and he said, "Why camest thou down hither? and with whom hast thou left those few sheep in the wilderness? I know thy pride, and the naughtiness of thine heart; for thou art come down that thou mightest see the battle." And David said, "What have I now done? Is there not a cause?" And he turned from him toward another, and spake after the same manner: and the people answered him again after the former manner.

And when the words were heard which David spake, they rehearsed them before Saul: and he sent for him. And David said to Saul, "Let no man's heart fail because of him; thy servant will go and fight with this Philistine". And Saul said to David, "Thou art not able to go against this Philistine to fight with him: for thou art but a youth, and he a man of war from his youth". And David said unto Saul, "Thy servant kept his father's sheep, and there came a lion, and a bear, and took a lamb out of the flock: and I went out after him, and smote him, and delivered it out of his mouth: and when he arose against me, I caught him by his beard, and smote him, and slew him. Thy servant slew both the lion and the bear: and this uncircumcised Philistine shall be as one of them, seeing he hath defied the armies of the living God." David said moreover, "The LORD that delivered me out of the paw of the lion, and out of the paw of the bear, he will deliver me out of the hand of this Philistine". And Saul said unto David, "Go, and the LORD be with thee". And Saul armed David with his armour, and he put an helmet of brass upon his head; also he armed him with a coat of mail. And David girded his sword upon his armour, and he assayed to go; for he had not proved it. And David said unto Saul, "I cannot go with these; for I have not proved them". And David put them off him.　　　　　　　　　　　　　　　　　　　　[17:17–39]

David Slays Goliath. And he took his staff in his hand, and chose him five smooth stones out of the brook, and put them in a shepherd's bag which he had, even in a scrip; and his sling was in his hand: and he drew near to the Philistine. And the Philistine came on and drew near unto David; and the man that bare the shield went before him. And when the Philistine looked about, and saw David, he disdained him: for he was but a youth, and ruddy, and of a fair countenance. And the Philistine said unto David, "Am I a dog, that thou comest to me with staves?" And the Philistine cursed David by his gods. And the Philistine said to David, "Come to me, and I will give thy flesh unto the fowls of the air, and to the beasts of the field". Then said David to the Philistine, "Thou comest to me with a sword, and with a spear, and with a shield: but I come to thee in the name of the LORD of hosts, the God of the armies of Israel, whom thou hast defied. This day will the LORD deliver thee into mine hand; and I will smite thee, and take thine head from thee; and I will give the carcases of the host of the Philistines this day unto the fowls of the air, and to the wild beasts of the earth; that all the earth may know that there is a God in Israel. And all this assembly shall know that the LORD saveth not with sword and spear: for the battle is the LORD's, and he will give you into our hands."

And it came to pass, when the Philistine arose, and came and drew nigh to meet David, that David hasted, and ran toward the army to meet the Philistine. And David put his hand in his bag, and took thence a stone, and slang it, and smote the Philistine in his forehead, that the stone sunk into his forehead; and he fell upon his face to the earth. So David prevailed over the Philistine with a sling and with a stone, and smote the Philistine, and slew him; but there was no sword in the hand of David. Therefore David ran, and stood upon the Philistine, and took his sword, and drew it out of the sheath thereof, and slew him, and cut off his head therewith. And when the Philistines saw their champion was dead, they fled. And the men of Israel and of Judah arose, and shouted, and pursued the

Philistines, until thou come to the valley, and to the gates of Ekron. And the wounded of the Philistines fell down by the way to Shaaraim, even unto Gath, and unto Ekron. And the children of Israel returned from chasing after the Philistines, and they spoiled their tents. And David took the head of the Philistine, and brought it to Jerusalem; but he put his armour in his tent.

And when Saul saw David go forth against the Philistine, he said unto Abner, the captain of the host, "Abner, whose son is this youth?" And Abner said, "As thy soul liveth, O king, I cannot tell". And the king said, "Enquire thou whose son the stripling is". And as David returned from the slaughter of the Philistine, Abner took him, and brought him before Saul with the head of the Philistine in his hand. And Saul said to him, "Whose son art thou, thou young man?" And David answered, "I am the son of thy servant Jesse the Beth-lehemite".   [17:40–58]

The Love of David and Jonathan. And it came to pass, when he had made an end of speaking unto Saul, that the soul of Jonathan was knit with the soul of David, and Jonathan loved him as his own soul. And Saul took him that day, and would let him go no more home to his father's house. Then Jonathan and David made a covenant, because he loved him as his own soul. And Jonathan stripped himself of the robe that was upon him, and gave it to David, and his garments, even to his sword, and to his bow, and to his girdle. And David went out whithersoever Saul sent him, and behaved himself wisely: and Saul set him over the men of war, and he was accepted in the sight of all the people, and also in the sight of Saul's servants.

And it came to pass as they came, when David was returned from the slaughter of the Philistine, that the women came out of all cities of Israel, singing and dancing, to meet king Saul, with tabrets, with joy, and with instruments of musick. And the women answered one another as they played, and said,

"Saul hath slain his thousands,
And David his ten thousands".

And Saul was very wroth, and the saying displeased him; and he said, "They have ascribed unto David ten thousands, and to me they have ascribed but thousands: and what can he have more but the kingdom?" And Saul eyed David from that day and forward.

And it came to pass on the morrow, that the evil spirit from God came upon Saul, and he prophesied in the midst of the house: and David played with his hand, as at other times: and there was a javelin in Saul's hand. And Saul cast the javelin; for he said, "I will smite David even to the wall with it". And David avoided out of his presence twice. And Saul was afraid of David, because the LORD was with him, and was departed from Saul. Therefore Saul removed him from him, and made him his captain over a thousand; and he went out and came in before the people. And David behaved himself wisely in all his ways; and the LORD was with him. Wherefore when Saul saw that he behaved himself very wisely, he was afraid of him. But all Israel and Judah loved David, because he went out and came in before them.   [18:1-16]

[Saul quarreled with David and sought his life. So David fled and became the leader of a band of outlaws until after Saul's death.]

Saul Consults the Witch of Endor. Now Samuel was dead, and all Israel had lamented him, and buried him in Ramah, even in his own city. And Saul had put away those that had familiar spirits, and the wizards, out of the land. And the Philistines gathered themselves together, and came and pitched in Shunem: and Saul gathered all Israel together, and they pitched in Gilboa. And when Saul saw the host of the Philistines, he was afraid, and his heart greatly trembled. And when Saul enquired of the LORD, the LORD answered him not, neither by dreams, nor by Urim, nor by prophets. Then said Saul unto his servants,

"Seek me a woman that hath a familiar spirit, that I may go to her, and enquire of her". And his servants said to him, "Behold, there is a woman that hath a familiar spirit at En-dor". And Saul disguised himself, and put on other raiment, and he went, and two men with him, and they came to the woman by night: and he said, "I pray thee, divine unto me by the familiar spirit, and bring me him up, whom I shall name unto thee". And the woman said unto him, "Behold, thou knowest what Saul hath done, how he hath cut off those that have familiar spirits, and the wizards, out of the land: wherefore then layest thou a snare for my life, to cause me to die?"

And Saul sware to her by the LORD, saying, "As the LORD liveth, there shall no punishment happen to thee for this thing". Then said the woman, "Whom shall I bring up unto thee?" And he said, "Bring me up Samuel". And when the woman saw Samuel, she cried with a loud voice: and the woman spake to Saul, saying, "Why hast thou deceived me? for thou art Saul". And the king said unto her, "Be not afraid: for what sawest thou?" And the woman said unto Saul, "I saw gods ascending out of the earth". And he said unto her, "What form is he of?" And she said, "An old man cometh up; and he is covered with a mantle". And Saul perceived that it was Samuel, and he stooped with his face to the ground, and bowed himself. And Samuel said to Saul, "Why hast thou disquieted me, to bring me up?" And Saul answered, "I am sore distressed; for the Philistines make war against me, and God is departed from me, and answereth me no more, neither by prophets, nor by dreams: therefore I have called thee, that thou mayest make known unto me what I shall do".

Then said Samuel, "Wherefore then dost thou ask of me, seeing the LORD is departed from thee, and is become thine enemy? And the LORD hath done to him, as he spake by me: for the LORD hath rent the kingdom out of thine hand, and given it to thy neighbour, even to David: because thou obeyedst not the voice of the LORD, nor executedst his fierce wrath upon Amalek, therefore hath the LORD done this thing unto thee this day. Moreover the LORD will also deliver Israel with thee into the hand of the Philistines: and to morrow shalt thou and thy sons be with me: the LORD also shall deliver the host of Israel into the hand of the Philistines."

Then Saul fell straightway all along on the earth, and was sore afraid, because of the words of Samuel: and there was no strength in him; for he had eaten no bread all the day, nor all the night. And the woman came unto Saul, and saw that he was sore troubled, and said unto him, "Behold, thine handmaid hath obeyed thy voice, and I have put my life in my hand, and have hearkened unto thy words which thou spakest unto me. Now therefore, I pray thee, hearken thou also unto the voice of thine handmaid, and let me set a morsel of bread before thee; and eat, that thou mayest have strength, when thou goest on thy way." But he refused, and said, "I will not eat". But his servants, together with the woman, compelled him; and he hearkened unto their voice. So he arose from the earth, and sat upon the bed. And the woman had a fat calf in the house; and she hasted, and killed it, and took flour, and kneaded it, and did bake unleavened bread thereof: and she brought it before Saul, and before his servants; and they did eat. Then they rose up, and went away that night. [28:3–25]

Saul and Jonathan Slain in Battle. Now the Philistines fought against Israel: and the men of Israel fled from before the Philistines, and fell down slain in mount Gilboa. And the Philistines followed hard upon Saul and upon his sons; and the Philistines slew Jonathan, and Abinadab, and Malchishua, Saul's sons. And the battle went sore against Saul, and the archers hit him; and he was sore wounded of the archers. Then said Saul unto his armour-bearer, "Draw thy sword, and thrust me through therewith; lest these uncircumcised come and thrust me through, and abuse me". But his armourbearer would not; for he was sore afraid. Therefore Saul took a sword, and fell upon it. And when his armourbearer saw that Saul was dead, he fell likewise upon his sword, and died with him. So Saul died, and his three sons, and his armourbearer, and all his men, that same day together. And when the men of Israel that were on the other side of the valley, and they that were on the other side Jordan, saw that the men of Israel fled, and that Saul and his sons were dead, they forsook the cities, and fled; and the Philistines came and dwelt in them.

And it came to pass on the morrow, when the Philistines came to strip the slain, that they found Saul and his three sons fallen in mount Gilboa. And they cut off his head, and stripped off his armour, and sent into the land of the Philistines round about, to publish it in the house of their idols, and among the people. And they put his armour in the house of Ashtaroth: and they fastened his body to the wall of Beth-shan. And when the inhabitants of Jabesh-gilead heard of that which the Philistines had done to Saul; all the valiant men arose, and went all night, and took the body of Saul and the bodies of his sons from the wall of Beth-shan, and came to Jabesh, and burnt them there. And they took their bones, and buried them under a tree at Jabesh, and fasted seven days.   [31:1–13]

From THE SECOND BOOK OF SAMUEL

David Hears of Saul's Death. Now it came to pass after the death of Saul, when David was returned from the slaughter of the Amalekites, and David had abode two days in Ziklag; it came even to pass on the third day, that, behold, a man came out of the camp from Saul with his clothes rent, and earth upon his head: and so it was, when he came to David, that he fell to the earth, and did obeisance. And David said unto him, "From whence comest thou?" And he said unto him, "Out of the camp of Israel am I escaped". And David said unto him, "How went the matter? I pray thee, tell me." And he answered, "That the people are fled from the battle, and many of the people also are fallen and dead; and Saul and Jonathan his son are dead also". And David said unto the young man that told him, "How knowest thou that Saul and Jonathan his son be dead?" And the young man that told him said, "As I happened by chance upon mount Gilboa, behold, Saul leaned upon his spear; and, lo, the chariots and horse-men followed hard after him. And when he looked behind him, he saw me, and called unto me. And I answered, Here am I. And he said unto me, 'Who art thou?' And I answered him, I am an Amalekite. He said unto me again, 'Stand, I pray thee, upon me, and slay me: for anguish is come upon me, because my life is yet whole in me'. So I stood upon him, and slew him, because I was sure that he could not live after that he was fallen: and I took the crown that was upon his head, and the bracelet that was on his arm, and have brought them hither unto my lord."

Then David took hold on his clothes, and rent them; and likewise all the men that were with him: and they mourned, and wept, and fasted until even, for Saul, and for Jonathan his son, and for the people of the LORD, and for the house of Israel; because they were fallen by the sword. And David said unto the young man that told him, "Whence art thou?" And he answered, "I am the son of a stranger, an Amalekite". And David said unto him, "How wast thou not afraid to stretch forth thine hand to destroy the LORD's anointed?" And David called one of the young men, and said, "Go near, and fall upon him". And he smote him that he died. And David said unto him, "Thy blood be upon thy head; for thy mouth hath testified against thee, saying, 'I have slain the LORD's anointed'".

[1:1–16]

David's Lament over Saul. And David lamented with this lamentation over Saul and over Jonathan his son: (also he bade them teach the children of Judah the use of the bow: behold, it is written in the book of Jasher.)

"The beauty of Israel is slain upon thy high places:
How are the mighty fallen!
Tell it not in Gath,
Publish it not in the streets of Askelon;
Lest the daughters of the Philistines rejoice,
Lest the daughters of the uncircumcised triumph.
Ye mountains of Gilboa, let there be no dew,
Neither let there be rain, upon you, nor fields of
   offerings:
For there the shield of the mighty is vilely cast away,
The shield of Saul, as though he had not been
   anointed with oil.
From the blood of the slain,
From the fat of the mighty,
The bow of Jonathan turned not back,
And the sword of Saul returned not empty.

Saul and Jonathan were lovely and pleasant in their
lives,
And in their death they were not divided:
They were swifter than eagles,
They were stronger than lions.
Ye daughters of Israel, weep over Saul,
Who clothed you in scarlet, with other delights,
Who put on ornaments of gold upon your apparel.
How are the mighty fallen in the midst of the battle!
O Jonathan, thou wast slain in thine high places.
I am distressed for thee, my brother Jonathan:
Very pleasant hast thou been unto me:
Thy love to me was wonderful,
Passing the love of women.
How are the mighty fallen,
And the weapons of war perished!"   [1:17–27]

David Made King of Judah.   And it came to pass after
this, that David enquired of the LORD, saying, "Shall I
go up into any of the cities of Judah?" And the LORD
said unto him, "Go up". And David said, "Whither shall
I go up?" And he said, "'Unto Hebron". So David went up
thither, and his two wives also, Ahinoam the Jezreelitess,
and Abigail Nabal's wife the Carmelite. And his men
that were with him did David bring up, every man with his
household: and they dwelt in the cities of Hebron. And the
men of Judah came, and there they anointed David king
over the house of Judah.   [2:1–4]

[Then there was war between David and the sons of
Saul, but Joab and Abishai, the sons of Zeruiah, David's
chief captains, prevailed; they slew Abner, the captain of
Saul's sons, by treachery; and Ish-bosheth, the son of
Jonathan, was slain by his own captains.]

David Anointed King over Israel.   Then came all the
tribes of Israel to David unto Hebron, and spake, saying,
"Behold, we are thy bone and thy flesh. Also in time
past, when Saul was king over us, thou wast he that led-

dest out and broughtest in Israel: and the LORD said to thee, 'Thou shalt feed my people Israel, and thou shalt be a captain over Israel'." So all the elders of Israel came to the king to Hebron; and king David made a league with them in Hebron before the LORD: and they anointed David king over Israel.

David was thirty years old when he began to reign, and he reigned forty years. In Hebron he reigned over Judah seven years and six months: and in Jerusalem he reigned thirty and three years over all Israel and Judah. And the king and his men went to Jerusalem unto the Jebusites, the inhabitants of the land: which spake unto David, saying, "Except thou take away the blind and the lame, thou shalt not come in hither": thinking, "David cannot come in hither". Nevertheless David took the strong hold of Zion: the same is the city of David. And David said on that day, "Whosoever getteth up to the gutter, and smiteth the Jebusites, and the lame and the blind, that are hated of David's soul, he shall be chief and captain". Wherefore they said, "The blind and the lame shall not come into the house". So David dwelt in the fort, and called it the city of David. And David built round about from Millo and inward. And David went on, and grew great, and the LORD God of hosts was with him.

[5:1-10]

David Fetches the Ark. Again, David gathered together all the chosen men of Israel, thirty thousand. And David arose, and went with all the people that were with him from Baale of Judah, to bring up from thence the ark of God, whose name is called by the name of the LORD of hosts that dwelleth between the cherubims. And they set the ark of God upon a new cart, and brought it out of the house of Abinadab that was in Gibeah: and Uzzah and Ahio, the sons of Abinadab, drave the new cart. And they brought it out of the house of Abinadab which was at Gibeah, accompanying the ark of God: and Ahio went before the ark. And David and all the house of

Israel played before the LORD on all manner of instruments made of fir wood, even on harps, and on psalteries, and on timbrels, and on cornets, and on cymbals. And when they came to Nachon's threshingfloor, Uzzah put forth his hand to the ark of God, and took hold of it; for the oxen shook it. And the anger of the LORD was kindled against Uzzah; and God smote him there for his error; and there he died by the ark of God. And David was displeased, because the LORD had made a breach upon Uzzah: and he called the name of the place Perez-uzzah to this day. And David was afraid of the LORD that day, and said, "How shall the ark of the LORD come to me?" So David would not remove the ark of the LORD unto him into the city of David: but David carried it aside into the house of Obed-edom the Gittite. And the ark of the LORD continued in the house of Obed-edom the Gittite three months: and the LORD blessed Obed-edom, and all his household. And it was told king David, saying, "The LORD hath blessed the house of Obed-edom, and all that pertaineth unto him, because of the ark of God". [6:1-12]

David Brings the Ark to Jerusalem. So David went and brought up the ark of God from the house of Obed-edom into the city of David with gladness. And it was so, that when they that bare the ark of the LORD had gone six paces, he sacrificed oxen and fatlings. And David danced before the LORD with all his might; and David was girded with a linen ephod. So David and all the house of Israel brought up the ark of the LORD with shouting, and with the sound of the trumpet. And as the ark of the LORD came into the city of David, Michal Saul's daughter looked through a window, and saw king David leaping and dancing before the LORD; and she despised him in her heart. And they brought in the ark of the LORD, and set it in his place, in the midst of the tabernacle that David had pitched for it: and David offered burnt offerings and peace offerings before the LORD. And as soon as David had made an end of offering burnt offerings and peace offerings, he blessed the people in the name of the LORD of hosts. And he dealt among all the people, even among the whole multitude of Israel, as well to the women as men, to every one a cake of bread, and a good piece of flesh, and a flagon of wine. So all the people departed every one to his house. Then David returned to bless his household.

And Michal the daughter of Saul came out to meet David, and said, "How glorious was the king of Israel to day, who uncovered himself to day in the eyes of the handmaids of his servants, as one of the vain fellows shamelessly uncovereth himself!" And David said unto Michal, "It was before the LORD, which chose me before thy father, and before all his house, to appoint me ruler over the people of the LORD, over Israel: therefore will I play before the LORD. And I will yet be more vile than thus, and will be base in mine own sight: and of the maidservants which thou hast spoken of, of them shall I be had in honour." Therefore Michal the daughter of Saul had no child unto the day of her death. [6:12–23]

David's Servants Shamed. And it came to pass after this, that the king of the children of Ammon died, and Hanun his son reigned in his stead. Then said David, "I will shew kindness unto Hanun the son of Nahash, as his father shewed kindness unto me". And David sent to comfort him by the hand of his servants for his father. And David's servants came into the land of the children of Ammon. And the princes of the children of Ammon said unto Hanun their lord, "Thinkest thou that David doth honour thy father, that he hath sent comforters unto thee? hath not David rather sent his servants unto thee, to search the city, and to spy it out, and to overthrow it?" Wherefore Hanun took David's servants, and shaved off the one half of their beards, and cut off their garments in the middle, even to their buttocks, and sent them away. When they told it unto David, he sent to meet them, because the men were greatly ashamed: and the king said, "Tarry at

Jericho until your beards be grown, and then return".
And when the children of Ammon saw that they stank
before David, the children of Ammon sent and hired the
Syrians of Beth-rehob, and the Syrians of Zoba, twenty
thousand footmen, and of king Maacah a thousand men,
and of Ish-tob twelve thousand men. And when David
heard of it, he sent Joab, and all the host of the mighty
men.   [10:1-7]

David and Bath-sheba. And it came to pass, after the
year was expired, at the time when kings go forth to
battle, that David sent Joab, and his servants with him,
and all Israel; and they destroyed the children of Ammon,
and besieged Rabbah. But David tarried still at Jerusalem.

And it came to pass in an eveningtide, that David
arose from off his bed, and walked upon the roof of
the king's house: and from the roof he saw a woman
washing herself; and the woman was very beautiful to
look upon. And David sent and enquired after the
woman. And one said, "Is not this Bath-sheba, the daughter of Eliam, the wife of Uriah the Hittite?" And David
sent messengers, and took her; and she came in unto him,
and he lay with her; for she was purified from her uncleanness: and she returned unto her house. And the
woman conceived, and sent and told David, and said, "I
am with child". And David sent to Joab, saying, "Send
me Uriah the Hittite". And Joab sent Uriah to David.
And when Uriah was come unto him, David demanded
of him how Joab did, and how the people did, and how
the war prospered. And David said to Uriah, "Go down
to thy house, and wash thy feet". And Uriah departed
out of the king's house, and there followed him a mess of
meat from the king. But Uriah slept at the door of the
king's house with all the servants of his lord, and went not
down to his house. And when they had told David, saying, "Uriah went not down unto his house", David said
unto Uriah, "Camest thou not from thy journey? why then
didst thou not go down unto thine house?" And Uriah

said unto David, "The ark, and Israel, and Judah, abide in tents; and my lord Joab, and the servants of my lord, are encamped in the open fields; shall I then go into mine house, to eat and to drink, and to lie with my wife? as thou livest, and as thy soul liveth, I will not do this thing". And David said to Uriah, "Tarry here to day also, and to morrow I will let thee depart". So Uriah abode in Jerusalem that day, and the morrow. And when David had called him, he did eat and drink before him; and he made him drunk: and at even he went out to lie on his bed with the servants of his lord, but went not down to his house.

[11:1–13]

David Causes the Death of Uriah. And it came to pass in the morning, that David wrote a letter to Joab, and sent it by the hand of Uriah. And he wrote in the letter, saying, "Set ye Uriah in the forefront of the hottest battle, and retire ye from him, that he may be smitten, and die". And it came to pass, when Joab observed the city, that he assigned Uriah unto a place where he knew that valiant men were. And the men of the city went out, and fought with Joab: and there fell some of the people of the servants of David; and Uriah the Hittite died also. Then Joab sent and told David all the things concerning the war; and charged the messenger, saying, "When thou hast made an end of telling the matters of the war unto the king, and if so be that the king's wrath arise, and he say unto thee, 'Wherefore approached ye so nigh unto the city when ye did fight? knew ye not that they would shoot from the wall? who smote Abimelech the son of Jerubbesheth? did not a woman cast a piece of a millstone upon him from the wall, that he died in Thebez? why went ye nigh the wall?' then say thou, 'Thy servant Uriah the Hittite is dead also'".

So the messenger went, and came and shewed David all that Joab had sent him for. And the messenger said unto David, "Surely the men prevailed against us, and came out unto us into the field, and we were upon them even unto the entering of the gate. And the shooters shot from off the wall upon thy servants; and some of the king's servants be dead, and thy servant Uriah the Hittite is dead also." Then David said unto the messenger, "Thus shalt thou say unto Joab, 'Let not this thing displease thee, for the sword devoureth one as well as another: make thy battle more strong against the city, and overthrow it': and encourage thou him". And when the wife of Uriah heard that Uriah her husband was dead, she mourned for her husband. And when the mourning was past, David sent and fetched her to his house, and she became his wife, and bare him a son. But the thing that David had done displeased the LORD.

[11:14–27]

Nathan's Parable. And the LORD sent Nathan unto David. And he came unto him, and said unto him, "There were two men in one city; the one rich, and the other poor. The rich man had exceeding many flocks and herds: but the poor man had nothing, save one little ewe lamb, which he had bought and nourished up: and it grew up together with him, and with his children; it did eat of his own meat, and drank of his own cup, and lay in his bosom, and was unto him as a daughter. And there came a traveller unto the rich man, and he spared to take of his own flock and of his own herd, to dress for the wayfaring man that was come unto him; but took the poor man's lamb, and dressed it for the man that was come to him." And David's anger was greatly kindled against the man; and he said to Nathan, "As the LORD liveth, the man that hath done this thing shall surely die: and he shall restore the lamb fourfold, because he did this thing, and because he had no pity".

And Nathan said to David, "Thou art the man. Thus saith the LORD God of Israel, 'I anointed thee king over Israel, and I delivered thee out of the hand of Saul; and I gave thee thy master's house, and thy master's wives into thy bosom, and gave thee the house of Israel and of Judah; and if that had been too little, I would moreover have given unto thee such and such things. Wherefore hast thou despised the commandment of the LORD, to do evil in his sight? thou hast killed Uriah the Hittite with the sword, and hast taken his wife to be thy wife, and hast slain him with the sword of the children of Ammon. Now therefore the sword shall never depart from thine house; because thou hast despised me, and hast taken the wife of Uriah the Hittite to be thy wife.' Thus saith the LORD, 'Behold, I will raise up evil against thee out of thine own house, and I will take thy wives before thine eyes, and give them unto thy neighbour, and he shall lie with thy wives in the sight of this sun. For thou didst it secretly: but I will do this thing before all Israel, and before the sun.'" And David said unto Nathan, "I have sinned against the LORD". And Nathan said unto David, "The LORD also hath put away thy sin; thou shalt not die. Howbeit, because by this deed thou hast given great occasion to the enemies of the LORD to blaspheme, the child also that is born unto thee shall surely die." And Nathan departed unto his house.

[12:1–15]

Bath-sheba's Child Dies. And the LORD struck the child that Uriah's wife bare unto David, and it was very sick. David therefore besought God for the child; and David fasted, and went in, and lay all night upon the earth. And the elders of his house arose, and went to him, to raise him up from the earth: but he would not, neither did he eat bread with them. And it came to pass on the seventh day, that the child died. And the servants of David feared to tell him that the child was dead: for they said, "Behold, while the child was yet alive, we spake unto him, and he would not hearken unto our voice: how will he then vex himself, if we tell him that the child is dead?" But when David saw that his servants whispered, David perceived that the child was dead: therefore David said unto his servants, "Is the child dead?" And they said, "He is dead". Then David arose from the earth, and washed, and anointed himself, and changed his apparel, and came into the house of the LORD, and worshipped: then he came to his own house; and when he required, they set bread before him, and he did eat. Then said his servants unto him, "What thing is this that thou hast done? thou didst fast and weep for the child, while it was alive; but when the child was dead, thou didst rise and eat bread". And he said, "While the child was yet alive, I fasted and wept: for I said, Who can tell whether GOD will be gracious to me, that the child may live? But now he is dead, wherefore should I fast? can I bring him back again? I shall go to him, but he shall not return to me." And David comforted Bath-sheba his wife, and went in unto her, and lay with her: and she bare a son, and he called his name Solomon: and the LORD loved him. And he sent by the hand of Nathan the prophet; and he called his name Jedidiah, because of the LORD.   [12:15–25]

Absalom. [Absalom, David's son by Maacah, was greatly beloved by his father. He slew his half brother Amnon, David's eldest son by Ahinoam, but David forgave him.]

But in all Israel there was none to be so much praised as Absalom for his beauty: from the sole of his foot even to the crown of his head there was no blemish in him. And when he polled his head, (for it was at every year's end that he polled it: because the hair was heavy on him, therefore he polled it:) he weighed the hair of his head at two hundred shekels after the king's weight. And unto Absalom there were born three sons, and one daughter, whose name was Tamar: she was a woman of a fair countenance.   [14:25–27]

Absalom Plots against David. And it came to pass after this, that Absalom prepared him chariots and horses, and fifty men to run before him. And Absalom rose up early, and stood beside the way of the gate: and it was so, that when any man that had a controversy came to the king for judgment, then Absalom called unto him, and said, "Of what city art thou?" And he said, "Thy servant is of one of the tribes of Israel". And Absalom said unto him, "See, thy matters are good and right; but there is no man deputed of the king to hear thee". Absalom said moreover, "Oh that I were made judge in the land, that every man which hath any suit or cause might come unto me, and I would do him justice!" And it was so, that when any man came nigh to him to do him obeisance, he put forth his hand, and took him, and kissed him. And on this manner did Absalom to all Israel that came to the king for judgment: so Absalom stole the hearts of the men of Israel.

And it came to pass after forty years,[1] that Absalom said unto the king, "I pray thee, let me go and pay my vow, which I have vowed unto the LORD, in Hebron. For thy servant vowed a vow while I abode at Geshur in Syria, saying, If the LORD shall bring me again indeed to Jerusalem, then I will serve the LORD." And the king said unto him, "Go in peace". So he arose, and went to Hebron. But Absalom sent spies throughout all the tribes of Israel, saying, "As soon as ye hear the sound of the trumpet, then ye shall say, 'Absalom reigneth in Hebron'". And with Absalom went two hundred men out of Jerusalem, that were called; and they went in their simplicity, and they knew not any thing. And Absalom sent for Ahithophel the Gilonite, David's counsellor, from his city, even from Giloh, while he offered sacrifices. And the conspiracy was strong; for the people increased continually with Absalom.
[15:1–12]

David Flees from Jerusalem. And there came a messenger to David, saying, "The hearts of the men of Israel are after Absalom". And David said unto all his servants that were with him at Jerusalem, "Arise, and let us flee; for we shall not else escape from Absalom: make speed to depart, lest he overtake us suddenly, and bring evil upon us, and smite the city with the edge of the sword". And

[1] "Forty years" was often used for "after some time."

the king's servants said unto the king, "Behold, thy servants are ready to do whatsoever my lord the king shall appoint". And the king went forth, and all his household after him. And the king left ten women, which were concubines, to keep the house. And the king went forth, and all the people after him, and tarried in a place that was far off. And all his servants passed on beside him; and all the Cherethites, and all the Pelethites, and all the Gittites, six hundred men which came after him from Gath, passed on before the king. Then said the king to Ittai the Gittite, "Wherefore goest thou also with us? return to thy place, and abide with the king: for thou art a stranger, and also an exile. Whereas thou camest but yesterday, should I this day make thee go up and down with us? seeing I go whither I may, return thou, and take back thy brethren: mercy and truth be with thee." And Ittai answered the king, and said, "As the LORD liveth, and as my lord the king liveth, surely in what place my lord the king shall be, whether in death or life, even there also will thy servant be". And David said to Ittai, "Go and pass over". And Ittai the Gittite passed over, and all his men, and all the little ones that were with him. And all the country wept with a loud voice, and all the people passed over: the king also himself passed over the brook Kidron, and all the people passed over, toward the way of the wilderness. And lo Zadok also, and all the Levites were with him, bearing the ark of the covenant of God: and they set down the ark of God; and Abiathar went up, until all the people had done passing out of the city. And the king said unto Zadok, "Carry back the ark of God into the city: if I shall find favour in the eyes of the LORD, he will bring me again, and shew me both it, and his habitation: but if he thus say, 'I have no delight in thee'; behold, here am I, let him do to me as seemeth good unto him". The king said also unto Zadok the priest, "Art not thou a seer? return into the city in peace, and your two sons with you, Ahimaaz thy son, and Jonathan the son of Abiathar. See, I will tarry in the plain of the wilderness, until there come word from you to certify me." Zadok therefore and Abiathar carried the ark of God again to Jerusalem: and they tarried there.   [15:13–29]

Ahithophel Joins Absalom.   And David went up by the ascent of mount Olivet, and wept as he went up, and had his head covered, and he went barefoot: and all the people that was with him covered every man his head, and they went up, weeping as they went up. And one told David, saying, "Ahithophel is among the conspirators with Absalom". And David said, "O LORD, I pray thee, turn the counsel of Ahithophel into foolishness". And it came to pass, that when David was come to the top of the mount, where he worshipped God, behold, Hushai the Archite came to meet him with his coat rent, and earth upon his head: unto whom David said, "If thou passest on with me, then thou shalt be a burden unto me: but if thou return to the city, and say unto Absalom, 'I will be thy servant, O king; as I have been thy father's servant hitherto, so will I now also be thy servant': then mayest thou for me defeat the counsel of Ahithophel. And hast thou not there with thee Zadok and Abiathar the priests? therefore it shall be, that what thing soever thou shalt hear out of the king's house, thou shalt tell it to Zadok and Abiathar the priests. Behold, they have there with them their two sons, Ahimaaz Zadok's son, and Jonathan Abiathar's son; and by them ye shall send unto me every thing that ye can hear." So Hushai David's friend came into the city, and Absalom came into Jerusalem.   [15:30–37]

Absalom Comes to Jerusalem.   And Absalom, and all the people the men of Israel, came to Jerusalem, and Ahithophel with him. And it came to pass, when Hushai the Archite, David's friend, was come unto Absalom, that Hushai said unto Absalom, "God save the king, God save the king". And Absalom said to Hushai, "Is this thy kindness to thy friend? why wentest thou not with thy friend?" And Hushai said unto Absalom, "Nay; but whom the

Lord, and this people, and all the men of Israel, choose, his will I be, and with him will I abide. And again, whom should I serve? should I not serve in the presence of his son? as I have served in thy father's presence, so will I be in thy presence." Then said Absalom to Ahithophel, "Give counsel among you what we shall do". And Ahithophel said unto Absalom, "Go in unto thy father's concubines, which he hath left to keep the house; and all Israel shall hear that thou art abhorred of thy father: then shall the hands of all that are with thee be strong". So they spread Absalom a tent upon the top of the house; and Absalom went in unto his father's concubines in the sight of all Israel.   [16:15-22]

Ahithophel's Counsel.   And the counsel of Ahithophel, which he counselled in those days, was as if a man had enquired at the oracle of God: so was all the counsel of Ahithophel both with David and with Absalom.

Moreover Ahithophel said unto Absalom, "Let me now choose out twelve thousand men, and I will arise and pursue after David this night: and I will come upon him while he is weary and weak handed, and will make him afraid: and all the people that are with him shall flee; and I will smite the king only: and I will bring back all the people unto thee: the man whom thou seekest is as if all returned: so all the people shall be in peace". And the saying pleased Absalom well, and all the elders of Israel.

                                                    [16:23; 17:1-4]

Hushai's Counsel Preferred.   Then said Absalom, "Call now Hushai the Archite also, and let us hear likewise what he saith". And when Hushai was come to Absalom, Absalom spake unto him, saying, "Ahithophel hath spoken after this manner: shall we do after his saying? if not; speak thou". And Hushai said unto Absalom, "The counsel that Ahithophel hath given is not good at this time. For", said Hushai, "thou knowest thy father and his men, that they be mighty men, and they be chafed in their minds, as a bear robbed of her whelps in the field: and thy father is a man of war, and will not lodge with the people. Behold, he is hid now in some pit, or in some other place: and it will come to pass, when some of them be overthrown at the first, that whosoever heareth it will say, 'There is a slaughter among the people that follow Absalom'. And he also that is valiant, whose heart is as the heart of a lion, shall utterly melt: for all Israel knoweth that thy father is a mighty man, and they which be with him are valiant men. Therefore I counsel that all Israel be generally gathered unto thee, from Dan even to Beer-sheba, as the sand that is by the sea for multitude; and that thou go to battle in thine own person. So shall we come upon him in some place where he shall be found, and we will light upon him as the dew falleth on the ground: and of him and of all the men that are with him there shall not be left so much as one. Moreover, if he be gotten into a city, then shall all Israel bring ropes to that city, and we will draw it into the river, until there be not one small stone found there." And Absalom and all the men of Israel said, "The counsel of Hushai the Archite is better than the counsel of Ahithophel". For the LORD had appointed to defeat the good counsel of Ahithophel, to the intent that the LORD might bring evil upon Absalom.

Then said Hushai unto Zadok and to Abiathar the priests, "Thus and thus did Ahithophel counsel Absalom and the elders of Israel; and thus and thus have I counselled. Now therefore send quickly, and tell David, saying, 'Lodge not this night in the plains of the wilderness, but speedily pass over; lest the king be swallowed up, and all the people that are with him'." Now Jonathan and Ahimaaz stayed by En-rogel; for they might not be seen to come into the city: and a wench went and told them; and they went and told king David. Nevertheless a lad saw them, and told Absalom: but they went both of them away quickly, and came to a man's house in Bahurim, which had a well in his court; whither they went down. And the woman took and spread a covering over the well's mouth, and spread ground corn thereon; and the thing was not known. And when Absalom's servants came to the woman to the house, they said, "Where is Ahimaaz and Jonathan?" And the woman said unto them, "They be gone over the brook of water". And when they had sought and could not find them, they returned to Jerusalem. And it came to pass, after they were departed, that they came up out of the well, and went and told king David, and said unto David, "Arise, and pass quickly over the water: for thus hath Ahithophel counselled against you". Then David arose, and all the people that were with him, and they passed over Jordan: by the morning light there lacked not one of them that was not gone over Jordan. And when Ahithophel saw that his counsel was not followed, he saddled his ass, and arose, and gat him home to his house, to his city, and put his household in order, and hanged himself, and died, and was buried in the sepulchre of his father.   [17:5–23]

Joab Defeats Absalom. And David numbered the people that were with him, and set captains of thousands and captains of hundreds over them. And David sent forth a third part of the people under the hand of Joab, and a third part under the hand of Abishai the son of Zeruiah, Joab's brother, and a third part under the hand of Ittai the Gittite. And the king said unto the people, "I will surely go forth with you myself also". But the people answered, "Thou shalt not go forth: for if we flee away, they will not care for us; neither if half of us die, will they care for us: but now thou art worth ten thousand of us: therefore now it is better that thou succour us out of the city". And the king said unto them, "What seemeth you best I will do". And the king stood by the gate side, and all the people came out by hundreds and by thousands. And the king commanded Joab and Abishai and Ittai, saying, "Deal gently for my sake with the young man, even with Absalom". And all the people heard when the king gave all the captains charge concerning Absalom. So the people went out into the field against Israel: and the battle was in the wood of Ephraim; where the people of Israel were slain before the servants of David, and there was there a great slaughter that day of twenty thousand men. For the battle was there scattered over the face of all the country: and the wood devoured more people that day than the sword devoured.   [18:1–8]

The Death of Absalom. And Absalom met the servants of David. And Absalom rode upon a mule, and the mule went under the thick boughs of a great oak, and his head caught hold of the oak, and he was taken up between the heaven and the earth; and the mule that was under him went away. And a certain man saw it, and told Joab, and said, "Behold, I saw Absalom hanged in an oak". And Joab said unto the man that told him, "And, behold, thou sawest him, and why didst thou not smite him there to the ground? and I would have given thee ten shekels of silver, and a girdle". And the man said unto Joab, "Though I should receive a thousand shekels of silver in mine hand, yet would I not put forth mine hand against the king's son: for in our hearing the king charged thee and Abishai and Ittai, saying, 'Beware that none touch the young man Absalom'. Otherwise I should have wrought falsehood against mine own life: for there is no matter hid from the king, and thou thyself wouldest have set thyself against me." Then said Joab, "I may not tarry thus with thee". And he took three darts in his hand, and thrust them through the heart of Absalom, while he was yet alive in the midst of the oak. And ten young men that bare Joab's armour compassed about and smote Absalom, and slew him. And Joab blew the trumpet, and the people returned from pursuing after Israel: for Joab held back the people. And they took Absalom, and cast him into a great pit in the wood, and laid a very great heap of stones upon him: and all Israel fled every one to his tent. Now Absalom in his lifetime had taken and reared up for himself a pillar, which is in the king's dale: for he said, "I have

no son to keep my name in remembrance": and he called
the pillar after his own name: and it is called unto this
day, Absalom's place.

Then said Ahimaaz the son of Zadok, "Let me now
run, and bear the king tidings, how that the LORD hath
avenged him of his enemies". And Joab said unto him,
"Thou shalt not bear tidings this day, but thou shalt bear
tidings another day: but this day thou shalt bear no tidings,
because the king's son is dead". Then said Joab to Cushi,
"Go tell the king what thou hast seen". And Cushi bowed
himself unto Joab, and ran. Then said Ahimaaz the son of
Zadok yet again to Joab, "But howsoever, let me, I pray
thee, also run after Cushi". And Joab said, "Wherefore
wilt thou run, my son, seeing that thou hast no tidings
ready?" "But howsoever," said he, "let me run." And he
said unto him, "Run". Then Ahimaaz ran by the way of
the plain, and overran Cushi.

And David sat between the two gates: and the watchman went up to the roof over the gate unto the wall, and
lifted up his eyes, and looked, and behold a man running
alone. And the watchman cried, and told the king. And
the king said, "If he be alone, there is tidings in his
mouth". And he came apace, and drew near. And the
watchman saw another man running: and the watchman
called unto the porter, and said, "Behold another man running alone". And the king said, "He also bringeth tidings".
And the watchman said, "Me thinketh the running of the
foremost is like the running of Ahimaaz the son of Zadok".
And the king said, "He is a good man, and cometh with
good tidings". And Ahimaaz called, and said unto the king,
"All is well". And he fell down to the earth upon his face
before the king, and said, "Blessed be the LORD thy God,
which hath delivered up the men that lifted up their hand
against my lord the king". And the king said, "Is the young
man Absalom safe?" And Ahimaaz answered, "When Joab
sent the king's servant, and me thy servant, I saw a great

tumult, but I knew not what it was". And the king said unto him, "Turn aside, and stand here". And he turned aside, and stood still. And, behold, Cushi came; and Cushi said, "Tidings, my lord the king: for the LORD hath avenged thee this day of all them that rose up against thee". And the king said unto Cushi, "Is the young man Absalom safe?" And Cushi answered, "The enemies of my lord the king, and all that rise against thee to do thee hurt, be as that young man is".　　　　　[18:9–32]

David Laments for Absalom.　And the king was much moved, and went up to the chamber over the gate, and wept: and as he went, thus he said, "O my son Absalom, my son, my son Absalom! would God I had died for thee, O Absalom, my son, my son!"

And it was told Joab, "Behold, the king weepeth and mourneth for Absalom". And the victory that day was turned into mourning unto all the people: for the people heard say that day how the king was grieved for his son. And the people gat them by stealth that day into the city, as people being ashamed steal away when they flee in battle. But the king covered his face, and the king cried with a loud voice, "O my son Absalom, O Absalom, my son, my son!" And Joab came into the house to the king, and said, "Thou hast shamed this day the faces of all thy servants, which this day have saved thy life, and the lives of thy sons and of thy daughters, and the lives of thy wives, and the lives of thy concubines; in that thou lovest thine enemies, and hatest thy friends. For thou hast declared this day, that thou regardest neither princes nor servants: for this day I perceive, that if Absalom had lived, and all we had died this day, then it had pleased thee well. Now therefore arise, go forth, and speak comfortably unto thy servants: for I swear by the LORD, if thou go not forth, there will not tarry one with thee this night: and that will be worse unto thee than all the evil that befell thee from thy youth until now." Then the king arose, and sat in the gate. And they told unto all the people, saying, "Behold, the king doth sit in the gate". And all the people came before the king: for Israel had fled every man to his tent.   [18:33; 19:1–8]

From THE FIRST BOOK OF THE KINGS

David's Old Age. Now king David was old and stricken in years; and they covered him with clothes, but he gat no heat. Wherefore his servants said unto him, "Let there be sought for my lord the king a young virgin: and let her stand before the king, and let her cherish him, and let her lie in thy bosom, that my lord the king may get heat". So they sought for a fair damsel throughout all the coasts of Israel, and found Abishag a Shunammite, and brought her to the king. And the damsel was very fair, and cherished the king, and ministered to him: but the king knew her not. Then Adonijah the son of Haggith exalted himself, saying, "I will be king": and he prepared him chariots and horsemen, and fifty men to run before him. And his father had not displeased him at any time in saying, "Why hast thou done so?" and he also was a very goodly man; and his mother bare him after Absalom. And he conferred with Joab the son of Zeruiah, and with Abiathar the priest: and they following Adonijah helped him. But Zadok the priest, and Benaiah the son of Jehoiada, and Nathan the prophet, and Shimei, and Rei, and the mighty men which belonged to David, were not with Adonijah.   [1:1–8]

[Hereupon Nathan the prophet urged Bath-sheba to tell David of Adonijah's actions.]

Solomon Anointed King. Then king David answered and said, "Call me Bath-sheba". And she came into the king's presence, and stood before the king. And the king sware, and said, "As the LORD liveth, that hath redeemed

my soul out of all distress, even as I sware unto thee by
the LORD God of Israel, saying, Assuredly Solomon thy
son shall reign after me, and he shall sit upon my throne
in my stead; even so will I certainly do this day". Then
Bath-sheba bowed with her face to the earth, and did
reverence to the king, and said, "Let my lord king David
live for ever". And king David said, "Call me Zadok the
priest, and Nathan the prophet, and Benaiah the son of
Jehoiada". And they came before the king. The king also
said unto them, "Take with you the servants of your lord,
and cause Solomon my son to ride upon mine own mule,
and bring him down to Gihon: and let Zadok the priest and
Nathan the prophet anoint him there king over Israel:
and blow ye with the trumpet, and say, 'God save king
Solomon'. Then ye shall come up after him, that he may
come and sit upon my throne; for he shall be king in my
stead: and I have appointed him to be ruler over Israel and
over Judah." And Benaiah the son of Jehoiada answered
the king, and said, "Amen: the LORD God of my lord the
king say so too. As the LORD hath been with my lord the
king, even so be he with Solomon, and make his throne
greater than the throne of my lord king David."

[So Zadok, Nathan, and Benaiah escorted Solomon to
Gihon where he was anointed king.]

And the king bowed himself upon the bed. And also
thus said the king, "Blessed be the LORD God of Israel,
which hath given one to sit on my throne this day, mine
eyes even seeing it." And all the guests that were with
Adonijah were afraid, and rose up, and went every man
his way. And Adonijah feared because of Solomon, and
arose, and went, and caught hold on the horns of the altar.
And it was told Solomon, saying, "Behold, Adonijah feareth king Solomon: for, lo, he hath caught hold on the
horns of the altar, saying, 'Let king Solomon swear unto
me to day that he will not slay his servant with the
sword' ". And Solomon said, "If he will shew himself a
worthy man, there shall not an hair of him fall to the

earth: but if wickedness shall be found in him, he shall
die". So king Solomon sent, and they brought him down
from the altar. And he came and bowed himself to king
Solomon: and Solomon said unto him, "Go to thine
house".   [1:28–37, 47–53]

David's Advice to Solomon. Now the days of David
drew nigh that he should die; and he charged Solomon his
son, saying, "I go the way of all the earth: be thou strong
therefore, and shew thyself a man; and keep the charge of
the LORD thy God, to walk in his ways, to keep his statutes,
and his commandments, and his judgments, and his testimonies, as it is written in the law of Moses, that thou
mayest prosper in all that thou doest, and whithersoever
thou turnest thyself: that the LORD may continue his
word which he spake concerning me, saying, 'If thy children take heed to their way, to walk before me in truth
with all their heart and with all their soul, there shall
not fail thee' (said he) a 'man on the throne of Israel'.
Moreover thou knowest also what Joab the son of Zeruiah
did to me, and what he did to the two captains of the hosts
of Israel, unto Abner the son of Ner, and unto Amasa the
son of Jether, whom he slew, and shed the blood of war in
peace, and put the blood of war upon his girdle that was
about his loins, and in his shoes that were on his feet.[1]
Do therefore according to thy wisdom, and let not his hoar
head go down to the grave in peace. But shew kindness
unto the sons of Barzillai the Gileadite, and let them be of
those that eat at thy table: for so they came to me when
I fled because of Absalom thy brother. And, behold, thou
hast with thee Shimei the son of Gera, a Benjamite of
Bahurim, which cursed me with a grievous curse in the
day when I went to Mahanaim: but he came down to
meet me at Jordan, and I sware to him by the LORD, saying, I will not put thee to death with the sword. Now
therefore hold him not guiltless: for thou art a wise man,

---

[1] See II Samuel 3 and 9.

and knowest what thou oughtest to do unto him; but his hoar head bring thou down to the grave with blood." So David slept with his fathers, and was buried in the city of David. And the days that David reigned over Israel were forty years: seven years reigned he in Hebron, and thirty and three years reigned he in Jerusalem.

Then sat Solomon upon the throne of David his father; and his kingdom was established greatly.   [2:1–12]

[Solomon's first acts were to cause Adonijah, Joab, and Shimei to be put to death.]

Solomon Allies with Egypt. And Solomon made affinity with Pharaoh king of Egypt, and took Pharaoh's daughter, and brought her into the city of David, until he had made an end of building his own house, and the house of the LORD, and the wall of Jerusalem round about. Only the people sacrificed in high places, because there was no house built unto the name of the LORD, until those days. And Solomon loved the LORD, walking in the statutes of David his father: only he sacrificed and burnt incense in high places.   [3:1–3]

Solomon Asks for Wisdom. And the king went to Gibeon to sacrifice there; for that was the great high place: a thousand burnt offerings did Solomon offer upon that altar. In Gibeon the LORD appeared to Solomon in a dream by night: and God said, "Ask what I shall give thee". And Solomon said, "Thou hast shewed unto thy servant David my father great mercy, according as he walked before thee in truth, and in righteousness, and in uprightness of heart with thee; and thou hast kept for him this great kindness, that thou hast given him a son to sit on his throne, as it is this day. And now, O LORD my God, thou hast made thy servant king instead of David my father: and I am but a little child: I know not how to go out or come in. And thy servant is in the midst of thy people which thou hast chosen, a great people, that cannot be numbered nor counted for multitude. Give therefore thy servant an understanding heart to judge thy people, that I may discern between good and bad: for who is able to judge this thy so great a people?" And the speech pleased the Lord, that Solomon had asked this thing. And God said unto him, "Because thou hast asked this thing, and hast not asked for thyself long life; neither hast asked riches for thyself, nor hast asked the life of thine enemies; but hast asked for thyself understanding to discern judgment; behold, I have done according to thy words: lo, I have given thee a wise and an understanding heart; so that there was none like thee before thee, neither after thee shall any arise like unto thee. And I have also given thee that which thou hast not asked, both riches, and honour: so that there shall not be any among the kings like unto thee all thy days. And if thou wilt walk in my ways, to keep my statutes and my commandments, as thy father David did walk, then I will lengthen thy days." And Solomon awoke; and, behold, it was a dream. And he came to Jerusalem, and stood before the ark of the covenant of the LORD, and offered up burnt offerings, and offered peace offerings, and made a feast to all his servants.   [3:4–15]

The Judgment of Solomon. Then came there two women, that were harlots, unto the king, and stood before him. And the one woman said, "O my lord, I and this woman dwell in one house; and I was delivered of a child with her in the house. And it came to pass the third day after that I was delivered, that this woman was delivered also: and we were together; there was no stranger with us in the house, save we two in the house. And this woman's child died in the night; because she overlaid it. And she arose at midnight, and took my son from beside me, while thine handmaid slept, and laid it in her bosom, and laid her dead child in my bosom. And when I rose in the morning to give my child suck, behold, it was dead: but when I had considered it in the morning, behold, it was not my son, which I did bear." And the other woman said, "Nay; but the living is my son, and the dead is thy son". And this said, "No; but the dead is thy son, and the living is my son". Thus they spake before the king. Then said the king, "The one saith, 'This is my son that liveth, and thy son is the dead': and the other saith, 'Nay; but thy son is the dead, and my son is the living'". And the king said, "Bring me a sword". And they brought a sword before the king. And the king said, "Divide the living child in two, and give half to the one, and half to the other". Then spake the woman whose the living child was unto the king, for her bowels yearned upon her son, and she said, "O my lord, give her the living child, and in no wise slay it". But the other said, "Let it be neither mine nor thine, but divide it". Then the king answered and said, "Give her the living child, and in no wise slay it: she is the mother thereof". And all Israel heard of the judgment which the king had judged; and they feared the king: for they saw that the wisdom of God was in him, to do judgment. [3:16–28]

In the fourth year of his reign Solomon began to build the Temple at Jerusalem. The inner shrine was after the pattern of the tabernacle, forty cubits in length, twenty cubits in breadth, and twenty cubits in height, with an inmost chamber—the sanctuary—for the ark, twenty cubits long by twenty cubits in breadth by twenty cubits in heighth. The whole was lined with cedar overlaid with gold. Within the sanctuary, the ark rested beneath two cherubim ten cubits high of carved cedar overlaid with gold with wings outstretched and touching. The Temple took seven years in the building.

Solomon also built for himself a palace at Jerusalem, "the house of the forest of Lebanon," and a house for Pharaoh's daughter.

The Queen of Sheba Visits Solomon. And when the queen of Sheba heard of the fame of Solomon concerning the name of the LORD, she came to prove him with hard questions. And she came to Jerusalem with a very great train, with camels that bare spices, and very much gold, and precious stones: and when she was come to Solomon, she communed with him of all that was in her heart. And Solomon told her all her questions: there was not any thing hid from the king, which he told her not. And when the queen of Sheba had seen all Solomon's wisdom, and the house that he had built, and the meat of his table, and the sitting of his servants, and the attendance of his ministers, and their apparel, and his cupbearers, and his ascent by which he went up unto the house of the LORD; there was no more spirit in her. And she said to the king, "It was a true report that I heard in mine own land of thy acts and of thy wisdom. Howbeit I believed not the words, until I came, and mine eyes had seen it: and, behold, the half was not told me: thy wisdom and prosperity exceedeth the fame which I heard. Happy are thy men, happy are these thy servants, which stand continually before thee, and that hear thy wisdom. Blessed be the LORD thy God, which delighted in thee, to set thee on the throne of Israel: because the LORD loved Israel for ever, therefore made he thee king, to do judgment and justice." And she gave the king an hundred and twenty talents of gold, and of spices very great store, and precious stones: there came no more such abundance of spices as these which the queen of Sheba gave to king Solomon. And the navy also of Hiram, that brought gold from Ophir, brought in from Ophir great plenty of almug trees, and precious stones. And the king made of the almug trees pillars for the house of the LORD, and for the king's house, harps also and psalteries for singers: there came no such almug trees, nor were seen unto this day. And king Solomon gave unto the queen of Sheba all her desire, whatsoever she asked, beside that which Solomon gave her of his royal bounty. So she turned and went to her own country, she and her servants. [10:1–13]

Solomon's Great Wealth. Now the weight of gold that came to Solomon in one year was six hundred threescore and six talents of gold, beside that he had of the merchantmen, and of the traffick of the spice merchants, and of all the kings of Arabia, and of the governors of the country. And king Solomon made two hundred targets of beaten gold: six hundred shekels of gold went to one target. And he made three hundred shields of beaten gold; three pound of gold went to one shield: and the king put them in the house of the forest of Lebanon. Moreover the king made a great throne of ivory, and overlaid it with the best gold. The throne had six steps, and the top of the throne was round behind: and there were stays on either side on the place of the seat, and two lions stood beside the stays. And twelve lions stood there on the one side and on the other upon the six steps: there was not the like made in any kingdom. And all king Solomon's drinking vessels were of gold, and all the vessels of the house of the forest of Lebanon were of pure gold; none were of silver: it was nothing accounted of in the days of Solomon. For the king had at sea a navy of Tharshish with the navy of Hiram: once in three years came the navy of Tharshish, bringing gold, and silver, ivory, and apes, and peacocks.

So king Solomon exceeded all the kings of the earth for riches and for wisdom. And all the earth sought to Solomon, to hear his wisdom, which God had put in his heart. And they brought every man his present, vessels of silver, and vessels of gold, and garments, and armour, and spices, horses, and mules, a rate year by year. And Solomon gathered together chariots and horsemen: and he had a thousand and four hundred chariots, and twelve thousand horsemen, whom he bestowed in the cities for chariots, and with the king at Jerusalem. And the king made silver to be in Jerusalem as stones, and cedars made he to be as the sycomore trees that are in the vale, for abundance. And Solomon had horses brought out of Egypt, and linen yarn: the king's merchants received the linen yarn at a price. And a chariot came up and went out of Egypt for six hundred shekels of silver, and an horse for an hundred and fifty: and so for all the kings of the Hittites, and for the kings of Syria, did they bring them out by their means.

[10:14–29]

Solomon's Sin. But king Solomon loved many strange women, together with the daughter of Pharaoh, women of the Moabites, Ammonites, Edomites, Zidonians, and Hittites; of the nations concerning which the LORD said unto the children of Israel, "Ye shall not go in to them, neither shall they come in unto you: for surely they will turn away your heart after their gods": Solomon clave unto these in love. And he had seven hundred wives, princesses, and three hundred concubines: and his wives turned away his heart. For it came to pass, when Solomon was old, that his wives turned away his heart after other gods: and his heart was not perfect with the LORD his God, as was the heart of David his father. For Solomon went after Ashtoreth the goddess of the Zidonians, and after Milcom the abomination of the Ammonites. And Solomon did evil in the sight of the LORD, and went not fully after the LORD, as did David his father. Then did Solomon build an high place for Chemosh, the abomination of Moab, in the hill that is before Jerusalem, and for Molech, the abomination of the children of Ammon. And likewise did he for all his strange wives, which burnt incense and sacrificed unto their gods.

And the LORD was angry with Solomon, because his heart was turned from the LORD God of Israel, which had appeared unto him twice, and had commanded him concerning this thing, that he should not go after other gods: but he kept not that which the LORD commanded. Wherefore the LORD said unto Solomon, "Forasmuch as this is done of thee, and thou hast not kept my covenant and my statutes, which I have commanded thee, I will surely rend the kingdom from thee, and will give it to thy servant. Notwithstanding in thy days I will not do it for David thy father's sake: but I will rend it out of the hand of thy son. Howbeit I will not rend away all the kingdom; but will

give one tribe to thy son for David my servant's sake, and
for Jerusalem's sake which I have chosen."   [11:1–13]

Jeroboam Anointed King of Israel.   And Jeroboam the
son of Nebat, an Ephrathite of Zereda, Solomon's servant,
whose mother's name was Zeruah, a widow woman, even
he lifted up his hand against the king. And this was the
cause that he lifted up his hand against the king: Solomon
built Millo, and repaired the breaches of the city of David
his father. And the man Jeroboam was a mighty man of
valour: and Solomon seeing the young man that he was
industrious, he made him ruler over all the charge of the
house of Joseph. And it came to pass at that time when
Jeroboam went out of Jerusalem, that the prophet Ahijah
the Shilonite found him in the way; and he had clad himself with a new garment; and they two were alone in the
field: and Ahijah caught the new garment that was on him,
and rent it in twelve pieces: and he said to Jeroboam,
"Take thee ten pieces: for thus saith the LORD, the God of
Israel, 'Behold, I will rend the kingdom out of the hand
of Solomon, and will give ten tribes to thee: (but he shall
have one tribe for my servant David's sake, and for Jerusalem's sake, the city which I have chosen out of all the
tribes of Israel:) because that they have forsaken me, and
have worshipped Ashtoreth the goddess of the Zidonians,
Chemosh the god of the Moabites, and Milcom the god of
the children of Ammon, and have not walked in my ways,
to do that which is right in mine eyes, and to keep my
statutes and my judgments, as did David his father. Howbeit I will not take the whole kingdom out of his hand: but
I will make him prince all the days of his life for David
my servant's sake, whom I chose, because he kept my
commandments and my statutes: but I will take the kingdom out of his son's hand, and will give it unto thee, even
ten tribes. And unto his son will I give one tribe, that David
my servant may have a light alway before me in Jerusalem,
the city which I have chosen me to put my name there.
And I will take thee, and thou shalt reign according to all

that thy soul desireth, and shalt be king over Israel. And
it shall be, if thou wilt hearken unto all that I command
thee, and wilt walk in my ways, and do that is right in my
sight, to keep my statutes and my commandments, as
David my servant did; that I will be with thee, and build
thee a sure house, as I built for David, and will give Israel
unto thee. And I will for this afflict the seed of David, but
not for ever.'" Solomon sought therefore to kill Jeroboam.
And Jeroboam arose, and fled into Egypt, unto Shishak
king of Egypt, and was in Egypt until the death of Solomon.
[11:26-40]

Solomon Succeeded by Rehoboam. And the rest of the
acts of Solomon, and all that he did, and his wisdom, are
they not written in the book of the acts of Solomon? And
the time that Solomon reigned in Jerusalem over all Israel
was forty years. And Solomon slept with his fathers, and
was buried in the city of David his father: and Rehoboam
his son reigned in his stead. [11:41-43]

Jeroboam's Rebellion. And Rehoboam went to Shechem: for all Israel were come to Shechem to make him
king. And it came to pass, when Jeroboam the son of
Nebat, who was yet in Egypt, heard of it, (for he was fled
from the presence of king Solomon, and Jeroboam dwelt in
Egypt;) that they sent and called him. And Jeroboam and
all the congregation of Israel came, and spake unto Rehoboam, saying, "Thy father made our yoke grievous: now
therefore make thou the grievous service of thy father, and
his heavy yoke which he put upon us, lighter, and we will
serve thee". And he said unto them, "Depart yet for three
days, then come again to me". And the people departed.

And king Rehoboam consulted with the old men, that
stood before Solomon his father while he yet lived, and
said, "How do ye advise that I may answer this people?"
And they spake unto him, saying, "If thou wilt be a servant unto this people this day, and wilt serve them, and
answer them, and speak good words to them, then they
will be thy servants for ever". But he forsook the coun-

sel of the old men, which they had given him, and consulted with the young men that were grown up with him, and which stood before him: and he said unto them, "What counsel give ye that we may answer this people, who have spoken to me, saying, 'Make the yoke which thy father did put upon us lighter'?" And the young men that were grown up with him spake unto him, saying, "Thus shalt thou speak unto this people that spake unto thee, saying, 'Thy father made our yoke heavy, but make thou it lighter unto us'; thus shalt thou say unto them, 'My little finger shall be thicker than my father's loins. And now whereas my father did lade you with a heavy yoke, I will add to your yoke: my father hath chastised you with whips, but I will chastise you with scorpions.'"

So Jeroboam and all the people came to Rehoboam the third day, as the king had appointed, saying, "Come to me again the third day". And the king answered the people roughly, and forsook the old men's counsel that they gave him; and spake to them after the counsel of the young men, saying, "My father made your yoke heavy, and I will add to your yoke: my father also chastised you with whips, but I will chastise you with scorpions". Wherefore the king hearkened not unto the people; for the cause was from the LORD, that he might perform his saying, which the LORD spake by Ahijah the Shilonite unto Jeroboam the son of Nebat. So when all Israel saw that the king hearkened not unto them, the people answered the king, saying, "What portion have we in David? neither have we inheritance in the son of Jesse: to your tents, O Israel: now see to thine own house, David". So Israel departed unto their tents. But as for the children of Israel which dwelt in the cities of Judah, Rehoboam reigned over them. Then king Rehoboam sent Adoram, who was over the tribute; and all Israel stoned him with stones, that he died. Therefore king Rehoboam made speed to get him up to his chariot, to flee to Jerusalem. [12:1-18]

The Kingdom Divided. So Israel rebelled against the house of David unto this day. And it came to pass, when all Israel heard that Jeroboam was come again, that they sent and called him unto the congregation, and made him king over all Israel: there was none that followed the house of David, but the tribe of Judah only.

And when Rehoboam was come to Jerusalem, he assembled all the house of Judah, with the tribe of Benjamin, an hundred and fourscore thousand chosen men, which were warriors, to fight against the house of Israel, to bring the kingdom again to Rehoboam the son of Solomon. But the word of God came unto Shemaiah the man of God, saying, "Speak unto Rehoboam, the son of Solomon, king of Judah, and unto all the house of Judah and Benjamin, and to the remnant of the people, saying, 'Thus saith the LORD, Ye shall not go up, nor fight against your brethren the children of Israel: return every man to his house; for this thing is from me'". They hearkened therefore to the word of the LORD, and returned to depart, according to the word of the LORD.   [12:19–24]

Jeroboam Establishes the Kingdom of Israel. Then Jeroboam built Shechem in mount Ephraim, and dwelt therein; and went out from thence, and built Penuel. And Jeroboam said in his heart, "Now shall the kingdom return to the house of David: if this people go up to do sacrifice in the house of the LORD at Jerusalem, then shall the heart of this people turn again unto their lord, even unto Rehoboam king of Judah, and they shall kill me, and go again to Rehoboam king of Judah". Whereupon the king took counsel, and made two calves of gold, and said unto them, "It is too much for you to go up to Jerusalem: behold thy gods, O Israel, which brought thee up out of the land of Egypt". And he set the one in Beth-el, and the other put he in Dan. And this thing became a sin: for the people went to worship before the one, even unto Dan. And he made an house of high places, and made priests of the lowest of the people, which were not of the sons of

Levi. And Jeroboam ordained a feast in the eighth month, on the fifteenth day of the month, like unto the feast that is in Judah, and he offered upon the altar. So did he in Beth-el, sacrificing unto the calves that he had made: and he placed in Beth-el the priests of the high places which he had made. So he offered upon the altar which he had made in Beth-el the fifteenth day of the eighth month, even in the month which he had devised of his own heart; and ordained a feast unto the children of Israel: and he offered upon the altar, and burnt incense.   [12:25–33]

[In the next fifty years there were two revolutions in the kingdom of Israel. In the second Zimri slew the reigning king Baasha but seven days later he was slain by Omri, who became king and reigned for seventeen years.]

Ahab King of Israel.   And in the thirty and eighth year of Asa king of Judah began Ahab the son of Omri to reign over Israel: and Ahab the son of Omri reigned over Israel in Samaria twenty and two years. And Ahab the son of Omri did evil in the sight of the LORD above all that were before him. And it came to pass, as if it had been a light thing for him to walk in the sins of Jeroboam the son of Nebat, that he took to wife Jezebel the daughter of Ethbaal king of the Zidonians, and went and served Baal, and worshipped him. And he reared up an altar for Baal in the house of Baal, which he had built in Samaria. And Ahab made a grove; and Ahab did more to provoke the LORD God of Israel to anger than all the kings of Israel that were before him. In his days did Hiel the Beth-elite build Jeri-cho: he laid the foundation thereof in Abiram his firstborn, and set up the gates thereof in his youngest son Segub, according to the word of the LORD, which he spake by Joshua the son of Nun.   [16:29–34]

Elijah the Prophet.   And Elijah the Tishbite, who was of the inhabitants of Gilead, said unto Ahab, "As the LORD God of Israel liveth, before whom I stand, there shall not be dew nor rain these years, but according to my word". And the word of the LORD came unto him, saying,

"Get thee hence, and turn thee eastward, and hide thyself by the brook Cherith, that is before Jordan. And it shall be, that thou shalt drink of the brook; and I have commanded the ravens to feed thee there." So he went and did according unto the word of the LORD: for he went and dwelt by the brook Cherith, that is before Jordan. And the ravens brought him bread and flesh in the morning, and bread and flesh in the evening; and he drank of the brook. And it came to pass after a while, that the brook dried up, because there had been no rain in the land.

[17:1–7]

Elijah and the Poor Widow. And the word of the LORD came unto him, saying, "Arise, get thee to Zarephath, which belongeth to Zidon, and dwell there: behold, I have commanded a widow woman there to sustain thee". So he arose and went to Zarephath. And when he came to the gate of the city, behold, the widow woman was there gathering of sticks: and he called to her, and said, "Fetch me, I pray thee, a little water in a vessel, that I may drink". And as she was going to fetch it, he called to her, and said, "Bring me, I pray thee, a morsel of bread in thine hand". And she said, "As the LORD thy God liveth, I have not a cake, but an handful of meal in a barrel, and a little oil in a cruse: and, behold, I am gathering two sticks, that I may go in and dress it for me and my son, that we may eat it, and die". And Elijah said unto her, "Fear not; go and do as thou hast said: but make me thereof a little cake first, and bring it unto me, and after make for thee and for thy son. For thus saith the LORD God of Israel, 'The barrel of meal shall not waste, neither shall the cruse of oil fail, until the day that the LORD sendeth rain upon the earth'." And she went and did according to the saying of Elijah: and she, and he, and her house, did eat many days. And the barrel of meal wasted not, neither did the cruse of oil fail, according to the word of the LORD, which he spake by Elijah. And it came to pass after these things, that the son of the woman, the mistress of the house, fell sick; and his sickness was so sore, that there was no breath left in him. And she said unto Elijah, "What have I to do with thee, O thou man of God? art thou come unto me to call my sin to remembrance, and to slay my son?" And he said unto her, "Give me thy son". And he took him out of her bosom, and carried him up into a loft, where he abode, and laid him upon his own bed. And he cried unto the LORD, and said, "O LORD my God, hast thou also brought evil upon the widow with whom I sojourn, by slaying her son?" And he stretched himself upon the child three times, and cried unto the LORD, and said, "O LORD my God, I pray thee, let this child's soul come into him again". And the LORD heard the voice of Elijah; and the soul of the child came into him again, and he revived. And Elijah took the child, and brought him down out of the chamber into the house, and delivered him unto his mother: and Elijah said, "See, thy son liveth". And the woman said to Elijah, "Now by this I know that thou art a man of God, and that the word of the LORD in thy mouth is truth". [17:8–24]

Elijah and Ahab. And it came to pass after many days, that the word of the LORD came to Elijah in the third year, saying, "Go, shew thyself unto Ahab; and I will send rain upon the earth". And Elijah went to shew himself unto Ahab. And there was a sore famine in Samaria. And Ahab called Obadiah, which was the governor of his house. (Now Obadiah feared the LORD greatly: for it was so, when Jezebel cut off the prophets of the LORD, that Obadiah took an hundred prophets, and hid them by fifty in a cave, and fed them with bread and water.) And Ahab said unto Obadiah, "Go into the land, unto all fountains of water, and unto all brooks: peradventure we may find grass to save the horses and mules alive, that we lose not all the beasts". So they divided the land between them to pass throughout it: Ahab went one way by himself, and Obadiah went another way by himself. And as Obadiah was in the way, behold, Elijah met him: and he knew him, and fell on his face, and said, "Art thou that my lord Elijah?" And he answered him, "I am: go, tell thy lord, Behold, Elijah is here". And he said, "What have I sinned, that thou wouldest deliver thy servant into the hand of Ahab, to slay me? As the LORD thy God liveth, there is no nation or kingdom, whither my lord hath not sent to seek thee: and when they said, 'He is not there'; he took an oath of the kingdom and nation, that they found thee not. And now thou sayest, 'Go, tell thy lord, Behold, Elijah is here'. And it shall come to pass, as soon as I am gone from thee, that the spirit of the LORD shall carry thee whither I know not; and so when I come and tell Ahab, and he cannot find thee, he shall slay me: but I thy servant fear the LORD from my youth. Was it not told my lord what I did when Jezebel slew the prophets of the LORD, how I hid an hundred men of the LORD's prophets by fifty in a cave, and fed them with bread and water? And now thou sayest, 'Go, tell thy lord, Behold, Elijah is here': and he shall slay me." And Elijah said, "As the LORD of hosts liveth, before whom I stand, I will surely shew myself unto him to day". So Obadiah went to meet Ahab, and told him: and Ahab went to meet Elijah. And it came to pass, when Ahab saw Elijah, that Ahab said unto him, "Art thou he that troubleth Israel?" And he answered, "I have not troubled Israel; but thou, and thy father's house, in that ye have forsaken the commandments of the LORD, and thou hast followed Baalim. Now therefore send, and gather to me all Israel unto mount Carmel, and the prophets of Baal four hundred and fifty, and the prophets of the groves four hundred, which eat at Jezebel's table." So Ahab sent unto all the children of Israel, and gathered the prophets together unto mount Carmel.   [18:1–20]

Elijah Challenges the Prophets of Baal. And Elijah came unto all the people, and said, "How long halt ye between two opinions? if the LORD be God, follow him: but if Baal, then follow him". And the people answered him not a word. Then said Elijah unto the people, "I, even

I only, remain a prophet of the LORD; but Baal's prophets are four hundred and fifty men. Let them therefore give us two bullocks; and let them choose one bullock for themselves, and cut it in pieces, and lay it on wood, and put no fire under: and I will dress the other bullock, and lay it on wood, and put no fire under: and call ye on the name of your gods, and I will call on the name of the LORD: and the God that answereth by fire, let him be God." And all the people answered and said, "It is well spoken". And Elijah said unto the prophets of Baal, "Choose you one bullock for yourselves, and dress it first; for ye are many; and call on the name of your gods, but put no fire under". And they took the bullock which was given them, and they dressed it, and called on the name of Baal from morning even until noon, saying, "O Baal, hear us". But there was no voice, nor any that answered. And they leaped upon the altar which was made. And it came to pass at noon, that Elijah mocked them, and said, "Cry aloud: for he is a god; either he is talking, or he is pursuing, or he is in a journey, or peradventure he sleepeth, and must be awaked". And they cried aloud, and cut themselves after their manner with knives and lancets, till the blood gushed out upon them. And it came to pass, when midday was past, and they prophesied until the time of the offering of the evening sacrifice, that there was neither voice, nor any to answer, nor any that regarded. And Elijah said unto all the people, "Come near unto me". And all the people came near unto him. And he repaired the altar of the LORD that was broken down.

And Elijah took twelve stones, according to the number of the tribes of the sons of Jacob, unto whom the word of the LORD came, saying, "Israel shall be thy name": and with the stones he built an altar in the name of the LORD: and he made a trench about the altar, as great as would contain two measures of seed. And he put the wood in order, and cut the bullock in pieces, and laid him on the wood, and said, "Fill four barrels with water, and pour it on the burnt sacrifice, and on the wood". And he said, "Do it the second time". And they did it the second time. And he said, "Do it the third time". And they did it the third time. And the water ran round about the altar; and he filled the trench also with water. And it came to pass at the time of the offering of the evening sacrifice, that Elijah the prophet came near, and said, "LORD God of Abraham, Isaac, and of Israel, let it be known this day that thou art God in Israel, and that I am thy servant, and that I have done all these things at thy word. Hear me, O LORD, hear me, that this people may know that thou art the LORD God, and that thou hast turned their heart back again." Then the fire of the LORD fell, and consumed the burnt sacrifice, and the wood, and the stones, and the dust, and licked up the water that was in the trench. And when all the people saw it, they fell on their faces: and they said, "The LORD, he is the God; the LORD, he is the God".

[18:21–39]

The Prophets of Baal Slain. And Elijah said unto them, "Take the prophets of Baal; let not one of them escape". And they took them: and Elijah brought them down to the brook Kishon, and slew them there. And Elijah said unto Ahab, "Get thee up, eat and drink; for there is a sound of abundance of rain". So Ahab went up to eat and to drink. And Elijah went up to the top of Carmel; and he cast himself down upon the earth, and put his face between his knees, and said to his servant, "Go up now, look toward the sea". And he went up, and looked, and said, "There is nothing". And he said, "Go again seven times". And it came to pass at the seventh time, that he said, "Behold, there ariseth a little cloud out of the sea, like a man's hand". And he said, "Go up, say unto Ahab, 'Prepare thy chariot, and get thee down, that the rain stop thee not'". And it came to pass in the mean while, that the heaven was black with clouds and wind, and there was a great rain. And Ahab rode, and went to Jezreel. And the hand of the LORD was on Elijah; and he

girded up his loins, and ran before Ahab to the entrance
of Jezreel.   [18:40–46]

Elijah Flees.   And Ahab told Jezebel all that Elijah had
done, and withal how he had slain all the prophets with
the sword. Then Jezebel sent a messenger unto Elijah,
saying, "So let the gods do to me, and more also, if I make
not thy life as the life of one of them by to morrow about
this time". And when he saw that, he arose, and went for
his life, and came to Beer-sheba, which belongeth to
Judah, and left his servant there. But he himself went a
day's journey into the wilderness, and came and sat down
under a juniper tree: and he requested for himself that he
might die; and said, "It is enough; now, O LORD, take
away my life; for I am not better than my fathers". And
as he lay and slept under a juniper tree, behold, then an
angel touched him, and said unto him, "Arise and eat".
And he looked, and, behold, there was a cake baken on
the coals, and a cruse of water at his head. And he did eat
and drink, and laid him down again. And the angel of the
LORD came again the second time, and touched him, and
said, "Arise and eat; because the journey is too great for
thee".   [19:1–7]

Elijah's Vision.   And he arose, and did eat and drink,
and went in the strength of that meat forty days and forty
nights unto Horeb the mount of God. And he came thither
unto a cave, and lodged there; and, behold, the word of
the LORD came to him, and he said unto him, "What doest
thou here, Elijah?" And he said, "I have been very jealous
for the LORD God of hosts: for the children of Israel have
forsaken thy covenant, thrown down thine altars, and
slain thy prophets with the sword; and I, even I only, am
left; and they seek my life, to take it away". And he said,
"Go forth, and stand upon the mount before the LORD".
And, behold, the LORD passed by, and a great and strong
wind rent the mountains, and brake in pieces the rocks
before the LORD; but the LORD was not in the wind: and
after the wind an earthquake; but the LORD was not in the

earthquake: and after the earthquake a fire; but the LORD was not in the fire: and after the fire a still small voice. And it was so, when Elijah heard it, that he wrapped his face in his mantle, and went out, and stood in the entering in of the cave. And, behold, there came a voice unto him, and said, "What doest thou here, Elijah?" And he said, "I have been very jealous for the LORD God of hosts: because the children of Israel have forsaken thy covenant, thrown down thine altars, and slain thy prophets with the sword; and I, even I only, am left; and they seek my life, to take it away". And the LORD said unto him, "Go, return on thy way to the wilderness of Damascus: and when thou comest, anoint Hazael to be king over Syria: and Jehu the son of Nimshi shalt thou anoint to be king over Israel: and Elisha the son of Shaphat of Abel-meholah shalt thou anoint to be prophet in thy room. And it shall come to pass, that him that escapeth the sword of Hazael shall Jehu slay: and him that escapeth from the sword of Jehu shall Elisha slay. Yet I have left me seven thousand in Israel, all the knees which have not bowed unto Baal, and every mouth which hath not kissed him." [19:8–18]

Elisha Chosen to Succeed Elijah. So he departed thence, and found Elisha the son of Shaphat, who was plowing with twelve yoke of oxen before him, and he with the twelfth: and Elijah passed by him, and cast his mantle upon him. And he left the oxen, and ran after Elijah, and said, "Let me, I pray thee, kiss my father and my mother, and then I will follow thee". And he said unto him, "Go back again: for what have I done to thee?" And he returned back from him, and took a yoke of oxen, and slew them, and boiled their flesh with the instruments of the oxen, and gave unto the people, and they did eat. Then he arose, and went after Elijah, and ministered unto him.

[19:19–21]

Naboth's Vineyard. And it came to pass after these things, that Naboth the Jezreelite had a vineyard, which was in Jezreel, hard by the palace of Ahab king of Samaria.

And Ahab spake unto Naboth, saying, "Give me thy vineyard, that I may have it for a garden of herbs, because it is near unto my house: and I will give thee for it a better vineyard than it; or, if it seem good to thee, I will give thee the worth of it in money". And Naboth said to Ahab, "The LORD forbid it me, that I should give the inheritance of my fathers unto thee". And Ahab came into his house heavy and displeased because of the word which Naboth the Jezreelite had spoken to him: for he had said, "I will not give thee the inheritance of my fathers". And he laid him down upon his bed, and turned away his face, and would eat no bread. But Jezebel his wife came to him, and said unto him, "Why is thy spirit so sad, that thou eatest no bread?" And he said unto her, "Because I spake unto Naboth the Jezreelite, and said unto him, Give me thy vineyard for money; or else, if it please thee, I will give thee another vineyard for it: and he answered, 'I will not give thee my vineyard' ". And Jezebel his wife said unto him, "Dost thou now govern the kingdom of Israel? arise, and eat bread, and let thine heart be merry: I will give thee the vineyard of Naboth the Jezreelite". So she wrote letters in Ahab's name, and sealed them with his seal, and sent the letters unto the elders and to the nobles that were in his city, dwelling with Naboth. And she wrote in the letters, saying, "Proclaim a fast, and set Naboth on high among the people: and set two men, sons of Belial, before him, to bear witness against him, saying, 'Thou didst blaspheme God and the king'. And then carry him out, and stone him, that he may die." And the men of his city, even the elders and the nobles who were the inhabitants in his city, did as Jezebel had sent unto them, and as it was written in the letters which she had sent unto them. They proclaimed a fast, and set Naboth on high among the people. And there came in two men, children of Belial, and sat before him: and the men of Belial witnessed against him, even against Naboth, in the presence of the people, saying, "Naboth did blaspheme God and the king".

Then they carried him forth out of the city, and stoned him with stones, that he died. Then they sent to Jezebel, saying, "Naboth is stoned, and is dead". And it came to pass, when Jezebel heard that Naboth was stoned, and was dead, that Jezebel said to Ahab, "Arise, take possession of the vineyard of Naboth the Jezreelite, which he refused to give thee for money: for Naboth is not alive, but dead". And it came to pass, when Ahab heard that Naboth was dead, that Ahab rose up to go down to the vineyard of Naboth the Jezreelite, to take possession of it. [21:1–16]

Ahab and Jezebel Cursed. And the word of the LORD came to Elijah the Tishbite, saying, "Arise, go down to meet Ahab king of Israel, which is in Samaria: behold, he is in the vineyard of Naboth, whither he is gone down to possess it. And thou shalt speak unto him, saying, 'Thus saith the LORD, Hast thou killed, and also taken possession?' And thou shalt speak unto him, saying, 'Thus saith the LORD, In the place where dogs licked the blood of Naboth shall dogs lick thy blood, even thine'." And Ahab said to Elijah, "Hast thou found me, O mine enemy?" And he answered, "I have found thee: because thou hast sold thyself to work evil in the sight of the LORD. Behold, I will bring evil upon thee, and will take away thy posterity, and will cut off from Ahab him that pisseth against the wall, and him that is shut up and left in Israel, and will make thine house like the house of Jeroboam the son of Nebat, and like the house of Baasha the son of Ahijah, for the provocation wherewith thou hast provoked me to anger, and made Israel to sin." And of Jezebel also spake the LORD, saying, "The dogs shall eat Jezebel by the wall of Jezreel. Him that dieth of Ahab in the city the dogs shall eat; and him that dieth in the field shall the fowls of the air eat." But there was none like unto Ahab, which did sell himself to work wickedness in the sight of the LORD, whom Jezebel his wife stirred up. And he did very abominably in following idols, according to all things as did the Amorites, whom the LORD cast out before the children of

Israel. And it came to pass, when Ahab heard those words, that he rent his clothes, and put sackcloth upon his flesh, and fasted, and lay in sackcloth, and went softly. And the word of the LORD came to Elijah the Tishbite, saying, "Seest thou how Ahab humbleth himself before me? because he humbleth himself before me, I will not bring the evil in his days: but in his son's days will I bring the evil upon his house". [21:17-29]

Ahab and Jehoshaphat in Alliance. And they continued three years without war between Syria and Israel. And it came to pass in the third year, that Jehoshaphat the king of Judah came down to the king of Israel. And the king of Israel said unto his servants, "Know ye that Ramoth in Gilead is ours, and we be still, and take it not out of the hand of the king of Syria?" And he said unto Jehoshaphat, "Wilt thou go with me to battle to Ramoth-gilead?" And Jehoshaphat said to the king of Israel, "I am as thou art, my people as thy people, my horses as thy horses". And Jehoshaphat said unto the king of Israel, "Enquire, I pray thee, at the word of the LORD to day". Then the king of Israel gathered the prophets together, about four hundred men, and said unto them, "Shall I go against Ramoth-gilead to battle, or shall I forbear?" And they said, "Go up; for the Lord shall deliver it into the hand of the king". And Jehoshaphat said, "Is there not here a prophet of the LORD besides, that we might enquire of him?" And the king of Israel said unto Jehoshaphat, "There is yet one man, Micaiah the son of Imlah, by whom we may enquire of the LORD: but I hate him; for he doth not prophesy good concerning me, but evil". And Jehoshaphat said, "Let not the king say so". Then the king of Israel called an officer, and said, "Hasten hither Micaiah the son of Imlah". And the king of Israel and Jehoshaphat the king of Judah sat each on his throne, having put on their robes, in a void place in the entrance of the gate of Samaria; and all the prophets prophesied before them. And Zedekiah the son of Chenaanah made him horns of iron:

and he said, "Thus saith the LORD, 'With these shalt thou push the Syrians, until thou have consumed them'". And all the prophets prophesied so, saying, "Go up to Ramoth-gilead, and prosper: for the LORD shall deliver it into the king's hand". And the messenger that was gone to call Micaiah spake unto him, saying, "Behold now, the words of the prophets declare good unto the king with one mouth: let thy word, I pray thee, be like the word of one of them, and speak that which is good". And Micaiah said, "As the LORD liveth, what the LORD saith unto me, that will I speak".   [22:1–15]

Ahab's Death Prophesied. So he came to the king. And the king said unto him, "Micaiah, shall we go against Ramoth-gilead to battle, or shall we forbear?" And he answered him, "Go, and prosper: for the LORD shall deliver it into the hand of the king". And the king said unto him, "How many times shall I adjure thee that thou tell me nothing but that which is true in the name of the LORD?" And he said, "I saw all Israel scattered upon the hills, as sheep that have not a shepherd: and the LORD said, 'These have no master: let them return every man to his house in peace'". And the king of Israel said unto Jehoshaphat, "Did I not tell thee that he would prophesy no good concerning me, but evil?" And he said, "Hear thou therefore the word of the LORD: I saw the LORD sitting on his throne, and all the host of heaven standing by him on his right hand and on his left. And the LORD said, 'Who shall persuade Ahab, that he may go up and fall at Ramoth-gilead?' And one said on this manner, and another said on that manner. And there came forth a spirit, and stood before the LORD, and said, 'I will persuade him'. And the LORD said unto him, 'Wherewith?' And he said, 'I will go forth, and I will be a lying spirit in the mouth of all his prophets'. And he said, 'Thou shalt persuade him, and prevail also: go forth, and do so'. Now therefore, behold, the LORD hath put a lying spirit in the mouth of all these thy prophets, and the LORD hath spoken evil concerning thee." But Zedekiah the son of Chenaanah went near, and smote Micaiah on the cheek, and said, "Which way went the spirit of the LORD from me to speak unto thee?" And Micaiah said, "Behold, thou shalt see in that day, when thou shalt go into an inner chamber to hide thyself". And the king of Israel said, "Take Micaiah, and carry him back unto Amon the governor of the city, and to Joash the king's son; and say, 'Thus saith the king, Put this fellow in the prison, and feed him with bread of affliction and with water of affliction, until I come in peace'". And Micaiah said, "If thou return at all in peace, the LORD hath not spoken by me". And he said, "Hearken, O people, every one of you".   [22:15–28]

The Death of Ahab.   So the king of Israel and Jehoshaphat the king of Judah went up to Ramoth-gilead. And the king of Israel said unto Jehoshaphat, "I will disguise myself, and enter into the battle; but put thou on thy robes". And the king of Israel disguised himself, and went into the battle. But the king of Syria commanded his thirty and two captains that had rule over his chariots, saying, "Fight neither with small nor great, save only with the king of Israel". And it came to pass, when the captains of the chariots saw Jehoshaphat, that they said, "Surely it is the king of Israel". And they turned aside to fight against him: and Jehoshaphat cried out. And it came to pass, when the captains of the chariots perceived that it was not the king of Israel, that they turned back from pursuing him. And a certain man drew a bow at a venture, and smote the king of Israel between the joints of the harness: wherefore he said unto the driver of his chariot, "Turn thine hand, and carry me out of the host; for I am wounded". And the battle increased that day: and the king was stayed up in his chariot against the Syrians, and died at even: and the blood ran out of the wound into the midst of the chariot. And there went a proclamation throughout the host about the going down of the sun, saying, "Every man to his city, and every man to his own country". So the king died, and

was brought to Samaria; and they buried the king in
Samaria. And one washed the chariot in the pool of
Samaria; and the dogs licked up his blood; and they
washed his armour; according unto the word of the LORD
which he spake. Now the rest of the acts of Ahab, and all
that he did, and the ivory house which he made, and all
the cities that he built, are they not written in the book of
the chronicles of the kings of Israel? So Ahab slept with
his fathers; and Ahaziah his son reigned in his stead.

[22:29–40]

From THE SECOND BOOK OF THE KINGS

Elijah and Elisha. And it came to pass, when the LORD would take up Elijah into heaven by a whirlwind, that Elijah went with Elisha from Gilgal. And Elijah said unto Elisha, "Tarry here, I pray thee; for the LORD hath sent me to Beth-el". And Elisha said unto him, "As the LORD liveth, and as thy soul liveth, I will not leave thee". So they went down to Beth-el. And the sons of the prophets that were at Beth-el came forth to Elisha, and said unto him, "Knowest thou that the LORD will take away thy master from thy head to day?" And he said, "Yea, I know it; hold ye your peace". And Elijah said unto him, "Elisha, tarry here, I pray thee; for the LORD hath sent me to Jericho". And he said, "As the LORD liveth, and as thy soul liveth, I will not leave thee". So they came to Jericho. And the sons of the prophets that were at Jericho came to Elisha, and said unto him, "Knowest thou that the LORD will take away thy master from thy head to day?" And he answered, "Yea, I know it; hold ye your peace". And Elijah said unto him, "Tarry, I pray thee, here; for the LORD hath sent me to Jordan". And he said, "As the LORD liveth, and as thy soul liveth, I will not leave thee". And they two went on. And fifty men of the sons of the prophets went, and stood to view afar off: and they two stood by Jordan. And Elijah took his mantle, and wrapped it together, and smote the waters, and they were divided hither and thither, so that they two went over on dry ground. And it came to pass, when they were gone over, that Elijah said unto Elisha, "Ask what I shall do for thee,

before I be taken away from thee". And Elisha said, "I
pray thee, let a double portion of thy spirit be upon me".
And he said, "Thou hast asked a hard thing: nevertheless,
if thou see me when I am taken from thee, it shall be so
unto thee; but if not, it shall not be so".   [2:1–10]

Elijah Carried into Heaven. And it came to pass, as
they still went on, and talked, that, behold, there appeared
a chariot of fire, and horses of fire, and parted them both
asunder; and Elijah went up by a whirlwind into heaven.
And Elisha saw it, and he cried, "My father, my father,
the chariot of Israel, and the horsemen thereof". And he
saw him no more: and he took hold of his own clothes,
and rent them in two pieces. He took up also the mantle
of Elijah that fell from him, and went back, and stood by
the bank of Jordan; and he took the mantle of Elijah that
fell from him, and smote the waters, and said, "Where is
the LORD God of Elijah?" and when he also had smitten
the waters, they parted hither and thither: and Elisha went
over. And when the sons of the prophets which were to
view at Jericho saw him, they said, "The spirit of Elijah
doth rest on Elisha". And they came to meet him, and
bowed themselves to the ground before him. And they said
unto him, "Behold now, there be with thy servants fifty
strong men; let them go, we pray thee, and seek thy master:
lest peradventure the spirit of the LORD hath taken him
up, and cast him upon some mountain, or into some valley". And he said, "Ye shall not send". And when they
urged him till he was ashamed, he said, "Send". They sent
therefore fifty men; and they sought three days, but found
him not. And when they came again to him, (for he tarried
at Jericho,) he said unto them, "Did I not say unto you,
Go not?"

And the men of the city said unto Elisha, "Behold, I
pray thee, the situation of this city is pleasant, as my lord
seeth: but the water is naught, and the ground barren".
And he said, "Bring me a new cruse, and put salt therein".
And they brought it to him. And he went forth unto the

spring of the waters, and cast the salt in there, and said, "Thus saith the LORD, 'I have healed these waters; there shall not be from thence any more death or barren land'". So the waters were healed unto this day, according to the saying of Elisha which he spake. [2:11–22]

Elisha Mocked. And he went up from thence unto Beth-el: and as he was going up by the way, there came forth little children out of the city, and mocked him, and said unto him, "Go up, thou bald head; go up, thou bald head". And he turned back, and looked on them, and cursed them in the name of the LORD. And there came forth two she bears out of the wood, and tare forty and two children of them. And he went from thence to mount Carmel, and from thence he returned to Samaria.

[2:23–25]

Elisha and the Poor Woman. Now there cried a certain woman of the wives of the sons of the prophets unto Elisha, saying, "Thy servant my husband is dead; and thou knowest that thy servant did fear the LORD: and the creditor is come to take unto him my two sons to be bondmen". And Elisha said unto her, "What shall I do for thee? tell me, what hast thou in the house?" And she said, "Thine handmaid hath not any thing in the house, save a pot of oil". Then he said, "Go, borrow thee vessels abroad of all thy neighbours, even empty vessels; borrow not a few. And when thou art come in, thou shalt shut the door upon thee and upon thy sons, and shalt pour out into all those vessels, and thou shalt set aside that which is full." So she went from him, and shut the door upon her and upon her sons, who brought the vessels to her; and she poured out. And it came to pass, when the vessels were full, that she said unto her son, "Bring me yet a vessel". And he said unto her, "There is not a vessel more". And the oil stayed. Then she came and told the man of God. And he said, "Go, sell the oil, and pay thy debt, and live thou and thy children of the rest". [4:1–7]

Elisha and the Widow of Shunem. And it fell on a day, that Elisha passed to Shunem, where was a great woman; and she constrained him to eat bread. And so it was, that as oft as he passed by, he turned in thither to eat bread. And she said unto her husband, "Behold now, I perceive that this is an holy man of God, which passeth by us continually. Let us make a little chamber, I pray thee, on the wall; and let us set for him there a bed, and a table, and a stool, and a candlestick: and it shall be, when he cometh to us, that he shall turn in thither." And it fell on a day, that he came thither, and he turned into the chamber, and lay there. And he said to Gehazi his servant, "Call this Shunammite". And when he had called her, she stood before him. And he said unto him, "Say now unto her, 'Behold, thou hast been careful for us with all this care; what is to be done for thee? wouldest thou be spoken for to the king, or to the captain of the host?'" And she answered, "I dwell among mine own people". And he said, "What then is to be done for her?" And Gehazi answered, "Verily she hath no child, and her husband is old". And he said, "Call her". And when he had called her, she stood in the door. And he said, "About this season, according to the time of life, thou shalt embrace a son". And she said, "Nay, my lord, thou man of God, do not lie unto thine handmaid". And the woman conceived, and bare a son at that season that Elisha had said unto her, according to the time of life. And when the child was grown, it fell on a day, that he went out to his father to the reapers. And he said unto his father, "My head, my head". And he said to a lad, "Carry him to his mother". And when he had taken him, and brought him to his mother, he sat on her knees till noon, and then died. And she went up, and laid him on the bed of the man of God, and shut the door upon him, and went out. And she called unto her husband, and said, "Send me, I pray thee, one of the young men, and one of the asses, that I may run to the man of God, and come again". And he said, "Wherefore wilt thou go to him to day? it is neither new moon, nor sabbath". And she said, "It shall be well". Then she saddled an ass, and said to her servant, "Drive, and go forward; slack not thy riding for me, except I bid thee". So she went and came unto the man of God to mount Carmel. And it came to pass, when the man of God saw her afar off, that he said to Gehazi his servant, "Behold, yonder is that Shunammite: run now, I pray thee, to meet her, and say unto her, 'Is it well with thee? is it well with thy husband? is it well with the child?'" And she answered, "It is well". And when she came to the man of God to the hill, she caught him by the feet: but Gehazi came near to thrust her away. And the man of God said, "Let her alone; for her soul is vexed within her: and the LORD hath hid it from me, and hath not told me". Then she said, "Did I desire a son of my lord? did I not say, Do not deceive me?" Then he said to Gehazi, "Gird up thy loins, and take my staff in thine hand, and go thy way: if thou meet any man, salute him not; and if any salute thee, answer him not again: and lay my staff upon the face of the child". And the mother of the child said, "As the LORD liveth, and as thy soul liveth, I will not leave thee". And he arose, and followed her. And Gehazi passed on before them, and laid the staff upon the face of the child; but there was neither voice, nor hearing. Wherefore he went again to meet him, and told him, saying, "The child is not awaked". [4:8-31]

Elisha Restores the Shunammite's Child to Life. And when Elisha was come into the house, behold, the child was dead, and laid upon his bed. He went in therefore, and shut the door upon them twain, and prayed unto the LORD. And he went up, and lay upon the child, and put his mouth upon his mouth, and his eyes upon his eyes, and his hands upon his hands: and he stretched himself upon the child; and the flesh of the child waxed warm. Then he returned, and walked in the house to and fro; and went up, and stretched himself upon him: and the child sneezed seven times, and the child opened his eyes. And he called

Gehazi, and said, "Call this Shunammite". So he called her. And when she was come in unto him, he said, "Take up thy son". Then she went in, and fell at his feet, and bowed herself to the ground, and took up her son, and went out. [4:32–37]

Elisha and the Poisoned Pottage. And Elisha came again to Gilgal: and there was a dearth in the land; and the sons of the prophets were sitting before him: and he said unto his servant, "Set on the great pot, and seethe pottage for the sons of the prophets". And one went out into the field to gather herbs, and found a wild vine, and gathered thereof wild gourds his lap full, and came and shred them into the pot of pottage: for they knew them not. So they poured out for the men to eat. And it came to pass, as they were eating of the pottage, that they cried out, and said, "O thou man of God, there is death in the pot". And they could not eat thereof. But he said, "Then bring meal". And he cast it into the pot; and he said, "Pour out for the people, that they may eat". And there was no harm in the pot.

And there came a man from Baal-shalisha, and brought the man of God bread of the firstfruits, twenty loaves of barley, and full ears of corn in the husk thereof. And he said, "Give unto the people, that they may eat". And his servitor said, "What, should I set this before an hundred men?" He said again, "Give the people, that they may eat: for thus saith the LORD, 'They shall eat, and shall leave thereof' ". So he set it before them, and they did eat, and left thereof, according to the word of the LORD.

[4:38–44]

The Leprosy of Naaman the Syrian. Now Naaman, captain of the host of the king of Syria, was a great man with his master, and honourable, because by him the LORD had given deliverance unto Syria: he was also a mighty man in valour, but he was a leper. And the Syrians had gone out by companies, and had brought away captive out of the land of Israel a little maid; and she waited on

Naaman's wife. And she said unto her mistress, "Would God my lord were with the prophet that is in Samaria! for he would recover him of his leprosy". And one went in, and told his lord, saying, "Thus and thus said the maid that is of the land of Israel". And the king of Syria said, "Go to, go, and I will send a letter unto the king of Israel". And he departed, and took with him ten talents of silver, and six thousand pieces of gold, and ten changes of raiment. And he brought the letter to the king of Israel, saying, "Now when this letter is come unto thee, behold, I have therewith sent Naaman my servant to thee, that thou mayest recover him of his leprosy". And it came to pass, when the king of Israel had read the letter, that he rent his clothes, and said, "Am I God, to kill and to make alive, that this man doth send unto me to recover a man of his leprosy? wherefore consider, I pray you, and see how he seeketh a quarrel against me".

And it was so, when Elisha the man of God had heard that the king of Israel had rent his clothes, that he sent to the king, saying, "Wherefore hast thou rent thy clothes? let him come now to me, and he shall know that there is a prophet in Israel". So Naaman came with his horses and with his chariot, and stood at the door of the house of Elisha. And Elisha sent a messenger unto him, saying, "Go and wash in Jordan seven times, and thy flesh shall come again to thee, and thou shalt be clean". But Naaman was wroth, and went away, and said, "Behold, I thought, He will surely come out to me, and stand, and call on the name of the LORD his God, and strike his hand over the place, and recover the leper. Are not Abana and Pharpar, rivers of Damascus, better than all the waters of Israel? may I not wash in them, and be clean?" So he turned and went away in a rage. And his servants came near, and spake unto him, and said, "My father, if the prophet had bid thee do some great thing, wouldest thou not have done it? how much rather then, when he saith to thee, 'Wash, and be clean'?" [5:1–13]

Naaman Healed. Then went he down, and dipped himself seven times in Jordan, according to the saying of the man of God: and his flesh came again like unto the flesh of a little child, and he was clean. And he returned to the man of God, he and all his company, and came, and stood before him: and he said, "Behold, now I know that there is no God in all the earth, but in Israel: now therefore, I pray thee, take a blessing of thy servant". But he said, "As the LORD liveth, before whom I stand, I will receive none". And he urged him to take it; but he refused. And Naaman said, "Shall there not then, I pray thee, be given to thy servant two mules' burden of earth? for thy servant will henceforth offer neither burnt offering nor sacrifice unto other gods, but unto the LORD. In this thing the LORD pardon thy servant, that when my master goeth into the house of Rimmon to worship there, and he leaneth on my hand, and I bow myself in the house of Rimmon: when I bow down myself in the house of Rimmon, the LORD pardon thy servant in this thing." And he said unto him, "Go in peace". So he departed from him a little way. [5:14–19]

Gehazi Punished. But Gehazi, the servant of Elisha the man of God, said, "Behold, my master hath spared Naaman this Syrian, in not receiving at his hands that which he brought: but, as the LORD liveth, I will run after him, and take somewhat of him". So Gehazi followed after Naaman. And when Naaman saw him running after him, he lighted down from the chariot to meet him, and said, "Is all well?" And he said, "All is well. My master hath sent me, saying, 'Behold, even now there be come to me from mount Ephraim two young men of the sons of the prophets: give them, I pray thee, a talent of silver, and two changes of garments'." And Naaman said, "Be content, take two talents". And he urged him, and bound two talents of silver in two bags, with two changes of garments, and laid them upon two of his servants; and they bare them before him. And when he came to the tower, he took them from their hand, and bestowed them in the house: and he let the men go, and they departed. But he went in, and stood before his master. And Elisha said unto him, "Whence comest thou, Gehazi?" And he said, "Thy servant went no whither". And he said unto him, "Went not mine heart with thee, when the man turned again from his chariot to meet thee? Is it a time to receive money, and to receive garments, and oliveyards, and vineyards, and sheep, and oxen, and menservants, and maidservants? The leprosy therefore of Naaman shall cleave unto thee, and unto thy seed for ever." And he went out from his presence a leper as white as snow.   [5:20–27]

Samaria Besieged. And it came to pass after this, that Ben-hadad king of Syria gathered all his host, and went up, and besieged Samaria. And there was a great famine in Samaria: and, behold, they besieged it, until an ass's head was sold for fourscore pieces of silver, and the fourth part of a cab of dove's dung for five pieces of silver. And as the king of Israel was passing by upon the wall, there cried a woman unto him, saying, "Help, my lord, O king". And he said, "If the Lord do not help thee, whence shall I help thee? out of the barnfloor, or out of the winepress?" And the king said unto her, "What aileth thee?" And she answered, "This woman said unto me, 'Give thy son, that we may eat him to day, and we will eat my son to morrow'. So we boiled my son, and did eat him: and I said unto her on the next day, Give thy son, that we may eat him: and she hath hid her son." And it came to pass, when the king heard the words of the woman, that he rent his clothes; and he passed by upon the wall, and the people looked, and, behold, he had sackcloth within upon his flesh. Then he said, "God do so and more also to me, if the head of Elisha the son of Shaphat shall stand on him this day". But Elisha sat in his house, and the elders sat with him; and the king sent a man from before him: but ere the messenger came to him, he said to the elders, "See ye how this son of a murderer hath sent to take away mine head? look, when the messenger cometh, shut the door, and hold him fast at the door: is not the sound of his master's feet behind him?" And while he yet talked with them, behold, the messenger came down unto him: and he said, "Behold, this evil is of the LORD; what should I wait for the LORD any longer?"   [6:24–33]

Elisha's Prophecy. Then Elisha said, "Hear ye the word of the LORD; 'Thus saith the LORD, To morrow about this time shall a measure of fine flour be sold for a shekel, and two measures of barley for a shekel, in the gate of Samaria'". Then a lord on whose hand the king leaned answered the man of God, and said, "Behold, if the LORD would make windows in heaven, might this thing be?" And he said, "Behold, thou shalt see it with thine eyes, but shalt not eat thereof".   [7:1–2]

The Prophecy Fulfilled. And there were four leprous men at the entering in of the gate: and they said one to another, "Why sit we here until we die? If we say, We will enter into the city, then the famine is in the city, and we shall die there: and if we sit still here, we die also. Now therefore come, and let us fall unto the host of the Syrians: if they save us alive, we shall live; and if they kill us, we shall but die." And they rose up in the twilight, to go unto the camp of the Syrians: and when they were come to the uttermost part of the camp of Syria, behold, there was no man there. For the Lord had made the host of the Syrians to hear a noise of chariots, and a noise of horses, even the noise of a great host: and they said one to another, "Lo, the king of Israel hath hired against us the kings of the Hittites, and the kings of the Egyptians, to come upon us". Wherefore they arose and fled in the twilight, and left their tents, and their horses, and their asses, even the camp as it was, and fled for their life. And when these lepers came to the uttermost part of the camp, they went into one tent, and did eat and drink, and carried thence silver, and gold, and raiment, and went and hid it; and came again, and entered into another tent, and carried thence also, and went and hid it. Then they said one to another, "We do not well: this day is a day of good tidings, and we hold our peace: if we tarry till the morning light, some mischief will come upon us: now therefore come, that we may go and tell the king's household". So they came and called unto the porter of the city: and they told them, saying, "We came to the camp of the Syrians, and, behold, there was no man there, neither voice of man, but horses tied, and asses tied, and the tents as they were". And he called the porters; and they told it to the king's house within. And the king arose in the night, and said unto his servants, "I will now shew you what the Syrians have done to us. They know that we be hungry; therefore are they gone out of the camp to hide themselves in the field, saying, 'When they come out of the city, we shall catch them alive, and get into the city'." And one of his servants answered and said, "Let some take, I pray thee, five of the horses that remain, which are left in the city, (behold, they are as all the multitude of Israel that are left in it: behold, I say, they are even as all the multitude of the Israelites that are consumed:) and let us send and see". They took therefore two chariot horses; and the king sent after the host of the Syrians, saying, "Go and see". And they went after them unto Jordan: and, lo, all the way was full of garments and vessels, which the Syrians had cast away in their haste. And the messengers returned, and told the king. And the people went out, and spoiled the tents of the Syrians. So a measure of fine flour was sold for a shekel, and two measures of barley for a shekel, according to the word of the LORD. And the king appointed the lord on whose hand he leaned to have the charge of the gate: and the people trode upon him in the gate, and he died, as the man of God had said, who spake when the king came down to him. And it came to pass as the man of God had spoken to the king, saying, "Two measures of barley for a shekel, and a measure of fine flour for a shekel, shall be to morrow about this time in the gate of Samaria":

and that lord answered the man of God, and said, "Now, behold, if the LORD should make windows in heaven, might such a thing be?" And he said, "Behold, thou shalt see it with thine eyes, but shalt not eat thereof". And so it fell out unto him: for the people trode upon him in the gate, and he died.   [7:3–20]

Jehu Anointed King of Israel. And Elisha the prophet called one of the children of the prophets, and said unto him, "Gird up thy loins, and take this box of oil in thine hand, and go to Ramoth-gilead: and when thou comest thither, look out there Jehu the son of Jehoshaphat the son of Nimshi, and go in, and make him arise up from among his brethren, and carry him to an inner chamber; then take the box of oil, and pour it on his head, and say, 'Thus saith the LORD, I have anointed thee king over Israel'. Then open the door, and flee, and tarry not." So the young man, even the young man the prophet, went to Ramoth-gilead. And when he came, behold, the captains of the host were sitting; and he said, "I have an errand to thee, O captain". And Jehu said, "Unto which of all us?" And he said, "To thee, O captain". And he arose, and went into the house; and he poured the oil on his head, and said unto him, "Thus saith the LORD God of Israel, 'I have anointed thee king over the people of the LORD, even over Israel. And thou shalt smite the house of Ahab thy master, that I may avenge the blood of my servants the prophets, and the blood of all the servants of the LORD, at the hand of Jezebel. For the whole house of Ahab shall perish: and I will cut off from Ahab him that pisseth against the wall, and him that is shut up and left in Israel: and I will make the house of Ahab like the house of Jeroboam the son of Nebat, and like the house of Baasha the son of Ahijah: and the dogs shall eat Jezebel in the portion of Jezreel, and there shall be none to bury her.'" And he opened the door, and fled. Then Jehu came forth to the servants of his lord: and one said unto him, "Is all well? wherefore came this mad fellow to thee?" And he said unto them, "Ye know the man, and his communication". And they said, "It is false; tell us now". And he said, "Thus and thus spake he to me, saying, 'Thus saith the LORD, I have anointed thee king over Israel'". Then they hasted, and took every man his garment, and put it under him on the top of the stairs, and blew with trumpets, saying, "Jehu is king". So Jehu the son of Jehoshaphat the son of Nimshi conspired against Joram. (Now Joram had kept Ramoth-gilead, he and all Israel, because of Hazael king of Syria. But king Joram was returned to be healed in Jezreel of the wounds which the Syrians had given him, when he fought with Hazael king of Syria.) And Jehu said, "If it be your minds, then let none go forth nor escape out of the city to go to tell it in Jezreel". So Jehu rode in a chariot, and went to Jezreel; for Joram lay there. And Ahaziah king of Judah was come down to see Joram. And there stood a watchman on the tower in Jezreel, and he spied the company of Jehu as he came, and said, "I see a company". And Joram said, "Take an horseman, and send to meet them, and let him say, 'Is it peace?'" So there went one on horseback to meet him, and said, "Thus saith the king, 'Is it peace?'" And Jehu said, "What hast thou to do with peace? turn thee behind me". And the watchman told, saying, "The messenger came to them, but he cometh not again". Then he sent out a second on horseback, which came to them, and said, "Thus saith the king, 'Is it peace?'" And Jehu answered, "What hast thou to do with peace? turn thee behind me". And the watchman told, saying, "He came even unto them, and cometh not again: and the driving is like the driving of Jehu the son of Nimshi; for he driveth furiously". And Joram said, "Make ready". And his chariot was made ready. And Joram king of Israel and Ahaziah king of Judah went out, each in his chariot, and they went out against Jehu, and met him in the portion of Naboth the Jezreelite. And it came to pass, when Joram saw Jehu, that he said, "Is it peace, Jehu?" And he answered, "What peace, so long as

the whoredoms of thy mother Jezebel and her witchcrafts
are so many?"   [9:1–22]

Jehu Victorious. And Joram turned his hands, and
fled, and said to Ahaziah, "There is treachery, O Ahaziah".
And Jehu drew a bow with his full strength, and smote
Jehoram between his arms, and the arrow went out at his
heart, and he sunk down in his chariot. Then said Jehu to
Bidkar his captain, "Take up, and cast him in the portion of
the field of Naboth the Jezreelite: for remember how that,
when I and thou rode together after Ahab his father, the
LORD laid this burden upon him; 'Surely I have seen yesterday the blood of Naboth, and the blood of his sons,' saith
the LORD; 'and I will requite thee in this plat,' saith the
LORD. Now therefore take and cast him into the plat of
ground, according to the word of the LORD." But when
Ahaziah the king of Judah saw this, he fled by the way of
the garden house. And Jehu followed after him, and said,
"Smite him also in the chariot". And they did so at the
going up to Gur, which is by Ibleam. And he fled to
Megiddo, and died there. And his servants carried him
in a chariot to Jerusalem, and buried him in his sepulchre
with his fathers in the city of David.

And in the eleventh year of Joram the son of Ahab
began Ahaziah to reign over Judah.   [9:23–29]

The End of Jezebel. And when Jehu was come to
Jezreel, Jezebel heard of it; and she painted her face, and
tired her head, and looked out at a window. And as Jehu
entered in at the gate, she said, "Had Zimri peace, who
slew his master?" And he lifted up his face to the window,
and said, "Who is on my side? who?" And there looked
out to him two or three eunuchs. And he said, "Throw her
down". So they threw her down: and some of her blood
was sprinkled on the wall, and on the horses: and he trode
her under foot. And when he was come in, he did eat and
drink, and said, "Go, see now this cursed woman, and
bury her: for she is a king's daughter". And they went to
bury her: but they found no more of her than the skull,

and the feet, and the palms of her hands. Wherefore they came again, and told him. And he said, "This is the word of the Lord, which he spake by his servant Elijah the Tishbite, saying, 'In the portion of Jezreel shall dogs eat the flesh of Jezebel: and the carcase of Jezebel shall be as dung upon the face of the field in the portion of Jezreel; so that they shall not say, This is Jezebel'".   [9:30–37]

The Death of Elisha. Now Elisha was fallen sick of his sickness whereof he died. And Joash the king of Israel came down unto him, and wept over his face, and said, "O my father, my father, the chariot of Israel, and the horsemen thereof". And Elisha said unto him, "Take bow and arrows". And he took unto him bow and arrows. And he said to the king of Israel, "Put thine hand upon the bow". And he put his hand upon it: and Elisha put his hands upon the king's hands. And he said, "Open the window eastward". And he opened it. Then Elisha said, "Shoot". And he shot. And he said, "The arrow of the Lord's deliverance, and the arrow of deliverance from Syria: for thou shalt smite the Syrians in Aphek, till thou have consumed them". And he said, "Take the arrows". And he took them. And he said unto the king of Israel, "Smite upon the ground". And he smote thrice, and stayed. And the man of God was wroth with him, and said, "Thou shouldest have smitten five or six times; then hadst thou smitten Syria till thou hadst consumed it: whereas now thou shalt smite Syria but thrice".

And Elisha died, and they buried him. And the bands of the Moabites invaded the land at the coming in of the year. And it came to pass, as they were burying a man, that, behold, they spied a band of men; and they cast the man into the sepulchre of Elisha: and when the man was let down, and touched the bones of Elisha, he revived, and stood up on his feet.   [13:14–21]

The End of the Kingdom of Israel. In the twelfth year of Ahaz king of Judah began Hoshea the son of Elah to reign in Samaria over Israel nine years. And he did that which was evil in the sight of the LORD, but not as the kings of Israel that were before him. Against him came up Shalmaneser king of Assyria; and Hoshea became his servant, and gave him presents. And the king of Assyria found conspiracy in Hoshea: for he had sent messengers to So king of Egypt, and brought no present to the king of Assyria, as he had done year by year: therefore the king of Assyria shut him up, and bound him in prison. Then the king of Assyria came up throughout all the land, and went up to Samaria, and besieged it three years. In the ninth year of Hoshea the king of Assyria took Samaria, and carried Israel away into Assyria, and placed them in Halah and in Habor by the river of Gozan, and in the cities of the Medes. For so it was, that the children of Israel had sinned against the LORD their God, which had brought them up out of the land of Egypt, from under the hand of Pharaoh king of Egypt, and had feared other gods, and walked in the statutes of the heathen, whom the LORD cast out from before the children of Israel, and of the kings of Israel, which they had made. And the children of Israel did secretly those things that were not right against the LORD their God, and they built them high places in all their cities, from the tower of the watchmen to the fenced city. And they set them up images and groves in every high hill, and under every green tree: and there they burnt incense in all the high places, as did the heathen whom the LORD carried away before them; and wrought wicked things to provoke the LORD to anger: for they served idols, whereof the LORD had said unto them, "Ye shall not do this thing". Yet the LORD testified against Israel, and against Judah, by all the prophets, and by all the seers, saying, "Turn ye from your evil ways, and keep my commandments and my statutes, according to all the law which I commanded your fathers, and which I sent to you by my servants the prophets". Notwithstanding they would not hear, but hardened their necks, like to the neck of their fathers, that did not believe in the LORD their God.

And they rejected his statutes, and his covenant that he made with their fathers, and his testimonies which he testified against them; and they followed vanity, and became vain, and went after the heathen that were round about them, concerning whom the LORD had charged them, that they should not do like them. And they left all the commandments of the LORD their God, and made them molten images, even two calves, and made a grove, and worshipped all the host of heaven, and served Baal. And they caused their sons and their daughters to pass through the fire, and used divination and enchantments, and sold themselves to do evil in the sight of the LORD, to provoke him to anger. [17:1-17]

The Israelites Carried Away. Therefore the LORD was very angry with Israel, and removed them out of his sight: there was none left but the tribe of Judah only. Also Judah kept not the commandments of the LORD their God, but walked in the statutes of Israel which they made. And the LORD rejected all the seed of Israel, and afflicted them, and delivered them into the hand of spoilers, until he had cast them out of his sight. For he rent Israel from the house of David; and they made Jeroboam the son of Nebat king: and Jeroboam drave Israel from following the LORD, and made them sin a great sin. For the children of Israel walked in all the sins of Jeroboam which he did; they departed not from them; until the LORD removed Israel out of his sight, as he had said by all his servants the prophets. So was Israel carried away out of their own land to Assyria unto this day. [17:18-23]

Strangers Occupy Samaria. And the king of Assyria brought men from Babylon, and from Cuthah, and from Ava, and from Hamath, and from Sepharvaim, and placed them in the cities of Samaria instead of the children of Israel: and they possessed Samaria, and dwelt in the cities thereof. And so it was at the beginning of their dwelling there, that they feared not the LORD: therefore the LORD sent lions among them, which slew some of them. Where-

fore they spake to the king of Assyria, saying, "The nations which thou hast removed, and placed in the cities of
Samaria, know not the manner of the God of the land:
therefore he hath sent lions among them, and, behold, they
slay them, because they know not the manner of the God
of the land". Then the king of Assyria commanded,
saying, "Carry thither one of the priests whom ye brought
from thence; and let them go and dwell there, and let
him teach them the manner of the God of the land". Then
one of the priests whom they had carried away from Samaria came and dwelt in Beth-el, and taught them how
they should fear the LORD. Howbeit every nation made
gods of their own, and put them in the houses of the high
places which the Samaritans had made, every nation in
their cities wherein they dwelt. And the men of Babylon
made Succoth-benoth, and the men of Cuth made Nergal,
and the men of Hamath made Ashima, and the Avites
made Nibhaz and Tartak, and the Sepharvites burnt their
children in fire to Adrammelech and Anammelech, the
gods of Sepharvaim. So they feared the LORD, and made
unto themselves of the lowest of them priests of the high
places, which sacrificed for them in the houses of the high
places. They feared the LORD, and served their own gods,
after the manner of the nations whom they carried away
from thence.   [17:24–33]

The Evil Manners of the Samaritans. Unto this day
they do after the former manners: they fear not the LORD,
neither do they after their statutes, or after their ordinances, or after the law and commandment which the
LORD commanded the children of Jacob, whom he named
Israel; with whom the LORD had made a covenant, and
charged them, saying, "Ye shall not fear other gods, nor
bow yourselves to them, nor serve them, nor sacrifice to
them: but the LORD, who brought you up out of the land
of Egypt with great power and a stretched out arm, him
shall ye fear, and him shall ye worship, and to him shall ye
do sacrifice. And the statutes, and the ordinances, and the

law, and the commandment, which he wrote for you, ye shall observe to do for evermore; and ye shall not fear other gods. And the covenant that I have made with you ye shall not forget; neither shall ye fear other gods. But the LORD your God ye shall fear; and he shall deliver you out of the hand of all your enemies." Howbeit they did not hearken, but they did after their former manner. So these nations feared the LORD, and served their graven images, both their children, and their children's children: as did their fathers, so do they unto this day. [17:34-41]

The End of the Kingdom of Judah. And it came to pass in the ninth year of his reign, in the tenth month, in the tenth day of the month, that Nebuchadnezzar king of Babylon came, he, and all his host, against Jerusalem, and pitched against it; and they built forts against it round about. And the city was besieged unto the eleventh year of king Zedekiah. And on the ninth day of the fourth month the famine prevailed in the city, and there was no bread for the people of the land. And the city was broken up, and all the men of war fled by night by the way of the gate between two walls, which is by the king's garden: (now the Chaldees were against the city round about:) and the king went the way toward the plain. And the army of the Chaldees pursued after the king, and overtook him in the plains of Jericho: and all his army were scattered from him. So they took the king, and brought him up to the king of Babylon to Riblah; and they gave judgment upon him. And they slew the sons of Zedekiah before his eyes, and put out the eyes of Zedekiah, and bound him with fetters of brass, and carried him to Babylon.

[25:1-7]

Jerusalem and the Temple Destroyed. And in the fifth month, on the seventh day of the month, which is the nine-teenth year of king Nebuchadnezzar king of Babylon, came Nebuzar-adan, captain of the guard, a servant of the king of Babylon, unto Jerusalem: and he burnt the house of the

LORD, and the king's house, and all the houses of Jerusalem, and every great man's house burnt he with fire. And all the army of the Chaldees, that were with the captain of the guard, brake down the walls of Jerusalem round about. Now the rest of the people that were left in the city, and the fugitives that fell away to the king of Babylon, with the remnant of the multitude, did Nebuzar-adan the captain of the guard carry away. But the captain of the guard left of the poor of the land to be vinedressers and husbandmen. And the pillars of brass that were in the house of the LORD, and the bases, and the brasen sea that was in the house of the LORD, did the Chaldees break in pieces, and carried the brass of them to Babylon. And the pots, and the shovels, and the snuffers, and the spoons, and all the vessels of brass wherewith they ministered, took they away. And the firepans, and the bowls, and such things as were of gold, in gold, and of silver, in silver, the captain of the guard took away. The two pillars, one sea, and the bases which Solomon had made for the house of the LORD; the brass of all these vessels was without weight. The height of the one pillar was eighteen cubits, and the chapiter upon it was brass: and the height of the chapiter three cubits; and the wreathen work, and pomegranates upon the chapiter round about, all of brass: and like unto these had the second pillar with wreathen work.

And the captain of the guard took Seraiah the chief priest, and Zephaniah the second priest, and the three keepers of the door: and out of the city he took an officer that was set over the men of war, and five men of them that were in the king's presence, which were found in the city, and the principal scribe of the host, which mustered the people of the land, and threescore men of the people of the land that were found in the city: and Nebuzar-adan captain of the guard took these, and brought them to the king of Babylon to Riblah: and the king of Babylon smote them, and slew them at Riblah in the land of Hamath. So

Judah was carried away out of their land. And as for the
people that remained in the land of Judah, whom Nebuchadnezzar king of Babylon had left, even over them he
made Gedaliah the son of Ahikam, the son of Shaphan,
ruler.   [25:8–22]

From THE BOOK OF ESTHER

The Anger of Ahasuerus.   Now it came to pass in the
days of Ahasuerus, (this is Ahasuerus which reigned, from
India even unto Ethiopia, over an hundred and seven and
twenty provinces:) that in those days, when the king
Ahasuerus sat on the throne of his kingdom, which was in
Shushan the palace, in the third year of his reign, he made
a feast unto all his princes and his servants; the power of
Persia and Media, the nobles and princes of the provinces,
being before him: when he shewed the riches of his
glorious kingdom and the honour of his excellent majesty
many days, even an hundred and fourscore days. And
when these days were expired, the king made a feast unto
all the people that were present in Shushan the palace,
both unto great and small, seven days, in the court of the
garden of the king's palace; where were white, green, and
blue, hangings, fastened with cords of fine linen and purple
to silver rings and pillars of marble: the beds were of
gold and silver, upon a pavement of red, and blue, and
white, and black, marble. And they gave them drink in
vessels of gold, (the vessels being diverse one from another,) and royal wine in abundance, according to the
state of the king. And the drinking was according to the
law; none did compel: for so the king had appointed to
all the officers of his house, that they should do according
to every man's pleasure. Also Vashti the queen made a
feast for the women in the royal house which belonged to
king Ahasuerus.   [1:1-9]

[On the seventh day, Ahasuerus sent for Vashti to show

the princes and the people her beauty; but she refused, wherefore the king was very wroth. Then the king sent for his wise men and asked them, "What shall we do unto the queen Vashti according to law?" And they advised him that Vashti should be put away and her royal estate given to another. And after this the king's servants caused fair young virgins to be brought to the palace at Shushan so that the maiden who best pleased the king should be queen instead of Vashti.

Now there was a certain Jew in the palace whose name was Mordecai, who had brought up Esther, his uncle's daughter, for she had no father or mother; and the maiden was very beautiful. Esther also was brought with the other virgins to the palace at Shushan, but she did not show her people or her kindred, for Mordecai had charged her that she should not show them. Now when the turn of Esther came to go unto the king, the king delighted in her.]

Esther Made Queen. And the king loved Esther above all the women, and she obtained grace and favour in his sight more than all the virgins; so that he set the royal crown upon her head, and made her queen instead of Vashti. Then the king made a great feast unto all his princes and his servants, even Esther's feast; and he made a release to the provinces, and gave gifts, according to the state of the king. And when the virgins were gathered together the second time, then Mordecai sat in the king's gate. Esther had not yet shewed her kindred nor her people; as Mordecai had charged her: for Esther did the commandment of Mordecai, like as when she was brought up with him. In those days, while Mordecai sat in the king's gate, two of the king's chamberlains, Bigthan and Teresh, of those which kept the door, were wroth, and sought to lay hand on the king Ahasuerus. And the thing was known to Mordecai, who told it unto Esther the queen; and Esther certified the king thereof in Mordecai's name. And when inquisition was made of the matter, it was found out; therefore they were both hanged on a tree:

and it was written in the book of the chronicles before the
king. [2:17–23]

[After this, king Ahasuerus promoted Haman the son
of Hammedatha and set his seat above all the princes.
And all the king's servants bowed and reverenced Haman,
but Mordecai bowed not nor did him reverence.]

Haman's Hatred of the Jews. And when Haman saw
that Mordecai bowed not, nor did him reverence, then was
Haman full of wrath. And he thought scorn to lay hands
on Mordecai alone; for they had shewed him the people of
Mordecai: wherefore Haman sought to destroy all the
Jews that were throughout the whole kingdom of Ahasuerus, even the people of Mordecai. In the first month, that
is, the month Nisan, in the twelfth year of king Ahasuerus,
they cast Pur, that is, the lot, before Haman from day to
day, and from month to month, to the twelfth month,
that is, the month Adar. And Haman said unto king
Ahasuerus, "There is a certain people scattered abroad
and dispersed among the people in all the provinces of thy
kingdom; and their laws are diverse from all people; neither keep they the king's laws: therefore it is not for the
king's profit to suffer them. If it please the king, let it be
written that they may be destroyed: and I will pay ten
thousand talents of silver to the hands of those that have
the charge of the business, to bring it into the king's
treasuries." And the king took his ring from his hand, and
gave it unto Haman the son of Hammedatha the Agagite,
the Jews' enemy. And the king said unto Haman, "The
silver is given to thee, the people also, to do with them as
it seemeth good to thee". [3:5–11]

[So orders were sent forth into every province that on
the thirteenth day of the twelfth month the Jews, young
and old, little children and women, should all be slain and
their goods taken for a prey. So Mordecai sent to charge
queen Esther that she go in to the king and make supplication unto him for her people. But Esther sent back
answer:]

"All the king's servants, and the people of the king's provinces, do know, that whosoever, whether man or woman, shall come unto the king into the inner court, who is not called, there is one law of his to put him to death, except such to whom the king shall hold out the golden sceptre, that he may live: but I have not been called to come in unto the king these thirty days". And they told to Mordecai Esther's words. Then Mordecai commanded to answer Esther, "Think not with thyself that thou shalt escape in the king's house, more than all the Jews. For if thou altogether holdest thy peace at this time, then shall there enlargement and deliverance arise to the Jews from another place; but thou and thy father's house shall be destroyed: and who knoweth whether thou art come to the kingdom for such a time as this?" Then Esther bade them return Mordecai this answer, "Go, gather together all the Jews that are present in Shushan, and fast ye for me, and neither eat nor drink three days, night or day: I also and my maidens will fast likewise; and so will I go in unto the king, which is not according to the law: and if I perish, I perish". So Mordecai went his way, and did according to all that Esther had commanded him. [4:11–17]

Esther Comes to the King. Now it came to pass on the third day, that Esther put on her royal apparel, and stood in the inner court of the king's house, over against the king's house: and the king sat upon his royal throne in the royal house, over against the gate of the house. And it was so, when the king saw Esther the queen standing in the court, that she obtained favour in his sight: and the king held out to Esther the golden sceptre that was in his hand. So Esther drew near, and touched the top of the sceptre. Then said the king unto her, "What wilt thou, queen Esther? and what is thy request? it shall be even given thee to the half of the kingdom". And Esther answered, "If it seem good unto the king, let the king and Haman come this day unto the banquet that I have prepared for him". Then the king said, "Cause Haman to make haste, that he may do as Esther hath said". So the king and Haman came to the banquet that Esther had prepared. And the king said unto Esther at the banquet of wine, "What is thy petition? and it shall be granted thee: and what is thy request? even to the half of the kingdom it shall be performed". Then answered Esther, and said, "My petition and my request is; If I have found favour in the sight of the king, and if it please the king to grant my petition, and to perform my request, let the king and Haman come to the banquet that I shall prepare for them, and I will do to morrow as the king hath said". Then went Haman forth that day joyful and with a glad heart: but when Haman saw Mordecai in the king's gate, that he stood not up, nor moved for him, he was full of indignation against Mordecai. Nevertheless Haman refrained himself: and when he came home, he sent and called for his friends, and Zeresh his wife. And Haman told them of the glory of his riches, and the multitude of his children, and all the things wherein the king had promoted him, and how he had advanced him above the princes and servants of the king. Haman said moreover, "Yea, Esther the queen did let no man come in with the king unto the banquet that she had prepared but myself; and to morrow am I invited unto her also with the king. Yet all this availeth me nothing, so long as I see Mordecai the Jew sitting at the king's gate." Then said Zeresh his wife and all his friends unto him, "Let a gallows be made of fifty cubits high, and to morrow speak thou unto the king that Mordecai may be hanged thereon: then go thou in merrily with the king unto the banquet". And the thing pleased Haman; and he caused the gallows to be made.   [5:1–14]

The King Honors Mordecai. On that night could not the king sleep, and he commanded to bring the book of records of the chronicles; and they were read before the king. And it was found written, that Mordecai had told of Bigthana and Teresh, two of the king's chamberlains, the keepers of the door, who sought to lay hand on the king Ahasuerus. And the king said, "What honour and dignity hath been done to Mordecai for this?" Then said the king's servants that ministered unto him, "There is nothing done for him". And the king said, "Who is in the court?" Now Haman was come into the outward court of the king's house, to speak unto the king to hang Mordecai on the gallows that he had prepared for him. And the king's servants said unto him, "Behold, Haman standeth in the court". And the king said, "Let him come in". So Haman came in. And the king said unto him, "What shall be done unto the man whom the king delighteth to honour?" Now Haman thought in his heart, "To whom would the king delight to do honour more than to myself?" And Haman answered the king, "For the man whom the king delighteth to honour, let the royal apparel be brought which the king useth to wear, and the horse that the king rideth upon, and the crown royal which is set upon his head: and let this apparel and horse be delivered to the hand of one of the king's most noble princes, that they may array the man withal whom the king delighteth to honour, and bring him on horseback through the street of the city, and proclaim before him, 'Thus shall it be done to the man whom the king delighteth to honour'". Then the king said to Haman, "Make haste, and take the apparel and the horse, as thou hast said, and do even so to Mordecai the Jew, that sitteth at the king's gate: let nothing fail of all that thou hast spoken". Then took Haman the apparel and the horse, and arrayed Mordecai, and brought him on horseback through the street of the city, and proclaimed before him, "Thus shall it be done unto the man whom the king delighteth to honour". And Mordecai came again to the king's gate. But Haman hasted to his house mourning, and having his head covered. And Haman told Zeresh his wife and all his friends every thing that had befallen him. Then said his wise men and Zeresh his wife unto him, "If Mordecai be of the seed of the Jews, before whom thou

hast begun to fall, thou shalt not prevail against him, but shalt surely fall before him". And while they were yet talking with him, came the king's chamberlains, and hasted to bring Haman unto the banquet that Esther had prepared.
[6:1–14]

Haman Hanged on His Own Gallows. So the king and Haman came to banquet with Esther the queen. And the king said again unto Esther on the second day at the banquet of wine, "What is thy petition, queen Esther? and it shall be granted thee: and what is thy request? and it shall be performed, even to the half of the kingdom". Then Esther the queen answered and said, "If I have found favour in thy sight, O king, and if it please the king, let my life be given me at my petition, and my people at my request: for we are sold, I and my people, to be destroyed, to be slain, and to perish. But if we had been sold for bondmen and bondwomen, I had held my tongue, although the enemy could not countervail the king's damage." Then the king Ahasuerus answered and said unto Esther the queen, "Who is he, and where is he, that durst presume in his heart to do so?" And Esther said, "The adversary and enemy is this wicked Haman". Then Haman was afraid before the king and the queen. And the king arising from the banquet of wine in his wrath went into the palace garden: and Haman stood up to make request for his life to Esther the queen; for he saw that there was evil determined against him by the king. Then the king returned out of the palace garden into the place of the banquet of wine; and Haman was fallen upon the bed whereon Esther was. Then said the king, "Will he force the queen also before me in the house?" As the word went out of the king's mouth, they covered Haman's face. And Harbonah, one of the chamberlains, said before the king, "Behold also, the gallows fifty cubits high, which Haman had made for Mordecai, who had spoken good for the king, standeth in the house of Haman". Then the king said, "Hang him thereon". So they hanged Haman on the gallows that he had prepared for Mordecai. Then was the king's wrath pacified.   [7:1–10]

Esther Saves Her People. On that day did the king Ahasuerus give the house of Haman the Jews' enemy unto Esther the queen. And Mordecai came before the king; for Esther had told what he was unto her. And the king took off his ring, which he had taken from Haman, and gave it unto Mordecai. And Esther set Mordecai over the house of Haman. And Esther spake yet again before the king, and fell down at his feet, and besought him with tears to put away the mischief of Haman the Agagite, and his device that he had devised against the Jews. Then the king held out the golden sceptre toward Esther. So Esther arose, and stood before the king, and said, "If it please the king, and if I have found favour in his sight, and the thing seem right before the king, and I be pleasing in his eyes, let it be written to reverse the letters devised by Haman the son of Hammedatha the Agagite, which he wrote to destroy the Jews which are in all the king's provinces: for how can I endure to see the evil that shall come unto my people? or how can I endure to see the destruction of my kindred?" Then the king Ahasuerus said unto Esther the queen and to Mordecai the Jew, "Behold, I have given Esther the house of Haman, and him they have hanged upon the gallows, because he laid his hand upon the Jews. Write ye also for the Jews, as it liketh you, in the king's name, and seal it with the king's ring: for the writing which is written in the king's name, and sealed with the king's ring, may no man reverse."

Then were the king's scribes called at that time in the third month, that is, the month Sivan, on the three and twentieth day thereof; and it was written according to all that Mordecai commanded unto the Jews, and to the lieutenants, and the deputies and rulers of the provinces which are from India unto Ethiopia, an hundred twenty and seven provinces, unto every province according to the writing thereof, and unto every people after their language, and to the Jews according to their writing, and according to their language. And he wrote in the king Ahasuerus' name, and sealed it with the king's ring, and sent letters by posts on horseback, and riders on mules, camels, and young dromedaries: wherein the king granted the Jews which were in every city to gather themselves together, and to stand for their life, to destroy, to slay, and to cause to perish, all the power of the people and province that would assault them, both little ones and women, and to take the spoil of them for a prey, upon one day in all the provinces of king Ahasuerus, namely, upon the thirteenth day of the twelfth month, which is the month Adar. The copy of the writing for a commandment to be given in every province was published unto all people, and that the Jews should be ready against that day to avenge themselves on their enemies. So the posts that rode upon mules and camels went out, being hastened and pressed on by the king's commandment. And the decree was given at Shushan the palace. And Mordecai went out from the presence of the king in royal apparel of blue and white, and with a great crown of gold, and with a garment of fine linen and purple: and the city of Shushan rejoiced and was glad. The Jews had light, and gladness, and joy, and honour. And in every province, and in every city, whithersoever the king's commandment and his decree came, the Jews had joy and gladness, a feast and a good day. And many of the people of the land became Jews; for the fear of the Jews fell upon them.   [8:1–17]

From JOB

The Book of Job is a long poem on the most difficult of theological problems—why God allows a good man to suffer. In the poem Job is reduced to abject misery. His three old friends, Eliphaz, Bildad, and Zophar, come to comfort him. They declare that since suffering is divine punishment for sin, Job must have sinned; but Job is conscious of his innocence, and he wishes to confront God and find the answer. A new speaker, a young man named Elihu, intervenes and blames all the speakers. Then the LORD answers Job, by asking how man can hope to know the mind of the Creator of the Universe. Job is abashed and repents, and is restored to prosperity.

The Sufferings of Job.   There was a man in the land of Uz, whose name was Job; and that man was perfect and upright, and one that feared God, and eschewed evil. And there were born unto him seven sons and three daughters. His substance also was seven thousand sheep, and three thousand camels, and five hundred yoke of oxen, and five hundred she asses, and a very great household; so that this man was the greatest of all the men of the east. And his sons went and feasted in their houses, every one his day; and sent and called for their three sisters to eat and to drink with them. And it was so, when the days of their feasting were gone about, that Job sent and sanctified them, and rose up early in the morning, and offered burnt offerings according to the number of them all: for Job said, "It may be that my sons have sinned, and cursed God in their hearts". Thus did Job continually.

Now there was a day when the sons of God came to present themselves before the LORD, and Satan came also among them. And the LORD said unto Satan, "Whence comest thou?" Then Satan answered the LORD, and said, "From going to and fro in the earth, and from walking up and down in it". And the LORD said unto Satan, "Hast thou considered my servant Job, that there is none like him in the earth, a perfect and an upright man, one that feareth God, and escheweth evil?" Then Satan answered the LORD, and said, "Doth Job fear God for nought? Hast not thou made an hedge about him, and about his house, and about all that he hath on every side? thou hast blessed the work of his hands, and his substance is increased in the land. But put forth thine hand now, and touch all that he hath, and he will curse thee to thy face." And the LORD said unto Satan, "Behold, all that he hath is in thy power; only upon himself put not forth thine hand". So Satan went forth from the presence of the LORD.

And there was a day when his sons and his daughters were eating and drinking wine in their eldest brother's house: and there came a messenger unto Job, and said, "The oxen were plowing, and the asses feeding beside them: and the Sabeans fell upon them, and took them away; yea, they have slain the servants with the edge of the sword; and I only am escaped alone to tell thee". While he was yet speaking, there came also another, and said, "The fire of God is fallen from heaven, and hath burned up the sheep, and the servants, and consumed them; and I only am escaped alone to tell thee". While he was yet speaking, there came also another, and said, "The Chaldeans made out three bands, and fell upon the camels, and have carried them away, yea, and slain the servants with the edge of the sword; and I only am escaped alone to tell thee". While he was yet speaking, there came also another, and said, "Thy sons and thy daughters were eating and drinking wine in their eldest brother's house: and, behold, there came a great wind from the wilderness, and smote the four corners of the house, and it fell upon the young men, and they are dead; and I only am escaped alone to tell thee". Then Job arose, and rent his mantle, and shaved his head, and fell down upon the ground, and worshipped, and said,

> "Naked came I out of my mother's womb,
> And naked shall I return thither:
> The LORD gave, and the LORD hath taken away;
> Blessed be the name of the LORD".

In all this Job sinned not, nor charged God foolishly.

[1:1–22]

Job's Sorrows Increased. Again there was a day when the sons of God came to present themselves before the LORD, and Satan came also among them to present himself before the LORD. And the LORD said unto Satan, "From whence comest thou?" And Satan answered the LORD, and said, "From going to and fro in the earth, and from walking up and down in it". And the LORD said unto Satan, "Hast thou considered my servant Job, that there is none like him in the earth, a perfect and an upright man, one that feareth God, and escheweth evil? and still he holdeth fast his integrity, although thou movedst me against him, to destroy him without cause". And Satan answered the LORD, and said, "Skin for skin, yea, all that a man hath will he give for his life. But put forth thine hand now, and touch his bone and his flesh, and he will curse thee to thy face." And the LORD said unto Satan, "Behold, he is in thine hand; but save his life". So went Satan forth from the presence of the LORD, and smote Job with sore boils from the sole of his foot unto his crown. And he took him a potsherd to scrape himself withal; and he sat down among the ashes. Then said his wife unto him, "Dost thou still retain thine integrity? curse God, and die". But he said unto her, "Thou speakest as one of the foolish women speaketh. What? shall we receive good at the hand of God, and shall we not receive evil?" In all this did not Job sin with his lips.   [2:1–10]

Job's Comforters. Now when Job's three friends heard of all this evil that was come upon him, they came every one from his own place; Eliphaz the Temanite, and Bildad the Shuhite, and Zophar the Naamathite: for they had made an appointment together to come to mourn with him and to comfort him. And when they lifted up their eyes afar off, and knew him not, they lifted up their voice, and wept; and they rent every one his mantle, and sprinkled dust upon their heads toward heaven. So they sat down with him upon the ground seven days and seven nights, and none spake a word unto him: for they saw that his grief was very great.   [2:11–13]

The Lamentation of Job. After this opened Job his mouth, and cursed his day. And Job spake, and said,

"Let the day perish wherein I was born,
    And the night in which it was said, 'There is a man
        child conceived'.
    Let that day be darkness;
    Let not God regard it from above,
    Neither let the light shine upon it.
    Let darkness and the shadow of death stain it;
    Let a cloud dwell upon it;
    Let the blackness of the day terrify it.
    As for that night, let darkness seize upon it;
    Let it not be joined unto the days of the year,
    Let it not come into the number of the months.
    Lo, let that night be solitary,
    Let no joyful voice come therein.
    Let them curse it that curse the day,
    Who are ready to raise up their mourning.
    Let the stars of the twilight thereof be dark;
    Let it look for light, but have none;

Neither let it see the dawning of the day:

Because it shut not up the doors of my mother's womb,

Nor hid sorrow from mine eyes.

Why died I not from the womb?

Why did I not give up the ghost when I came out of the belly?

Why did the knees prevent me?

Or why the breasts that I should suck?

For now should I have lain still and been quiet,

I should have slept: then had I been at rest,

With kings and counsellors of the earth,

Which built desolate places for themselves;

Or with princes that had gold,

Who filled their houses with silver:

Or as an hidden untimely birth I had not been;

As infants which never saw light.

There the wicked cease from troubling;

And there the weary be at rest.

There the prisoners rest together;

They hear not the voice of the oppressor.

The small and great are there;

And the servant is free from his master.

Wherefore is light given to him that is in misery,

And life unto the bitter in soul;

Which long for death, but it cometh not;

And dig for it more than for hid treasures;

Which rejoice exceedingly,

And are glad, when they can find the grave?

Why is light given to a man whose way is hid,

And whom God hath hedged in?

For my sighing cometh before I eat,

And my roarings are poured out like the waters.

For the thing which I greatly feared is come upon me,

And that which I was afraid of is come unto me.

I was not in safety, neither had I rest, neither was I
     quiet;
Yet trouble came."   [3:1–26]

Words of Eliphaz. Then Eliphaz the Temanite answered and said,

"If we assay to commune with thee, wilt thou be
     grieved?
But who can withhold himself from speaking?
Behold, thou hast instructed many,
And thou hast strengthened the weak hands.
Thy words have upholden him that was falling,
And thou hast strengthened the feeble knees.
But now it is come upon thee, and thou faintest;
It toucheth thee, and thou art troubled.
Is not this thy fear, thy confidence,
Thy hope, and the uprightness of thy ways?
Remember, I pray thee, who ever perished, being
     innocent?
Or where were the righteous cut off?
Even as I have seen, they that plow iniquity,
And sow wickedness, reap the same.
By the blast of God they perish,
And by the breath of his nostrils are they consumed.

            . . . . .

"Call now, if there be any that will answer thee;
And to which of the saints wilt thou turn?
For wrath killeth the foolish man,
And envy slayeth the silly one.
I have seen the foolish taking root:
But suddenly I cursed his habitation.
His children are far from safety,
And they are crushed in the gate, neither is there any
     to deliver them.
Whose harvest the hungry eateth up,
And taketh it even out of the thorns,

And the robber swalloweth up their substance.
Although affliction cometh not forth of the dust,
Neither doth trouble spring out of the ground;
Yet man is born unto trouble,
As the sparks fly upward.
I would seek unto God,
And unto God would I commit my cause:
Which doeth great things and unsearchable;
Marvellous things without number:
Who giveth rain upon the earth,
And sendeth waters upon the fields:
To set up on high those that be low;
That those which mourn may be exalted to safety.
He disappointeth the devices of the crafty,
So that their hands cannot perform their enterprise.
He taketh the wise in their own craftiness:
And the counsel of the froward is carried headlong."

[4:1–9; 5:1–13]

Job's Answer. But Job answered and said,

"Oh that my grief were throughly weighed,
And my calamity laid in the balances together!
For now it would be heavier than the sand of the sea:
Therefore my words are swallowed up.

. . . . .

For now ye are nothing;
Ye see my casting down, and are afraid.
Did I say, Bring unto me?
Or, Give a reward for me of your substance?
Or, Deliver me from the enemy's hand?
Or, Redeem me from the hand of the mighty?
Teach me, and I will hold my tongue:
And cause me to understand wherein I have erred.
How forcible are right words!
But what doth your arguing reprove?

. . . . .

What is man, that thou shouldest magnify him?
And that thou shouldest set thine heart upon him?
And that thou shouldest visit him every morning,
And try him every moment?
How long wilt thou not depart from me,
Nor let me alone till I swallow down my spittle?
I have sinned; what shall I do unto thee,
O thou preserver of men?
Why hast thou set me as a mark against thee,
So that I am a burden to myself?
And why dost thou not pardon my transgression,
And take away mine iniquity?
For now shall I sleep in the dust;
And thou shalt seek me in the morning, but I shall
    not be."   [6:1-3, 21-25; 7:17-21]

Words of Bildad.   Then answered Bildad the Shuhite,
and said,

"How long wilt thou speak these things?
And how long shall the words of thy mouth be like
    a strong wind?
Doth God pervert judgment?
Or doth the Almighty pervert justice?

Behold, God will not cast away a perfect man,
Neither will he help the evil doers:
Till he fill thy mouth with laughing,
And thy lips with rejoicing.
They that hate thee shall be clothed with shame;
And the dwelling place of the wicked shall come to
    nought."   [8:1-3, 20-22]

Job's Answer.   Then Job answered and said,

"I know it is so of a truth:
But how should man be just with God?
If he will contend with him,

He cannot answer him one of a thousand.
He is wise in heart, and mighty in strength:
Who hath hardened himself against him, and hath
   prospered?
Which removeth the mountains, and they know not:
Which overturneth them in his anger.
Which shaketh the earth out of her place,
And the pillars thereof tremble.

     . . . . . .

"My soul is weary of my life;
I will leave my complaint upon myself;
I will speak in the bitterness of my soul.
I will say unto God, Do not condemn me;
Shew me wherefore thou contendest with me.
Is it good unto thee that thou shouldest oppress,
That thou shouldest despise the work of thine hands,
And shine upon the counsel of the wicked?
Hast thou eyes of flesh?
Or seest thou as man seeth?
Are thy days as the days of man?
Are thy years as man's days,
That thou enquirest after mine iniquity,
And searchest after my sin?
Thou knowest that I am not wicked;
And there is none that can deliver out of thine hand.
Thine hands have made me and fashioned me
Together round about; yet thou dost destroy me."

                             [9:1–6; 10:1–8]

Words of Zophar. Then answered Zophar the Naamathite, and said,

"Should not the multitude of words be answered?
And should a man full of talk be justified?
Should thy lies make men hold their peace?
And when thou mockest, shall no man make thee
   ashamed?

For thou hast said, 'My doctrine is pure,
And I am clean in thine eyes'.
But oh that God would speak,
And open his lips against thee;
And that he would shew thee the secrets of wisdom,
That they are double to that which is!
Know therefore that God exacteth of thee less than
    thine iniquity deserveth.
Canst thou by searching find out God?
Canst thou find out the Almighty unto perfection?
It is as high as heaven; what canst thou do?
Deeper than hell; what canst thou know?" [11:1-8]

Job's Answer.   And Job answered and said,

"No doubt but ye are the people,
And wisdom shall die with you.
But I have understanding as well as you;
I am not inferior to you:
Yea, who knoweth not such things as these?
I am as one mocked of his neighbour,
Who calleth upon God, and he answereth him:
The just upright man is laughed to scorn.
He that is ready to slip with his feet
Is as a lamp despised in the thought of him that is
    at ease.

        .   .   .   .   .   .

"Lo, mine eye hath seen all this,
Mine ear hath heard and understood it.
What ye know, the same do I know also:
I am not inferior unto you.
Surely I would speak to the Almighty,
And I desire to reason with God.
But ye are forgers of lies,
Ye are all physicians of no value.
O that ye would altogether hold your peace!
And it should be your wisdom.

        .   .   .   .

"Hold your peace, let me alone, that I may speak,
  And let come on me what will.
  Wherefore do I take my flesh in my teeth,
  And put my life in mine hand?
  Though he slay me, yet will I trust in him: N B
  But I will maintain mine own ways before him.
  He also shall be my salvation:
  For an hypocrite shall not come before him.

                . . . . . .

"Man that is born of a woman
  Is of few days, and full of trouble.
  He cometh forth like a flower, and is cut down:
  He fleeth also as a shadow, and continueth not.
  And dost thou open thine eyes upon such an one,
  And bringest me into judgment with thee?
  Who can bring a clean thing out of an unclean?
  Not one."   [12:1–5; 13:1–5, 13–16; 14:1–4]

Words of Eliphaz. Then answered Eliphaz the Temanite, and said,

"Should a wise man utter vain knowledge,
  And fill his belly with the east wind?
  Should he reason with unprofitable talk?
  Or with speeches wherewith he can do no good?
  Yea, thou castest off fear,
  And restrainest prayer before God.
  For thy mouth uttereth thine iniquity,
  And thou choosest the tongue of the crafty.
  Thine own mouth condemneth thee, and not I:
  Yea, thine own lips testify against thee.
  Art thou the first man that was born?
  Or wast thou made before the hills?
  Hast thou heard the secret of God?
  And dost thou restrain wisdom to thyself?
  What knowest thou, that we know not?
  What understandest thou, which is not in us?
  With us are both the grayheaded and very aged men,

Much elder than thy father.
Are the consolations of God small with thee?
Is there any secret thing with thee?
Why doth thine heart carry thee away?
And what do thy eyes wink at,
That thou turnest thy spirit against God,
And lettest such words go out of thy mouth?"

[15:1–13]

Job's Answer. Then Job answered and said,

"I have heard many such things:
Miserable comforters are ye all.
Shall vain words have an end?

"For I know that my redeemer liveth,
And that he shall stand at the latter day upon the
    earth:
And though after my skin worms destroy this body,
Yet in my flesh shall I see God:
Whom I shall see for myself,
And mine eyes shall behold, and not another;
Though my reins be consumed within me.
But ye should say, 'Why persecute we him,
Seeing the root of the matter is found in me?'
Be ye afraid of the sword:
For wrath bringeth the punishments of the sword,
That ye may know there is a judgment."

. . . .

But Job answered and said,

"Hear diligently my speech,
And let this be your consolations.
Suffer me that I may speak;
And after that I have spoken, mock on.
As for me, is my complaint to man?
And if it were so, why should not my spirit be
    troubled?

Mark me, and be astonished,
And lay your hand upon your mouth.
Even when I remember I am afraid,
And trembling taketh hold on my flesh.
Wherefore do the wicked live,
Become old, yea, are mighty in power?
Their seed is established in their sight with them,
And their offspring before their eyes.
Their houses are safe from fear,
Neither is the rod of God upon them.

. . . .

"Therefore they say unto God, 'Depart from us;
For we desire not the knowledge of thy ways.
What is the Almighty, that we should serve him?
And what profit should we have, if we pray unto
him?'
Lo, their good is not in their hand:
The counsel of the wicked is far from me."

. . . .

Then Job answered and said,

"Even to day is my complaint bitter:
My stroke is heavier than my groaning.
Oh that I knew where I might find him!
That I might come even to his seat!
I would order my cause before him,
And fill my mouth with arguments.
I would know the words which he would answer me,
And understand what he would say unto me.
Will he plead against me with his great power?
No; but he would put strength in me.
There the righteous might dispute with him;
So should I be delivered for ever from my judge."
        [16:1–3; 19:25–29; 21:1–9, 14–16; 23:1–7]

Elihu Rebukes His Elders. So these three men ceased
to answer Job, because he was righteous in his own eyes.

Then was kindled the wrath of Elihu the son of Barachel the Buzite, of the kindred of Ram: against Job was his wrath kindled, because he justified himself rather than God. Also against his three friends was his wrath kindled, because they had found no answer, and yet had condemned Job. Now Elihu had waited till Job had spoken, because they were elder than he. When Elihu saw that there was no answer in the mouth of these three men, then his wrath was kindled.

And Elihu the son of Barachel the Buzite answered and said,

"I am young, and ye are very old;
  Wherefore I was afraid, and durst not shew you
    mine opinion.
I said, Days should speak,
And multitude of years should teach wisdom.
But there is a spirit in man:
And the inspiration of the Almighty giveth them
    understanding.
Great men are not always wise:
Neither do the aged understand judgment.
Therefore I said, Hearken to me;
I also will shew mine opinion.
       . . . . .
"Wherefore, Job, I pray thee, hear my speeches,
And hearken to all my words.
Behold, now I have opened my mouth,
My tongue hath spoken in my mouth.
My words shall be of the uprightness of my heart:
And my lips shall utter knowledge clearly.
The spirit of God hath made me,
And the breath of the Almighty hath given me life.
If thou canst answer me,
Set thy words in order before me, stand up.
Behold, I am according to thy wish in God's stead:
I also am formed out of the clay.

Behold, my terror shall not make thee afraid,
Neither shall my hand be heavy upon thee.
Surely thou hast spoken in mine hearing,
And I have heard the voice of thy words, saying,
'I am clean without transgression,
I am innocent; neither is there iniquity in me.
Behold, he findeth occasions against me,
He counteth me for his enemy,
He putteth my feet in the stocks,
He marketh all my paths.'
Behold, in this thou art not just: I will answer thee,
That God is greater than man.
Why dost thou strive against him?
For he giveth not account of any of his matters.
For God speaketh once,
Yea twice, yet man perceiveth it not.
In a dream, in a vision of the night,
When deep sleep falleth upon men,
In slumberings upon the bed;
Then he openeth the ears of men,
And sealeth their instruction,
That he may withdraw man from his purpose,
And hide pride from man."

. . . .

Elihu spake moreover, and said,

"Thinkest thou this to be right,
That thou saidst, 'My righteousness is more than
    God's'?
For thou saidst, 'What advantage will it be unto
    thee?'
And, 'What profit shall I have, if I be cleansed from
    my sin?'
I will answer thee,
And thy companions with thee.
Look unto the heavens, and see;
And behold the clouds which are higher than thou.

If thou sinnest, what doest thou against him?
Or if thy transgressions be multiplied, what doest
    thou unto him?
If thou be righteous, what givest thou him?
Or what receiveth he of thine hand?
Thy wickedness may hurt a man as thou art;
And thy righteousness may profit the son of man.
By reason of the multitude of oppressions they make
    the oppressed to cry:
They cry out by reason of the arm of the mighty.
But none saith, 'Where is God my Maker,
Who giveth songs in the night;
Who teacheth us more than the beasts of the earth,
And maketh us wiser than the fowls of heaven?'
There they cry, but none giveth answer,
Because of the pride of evil men.
Surely God will not hear vanity,
Neither will the Almighty regard it.
Although thou sayest thou shalt not see him,
Yet judgment is before him; therefore trust thou in
    him.
But now, because it is not so, he hath visited in his
    anger;
Yet he knoweth it not in great extremity:
Therefore doth Job open his mouth in vain;
He multiplieth words without knowledge."
[32:1–10; 33:1–17; 35:1–16]

The Lord Answers Job. Then the LORD answered Job
out of the whirlwind, and said,

"Who is this that darkeneth counsel
    By words without knowledge?
    Gird up now thy loins like a man;
    For I will demand of thee, and answer thou me.
    Where wast thou when I laid the foundations of the
        earth?

Declare, if thou hast understanding.
Who hath laid the measures thereof, if thou knowest?
Or who hath stretched the line upon it?
Whereupon are the foundations thereof fastened?
Or who laid the corner stone thereof;
When the morning stars sang together,
And all the sons of God shouted for joy?
Or who shut up the sea with doors,
When it brake forth, as if it had issued out of the
    womb?
When I made the cloud the garment thereof,
And thick darkness a swaddlingband for it,
And brake up for it my decreed place,
And set bars and doors,
And said, Hitherto shalt thou come, but no further:
And here shall thy proud waves be stayed?
Hast thou commanded the morning since thy days;
And caused the dayspring to know his place;
That it might take hold of the ends of the earth,
That the wicked might be shaken out of it?
It is turned as clay to the seal;
And they stand as a garment.
And from the wicked their light is withholden,
And the high arm shall be broken.
Hast thou entered into the springs of the sea?
Or hast thou walked in the search of the depth?
Have the gates of death been opened unto thee?
Or hast thou seen the doors of the shadow of death?
Hast thou perceived the breadth of the earth?
Declare if thou knowest it all.
Where is the way where light dwelleth?
And as for darkness, where is the place thereof,
That thou shouldest take it to the bound thereof,
And that thou shouldest know the paths to the house
    thereof?
Knowest thou it, because thou wast then born?
Or because the number of thy days is great?

Hast thou entered into the treasures of the snow?
Or hast thou seen the treasures of the hail,
Which I have reserved against the time of trouble,
Against the day of battle and war?
By what way is the light parted,
Which scattereth the east wind upon the earth?
Who hath divided a watercourse for the overflowing
    of waters,
Or a way for the lightning of thunder;
To cause it to rain on the earth, where no man is;
On the wilderness, wherein there is no man;
To satisfy the desolate and waste ground;
And to cause the bud of the tender herb to spring
    forth?
Hath the rain a father?
Or who hath begotten the drops of dew?
Out of whose womb came the ice?
And the hoary frost of heaven, who hath gendered
    it?
The waters are hid as with a stone,
And the face of the deep is frozen.
Canst thou bind the sweet influences of Pleiades,
Or loose the bands of Orion?
Canst thou bring forth Mazzaroth in his season?
Or canst thou guide Arcturus with his sons?
Knowest thou the ordinances of heaven?
Canst thou set the dominion thereof in the earth?
Canst thou lift up thy voice to the clouds,
That abundance of waters may cover thee?
Canst thou send lightnings, that they may go,
And say unto thee, 'Here we are'?
Who hath put wisdom in the inward parts?
Or who hath given understanding to the heart?
Who can number the clouds in wisdom?
Or who can stay the bottles of heaven,
When the dust groweth into hardness,
And the clods cleave fast together?

"Wilt thou hunt the prey for the lion?
Or fill the appetite of the young lions,
When they couch in their dens,
And abide in the covert to lie in wait?

"Who provideth for the raven his food?
When his young-ones cry unto God,
They wander for lack of meat."

. . . .

Moreover the LORD answered Job, and said,

"Shall he that contendeth with the Almighty instruct
him?
He that reproveth God, let him answer it".

Then Job answered the LORD, and said,

"Behold, I am vile; what shall I answer thee?
I will lay mine hand upon my mouth.
Once have I spoken; but I will not answer:
Yea, twice; but I will proceed no further."

Then answered the LORD unto Job out of the whirlwind,
and said,

"Gird up thy loins now like a man:
I will demand of thee, and declare thou unto me.
Wilt thou also disannul my judgment?
Wilt thou condemn me, that thou mayest be
righteous?
Hast thou an arm like God?
Or canst thou thunder with a voice like him?
Deck thyself now with majesty and excellency;
And array thyself with glory and beauty.
Cast abroad the rage of thy wrath:
And behold every one that is proud, and abase him.
Look on every one that is proud, and bring him low;
And tread down the wicked in their place.
Hide them in the dust together;

And bind their faces in secret.
Then will I also confess unto thee
That thine own right hand can save thee.

"Behold now behemoth, *beast of plains*
Which I made with thee;
He eateth grass as an ox.
Lo now, his strength is in his loins,
And his force is in the navel of his belly.
He moveth his tail like a cedar:
The sinews of his stones are wrapped together.
His bones are as strong pieces of brass;
His bones are like bars of iron.
He is the chief of the ways of God:
He that made him can make his sword to approach
 unto him.
Surely the mountains bring him forth food,
Where all the beasts of the field play.
He lieth under the shady trees,
In the covert of the reed, and fens.
The shady trees cover him with their shadow;
The willows of the brook compass him about.
Behold, he drinketh up a river, and hasteth not:
He trusteth that he can draw up Jordan into his
 mouth.
He taketh it with his eyes:
His nose pierceth through snares." *beast of waters*

"Canst thou draw out leviathan with an hook?
Or his tongue with a cord which thou lettest down?
Canst thou put an hook into his nose?
Or bore his jaw through with a thorn?
Will he make many supplications unto thee?
Will he speak soft words unto thee?
Will he make a covenant with thee?
Wilt thou take him for a servant for ever?
Wilt thou play with him as with a bird?
Or wilt thou bind him for thy maidens?

Shall the companions make a banquet of him?
Shall they part him among the merchants?
Canst thou fill his skin with barbed irons?
Or his head with fish spears?"

[38:1–41; 40:1–24; 41:1–7]

Job Repents of His Rash Words.   Then Job answered
the LORD, and said,

"I know that thou canst do every thing,
And that no thought can be withholden from thee.
Who is he that hideth counsel
Without knowledge?
Therefore have I uttered that I understood not;
Things too wonderful for me, which I knew not.
Hear, I beseech thee, and I will speak:
I will demand of thee, and declare thou unto me.
I have heard of thee by the hearing of the ear:
But now mine eye seeth thee.
Wherefore I abhor myself, and repent
In dust and ashes."   [42:1–6]

Job's Prosperity Restored.   And it was so, that after the
LORD had spoken these words unto Job, the LORD said to
Eliphaz the Temanite, "My wrath is kindled against thee,
and against thy two friends: for ye have not spoken of
me the thing that is right, as my servant Job hath. Therefore take unto you now seven bullocks and seven rams,
and go to my servant Job, and offer up for yourselves a
burnt offering; and my servant Job shall pray for you: for
him will I accept: lest I deal with you after your folly, in
that ye have not spoken of me the thing which is right, like
my servant Job." So Eliphaz the Temanite and Bildad the
Shuhite and Zophar the Naamathite went, and did according as the LORD commanded them: the LORD also accepted
Job. And the LORD turned the captivity of Job, when he
prayed for his friends: also the LORD gave Job twice as
much as he had before. Then came there unto him all his

brethren, and all his sisters, and all they that had been of
his acquaintance before, and did eat bread with him in his
house: and they bemoaned him, and comforted him over
all the evil that the LORD had brought upon him: every man
also gave him a piece of money, and every one an earring
of gold. So the LORD blessed the latter end of Job more
than his beginning: for he had fourteen thousand sheep,
and six thousand camels, and a thousand yoke of oxen,
and a thousand she asses. He had also seven sons and three
daughters. And he called the name of the first, Jemima;
and the name of the second, Kezia; and the name of the
third, Kerenhappuch. And in all the land were no women
found so fair as the daughters of Job: and their father
gave them inheritance among their brethren. After this
lived Job an hundred and forty years, and saw his sons,
and his sons' sons, even four generations. So Job died, being old and full of days.   [42:7–17]

From THE BOOK OF PSALMS[1]

1. Blessed is the man
   That walketh not in the counsel of the ungodly,
   Nor standeth in the way of sinners,
   Nor sitteth in the seat of the scornful.
   But his delight is in the law of the LORD;
   And in his law doth he meditate day and night.
   And he shall be like a tree planted by the rivers of
      water,
   That bringeth forth his fruit in his season;
   His leaf also shall not wither;
   And whatsoever he doeth shall prosper.
   The ungodly are not so:
   But are like the chaff which the wind driveth away.
   Therefore the ungodly shall not stand in the judgment,
   Nor sinners in the congregation of the righteous.
   For the LORD knoweth the way of the righteous:
   But the way of the ungodly shall perish.

2. Why do the heathen rage,
   And the people imagine a vain thing?
   The kings of the earth set themselves,
   And the rulers take counsel together,
   Against the LORD, and against his anointed, saying,
   "Let us break their bands asunder,
   And cast away their cords from us".

   He that sitteth in the heavens shall laugh:
   The LORD shall have them in derision.

---

[1] See Appendix 5.

Then shall he speak unto them in his wrath,
And vex them in his sore displeasure.
Yet have I set my king
Upon my holy hill of Zion.

I will declare the decree:
The LORD hath said unto me, "Thou art my son;
This day have I begotten thee.
Ask of me, and I shall give thee the heathen for thine
    inheritance,
And the uttermost parts of the earth for thy pos-
    session.
Thou shalt break them with a rod of iron;
Thou shalt dash them in pieces like a potter's vessel."

Be wise now therefore, O ye kings:
Be instructed, ye judges of the earth.
Serve the LORD with fear,
And rejoice with trembling.
Kiss the son, lest he be angry,
And ye perish from the way,
When his wrath is kindled but a little.
Blessed are all they that put their trust in him.

8. O LORD our Lord,
How excellent is thy name in all the earth!
Who hast set thy glory above the heavens.
Out of the mouth of babes and sucklings hast thou
    ordained strength
Because of thine enemies,
That thou mightest still the enemy and the avenger.
When I consider thy heavens, the work of thy fingers,
The moon and the stars, which thou hast ordained;
What is man, that thou art mindful of him?
And the son of man, that thou visitest him?
For thou hast made him a little lower than the angels,
And hast crowned him with glory and honour.

Thou madest him to have dominion over the works of
    thy hands;
Thou hast put all things under his feet:
All sheep and oxen,
Yea, and the beasts of the field;
The fowl of the air, and the fish of the sea,
And whatsoever passeth through the paths of the seas.
O LORD our Lord, how excellent is thy name in all the
    earth!

11. In the LORD put I my trust:
    How say ye to my soul,
  "Flee as a bird to your mountain"?
For, lo, the wicked bend their bow,
They make ready their arrow upon the string,
That they may privily shoot at the upright in heart.
If the foundations be destroyed,
What can the righteous do?
The LORD is in his holy temple,
The LORD'S throne is in heaven:
His eyes behold,
His eyelids try, the children of men.
The LORD trieth the righteous:
But the wicked and him that loveth violence his soul
    hateth.
Upon the wicked he shall rain snares, fire and brim-
    stone,
And an horrible tempest: this shall be the portion of
    their cup.
For the righteous LORD loveth righteousness;
His countenance doth behold the upright.

14. The fool hath said in his heart, "There is no God".
They are corrupt, they have done abominable works,
There is none that doeth good.
    The LORD looked down from heaven upon the
    children of men,

To see if there were any that did understand, and seek
    God.
They are all gone aside, they are all together become
    filthy:
There is none that doeth good, no, not one.
Have all the workers of iniquity no knowledge?
Who eat up my people as they eat bread,
And call not upon the LORD.
There were they in great fear:
For God is in the generation of the righteous.
Ye have shamed the counsel of the poor,
Because the LORD is his refuge.
Oh that the salvation of Israel were come out of Zion!
When the LORD bringeth back the captivity of his
    people,
Jacob shall rejoice, and Israel shall be glad.

19. The heavens declare the glory of God;
And the firmament sheweth his handywork.
Day unto day uttereth speech,
And night unto night sheweth knowledge.
There is no speech nor language,
Where their voice is not heard.
Their line is gone out through all the earth,
And their words to the end of the world.
In them hath he set a tabernacle for the sun,
Which is as a bridegroom coming out of his chamber,
And rejoiceth as a strong man to run a race.
His going forth is from the end of the heaven,
And his circuit unto the ends of it:
And there is nothing hid from the heat thereof.

The law of the LORD is perfect, converting the soul:
The testimony of the LORD is sure, making wise the
    simple.
The statutes of the LORD are right, rejoicing the heart:

The commandment of the LORD is pure, enlightening
the eyes.
The fear of the LORD is clean, enduring for ever:
The judgments of the LORD are true and righteous
altogether.
More to be desired are they than gold, yea, than much
fine gold:
Sweeter also than honey and the honeycomb.
Moreover by them is thy servant warned:
And in keeping of them there is great reward.
Who can understand his errors?
Cleanse thou me from secret faults.
Keep back thy servant also from presumptuous sins;
Let them not have dominion over me:
Then shall I be upright,
And I shall be innocent from the great transgression.
Let the words of my mouth,
And the meditation of my heart, be acceptable in thy
sight,
O LORD, my strength, and my redeemer.

22. My God, my God, why hast thou forsaken me?
Why art thou so far from helping me, and from the
words of my roaring?
O my God, I cry in the daytime, but thou hearest not;
And in the night season, and am not silent.
But thou art holy, O thou that inhabitest the praises of
Israel.
Our fathers trusted in thee:
They trusted, and thou didst deliver them.
They cried unto thee, and were delivered:
They trusted in thee, and were not confounded.
But I am a worm, and no man;
A reproach of men, and despised of the people.
All they that see me laugh me to scorn:
They shoot out the lip, they shake the head, saying,
"He trusted on the LORD that he would deliver him:

Let him deliver him, seeing he delighted in him".
But thou art he that took me out of the womb:
Thou didst make me hope when I was upon my
    mother's breasts.
I was cast upon thee from the womb:
Thou art my God from my mother's belly.
Be not far from me; for trouble is near;
For there is none to help.
Many bulls have compassed me:
Strong bulls of Bashan have beset me round.
They gaped upon me with their mouths,
As a ravening and a roaring lion.
I am poured out like water,
And all my bones are out of joint:
My heart is like wax;
It is melted in the midst of my bowels.
My strength is dried up like a potsherd;
And my tongue cleaveth to my jaws;
And thou hast brought me into the dust of death.
For dogs have compassed me:
The assembly of the wicked have inclosed me:
They pierced my hands and my feet.
I may tell all my bones:
They look and stare upon me.
They part my garments among them,
And cast lots upon my vesture.
But be not thou far from me, O Lord:
O my strength, haste thee to help me.
Deliver my soul from the sword;
My darling from the power of the dog.
Save me from the lion's mouth:
For thou hast heard me from the horns of the
    unicorns.

I will declare thy name unto my brethren:
In the midst of the congregation will I praise thee.
Ye that fear the Lord, praise him;

All ye the seed of Jacob, glorify him;
And fear him, all ye the seed of Israel.
For he hath not despised nor abhorred the affliction
   of the afflicted;
Neither hath he hid his face from him;
But when he cried unto him, he heard.
My praise shall be of thee in the great congregation:
I will pay my vows before them that fear him.
The meek shall eat and be satisfied:
They shall praise the LORD that seek him:
Your heart shall live for ever.
All the ends of the world shall remember and turn
   unto the LORD:
And all the kindreds of the nations shall worship be-
   fore thee.
For the kingdom is the LORD'S:
And he is the governor among the nations.
All they that be fat upon earth shall eat and worship:
All they that go down to the dust shall bow before
   him:
And none can keep alive his own soul.
A seed shall serve him;
It shall be accounted to the Lord for a generation.
They shall come, and shall declare his righteousness
Unto a people that shall be born, that he hath done
   this.

23. The LORD is my shepherd; I shall not want.
   He maketh me to lie down in green pastures:
   He leadeth me beside the still waters.
   He restoreth my soul:
   He leadeth me in the paths of righteousness for his
      name's sake.
   Yea, though I walk through the valley of the shadow
      of death,
   I will fear no evil: for thou art with me;
   Thy rod and thy staff they comfort me.

Thou preparest a table before me in the presence of
mine enemies:
Thou anointest my head with oil; my cup runneth
over.
Surely goodness and mercy shall follow me all the
days of my life:
And I will dwell in the house of the LORD for ever.

24. The earth is the LORD's, and the fulness thereof;
The world, and they that dwell therein.
For he hath founded it upon the seas,
And established it upon the floods.
Who shall ascend into the hill of the LORD?
And who shall stand in his holy place?
He that hath clean hands, and a pure heart;
Who hath not lifted up his soul unto vanity,
Nor sworn deceitfully.
He shall receive the blessing from the LORD,
And righteousness from the God of his salvation.
This is the generation of them that seek him,
That seek thy face, O Jacob. Selah.

Lift up your heads, O ye gates;
And be ye lift up, ye everlasting doors;
And the King of glory shall come in.
Who is this King of glory?
The LORD strong and mighty,
The LORD mighty in battle.
Lift up your heads, O ye gates;
Even lift them up, ye everlasting doors;
And the King of glory shall come in.
Who is this King of glory?
The LORD of hosts, he is the King of glory. Selah.

38. O LORD, rebuke me not in thy wrath:
Neither chasten me in thy hot displeasure.
For thine arrows stick fast in me,

And thy hand presseth me sore.
There is no soundness in my flesh because of thine
  anger;
Neither is there any rest in my bones because of my
  sin.
For mine iniquities are gone over mine head:
As an heavy burden they are too heavy for me.
My wounds stink and are corrupt
Because of my foolishness.
I am troubled; I am bowed down greatly;
I go mourning all the day long.
For my loins are filled with a loathsome disease:
And there is no soundness in my flesh.
I am feeble and sore broken:
I have roared by reason of the disquietness of my
  heart
Lord, all my desire is before thee;
And my groaning is not hid from thee.
My heart panteth, my strength faileth me:
As for the light of mine eyes, it also is gone from me.
My lovers and my friends stand aloof from my sore;
And my kinsmen stand afar off.
They also that seek after my life lay snares for me:
And they that seek my hurt speak mischievous things,
And imagine deceits all the day long.
But I, as a deaf man, heard not;
And I was as a dumb man that openeth not his mouth.
Thus I was as a man that heareth not,
And in whose mouth are no reproofs.
For in thee, O LORD, do I hope:
Thou wilt hear, O Lord my God.
For I said, Hear me, lest otherwise they should re-
  joice over me:
When my foot slippeth, they magnify themselves
  against me.
For I am ready to halt,
And my sorrow is continually before me.

For I will declare mine iniquity;
I will be sorry for my sin.
But mine enemies are lively, and they are strong:
And they that hate me wrongfully are multiplied.
They also that render evil for good are mine adversaries;
Because I follow the thing that good is.
Forsake me not, O LORD:
O my God, be not far from me.
Make haste to help me,
O Lord my salvation.

40. I waited patiently for the LORD;
And he inclined unto me, and heard my cry.
He brought me up also out of an horrible pit, out of the miry clay,
And set my feet upon a rock, and established my goings.
And he hath put a new song in my mouth, even praise unto our God:
Many shall see it, and fear, and shall trust in the LORD.
Blessed is that man that maketh the LORD his trust,
And respecteth not the proud, nor such as turn aside to lies.
Many, O LORD my God, are thy wonderful works which thou hast done,
And thy thoughts which are to us-ward:
They cannot be reckoned up in order unto thee:
If I would declare and speak of them,
They are more than can be numbered.
Sacrifice and offering thou didst not desire;
Mine ears hast thou opened:
Burnt offering and sin offering hast thou not required.
Then said I, Lo, I come:
In the volume of the book it is written of me,
I delight to do thy will, O my God:

Yea, thy law is within my heart.

I have preached righteousness in the great congregation:

Lo, I have not refrained my lips,

O Lord, thou knowest.

I have not hid thy righteousness within my heart;

I have declared thy faithfulness and thy salvation:

I have not concealed thy lovingkindness and thy truth
from the great congregation.

Withhold not thou thy tender mercies from me, O
Lord:

Let thy lovingkindness and thy truth continually
preserve me.

For innumerable evils have compassed me about:

Mine iniquities have taken hold upon me, so that I
am not able to look up;

They are more than the hairs of mine head: therefore
my heart faileth me.

Be pleased, O Lord, to deliver me:

O Lord, make haste to help me.

Let them be ashamed and confounded together that
seek after my soul to destroy it;

Let them be driven backward and put to shame that
wish me evil.

Let them be desolate for a reward of their shame

That say unto me, "Aha, aha".

Let all those that seek thee rejoice and be glad in thee:

Let such as love thy salvation say continually, "The
Lord be magnified".

But I am poor and needy; yet the Lord thinketh upon
me:

Thou art my help and my deliverer;

Make no tarrying, O my God.

42. As the hart panteth after the water brooks,
So panteth my soul after thee, O God.
My soul thirsteth for God, for the living God:

When shall I come and appear before God?

My tears have been my meat day and night,

While they continually say unto me, "Where is thy
God?"

When I remember these things, I pour out my soul
in me:

For I had gone with the multitude, I went with them
to the house of God,

With the voice of joy and praise, with a multitude
that kept holyday.

Why art thou cast down, O my soul? and why art
thou disquieted in me?

Hope thou in God: for I shall yet praise him

For the help of his countenance.

O my God, my soul is cast down within me: therefore
will I remember thee

From the land of Jordan, and of the Hermonites, from
the hill Mizar.

Deep calleth unto deep at the noise of thy water-
spouts:

All thy waves and thy billows are gone over me.

Yet the LORD will command his lovingkindness in
the daytime,

And in the night his song shall be with me,

And my prayer unto the God of my life.

I will say unto God my rock, Why hast thou forgotten
me?

Why go I mourning because of the oppression of the
enemy?

As with a sword in my bones, mine enemies reproach
me;

While they say daily unto me, "Where is thy God?"

Why art thou cast down, O my soul? and why art
thou disquieted within me?

Hope thou in God: for I shall yet praise him,

Who is the health of my countenance, and my God.

45. My heart is inditing a good matter:
   I speak of the things which I have made touching the
      king:
   My tongue is the pen of a ready writer.
   Thou art fairer than the children of men:
   Grace is poured into thy lips:
   Therefore God hath blessed thee for ever.
   Gird thy sword upon thy thigh, O most mighty,
   With thy glory and thy majesty.
   And in thy majesty ride prosperously
   Because of truth and meekness and righteousness;
   And thy right hand shall teach thee terrible things.
   Thine arrows are sharp
   In the heart of the king's enemies;
   Whereby the people fall under thee.
   Thy throne, O God, is for ever and ever:
   The sceptre of thy kingdom is a right sceptre.
   Thou lovest righteousness, and hatest wickedness:
   Therefore God, thy God, hath anointed thee
   With the oil of gladness above thy fellows.
   All thy garments smell of myrrh, and aloes, and
      cassia,
   Out of the ivory palaces, whereby they have made
      thee glad.
   Kings' daughters were among thy honourable women:
   Upon thy right hand did stand the queen in gold of
      Ophir.
   Hearken, O daughter, and consider, and incline thine
      ear;
   Forget also thine own people, and thy father's house;
   So shall the king greatly desire thy beauty:
   For he is thy Lord; and worship thou him.
   And the daughter of Tyre shall be there with a gift;
   Even the rich among the people shall intreat thy
      favour.
   The king's daughter is all glorious within:
   Her clothing is of wrought gold.

She shall be brought unto the king in raiment of
    needlework:
The virgins her companions that follow her shall be
    brought unto thee.
With gladness and rejoicing shall they be brought:
They shall enter into the king's palace.
Instead of thy fathers shall be thy children,
Whom thou mayest make princes in all the earth.
I will make thy name to be remembered in all
    generations:
Therefore shall the people praise thee for ever and
    ever.

46. God is our refuge and strength,
    A very present help in trouble.
Therefore will not we fear, though the earth be re-
    moved,
And though the mountains be carried into the midst
    of the sea;
Though the waters thereof roar and be troubled,
Though the mountains shake with the swelling thereof.
    Selah.

There is a river, the streams whereof shall make glad
    the city of God,
The holy place of the tabernacles of the Most High.
God is in the midst of her; she shall not be moved:
God shall help her, and that right early.
The heathen raged, the kingdoms were moved:
He uttered his voice, the earth melted.
The LORD of hosts is with us;
The God of Jacob is our refuge. Selah.

Come, behold the works of the LORD,
What desolations he hath made in the earth.
He maketh wars to cease unto the end of the earth;
He breaketh the bow, and cutteth the spear in sunder;
He burneth the chariot in the fire.

"Be still, and know that I am God:
I will be exalted among the heathen, I will be exalted
   in the earth."
The LORD of hosts is with us;
The God of Jacob is our refuge. Selah.

51. A Psalm of David, when Nathan the prophet came
unto him, after he had gone in to Bath-sheba.[2]

Have mercy upon me, O God, according to thy
   lovingkindness:
According unto the multitude of thy tender mercies
   blot out my transgressions.
Wash me throughly from mine iniquity,
And cleanse me from my sin.
For I acknowledge my transgressions:
And my sin is ever before me.
Against thee, thee only, have I sinned,
And done this evil in thy sight:
That thou mightest be justified when thou speakest,
And be clear when thou judgest.
Behold, I was shapen in iniquity;
And in sin did my mother conceive me.
Behold, thou desirest truth in the inward parts:
And in the hidden part thou shalt make me to know
   wisdom.
Purge me with hyssop, and I shall be clean:
Wash me, and I shall be whiter than snow.
Make me to hear joy and gladness;
That the bones which thou hast broken may rejoice.
Hide thy face from my sins,
And blot out all mine iniquities.
Create in me a clean heart, O God;
And renew a right spirit within me.
Cast me not away from thy presence;
And take not thy holy spirit from me.

[2] See pp. 165–68.

Restore unto me the joy of thy salvation;
And uphold me with thy free spirit.
Then will I teach transgressors thy ways;
And sinners shall be converted unto thee.
Deliver me from bloodguiltiness, O God, thou God
of my salvation:
And my tongue shall sing aloud of thy righteousness.
O Lord, open thou my lips;
And my mouth shall shew forth thy praise.
For thou desirest not sacrifice; else would I give it:
Thou delightest not in burnt offering.
The sacrifices of God are a broken spirit:
A broken and a contrite heart, O God, thou wilt not
despise.

Do good in thy good pleasure unto Zion:
Build thou the walls of Jerusalem.
Then shalt thou be pleased with the sacrifices of
righteousness, with burnt offering and whole burnt
offering:
Then shall they offer bullocks upon thine altar.

63. O God, thou art my God; early will I seek thee:
My soul thirsteth for thee,
My flesh longeth for thee
In a dry and thirsty land, where no water is;
To see thy power and thy glory,
So as I have seen thee in the sanctuary.
Because thy lovingkindness is better than life,
My lips shall praise thee.
Thus will I bless thee while I live:
I will lift up my hands in thy name.
My soul shall be satisfied as with marrow and fatness;
And my mouth shall praise thee with joyful lips:
When I remember thee upon my bed,
And meditate on thee in the night watches.
Because thou hast been my help,

Therefore in the shadow of thy wings will I rejoice.
My soul followeth hard after thee:
Thy right hand upholdeth me.
But those that seek my soul, to destroy it,
Shall go into the lower parts of the earth.
They shall fall by the sword:
They shall be a portion for foxes.
But the king shall rejoice in God;
Every one that sweareth by him shall glory:
But the mouth of them that speak lies shall be stopped.

90. LORD, thou hast been our dwelling place in all
generations.
Before the mountains were brought forth,
Or ever thou hadst formed the earth and the world,
Even from everlasting to everlasting, thou art God.
Thou turnest man to destruction;
And sayest, "Return, ye children of men".
For a thousand years in thy sight
Are but as yesterday when it is past,
And as a watch in the night.
Thou carriest them away as with a flood; they are as
a sleep:
In the morning they are like grass which groweth up.
In the morning it flourisheth, and groweth up;
In the evening it is cut down, and withereth.
For we are consumed by thine anger,
And by thy wrath are we troubled.
Thou hast set our iniquities before thee,
Our secret sins in the light of thy countenance.
For all our days are passed away in thy wrath:
We spend our years as a tale that is told.
The days of our years are threescore years and ten;
And if by reason of strength they be fourscore years,
Yet is their strength labour and sorrow;
For it is soon cut off, and we fly away.
Who knoweth the power of thine anger?

Even according to thy fear, so is thy wrath.
So teach us to number our days,
That we may apply our hearts unto wisdom.
Return, O LORD, how long?
And let it repent thee concerning thy servants.
O satisfy us early with thy mercy;
That we may rejoice and be glad all our days.
Make us glad according to the days wherein thou
    hast afflicted us,
And the years wherein we have seen evil.
Let thy work appear unto thy servants,
And thy glory unto their children.
And let the beauty of the LORD our God be upon us:
And establish thou the work of our hands upon us;
Yea, the work of our hands establish thou it.

91. He that dwelleth in the secret place of the Most High
    Shall abide under the shadow of the Almighty.
I will say of the LORD, He is my refuge and my
    fortress:
My God; in him will I trust.
Surely he shall deliver thee from the snare of the
    fowler,
And from the noisome pestilence.
He shall cover thee with his feathers,
And under his wings shalt thou trust:
His truth shall be thy shield and buckler.
Thou shalt not be afraid for the terror by night;
Nor for the arrow that flieth by day;
Nor for the pestilence that walketh in darkness;
Nor for the destruction that wasteth at noonday.
A thousand shall fall at thy side,
And ten thousand at thy right hand;
But it shall not come nigh thee.
Only with thine eyes shalt thou behold
And see the reward of the wicked.
Because thou hast made the LORD, which is my refuge,

Even the Most High, thy habitation;
There shall no evil befall thee,
Neither shall any plague come nigh thy dwelling.
For he shall give his angels charge over thee,
To keep thee in all thy ways.
They shall bear thee up in their hands,
Lest thou dash thy foot against a stone.
Thou shalt tread upon the lion and adder:
The young lion and the dragon shalt thou trample
    under feet.
"Because he hath set his love upon me, therefore will
    I deliver him:
I will set him on high, because he hath known my
    name.
He shall call upon me, and I will answer him:
I will be with him in trouble;
I will deliver him, and honour him.
With long life will I satisfy him,
And shew him my salvation."

96. O sing unto the LORD a new song:
Sing unto the LORD, all the earth.
Sing unto the LORD, bless his name;
Shew forth his salvation from day to day.
Declare his glory among the heathen,
His wonders among all people.
For the LORD is great, and greatly to be praised:
He is to be feared above all gods.
For all the gods of the nations are idols:
But the LORD made the heavens.
Honour and majesty are before him:
Strength and beauty are in his sanctuary.
Give unto the LORD, O ye kindreds of the people,
Give unto the LORD glory and strength.
Give unto the LORD the glory due unto his name:
Bring an offering, and come into his courts.
O worship the LORD in the beauty of holiness:

Fear before him, all the earth.
Say among the heathen that the LORD reigneth:
The world also shall be established that it shall not
    be moved:
He shall judge the people righteously.
Let the heavens rejoice, and let the earth be glad;
Let the sea roar, and the fulness thereof.
Let the field be joyful, and all that is therein:
Then shall all the trees of the wood rejoice
Before the LORD: for he cometh,
For he cometh to judge the earth:
He shall judge the world with righteousness,
And the people with his truth.

103. Bless the LORD, O my soul:
And all that is within me, bless his holy name.
Bless the LORD, O my soul,
And forget not all his benefits:
Who forgiveth all thine iniquities;
Who healeth all thy diseases;
Who redeemeth thy life from destruction;
Who crowneth thee with lovingkindness and
    tender mercies:
Who satisfieth thy mouth with good things;
So that thy youth is renewed like the eagle's.
The LORD executeth righteousness
And judgment for all that are oppressed.
He made known his ways unto Moses,
His acts unto the children of Israel.
The LORD is merciful and gracious,
Slow to anger, and plenteous in mercy.
He will not always chide:
Neither will he keep his anger for ever.
He hath not dealt with us after our sins;
Nor rewarded us according to our iniquities.
For as the heaven is high above the earth,
So great is his mercy toward them that fear him.

As far as the east is from the west,
So far hath he removed our transgressions from us.
Like as a father pitieth his children,
So the LORD pitieth them that fear him.
For he knoweth our frame;
He remembereth that we are dust.
As for man, his days are as grass:
As a flower of the field, so he flourisheth.
For the wind passeth over it, and it is gone;
And the place thereof shall know it no more.
But the mercy of the LORD is from everlasting to
    everlasting upon them that fear him,
And his righteousness unto children's children;
To such as keep his covenant,
And to those that remember his commandments
    to do them.
The LORD hath prepared his throne in the heavens;
And his kingdom ruleth over all.
Bless the LORD, ye his angels,
That excel in strength, that do his commandments,
Hearkening unto the voice of his word.
Bless ye the LORD, all ye his hosts;
Ye ministers of his, that do his pleasure.
Bless the LORD, all his works
In all places of his dominion:
Bless the LORD, O my soul.

110. The LORD said unto my Lord,
    "Sit thou at my right hand,
    Until I make thine enemies thy footstool".
The LORD shall send the rod of thy strength out
    of Zion:
Rule thou in the midst of thine enemies.
Thy people shall be willing in the day of thy power,
    in the beauties of holiness
From the womb of the morning: thou hast the dew
    of thy youth.

The LORD hath sworn, and will not repent,
"Thou art a priest for ever
After the order of Melchizedek".
The Lord at thy right hand
Shall strike through kings in the day of his wrath.
He shall judge among the heathen, he shall fill the
    places with the dead bodies;
He shall wound the heads over many countries.
He shall drink of the brook in the way:
Therefore shall he lift up the head.

114. When Israel went out of Egypt,
The house of Jacob from a people of strange
    language;
Judah was his sanctuary,
And Israel his dominion.
The sea saw it, and fled:
Jordan was driven back.
The mountains skipped like rams,
And the little hills like lambs.
What ailed thee, O thou sea, that thou fleddest?
Thou Jordan, that thou wast driven back?
Ye mountains, that ye skipped like rams;
And ye little hills, like lambs?
Tremble, thou earth, at the presence of the LORD,
At the presence of the God of Jacob;
Which turned the rock into a standing water,
The flint into a fountain of waters.

115. Not unto us, O LORD, not unto us,
But unto thy name give glory,
For thy mercy, and for thy truth's sake.
Wherefore should the heathen say,
"Where is now their God"?
But our God is in the heavens:
He hath done whatsoever he hath pleased.
Their idols are silver and gold,

The work of men's hands.
They have mouths, but they speak not:
Eyes have they, but they see not:
They have ears, but they hear not:
Noses have they, but they smell not:
They have hands, but they handle not:
Feet have they, but they walk not:
Neither speak they through their throat.
They that make them are like unto them;
So is every one that trusteth in them.
O Israel, trust thou in the LORD:
He is their help and their shield.
O house of Aaron, trust in the LORD:
He is their help and their shield.
Ye that fear the LORD, trust in the LORD:
He is their help and their shield.
The LORD hath been mindful of us: he will bless us;
He will bless the house of Israel;
He will bless the house of Aaron.
He will bless them that fear the LORD,
Both small and great.
The LORD shall increase you more and more,
You and your children.
Ye are blessed of the LORD
Which made heaven and earth.
The heaven, even the heavens, are the LORD's:
But the earth hath he given to the children of men.
The dead praise not the LORD,
Neither any that go down into silence.
But we will bless the LORD
From this time forth and for evermore.
Praise the LORD.

121. I will lift up mine eyes unto the hills,
From whence cometh my help.
My help cometh from the LORD,
Which made heaven and earth.

He will not suffer thy foot to be moved:
He that keepeth thee will not slumber.
Behold, he that keepeth Israel
Shall neither slumber nor sleep.
The LORD is thy keeper:
The LORD is thy shade upon thy right hand.
The sun shall not smite thee by day,
Nor the moon by night.
The LORD shall preserve thee from all evil:
He shall preserve thy soul.
The LORD shall preserve thy going out and thy coming
    in
From this time forth, and even for evermore.

122. I was glad when they said unto me,
    "Let us go into the house of the LORD".
    Our feet shall stand
    Within thy gates, O Jerusalem.
    Jerusalem is builded
    As a city that is compact together:
    Whither the tribes go up, the tribes of the LORD,
    Unto the testimony of Israel,
    To give thanks unto the name of the LORD.
    For there are set thrones of judgment,
    The thrones of the house of David.
    Pray for the peace of Jerusalem:
    They shall prosper that love thee.
    Peace be within thy walls,
    And prosperity within thy palaces.
    For my brethren and companions' sakes,
    I will now say, Peace be within thee.
    Because of the house of the LORD our God
    I will seek thy good.

127. Except the LORD build the house, they labour in
    vain that build it:

Except the LORD keep the city, the watchman
    waketh but in vain.
It is vain for you to rise up early, to sit up late,
To eat the bread of sorrows:
For so he giveth his beloved sleep.
Lo, children are an heritage of the LORD:
And the fruit of the womb is his reward.
As arrows are in the hand of a mighty man;
So are children of the youth.
Happy is the man that hath his quiver full of them:
They shall not be ashamed,
But they shall speak with the enemies in the gate.

130. Out of the depths have I cried unto thee, O LORD.
    Lord, hear my voice:
Let thine ears be attentive to the voice of my
    supplications.
If thou, LORD, shouldest mark iniquities,
O Lord, who shall stand?
But there is forgiveness with thee,
That thou mayest be feared.
I wait for the LORD, my soul doth wait,
And in his word do I hope.
My soul waiteth for the Lord
More than they that watch for the morning:
I say, more than they that watch for the morning.
Let Israel hope in the LORD:
For with the LORD there is mercy,
And with him is plenteous redemption.
And he shall redeem Israel
From all his iniquities.

133. Behold, how good and how pleasant it is
    For brethren to dwell together in unity!
It is like the precious ointment upon the head,
That ran down upon the beard, even Aaron's beard:
That went down to the skirts of his garments;

As the dew of Hermon, and as the dew that descended
    upon the mountains of Zion:
For there the LORD commanded the blessing,
Even life for evermore.

137. By the rivers of Babylon, there we sat down, yea, we
       wept,
    When we remembered Zion.
    We hanged our harps
    Upon the willows in the midst thereof.
    For there they that carried us away captive required
      of us a song;
    And they that wasted us required of us mirth,
    Saying, "Sing us one of the songs of Zion".
    How shall we sing the LORD's song
    In a strange land?
    If I forget thee, O Jerusalem,
    Let my right hand forget her cunning.
    If I do not remember thee,
    Let my tongue cleave to the roof of my mouth;
    If I prefer not Jerusalem above my chief joy.
    Remember, O LORD, the children of Edom in the day
      of Jerusalem;
    Who said, "Rase it, rase it, even to the foundation
      thereof".
    O daughter of Babylon, who art to be destroyed;
    Happy shall he be, that rewardeth thee
    As thou hast served us.
    Happy shall he be, that taketh
    And dasheth thy little ones against the stones.

139. O LORD, thou hast searched me, and known me.
    Thou knowest my downsitting and mine uprising.
    Thou understandest my thought afar off.
    Thou compassest my path and my lying down,
    And art acquainted with all my ways.
    For there is not a word in my tongue,

But, lo, O LORD, thou knowest it altogether.
Thou hast beset me behind and before,
And laid thine hand upon me.
Such knowledge is too wonderful for me;
It is high, I cannot attain unto it.
Whither shall I go from thy spirit?
Or whither shall I flee from thy presence?
If I ascend up into heaven, thou art there:
If I make my bed in hell, behold, thou art there.
If I take the wings of the morning,
And dwell in the uttermost parts of the sea;
Even there shall thy hand lead me,
And thy right hand shall hold me.
If I say, Surely the darkness shall cover me;
Even the night shall be light about me.
Yea, the darkness hideth not from thee;
But the night shineth as the day:
The darkness and the light are both alike to thee.
For thou hast possessed my reins:
Thou hast covered me in my mother's womb.
I will praise thee; for I am fearfully and wonderfully
    made:
Marvellous are thy works;
And that my soul knoweth right well.
My substance was not hid from thee,
When I was made in secret,
And curiously wrought in the lowest parts of the earth.
Thine eyes did see my substance, yet being unperfect;
And in thy book all my members were written,
Which in continuance were fashioned, when as yet
    there was none of them.
How precious also are thy thoughts unto me, O God!
How great is the sum of them!
If I should count them, they are more in number than
    the sand:
When I awake, I am still with thee.
Surely thou wilt slay the wicked, O God:

Depart from me therefore, ye bloody men.
For they speak against thee wickedly,
And thine enemies take thy name in vain.
Do not I hate them, O LORD, that hate thee?
And am not I grieved with those that rise up against
    thee?
I hate them with perfect hatred:
I count them mine enemies.
Search me, O God, and know my heart:
Try me, and know my thoughts:
And see if there be any wicked way in me,
And lead me in the way everlasting.

150. Praise ye the LORD.
Praise God in his sanctuary:
Praise him in the firmament of his power.
Praise him for his mighty acts:
Praise him according to his excellent greatness.
Praise him with the sound of the trumpet:
Praise him with the psaltery and harp.
Praise him with the timbrel and dance:
Praise him with stringed instruments and organs.
Praise him upon the loud cymbals:
Praise him upon the high sounding cymbals.
Let every thing that hath breath praise the LORD.
Praise ye the LORD.

From THE PROVERBS

The proverbs of Solomon the son of David, king of
Israel;

To know wisdom and instruction;
To perceive the words of understanding;
To receive the instruction of wisdom,
Justice, and judgment, and equity;
To give subtilty to the simple,
To the young man knowledge and discretion.
A wise man will hear, and will increase learning;
And a man of understanding shall attain unto wise
    counsels:
To understand a proverb, and the interpretation;
The words of the wise, and their dark sayings.

The fear of the LORD is the beginning of knowledge:
But fools despise wisdom and instruction.
My son, hear the instruction of thy father,
And forsake not the law of thy mother:
For they shall be an ornament of grace unto thy head,
And chains about thy neck.
My son, if sinners entice thee,
Consent thou not.   [1:1–10]

My son, forget not my law;
But let thine heart keep my commandments:
For length of days, and long life,
And peace, shall they add to thee.
Let not mercy and truth forsake thee:

Bind them about thy neck;
Write them upon the table of thine heart:
So shalt thou find favour and good understanding
In the sight of God and man.
Trust in the LORD with all thine heart;
And lean not unto thine own understanding.
In all thy ways acknowledge him,
And he shall direct thy paths.
Be not wise in thine own eyes:
Fear the LORD, and depart from evil.
It shall be health to thy navel,
And marrow to thy bones.
Honour the LORD with thy substance,
And with the firstfruits of all thine increase:
So shall thy barns be filled with plenty,
And thy presses shall burst out with new wine.

My son, despise not the chastening of the LORD;
Neither be weary of his correction:
For whom the LORD loveth he correcteth;
Even as a father the son in whom he delighteth.
Happy is the man that findeth wisdom,
And the man that getteth understanding.
For the merchandise of it is better than the merchandise of silver,
And the gain thereof than fine gold.
She is more precious than rubies:
And all the things thou canst desire are not to be compared unto her.
Length of days is in her right hand;
And in her left hand riches and honour.
Her ways are ways of pleasantness,
And all her paths are peace.
She is a tree of life to them that lay hold upon her:
And happy is every one that retaineth her.
The LORD by wisdom hath founded the earth;

By understanding hath he established the heavens.
By his knowledge the depths are broken up,
And the clouds drop down the dew.   [3:1–20]

A soft answer turneth away wrath:
But grievous words stir up anger.
The tongue of the wise useth knowledge aright:
But the mouth of fools poureth out foolishness.
The eyes of the LORD are in every place,
Beholding the evil and the good.
A wholesome tongue is a tree of life:
But perverseness therein is a breach in the spirit.
A fool despiseth his father's instruction:
But he that regardeth reproof is prudent.   [15:1–5]

The king's heart is in the hand of the LORD, as the
    rivers of water:
He turneth it whithersoever he will.
Every way of a man is right in his own eyes:
But the LORD pondereth the hearts.
To do justice and judgment
Is more acceptable to the LORD than sacrifice.
An high look, and a proud heart,
And the plowing of the wicked, is sin.   [21:1–4]

As snow in summer, and as rain in harvest,
So honour is not seemly for a fool.
As the bird by wandering, as the swallow by flying,
So the curse causeless shall not come.
A whip for the horse, a bridle for the ass,
And a rod for the fool's back.
Answer not a fool according to his folly,
Lest thou also be like unto him.
Answer a fool according to his folly,
Lest he be wise in his own conceit.
He that sendeth a message by the hand of a fool
Cutteth off the feet, and drinketh damage.

The legs of the lame are not equal:
So is a parable in the mouth of fools.
As he that bindeth a stone in a sling,
So is he that giveth honour to a fool.
As a thorn goeth up into the hand of a drunkard,
So is a parable in the mouth of fools.
The great God that formed all things
Both rewardeth the fool, and rewardeth transgressors.
As a dog returneth to his vomit,
So a fool returneth to his folly.
Seest thou a man wise in his own conceit?
There is more hope of a fool than of him.
The slothful man saith, "There is a lion in the way;
A lion is in the streets".
As the door turneth upon his hinges,
So doth the slothful upon his bed.   [26:1–14]

The horseleach hath two daughters, crying, "Give,
    give".
There are three things that are never satisfied,
Yea, four things say not, "It is enough":
The grave; and the barren womb;
The earth that is not filled with water;
And the fire that saith not, "It is enough".

The eye that mocketh at his father,
And despiseth to obey his mother,
The ravens of the valley shall pick it out,
And the young eagles shall eat it.

There be three things which are too wonderful for me,
Yea, four which I know not:
The way of an eagle in the air;
The way of a serpent upon a rock;
The way of a ship in the midst of the sea;
And the way of a man with a maid.
Such is the way of an adulterous woman;

She eateth, and wipeth her mouth,
And saith, "I have done no wickedness".

For three things the earth is disquieted,
And for four which it cannot bear:
For a servant when he reigneth;
And a fool when he is filled with meat;
For an odious woman when she is married;
And an handmaid that is heir to her mistress.

There be four things which are little upon the earth,
But they are exceeding wise:
The ants are a people not strong,
Yet they prepare their meat in the summer;
The conies[1] are but a feeble folk,
Yet make they their houses in the rocks;
The locusts have no king,
Yet go they forth all of them by bands;
The spider taketh hold with her hands,
And is in kings' palaces.   [30:15–28]

Who can find a virtuous woman?
For her price is far above rubies.
The heart of her husband doth safely trust in her,
So that he shall have no need of spoil.
She will do him good and not evil
All the days of her life.
She seeketh wool, and flax,
And worketh willingly with her hands.
She is like the merchants' ships;
She bringeth her food from afar.
She riseth also while it is yet night,
And giveth meat to her household,
And a portion to her maidens.
She considereth a field, and buyeth it:
With the fruit of her hands she planteth a vineyard.

---

[1] Rabbits.

She girdeth her loins with strength,
And strengtheneth her arms.
She perceiveth that her merchandise is good:
Her candle goeth not out by night.
She layeth her hands to the spindle,
And her hands hold the distaff.
She stretcheth out her hand to the poor;
Yea, she reacheth forth her hands to the needy.
She is not afraid of the snow for her household:
For all her household are clothed with scarlet.
She maketh herself coverings of tapestry;
Her clothing is silk and purple.
Her husband is known in the gates,
When he sitteth among the elders of the land.
She maketh fine linen, and selleth it;
And delivereth girdles unto the merchant.
Strength and honour are her clothing;
And she shall rejoice in time to come.
She openeth her mouth with wisdom;
And in her tongue is the law of kindness.
She looketh well to the ways of her household,
And eateth not the bread of idleness.
Her children arise up, and call her blessed;
Her husband also, and he praiseth her.
Many daughters have done virtuously,
But thou excellest them all.
Favour is deceitful, and beauty is vain:
But a woman that feareth the LORD, she shall be
    praised.
Give her of the fruit of her hands;
And let her own works praise her in the gates.

                                        [31:10–31]

From ECCLESIASTES
OR, THE PREACHER

The words of the Preacher, the son of David, king in Jerusalem.

Vanity of vanities, saith the Preacher, vanity of vanities; all is vanity. What profit hath a man of all his labour which he taketh under the sun? One generation passeth away, and another generation cometh: but the earth abideth for ever. The sun also ariseth, and the sun goeth down, and hasteth to his place where he arose. The wind goeth toward the south, and turneth about unto the north; it whirleth about continually, and the wind returneth again according to his circuits. All the rivers run into the sea; yet the sea is not full; unto the place from whence the rivers come, thither they return again. All things are full of labour; man cannot utter it: the eye is not satisfied with seeing, nor the ear filled with hearing. The thing that hath been, it is that which shall be; and that which is done is that which shall be done: and there is no new thing under the sun. Is there any thing whereof it may be said, "See, this is new"? it hath been already of old time, which was before us. There is no remembrance of former things; neither shall there be any remembrance of things that are to come with those that shall come after.

I the Preacher was king over Israel in Jerusalem. And I gave my heart to seek and search out by wisdom concerning all things that are done under heaven: this sore travail hath God given to the sons of man to be exercised therewith. I have seen all the works that are done under the sun; and, behold, all is vanity and vexation of spirit. That which is crooked cannot be made straight: and that which is wanting cannot be numbered. I communed with mine own heart, saying, "Lo, I am come to great estate, and have gotten more wisdom than all they that have been before me in Jerusalem": yea, my heart had great experience of wisdom and knowledge. And I gave my heart to know wisdom, and to know madness and folly: I perceived that this also is vexation of spirit. For in much wisdom is much grief; and he that increaseth knowledge increaseth sorrow.

[1:1–17]

To every thing there is a season, and a time to every purpose under the heaven:

A time to be born, and a time to die;

A time to plant, and a time to pluck up that which is planted;

A time to kill, and a time to heal;

A time to break down, and a time to build up;

A time to weep, and a time to laugh;

A time to mourn, and a time to dance;

A time to cast away stones, and a time to gather stones together;

A time to embrace, and a time to refrain from embracing;

A time to get, and a time to lose;

A time to keep, and a time to cast away;

A time to rend, and a time to sew;

A time to keep silence, and a time to speak;

A time to love, and a time to hate;

A time of war, and a time of peace.

What profit hath he that worketh in that wherein he laboureth? I have seen the travail, which God hath given to the sons of men to be exercised in it. He hath made every thing beautiful in his time: also he hath set the world in their heart, so that no man can find out the work that God maketh from the beginning to the end. I know that there is no good in them, but for a man to rejoice, and to do good in his life. And also that every man should eat and drink, and enjoy the good of all his labour, it is the gift of God. I know that, whatsoever God doeth, it shall be for ever: nothing can be put to it, nor any thing taken from it: and God doeth it, that men should fear before him. That which hath been is now; and that which is to be hath already been; and God requireth that which is past.

[3:1–15]

Cast thy bread upon the waters: for thou shalt find it after many days. Give a portion to seven, and also to eight; for thou knowest not what evil shall be upon the earth. If the clouds be full of rain, they empty themselves upon the earth: and if the tree fall toward the south, or toward the north, in the place where the tree falleth, there it shall be. He that observeth the wind shall not sow; and he that regardeth the clouds shall not reap. As thou knowest not what is the way of the spirit, nor how the bones do grow in the womb of her that is with child: even so thou knowest not the works of God who maketh all. In the morning sow thy seed, and in the evening withhold not thine hand: for thou knowest not whether shall prosper, either this or that, or whether they both shall be alike good. Truly the light is sweet, and a pleasant thing it is for the eyes to behold the sun: but if a man live many years, and rejoice in them all; yet let him remember the days of darkness; for they shall be many. All that cometh is vanity.

Rejoice, O young man, in thy youth; and let thy heart cheer thee in the days of thy youth, and walk in the ways of thine heart, and in the sight of thine eyes: but know thou, that for all these things God will bring thee into judgment. Therefore remove sorrow from thy heart, and put away evil from thy flesh: for childhood and youth are vanity.   [11:1–10]

Remember now thy Creator in the days of thy youth, while the evil days come not, nor the years draw nigh, when thou shalt say, "I have no pleasure in them"; while the sun, or the light, or the moon, or the stars, be not darkened, nor the clouds return after the rain: in the day when the keepers of the house shall tremble, and the strong men shall bow themselves, and the grinders cease because they are few, and those that look out of the windows be darkened, and the doors shall be shut in the streets, when the sound of the grinding is low, and he shall rise up at the voice of the bird, and all the daughters of musick shall be brought low; also when they shall be afraid of that which is high, and fears shall be in the way, and the almond tree shall flourish, and the grasshopper shall be a burden, and desire shall fail: because man goeth to his long home, and the mourners go about the streets: or ever the silver cord be loosed, or the golden bowl be broken, or the pitcher be broken at the fountain, or the wheel broken at the cistern. Then shall the dust return to the earth as it was: and the spirit shall return unto God who gave it. Vanity of vanities, saith the Preacher; all is vanity.

And moreover, because the Preacher was wise, he still taught the people knowledge; yea, he gave good heed, and sought out, and set in order many proverbs. The Preacher sought to find out acceptable words: and that which was written was upright, even words of truth.

The words of the wise are as goads, and as nails fastened by the masters of assemblies, which are given from one shepherd. And further, by these, my son, be admonished: of making many books there is no end; and much study is a weariness of the flesh.

Let us hear the conclusion of the whole matter: Fear God, and keep his commandments: for this is the whole duty of man. For God shall bring every work into judgment, with every secret thing, whether it be good, or whether it be evil.   [12:1–14]

From THE SONG OF SOLOMON

This book is also called "The Canticle of Canticles"
and "The Song of Songs." There is considerable disagree-
ment whether the book is a collection of love songs or a
kind of lyric dialogue between lover and beloved. Many
theologians, both Jewish and Christian, interpret the book
as an allegory of the love of Yahweh and his Chosen
People.

I am the rose of Sharon,
And the lily of the valleys.

As the lily among thorns,
So is my love among the daughters.

As the apple tree among the trees of the wood,
So is my beloved among the sons.
I sat down under his shadow with great delight,
And his fruit was sweet to my taste.
He brought me to the banqueting house,
And his banner over me was love.
Stay me with flagons, comfort me with apples:
For I am sick of love.
His left hand is under my head,
And his right hand doth embrace me.
I charge you, O ye daughters of Jerusalem,
By the roes, and by the hinds of the field,
That ye stir not up, nor awake my love, till he please.

The voice of my beloved! behold, he cometh
Leaping upon the mountains, skipping upon the hills.

My beloved is like a roe or a young hart:
Behold, he standeth behind our wall,
He looketh forth at the windows,
Shewing himself through the lattice.
My beloved spake, and said unto me,
"Rise up, my love, my fair one, and come away.
For, lo, the winter is past,
The rain is over and gone;
The flowers appear on the earth;
The time of the singing of birds is come,
And the voice of the turtle is heard in our land;
The fig tree putteth forth her green figs,
And the vines with the tender grape give a good smell.
Arise, my love, my fair one, and come away.
O my dove, that art in the clefts of the rock, in the
     secret places of the stairs,
Let me see thy countenance, let me hear thy voice;
For sweet is thy voice, and thy countenance is
     comely."

          "Take us the foxes,
               The little foxes, that spoil the vines:
               For our vines have tender grapes."

My beloved is mine, and I am his:
He feedeth among the lilies.
Until the day break, and the shadows flee away,
Turn, my beloved,
And be thou like a roe or a young hart
Upon the mountains of Bether.   [2:1–17]

From THE BOOK OF THE PROPHET ISAIAH

The word that Isaiah the son of Amoz saw concerning Judah and Jerusalem.

And it shall come to pass in the last days,
That the mountain of the LORD's house shall be established in the top of the mountains,
And shall be exalted above the hills;
And all nations shall flow unto it.
And many people shall go and say,
"Come ye, and let us go up to the mountain of the LORD,
To the house of the God of Jacob;
And he will teach us of his ways,
And we will walk in his paths:
For out of Zion shall go forth the law,
And the word of the LORD from Jerusalem".
And he shall judge among the nations,
And shall rebuke many people:
And they shall beat their swords into plowshares,
And their spears into pruninghooks:
Nation shall not lift up sword against nation,
Neither shall they learn war any more.   [2:1–4]

Now will I sing to my wellbeloved a song of my beloved touching his vineyard.

My wellbeloved hath a vineyard in a very fruitful hill:
And he fenced it, and gathered out the stones thereof,
And planted it with the choicest vine,

And built a tower in the midst of it,
And also made a winepress therein:
And he looked that it should bring forth grapes,
And it brought forth wild grapes.
And now, O inhabitants of Jerusalem, and men of
 Judah,
Judge, I pray you, betwixt me and my vineyard.
What could have been done more to my vineyard,
That I have not done in it?
Wherefore, when I looked that it should bring forth
 grapes,
Brought it forth wild grapes?
And now go to; I will tell you what I will do to my
 vineyard:
I will take away the hedge thereof, and it shall be
 eaten up;
And break down the wall thereof, and it shall be
 trodden down:
And I will lay it waste:
It shall not be pruned, nor digged;
But there shall come up briers and thorns:
I will also command the clouds that they rain no rain
 upon it.
For the vineyard of the LORD of hosts is the house of
 Israel,
And the men of Judah his pleasant plant:
And he looked for judgment, but behold oppression;
For righteousness, but behold a cry.   [5:1–7]

In the year that king Uzziah died I saw also the Lord
sitting upon a throne, high and lifted up, and his train
filled the temple. Above it stood the seraphims: each one
had six wings; with twain he covered his face, and with
twain he covered his feet, and with twain he did fly. And
one cried unto another, and said,

"Holy, holy, holy, is the LORD of hosts:
The whole earth is full of his glory".

And the posts of the door moved at the voice of him that cried, and the house was filled with smoke. Then said I, "Woe is me! for I am undone; because I am a man of unclean lips, and I dwell in the midst of a people of unclean lips: for mine eyes have seen the King, the LORD of hosts". Then flew one of the seraphims unto me, having a live coal in his hand, which he had taken with the tongs from off the altar: and he laid it upon my mouth, and said, "Lo, this hath touched thy lips; and thine iniquity is taken away, and thy sin purged". Also I heard the voice of the Lord, saying, "Whom shall I send, and who will go for us?" Then said I, "Here am I; send me". And he said, "Go, and tell this people,

'Hear ye indeed, but understand not;
And see ye indeed, but perceive not'.
Make the heart of this people fat,
And make their ears heavy, and shut their eyes;
Lest they see with their eyes, and hear with their ears,
And understand with their heart, and convert, and be healed."

Then said I, "Lord, how long?" And he answered,

"Until the cities be wasted without inhabitant,
And the houses without man,
And the land be utterly desolate,
And the LORD have removed men far away,
And there be a great forsaking in the midst of the land.
But yet in it shall be a tenth, and it shall return, and shall be eaten:
As a teil tree, and as an oak, whose substance is in them, when they cast their leaves:
So the holy seed shall be the substance thereof."

[6:1–13]

[Jerusalem was attacked by the armies of the kings of Syria and of Israel, and Ahaz king of Judah was afraid. Isaiah was commanded by the LORD to tell Ahaz that his enemies would not prevail.]

Moreover the LORD spake again unto Ahaz, saying,
"Ask thee a sign of the LORD thy God;
Ask it either in the depth, or in the height above".

But Ahaz said, "I will not ask, neither will I tempt the LORD". And he said,

"Hear ye now, O house of David;
Is it a small thing for you to weary men, but will ye weary my God also?
Therefore the Lord himself shall give you a sign;
Behold, a virgin shall conceive, and bear a son,
And shall call his name Immanuel.
Butter and honey shall he eat,
That he may know to refuse the evil, and choose the good.
For before the child shall know to refuse the evil, and choose the good,
The land that thou abhorrest shall be forsaken of both her kings.
The LORD shall bring upon thee,
And upon thy people, and upon thy father's house,
Days that have not come,
From the day that Ephraim departed from Judah;
Even the king of Assyria."   [7:10–17]

Nevertheless the dimness shall not be such as was in her vexation,
When at the first he lightly afflicted the land of Zebulun and the land of Naphtali,
And afterward did more grievously afflict her by the way of the sea,
Beyond Jordan, in Galilee of the nations.

The people that walked in darkness have seen a great
    light:
They that dwell in the land of the shadow of death,
    upon them hath the light shined.
Thou hast multiplied the nation, and not increased
    the joy:
They joy before thee according to the joy in harvest,
And as men rejoice when they divide the spoil.
For thou hast broken the yoke of his burden, and the
    staff of his shoulder,
The rod of his oppressor, as in the day of Midian.
For every battle of the warrior is with confused noise,
And garments rolled in blood;
But this shall be with burning and fuel of fire.
For unto us a child is born, unto us a son is given:
And the government shall be upon his shoulder:
And his name shall be called Wonderful, Counsellor,
    The Mighty God,
The Everlasting Father, The Prince of Peace.
Of the increase of his government and peace there
    shall be no end,
Upon the throne of David, and upon his kingdom,
To order it, and to establish it with judgment and with
    justice
From henceforth even for ever.
The zeal of the LORD of hosts will perform this.

[9:1-7]

And there shall come forth a rod out of the stem of
    Jesse,
And a branch shall grow out of his roots:
And the spirit of the LORD shall rest upon him,
The spirit of wisdom and understanding,
The spirit of counsel and might,
The spirit of knowledge and of the fear of the LORD;
And shall make him of quick understanding in the
    fear of the LORD:

And he shall not judge after the sight of his eyes,
Neither reprove after the hearing of his ears:
But with righteousness shall he judge the poor,
And reprove with equity for the meek of the earth:
And he shall smite the earth with the rod of his mouth,
And with the breath of his lips shall he slay the
    wicked.
And righteousness shall be the girdle of his loins,
And faithfulness the girdle of his reins.
The wolf also shall dwell with the lamb,
And the leopard shall lie down with the kid;
And the calf and the young lion and the fatling
    together;
And a little child shall lead them.
And the cow and the bear shall feed;
Their young ones shall lie down together:
And the lion shall eat straw like the ox.
And the sucking child shall play on the hole of the asp,
And the weaned child shall put his hand on the cock-
    atrice' den.
They shall not hurt nor destroy in all my holy
    mountain:
For the earth shall be full of the knowledge of the
    LORD,
As the waters cover the sea.   [11:1–9]

Behold, a king shall reign in righteousness,
And princes shall rule in judgment.
And a man shall be as an hiding place from the wind,
And a covert from the tempest;
As rivers of water in a dry place,
As the shadow of a great rock in a weary land.
And the eyes of them that see shall not be dim,
And the ears of them that hear shall hearken.
The heart also of the rash shall understand knowledge,
And the tongue of the stammerers shall be ready to
    speak plainly.

The vile person shall be no more called liberal,
Nor the churl said to be bountiful.
For the vile person will speak villany,
And his heart will work iniquity,
To practise hypocrisy, and to utter error against the
    LORD,
To make empty the soul of the hungry,
And he will cause the drink of the thirsty to fail.
The instruments also of the churl are evil:
He deviseth wicked devices
To destroy the poor with lying words,
Even when the needy speaketh right.
But the liberal deviseth liberal things;
And by liberal things shall he stand.   [32:1-8]

Then Isaiah the son of Amoz sent unto Hezekiah, saying, "Thus saith the LORD God of Israel, 'Whereas thou hast prayed to me against Sennacherib king of Assyria: this is the word which the LORD hath spoken concerning him;

The virgin, the daughter of Zion, hath despised thee,
    and laughed thee to scorn;
The daughter of Jerusalem hath shaken her head at
    thee.
Whom hast thou reproached and blasphemed?
And against whom hast thou exalted thy voice,
And lifted up thine eyes on high?
Even against the Holy One of Israel.
By thy servants hast thou reproached the Lord, and
    hast said,
By the multitude of my chariots am I come up
To the height of the mountains, to the sides of
    Lebanon;
And I will cut down the tall cedars thereof, and the
    choice fir trees thereof:

And I will enter into the height of his border, and the forest of his Carmel.

I have digged, and drunk water;

And with the sole of my feet have I dried up all the rivers of the besieged places.

Hast thou not heard long ago, how I have done it;

And of ancient times, that I have formed it?

Now have I brought it to pass, that thou shouldest be to lay waste

Defenced cities into ruinous heaps.

Therefore their inhabitants were of small power,

They were dismayed and confounded:

They were as the grass of the field, and as the green herb,

As the grass on the housetops, and as corn blasted before it be grown up.

But I know thy abode, and thy going out, and thy coming in,

And thy rage against me.

Because thy rage against me, and thy tumult, is come up into mine ears,

Therefore will I put my hook in thy nose, and my bridle in thy lips,

And I will turn thee back by the way by which thou camest.

And this shall be a sign unto thee,

Ye shall eat this year such as groweth of itself;

And the second year that which springeth of the same:

And in the third year sow ye, and reap,

And plant vineyards, and eat the fruit thereof.

And the remnant that is escaped of the house of Judah

Shall again take root downward, and bear fruit upward:

For out of Jerusalem shall go forth a remnant,

And they that escape out of mount Zion:

The zeal of the LORD of hosts shall do this.

Therefore thus saith the LORD concerning the king of
   Assyria,
He shall not come into this city,
Nor shoot an arrow there,
Nor come before it with shields,
Nor cast a bank against it.
By the way that he came, by the same shall he return,
And shall not come into this city, saith the LORD.
For I will defend this city to save it
For mine own sake, and for my servant David's
   sake.' "

Then the angel of the LORD went forth, and smote in the
camp of the Assyrians a hundred and fourscore and five
thousand: and when they arose early in the morning, behold, they were all dead corpses. So Sennacherib king of
Assyria departed, and went and returned, and dwelt at
Nineveh. And it came to pass, as he was worshipping in
the house of Nisroch his god, that Adrammelech and
Sharezer his sons smote him with the sword; and they escaped into the land of Armenia: and Esar-haddon his son
reigned in his stead.   [37:21–38]

"Comfort ye, comfort ye my people," saith your God,
"Speak ye comfortably to Jerusalem, and cry unto
   her,
That her warfare is accomplished,
That her iniquity is pardoned:
For she hath received of the LORD's hand double for
   all her sins."

The voice of him that crieth in the wilderness, "Pre-
   pare ye the way of the LORD,
Make straight in the desert a highway for our God.
Every valley shall be exalted,
And every mountain and hill shall be made low:
And the crooked shall be made straight,
And the rough places plain:

And the glory of the LORD shall be revealed,
And all flesh shall see it together:
For the mouth of the LORD hath spoken it."
The voice said, "Cry".
And he said, "What shall I cry?"
"All flesh is grass,
And all the goodliness thereof is as the flower of the
field:
The grass withereth, the flower fadeth:
Because the spirit of the LORD bloweth upon it:
Surely the people is grass.
The grass withereth, the flower fadeth:
But the word of our God shall stand for ever."

[40:1–8]

"Behold my servant, whom I uphold;
Mine elect, in whom my soul delighteth;
I have put my spirit upon him:
He shall bring forth judgment to the Gentiles.
He shall not cry, nor lift up,
Nor cause his voice to be heard in the street.
A bruised reed shall he not break,
And the smoking flax shall he not quench:
He shall bring forth judgment unto truth.
He shall not fail nor be discouraged,
Till he have set judgment in the earth:
And the isles shall wait for his law."
Thus saith God the LORD,
He that created the heavens, and stretched them out;
He that spread forth the earth, and that which cometh
out of it;
He that giveth breath unto the people upon it,
And spirit to them that walk therein:
"I the LORD have called thee in righteousness,
And will hold thine hand, and will keep thee,
And give thee for a covenant of the people, for a light
of the Gentiles;

To open the blind eyes,
To bring out the prisoners from the prison,
And them that sit in darkness out of the prison house.
I am the LORD: that is my name:
And my glory will I not give to another,
Neither my praise to graven images.
Behold, the former things are come to pass,
And new things do I declare:
Before they spring forth I tell you of them."

[42:1-9]

Who hath believed our report?
And to whom is the arm of the LORD revealed?
For he shall grow up before him as a tender plant,
And as a root out of a dry ground:
He hath no form nor comeliness;
And when we shall see him, there is no beauty that
    we should desire him.
He is despised and rejected of men;
A man of sorrows, and acquainted with grief:
And we hid as it were our faces from him;
He was despised, and we esteemed him not.

Surely he hath borne our griefs,
And carried our sorrows:
Yet we did esteem him stricken,
Smitten of God, and afflicted.
But he was wounded for our transgressions,
He was bruised for our iniquities:
The chastisement of our peace was upon him;
And with his stripes we are healed.
All we like sheep have gone astray;
We have turned every one to his own way;
And the LORD hath laid on him the iniquity of us all.

He was oppressed, and he was afflicted,
Yet he opened not his mouth:
He is brought as a lamb to the slaughter,

And as a sheep before her shearers is dumb,
So he openeth not his mouth.
He was taken from prison and from judgment:
And who shall declare his generation?
For he was cut off out of the land of the living:
For the transgression of my people was he stricken.
And he made his grave with the wicked,
And with the rich in his death;
Because he had done no violence,
Neither was any deceit in his mouth.

Yet it pleased the LORD to bruise him; he hath put
    him to grief:
When thou shalt make his soul an offering for sin,
He shall see his seed, he shall prolong his days,
And the pleasure of the LORD shall prosper in his
    hand.
He shall see of the travail of his soul, and shall be
    satisfied:
By his knowledge shall my righteous servant justify
    many;
For he shall bear their iniquities.
Therefore will I divide him a portion with the great,
And he shall divide the spoil with the strong;
Because he hath poured out his soul unto death:
And he was numbered with the transgressors;
And he bare the sin of many,
And made intercession for the transgressors.

[53:1–12]

"Ho, every one that thirsteth, come ye to the waters,
And he that hath no money;
Come ye, buy, and eat;
Yea, come, buy wine and milk without money and
    without price.
Wherefore do ye spend money for that which is not
    bread?

And your labour for that which satisfieth not?

Hearken diligently unto me, and eat ye that which is
good,

And let your soul delight itself in fatness.

Incline your ear, and come unto me:

Hear, and your soul shall live;

And I will make an everlasting covenant with you,

Even the sure mercies of David.

Behold, I have given him for a witness to the people,

A leader and commander to the people.

Behold, thou shalt call a nation that thou knowest not,

And nations that knew not thee shall run unto thee

Because of the LORD thy God,

And for the Holy One of Israel; for he hath glorified
thee.

"Seek ye the LORD while he may be found,

Call ye upon him while he is near:

Let the wicked forsake his way,

And the unrighteous man his thoughts:

And let him return unto the LORD, and he will have
mercy upon him;

And to our God, for he will abundantly pardon.

For my thoughts are not your thoughts,

Neither are your ways my ways," saith the LORD.

"For as the heavens are higher than the earth,

So are my ways higher than your ways,

And my thoughts than your thoughts.

For as the rain cometh down,

And the snow from heaven,

And returneth not thither,

But watereth the earth,

And maketh it bring forth and bud,

That it may give seed to the sower, and bread to the
eater:

So shall my word be that goeth forth out of my mouth:

It shall not return unto me void,

But it shall accomplish that which I please,

And it shall prosper in the thing whereto I sent it.
For ye shall go out with joy,
And be led forth with peace:
The mountains and the hills shall break forth before
    you into singing,
And all the trees of the field shall clap their hands.
Instead of the thorn shall come up the fir tree,
And instead of the brier shall come up the myrtle tree:
And it shall be to the LORD for a name,
For an everlasting sign that shall not be cut off."

                                     [55:1–13]

The spirit of the Lord GOD is upon me;
Because the LORD hath anointed me to preach good
    tidings unto the meek;
He hath sent me to bind up the brokenhearted,
To proclaim liberty to the captives,
And the opening of the prison to them that are bound;
To proclaim the acceptable year of the LORD,
And the day of vengeance of our God;
To comfort all that mourn;
To appoint unto them that mourn in Zion,
To give unto them beauty for ashes,
The oil of joy for mourning,
The garment of praise for the spirit of heaviness;
That they might be called trees of righteousness,
The planting of the LORD, that he might be glorified.
And they shall build the old wastes,
They shall raise up the former desolations,
And they shall repair the waste cities,
The desolations of many generations.
And strangers shall stand and feed your flocks,
And the sons of the alien shall be your plowmen and
    your vinedressers.
But ye shall be named the Priests of the LORD:
Men shall call you the Ministers of our God:
Ye shall eat the riches of the Gentiles,

And in their glory shall ye boast yourselves.
For your shame ye shall have double;
And for confusion they shall rejoice in their portion:
Therefore in their land they shall possess the double:
Everlasting joy shall be unto them.
For I the LORD love judgment,
I hate robbery for burnt offering;
And I will direct their work in truth,
And I will make an everlasting covenant with them.
And their seed shall be known among the Gentiles,
And their offspring among the people:
All that see them shall acknowledge them,
That they are the seed which the LORD hath blessed.

[61:1–9]

From THE BOOK OF DANIEL

Daniel and His Companions Chosen.   In the third year
of the reign of Jehoiakim king of Judah came Nebuchadnezzar king of Babylon unto Jerusalem, and besieged it.
And the Lord gave Jehoiakim king of Judah into his hand,
with part of the vessels of the house of God: which he carried into the land of Shinar to the house of his god; and he
brought the vessels into the treasure house of his god. And
the king spake unto Ashpenaz the master of his eunuchs,
that he should bring certain of the children of Israel, and
of the king's seed, and of the princes; children in whom
was no blemish, but well favoured, and skilful in all wisdom, and cunning in knowledge, and understanding sci-
ence, and such as had ability in them to stand in the
king's palace, and whom they might teach the learning and
the tongue of the Chaldeans. And the king appointed them
a daily provision of the king's meat, and of the wine which
he drank: so nourishing them three years, that at the end
thereof they might stand before the king.

Now among these were of the children of Judah, Daniel,
Hananiah, Mishael, and Azariah: unto whom the prince
of the eunuchs gave names: for he gave unto Daniel the
name of Belteshazzar; and to Hananiah, of Shadrach; and
to Mishael, of Meshach; and to Azariah, of Abed-nego.
But Daniel purposed in his heart that he would not defile
himself with the portion of the king's meat, nor with the
wine which he drank: therefore he requested of the prince
of the eunuchs that he might not defile himself. Now God
had brought Daniel into favour and tender love with the

prince of the eunuchs. And the prince of the eunuchs said unto Daniel, "I fear my lord the king, who hath appointed your meat and your drink: for why should he see your faces worse liking than the children which are of your sort? then shall ye make me endanger my head to the king". Then said Daniel to Melzar, whom the prince of the eunuchs had set over Daniel, Hananiah, Mishael, and Azariah, "Prove thy servants, I beseech thee, ten days; and let them give us pulse to eat, and water to drink. Then let our countenances be looked upon before thee, and the countenance of the children that eat of the portion of the king's meat: and as thou seest, deal with thy servants." So he consented to them in this matter, and proved them ten days.

And at the end of ten days their countenances appeared fairer and fatter in flesh than all the children which did eat the portion of the king's meat. Thus Melzar took away the portion of their meat, and the wine that they should drink; and gave them pulse. As for these four children, God gave them knowledge and skill in all learning and wisdom: and Daniel had understanding in all visions and dreams. Now at the end of the days that the king had said he should bring them in, then the prince of the eunuchs brought them in before Nebuchadnezzar. And the king communed with them; and among them all was found none like Daniel, Hananiah, Mishael, and Azariah: therefore stood they before the king. And in all matters of wisdom and understanding, that the king enquired of them, he found them ten times better than all the magicians and astrologers that were in all his realm. And Daniel continued even unto the first year of king Cyrus.   [1:1–21]

The Image with the Feet of Clay. [Nebuchadnezzar the king was troubled with a dream which he could not remember. So he summoned the astrologers and the Chaldeans and commanded them to tell him his dream and its interpretation; but they could not. So the king was angry and very furious, and commanded to destroy the wise men of Babylon; and they sought Daniel and his fellows to be slain. Then Daniel said to Arioch the captain of the king's guard, "Why is the decree so hasty from the king?"]

Then Arioch brought in Daniel before the king in haste, and said thus unto him, "I have found a man of the captives of Judah, that will make known unto the king the interpretation". The king answered and said to Daniel, whose name was Belteshazzar, "Art thou able to make known unto me the dream which I have seen, and the interpretation thereof?" Daniel answered in the presence of the king, and said, "The secret which the king hath demanded cannot the wise men, the astrologers, the magicians, the soothsayers, shew unto the king; but there is a God in heaven that revealeth secrets, and maketh known to the king Nebuchadnezzar what shall be in the latter days. Thy dream, and the visions of thy head upon thy bed, are these; as for thee, O king, thy thoughts came into thy mind upon thy bed, what should come to pass hereafter: and he that revealeth secrets maketh known to thee what shall come to pass. But as for me, this secret is not revealed to me for any wisdom that I have more than any living, but for their sakes that shall make known the interpretation to the king, and that thou mightest know the thoughts of thy heart. Thou, O king, sawest, and behold a great image. This great image, whose brightness was excellent, stood before thee; and the form thereof was terrible. This image's head was of fine gold, his breast and his arms of silver, his belly and his thighs of brass, his legs of iron, his feet part of iron and part of clay. Thou sawest till that a stone was cut out without hands, which smote the image upon his feet that were of iron and clay, and brake them to pieces. Then was the iron, the clay, the brass, the silver, and the gold, broken to pieces together, and became like the chaff of the summer threshingfloors; and the wind carried them away, that no place was found for them: and the stone that smote the image became a great mountain, and filled the whole earth. This is the dream; and we will tell the interpretation thereof before the king. Thou, O king, art a king of kings: for the God of heaven hath given thee a kingdom, power, and strength, and glory. And wheresoever the children of men dwell, the beasts of the field and the fowls of the heaven hath he given into thine hand, and hath made thee ruler over them all. Thou art this head of gold. And after thee shall arise another kingdom inferior to thee, and another third kingdom of brass, which shall bear rule over all the earth. And the fourth kingdom shall be strong as iron: forasmuch as iron breaketh in pieces and subdueth all things: and as iron that breaketh all these, shall it break in pieces and bruise. And whereas thou sawest the feet and toes, part of potters' clay, and part of iron, the kingdom shall be divided; but there shall be in it of the strength of the iron, forasmuch as thou sawest the iron mixed with miry clay. And as the toes of the feet were part of iron, and part of clay, so the kingdom shall be partly strong, and partly broken. And whereas thou sawest iron mixed with miry clay, they shall mingle themselves with the seed of men: but they shall not cleave one to another, even as iron is not mixed with clay. And in the days of these kings shall the God of heaven set up a kingdom, which shall never be destroyed: and the kingdom shall not be left to other people, but it shall break in pieces and consume all these kingdoms, and it shall stand for ever. Forasmuch as thou sawest that the stone was cut out of the mountain without hands, and that it brake in pieces the iron, the brass, the clay, the silver, and the gold; the great God hath made known to the king what shall come to pass hereafter: and the dream is certain, and the interpretation thereof sure."

Then the king Nebuchadnezzar fell upon his face, and worshipped Daniel, and commanded that they should offer an oblation and sweet odours unto him. The king answered unto Daniel, and said, "Of a truth it is, that your God is a God of gods, and a Lord of kings, and a revealer of secrets,

seeing thou couldest reveal this secret". Then the king
made Daniel a great man, and gave him many great gifts,
and made him ruler over the whole province of Babylon,
and chief of the governors over all the wise men of Babylon. Then Daniel requested of the king, and he set Shadrach, Meshach, and Abed-nego, over the affairs of the
province of Babylon: but Daniel sat in the gate of the king.

[2:25–49]

The Burning Fiery Furnace. Nebuchadnezzar the king
made an image of gold, whose height was threescore cubits, and the breadth thereof six cubits: he set it up in the
plain of Dura, in the province of Babylon. Then Nebuchadnezzar the king sent to gather together the princes, the
governors, and the captains, the judges, the treasurers, the
counsellors, the sheriffs, and all the rulers of the provinces,
to come to the dedication of the image which Nebuchadnezzar the king had set up. Then the princes, the governors, and captains, the judges, the treasurers, the counsellors, the sheriffs, and all the rulers of the provinces, were
gathered together unto the dedication of the image that
Nebuchadnezzar the king had set up; and they stood before the image that Nebuchadnezzar had set up. Then an
herald cried aloud, "To you it is commanded, O people,
nations, and languages, that at what time ye hear the
sound of the cornet, flute, harp, sackbut, psaltery, dulcimer, and all kinds of musick, ye fall down and worship the
golden image that Nebuchadnezzar the king hath set up:
and whoso falleth not down and worshippeth shall the
same hour be cast into the midst of a burning fiery
furnace".

[Then certain Chaldeans declared to Nebuchadnezzar
that three Jews, Shadrach, Meshach, and Abed-nego,
whom the king had set over the affairs of Babylon, would
not worship the golden image. So the king in his rage
commanded that they should be brought before him.]

Nebuchadnezzar spake and said unto them, "Is it true,
O Shadrach, Meshach, and Abed-nego, do not ye serve

my gods, nor worship the golden image which I have set up? Now if ye be ready that at what time ye hear the sound of the cornet, flute, harp, sackbut, psaltery, and dulcimer, and all kinds of musick, ye fall down and worship the image which I have made; well: but if ye worship not, ye shall be cast the same hour into the midst of a burning fiery furnace; and who is that God that shall deliver you out of my hands?" Shadrach, Meshach, and Abed-nego, answered and said to the king, "O Nebuchadnezzar, we are not careful to answer thee in this matter. If it be so, our God whom we serve is able to deliver us from the burning fiery furnace, and he will deliver us out of thine hand, O king. But if not, be it known unto thee, O king, that we will not serve thy gods, nor worship the golden image which thou hast set up." Then was Nebuchadnezzar full of fury, and the form of his visage was changed against Shadrach, Meshach, and Abed-nego: therefore he spake, and commanded that they should heat the furnace one seven times more than it was wont to be heated. And he commanded the most mighty men that were in his army to bind Shadrach, Meshach, and Abed-nego, and to cast them into the burning fiery furnace. Then these men were bound in their coats, their hosen, and their hats, and their other garments, and were cast into the midst of the burning fiery furnace. Therefore because the king's commandment was urgent, and the furnace exceeding hot, the flame of the fire slew those men that took up Shadrach, Meshach, and Abed-nego. And these three men, Shadrach, Meshach, and Abed-nego, fell down bound into the midst of the burning fiery furnace.

Then Nebuchadnezzar the king was astonied, and rose up in haste, and spake, and said unto his counsellors, "Did not we cast three men bound into the midst of the fire?" They answered and said unto the king, "True, O king". He answered and said, "Lo, I see four men loose, walking in the midst of the fire, and they have no hurt; and the form of the fourth is like the Son of God". Then

Nebuchadnezzar came near to the mouth of the burning fiery furnace, and spake, and said, "Shadrach, Meshach, and Abed-nego, ye servants of the Most High God, come forth, and come hither". Then Shadrach, Meshach, and Abed-nego, came forth of the midst of the fire. And the princes, governors, and captains, and the king's counsellors, being gathered together, saw these men, upon whose bodies the fire had no power, nor was an hair of their head singed, neither were their coats changed, nor the smell of fire had passed on them. Then Nebuchadnezzar spake, and said, "Blessed be the God of Shadrach, Meshach, and Abed-nego, who hath sent his angel, and delivered his servants that trusted in him, and have changed the king's word, and yielded their bodies, that they might not serve nor worship any god, except their own God. Therefore I make a decree, that every people, nation, and language, which speak any thing amiss against the God of Shadrach, Meshach, and Abed-nego, shall be cut in pieces, and their houses shall be made a dunghill: because there is no other God that can deliver after this sort." Then the king promoted Shadrach, Meshach, and Abed-nego, in the province of Babylon.   [3:1-6, 14-30]

Nebuchadnezzar's Madness. [Nebuchadnezzar had another dream which his astrologers and soothsayers could not interpret. But at last Daniel came in, and the king told his dream.]

"Thus were the visions of mine head in my bed; I saw, and behold a tree in the midst of the earth, and the height thereof was great. The tree grew, and was strong, and the height thereof reached unto heaven, and the sight thereof to the end of all the earth: the leaves thereof were fair, and the fruit thereof much, and in it was meat for all: the beasts of the field had shadow under it, and the fowls of the heaven dwelt in the boughs thereof, and all flesh was fed of it. I saw in the visions of my head upon my bed, and, behold, a watcher and an holy one came down from heaven; he cried aloud, and said thus, 'Hew down the tree, and cut off his branches, shake off his leaves, and scatter his fruit: let the beasts get away from under it, and the fowls from his branches: nevertheless leave the stump of his roots in the earth, even with a band of iron and brass, in the tender grass of the field; and let it be wet with the dew of heaven, and let his portion be with the beasts in the grass of the earth: let his heart be changed from man's, and let a beast's heart be given unto him; and let seven times pass over him. This matter is by the decree of the watchers, and the demand by the word of the holy ones: to the intent that the living may know that the Most High ruleth in the kingdom of men, and giveth it to whomsoever he will, and setteth up over it the basest of men.' This dream I king Nebuchadnezzar have seen. Now thou, O Belteshazzar, declare the interpretation thereof, forasmuch as all the wise men of my kingdom are not able to make known unto me the interpretation: but thou art able; for the spirit of the holy gods is in thee."

Then Daniel, whose name was Belteshazzar, was astonied for one hour, and his thoughts troubled him. The king spake, and said, "Belteshazzar, let not the dream, or the interpretation thereof, trouble thee". Belteshazzar answered and said, "My lord, the dream be to them that hate thee, and the interpretation thereof to thine enemies. The tree that thou sawest, which grew, and was strong, whose height reached unto the heaven, and the sight thereof to all the earth; whose leaves were fair, and the fruit thereof much, and in it was meat for all; under which the beasts of the field dwelt, and upon whose branches the fowls of the heaven had their habitation: it is thou, O king, that art grown and become strong: for thy greatness is grown, and reacheth unto heaven, and thy dominion to the end of the earth. And whereas the king saw a watcher and an holy one coming down from heaven, and saying, 'Hew the tree down, and destroy it; yet leave the stump of the roots thereof in the earth, even with a band of iron and brass, in the tender grass of the field; and let it be wet with the dew of heaven, and let his portion be with the beasts of the field, till seven times pass over him'; this is the interpretation, O king, and this is the decree of the Most High, which is come upon my lord the king: that they shall drive thee from men, and thy dwelling shall be with the beasts of the field, and they shall make thee to eat grass as oxen, and they shall wet thee with the dew of heaven, and seven times shall pass over thee, till thou know that the Most High ruleth in the kingdom of men, and giveth it to whomsoever he will. And whereas they commanded to leave the stump of the tree roots; thy kingdom shall be sure unto thee, after that thou shalt have known that the heavens do rule. Wherefore, O king, let my counsel be acceptable unto thee, and break off thy sins by righteousness, and thine iniquities by shewing mercy to the poor; if it may be a lengthening of thy tranquillity." All this came upon the king Nebuchadnezzar. At the end of twelve months he walked in the palace of the kingdom of Babylon. The king spake, and said, "Is not this great Babylon, that I have built for the house of the kingdom by the might of my power, and for the honour of my majesty?"

While the word was in the king's mouth, there fell a voice from heaven, saying, "O king Nebuchadnezzar, to thee it is spoken; 'The kingdom is departed from thee'. And they shall drive thee from men, and thy dwelling shall be with the beasts of the field: they shall make thee to eat grass as oxen, and seven times shall pass over thee, until thou know that the Most High ruleth in the kingdom of men, and giveth it to whomsoever he will." The same hour was the thing fulfilled upon Nebuchadnezzar: and he was driven from men, and did eat grass as oxen, and his body was wet with the dew of heaven, till his hairs were grown like eagles' feathers, and his nails like birds' claws. And at the end of the days I Nebuchadnezzar lifted up mine eyes unto heaven, and mine understanding returned unto me, and I blessed the Most High, and I praised and honoured him that liveth for ever, whose dominion is an everlasting dominion, and his kingdom is from generation to generation: and all the inhabitants of the earth are reputed as nothing: and he doeth according to his will in the army of heaven, and among the inhabitants of the earth: and none can stay his hand, or say unto him, "What doest thou?" At the same time my reason returned unto me; and for the glory of my kingdom, mine honour and brightness returned unto me; and my counsellors and my lords sought unto me; and I was established in my kingdom, and excellent majesty was added unto me. Now I Nebuchadnezzar praise and extol and honour the King of heaven, all whose works are truth, and his ways judgment: and those that walk in pride he is able to abase.

[4:10–37]

Belshazzar's Feast. Belshazzar the king made a great feast to a thousand of his lords, and drank wine before the thousand. Belshazzar, whiles he tasted the wine, commanded to bring the golden and silver vessels which his father Nebuchadnezzar had taken out of the temple which was in Jerusalem; that the king, and his princes, his wives, and his concubines, might drink therein. Then they brought the golden vessels that were taken out of the temple of the house of God which was at Jerusalem; and the king, and his princes, his wives, and his concubines, drank in them. They drank wine, and praised the gods of gold, and of silver, of brass, of iron, of wood, and of stone. In the same hour came forth fingers of a man's hand, and wrote over against the candlestick upon the plaister of the wall of the king's palace: and the king saw the part of the hand that wrote. Then the king's countenance was changed, and his thoughts troubled him, so that the joints of his loins were loosed, and his knees smote one against another. The king cried aloud to bring in the astrologers, the Chaldeans, and the soothsayers. And the king spake, and said to the wise men of Babylon, "Whosoever shall read this writing, and shew me the interpretation thereof, shall be clothed with scarlet, and have a chain of gold about his neck, and shall be the third ruler in the kingdom". Then came in all the king's wise men: but they could not read the writing, nor make known to the king the interpretation thereof.

[So the queen came to Belshazzar and told him of Daniel.]

Then was Daniel brought in before the king. And the king spake and said unto Daniel, "Art thou that Daniel, which art of the children of the captivity of Judah, whom the king my father brought out of Jewry? I have even heard of thee, that the spirit of the gods is in thee, and that light and understanding and excellent wisdom is found in thee. And now the wise men, the astrologers, have been brought in before me, that they should read this writing, and make known unto me the interpretation thereof: but they could not shew the interpretation of the thing: and I have heard of thee, that thou canst make interpretations, and dissolve doubts: now if thou canst read the writing, and make known to me the interpretation thereof, thou shalt be clothed with scarlet, and have a chain of gold about thy neck, and shalt be the third ruler in the kingdom."

Then Daniel answered and said before the king, "Let thy gifts be to thyself, and give thy rewards to another; yet I will read the writing unto the king, and make known to him the interpretation. O thou king, the Most High God gave Nebuchadnezzar thy father a kingdom, and majesty, and glory, and honour: and for the majesty that he gave him, all people, nations, and languages, trembled and feared before him: whom he would he slew; and whom he would he kept alive; and whom he would he set up; and whom he would he put down. But when his heart was lifted up, and his mind hardened in pride, he was deposed from his kingly throne, and they took his glory from him: and he was driven from the sons of men; and his heart was made like the beasts, and his dwelling was with the wild asses: they fed him with grass like oxen, and his body was wet with the dew of heaven; till he knew that the Most High God ruled in the kingdom of men, and that he appointeth over it whomsoever he will. And thou his son, O Belshazzar, hast not humbled thine heart, though thou knewest all this; but hast lifted up thyself against the LORD of heaven; and they have brought the vessels of his house before thee, and thou, and thy lords, thy wives, and thy concubines, have drunk wine in them; and thou hast praised the gods of silver, and gold, of brass, iron, wood, and stone, which see not, nor hear, nor know: and the God in whose hand thy breath is, and whose are all thy ways, hast thou not glorified: then was the part of the hand sent from him; and this writing was written. And this is the writing that was written, MENE, MENE, TEKEL, UPHARSIN. This is the interpretation of the thing: MENE; God hath numbered thy kingdom, and finished it. TEKEL; Thou art weighed in the balances, and art found wanting. PERES; Thy kingdom is divided, and given to the Medes and Persians." Then commanded Belshazzar, and they clothed Daniel with scarlet, and put a chain of gold about his neck, and made a proclamation concerning him, that he should be the third ruler in the kingdom. In that night was Belshazzar the king of the Chaldeans slain. And Darius the Median took the kingdom, being about threescore and two years old.   [5:1-8, 13-31]

Daniel in the Lions' Den. It pleased Darius to set over the kingdom an hundred and twenty princes, which should be over the whole kingdom; and over these three presidents; of whom Daniel was first: that the princes might give accounts unto them, and the king should have no damage. Then this Daniel was preferred above the presidents and princes, because an excellent spirit was in him; and the king thought to set him over the whole realm. Then the presidents and princes sought to find occasion against Daniel concerning the kingdom; but they could find none occasion nor fault; forasmuch as he was faithful, neither was there any error or fault found in him. Then said these men, "We shall not find any occasion against this Daniel, except we find it against him concerning the law of his God". Then these presidents and princes assembled together to the king, and said thus unto him, "King Darius, live for ever. All the presidents of the kingdom, the governors, and the princes, the counsellors, and the captains, have consulted together to establish a royal statute, and to make a firm decree, that whosoever shall ask a petition of any god or man for thirty days, save of thee, O king, he shall be cast into the den of lions. Now, O king, establish the decree, and sign the writing, that it be not changed, according to the law of the Medes and Persians, which altereth not." Wherefore king Darius signed the writing and the decree.

Now when Daniel knew that the writing was signed, he went into his house; and his windows being open in his chamber toward Jerusalem, he kneeled upon his knees three times a day, and prayed, and gave thanks before his God, as he did aforetime. Then these men assembled, and found Daniel praying and making supplication before his God. Then they came near, and spake before the king concerning the king's decree; "Hast thou not signed a decree, that every man that shall ask a petition of any god or man within thirty days, save of thee, O king, shall be cast into the den of lions?" The king answered and said, "The thing is true, according to the law of the Medes and Persians, which altereth not". Then answered they and said before the king, "That Daniel, which is of the children of the captivity of Judah, regardeth not thee, O king, nor the decree that thou hast signed, but maketh his petition three times a day". Then the king, when he heard these words, was sore displeased with himself, and set his heart on Daniel to deliver him: and he laboured till the going down of the sun to deliver him. Then these men assembled unto the king, and said unto the king, "Know, O king, that the law of the Medes and Persians is, that no decree nor statute which the king establisheth may be changed".

Then the king commanded, and they brought Daniel, and cast him into the den of lions. Now the king spake and said unto Daniel, "Thy God whom thou servest continually, he will deliver thee". And a stone was brought, and laid upon the mouth of the den; and the king sealed it with his own signet, and with the signet of his lords; that the purpose might not be changed concerning Daniel. Then the king went to his palace, and passed the night fasting: neither were instruments of musick brought before him: and his sleep went from him. Then the king arose very early in the morning, and went in haste unto the den of lions. And when he came to the den, he cried with a lamentable voice unto Daniel: and the king spake and said to Daniel, "O Daniel, servant of the living God, is thy God, whom thou servest continually, able to deliver thee from the lions?" Then said Daniel unto the king, "O king, live for ever. My God hath sent his angel, and hath shut the lions' mouths, that they have not hurt me: forasmuch as before him innocency was found in me; and also before thee, O king, have I done no hurt." Then was the king exceeding glad for him, and commanded that they should take Daniel up out of the den. So Daniel was taken up out of the den, and no manner of hurt was found upon him, because he believed in his God. And the king commanded, and they brought those men which had accused Daniel, and they cast them into the den of lions, them, their children, and their wives; and the lions had the mastery of them, and brake all their bones in pieces or ever they came at the bottom of the den.   [6:1–24]

The History of Susanna

The story of Susanna *is found only in the* Apocrypha *where it is part of the* Book of Daniel.

There dwelt a man in Babylon, called Joacim: and he took a wife, whose name was Susanna, the daughter of

Chelcias, a very fair woman, and one that feared the Lord. Her parents also were righteous, and taught their daughter according to the law of Moses. Now Joacim was a great rich man, and had a fair garden joining unto his house: and to him resorted the Jews; because he was more honourable than all others. The same year were appointed two of the ancients of the people to be judges, such as the Lord spake of, that wickedness came from Babylon from ancient judges, who seemed to govern the people. These kept much at Joacim's house: and all that had any suits in law came unto them. Now when the people departed away at noon, Susanna went into her husband's garden to walk. And the two elders saw her going in every day, and walking; so that their lust was inflamed toward her. And they perverted their own mind, and turned away their eyes, that they might not look unto heaven, nor remember just judgments. And albeit they both were wounded with her love, yet durst not one shew another his grief. For they were ashamed to declare their lust, that they desired to have to do with her. Yet they watched diligently from day to day to see her. And the one said to the other, "Let us now go home: for it is dinner time". So when they were gone out, they parted the one from the other, and turning back again they came to the same place; and after that they had asked one another the cause, they acknowledged their lust: then appointed they a time both together, when they might find her alone.

And it fell out, as they watched a fit time, she went in as before with two maids only, and she was desirous to wash herself in the garden: for it was hot. And there was no body there save the two elders, that had hid themselves, and watched her. Then she said to her maids, "Bring me oil and washing balls, and shut the garden doors, that I may wash me". And they did as she bade them, and shut the garden doors, and went out themselves at privy doors to fetch the things that she had commanded them: but they saw not the elders, because they were hid. Now when

the maids were gone forth, the two elders rose up, and ran
unto her, saying, "Behold, the garden doors are shut, that
no man can see us, and we are in love with thee; therefore
consent unto us, and lie with us. If thou wilt not, we will
bear witness against thee, that a young man was with thee:
and therefore thou didst send away thy maids from thee."
Then Susanna sighed, and said, "I am straitened on every
side: for if I do this thing, it is death unto me: and if I do
it not, I cannot escape your hands. It is better for me to
fall into your hands, and not do it, than to sin in the sight
of the Lord." With that Susanna cried with a loud voice:
and the two elders cried out against her. Then ran the one,
and opened the garden door. So when the servants of the
house heard the cry in the garden, they rushed in at a
privy door, to see what was done unto her. But when the
elders had declared their matter, the servants were greatly
ashamed: for there was never such a report made of Susanna.

And it came to pass the next day, when the people
were assembled to her husband Joacim, the two elders
came also full of mischievous imagination against Susanna
to put her to death; and said before the people, "Send for
Susanna, the daughter of Chelcias, Joacim's wife". And
so they sent. So she came with her father and mother, her
children, and all her kindred. Now Susanna was a very
delicate woman, and beauteous to behold. And these
wicked men commanded to uncover her face, (for she was
covered) that they might be filled with her beauty. Therefore her friends and all that saw her wept. Then the two
elders stood up in the midst of the people, and laid their
hands upon her head. And she weeping looked up toward
heaven: for her heart trusted in the Lord. And the elders
said, "As we walked in the garden alone, this woman came
in with two maids, and shut the garden doors, and sent the
maids away. Then a young man, who there was hid, came
unto her, and lay with her. Then we that stood in a corner
of the garden, seeing this wickedness, ran unto them. And

when we saw them together, the man we could not hold: for he was stronger than we, and opened the door, and leaped out. But having taken this woman, we asked who the young man was, but she would not tell us: these things do we testify." Then the assembly believed them, as those that were the elders and judges of the people: so they condemned her to death.

Then Susanna cried out with a loud voice, and said, "O everlasting God, that knowest the secrets, and knowest all things before they be: thou knowest that they have borne false witness against me, and, behold, I must die; whereas I never did such things as these men have maliciously invented against me". And the Lord heard her voice. Therefore when she was led to be put to death, the Lord raised up the holy spirit of a young youth, whose name was Daniel: who cried with a loud voice, "I am clear from the blood of this woman". Then all the people turned them toward him, and said, "What mean these words that thou hast spoken?" So he standing in the midst of them, said, "Are ye such fools, ye sons of Israel, that without examination or knowledge of the truth ye have condemned a daughter of Israel? Return again to the place of judgment: for they have borne false witness against her." Wherefore all the people turned again in haste, and the elders said unto him, "Come, sit down among us, and shew it us, seeing God hath given thee the honour of an elder".

Then said Daniel unto them, "Put these two aside one far from another, and I will examine them". So when they were put asunder one from another, he called one of them, and said unto him, "O thou that art waxen old in wickedness, now thy sins which thou hast committed aforetime are come to light: for thou hast pronounced false judgment, and hast condemned the innocent, and hast let the guilty go free; albeit the Lord saith, 'The innocent and righteous shalt thou not slay'. Now then, if thou hast seen her, tell me, Under what tree sawest thou them company-

ing together?" Who answered, "Under a mastick tree".
And Daniel said, "Very well; thou hast lied against thine
own head; for even now the angel of God hath received
the sentence of God to cut thee in two". So he put him
aside, and commanded to bring the other, and said unto
him, "O thou seed of Chanaan, and not of Juda, beauty
hath deceived thee, and lust hath perverted thine heart.
Thus have ye dealt with the daughters of Israel, and they
for fear companied with you: but the daughter of Juda
would not abide your wickedness. Now therefore tell me,
Under what tree didst thou take them companying together?" Who answered, "Under a holm tree". Then said
Daniel unto him, "Well; thou hast also lied against thine
own head: for the angel of God waiteth with the sword to
cut thee in two, that he may destroy you". With that all the
assembly cried out with a loud voice, and praised God,
who saveth them that trust in him.

And they arose against the two elders, (for Daniel had
convicted them of false witness by their own mouth;) and
according to the law of Moses they did unto them in such
sort as they maliciously intended to do to their neighbour:
and they put them to death. Thus the innocent blood was
saved the same day. Therefore Chelcias and his wife
praised God for their daughter Susanna, with Joacim her
husband, and all the kindred, because there was no dis-
honesty found in her. From that day forth was Daniel had
in great reputation in the sight of the people.

JONAH

1. Jonah Swallowed by a Great Fish. Now the word of the LORD came unto Jonah the son of Amittai, saying, "Arise, go to Nineveh, that great city, and cry against it; for their wickedness is come up before me". But Jonah rose up to flee unto Tarshish from the presence of the LORD, and went down to Joppa; and he found a ship going to Tarshish: so he paid the fare thereof, and went down into it, to go with them unto Tarshish from the presence of the LORD. But the LORD sent out a great wind into the sea, and there was a mighty tempest in the sea, so that the ship was like to be broken. Then the mariners were afraid, and cried every man unto his god, and cast forth the wares that were in the ship into the sea, to lighten it of them. But Jonah was gone down into the sides of the ship; and he lay, and was fast asleep.

So the shipmaster came to him, and said unto him, "What meanest thou, O sleeper? arise, call upon thy God, if so be that God will think upon us, that we perish not". And they said every one to his fellow, "Come, and let us cast lots, that we may know for whose cause this evil is upon us". So they cast lots, and the lot fell upon Jonah. Then said they unto him, "Tell us, we pray thee, for whose cause this evil is upon us; What is thine occupation? and whence comest thou? what is thy country? and of what people art thou?" And he said unto them, "I am an Hebrew; and I fear the LORD, the God of heaven, which hath made the sea and the dry land". Then were the men exceedingly afraid, and said unto him, "Why hast thou done this?" For the men knew that he fled from the presence of the LORD, because he had told them. Then said they unto him, "What shall we do unto thee, that the sea may be calm unto us?" for the sea wrought, and was tempestuous. And he said unto them, "Take me up, and cast me forth into the sea; so shall the sea be calm unto you: for I know that for my sake this great tempest is upon you".

Nevertheless the men rowed hard to bring it to the land; but they could not: for the sea wrought, and was tempestuous against them. Wherefore they cried unto the LORD, and said, "We beseech thee, O LORD, we beseech thee, let us not perish for this man's life, and lay not upon us innocent blood: for thou, O LORD, hast done as it pleased thee". So they took up Jonah, and cast him forth into the sea: and the sea ceased from her raging. Then the men feared the LORD exceedingly, and offered a sacrifice unto the LORD, and made vows. Now the LORD had prepared a great fish to swallow up Jonah. And Jonah was in the belly of the fish three days and three nights.

2. Then Jonah prayed unto the LORD his God out of the fish's belly, and said,

"I cried by reason of mine affliction unto the LORD, and he heard me;
Out of the belly of hell cried I, and thou heardest my voice.
For thou hadst cast me into the deep, in the midst of the seas;
And the floods compassed me about:
All thy billows and thy waves passed over me.
Then I said, I am cast out of thy sight;
Yet I will look again toward thy holy temple.
The waters compassed me about, even to the soul:
The depth closed me round about,
The weeds were wrapped about my head.
I went down to the bottoms of the mountains;
The earth with her bars was about me for ever:

Yet hast thou brought up my life from corruption,
O LORD my God.

When my soul fainted within me I remembered the
LORD:

And my prayer came in unto thee, into thine holy
temple.

They that observe lying vanities forsake their own
mercy.

But I will sacrifice unto thee with the voice of thanksgiving;

I will pay that that I have vowed.

Salvation is of the LORD."

And the LORD spake unto the fish, and it vomited out
Jonah upon the dry land.

3. Jonah Calls on the People of Nineveh to Repent.
And the word of the LORD came unto Jonah the second
time, saying, "Arise, go unto Nineveh, that great city, and
preach unto it the preaching that I bid thee". So Jonah
arose, and went unto Nineveh, according to the word of
the LORD. Now Nineveh was an exceeding great city of
three days' journey. And Jonah began to enter into the
city a day's journey, and he cried, and said, "Yet forty
days, and Nineveh shall be overthrown". So the people of
Nineveh believed God, and proclaimed a fast, and put on
sackcloth, from the greatest of them even to the least of
them. For word came unto the king of Nineveh, and he
arose from his throne, and he laid his robe from him, and
covered him with sackcloth, and sat in ashes. And he
caused it to be proclaimed and published through Nineveh
by the decree of the king and his nobles, saying, "Let neither man nor beast, herd nor flock, taste any thing: let
them not feed, nor drink water: but let man and beast be
covered with sackcloth, and cry mightily unto God: yea,
let them turn every one from his evil way, and from the
violence that is in their hands. Who can tell if God will
turn and repent, and turn away from his fierce anger, that

we perish not?" And God saw their works, that they turned from their evil way; and God repented of the evil, that he had said that he would do unto them; and he did it not.

4. Jonah Rebuked. But it displeased Jonah exceedingly, and he was very angry. And he prayed unto the LORD, and said, "I pray thee, O LORD, was not this my saying, when I was yet in my country? Therefore I fled before unto Tarshish: for I knew that thou art a gracious God, and merciful, slow to anger, and of great kindness, and repentest thee of the evil. Therefore now, O LORD, take, I beseech thee, my life from me; for it is better for me to die than to live." Then said the LORD, "Doest thou well to be angry?" So Jonah went out of the city, and sat on the east side of the city, and there made him a booth, and sat under it in the shadow, till he might see what would become of the city. And the LORD God prepared a gourd, and made it to come up over Jonah, that it might be a shadow over his head, to deliver him from his grief. So Jonah was exceeding glad of the gourd. But God prepared a worm when the morning rose the next day, and it smote the gourd that it withered. And it came to pass, when the sun did arise, that God prepared a vehement east wind; and the sun beat upon the head of Jonah, that he fainted, and wished in himself to die, and said, "It is better for me to die than to live". And God said to Jonah, "Doest thou well to be angry for the gourd?" And he said, "I do well to be angry, even unto death". Then said the LORD, "Thou hast had pity on the gourd, for the which thou hast not laboured, neither madest it grow; which came up in a night, and perished in a night: and should not I spare Nineveh, that great city, wherein are more than sixscore thousand persons that cannot discern between their right hand and their left hand; and also much cattle?"

From JUDITH

The Book of Judith *is found only in the* Apocrypha.

[Nabuchodonosor, who reigned in Nineve, the great city, sent ambassadors to all the peoples to come to his aid in his war against Arphaxad, king of the Medes, but they would not. When Nabuchodonosor had overcome Arphaxad, he sent Holofernes, the chief captain of his army, to put to the sword all those who refused him. So Holofernes came against the Israelites and surrounded the city of Bethulia in the hill country; and the cisterns of water in the city failed. Then all the people came to Ozias and the ancients of the city that he should yield to Holofernes. Now there was a widow of Bethulia by name Judith, who was rich and very beautiful. She went to Ozias and the ancients of the city.]

Then said Judith unto them, "Hear me, and I will do a thing, which shall go throughout all generations to the children of our nation. Ye shall stand this night in the gate, and I will go forth with my waitingwoman: and within the days that ye have promised to deliver the city to our enemies the Lord will visit Israel by mine hand. But enquire not ye of mine act: for I will not declare it unto you, till the things be finished that I do." Then said Ozias and the princes unto her, "Go in peace, and the Lord God be before thee, to take vengeance on our enemies". So they returned from the tent, and went to their wards. [8:32–36]

[Then Judith fell upon her face and prayed.]

Now after that she had ceased to cry unto the God of Israel, and had made an end of all these words, she rose where she had fallen down, and called her maid, and went down into the house, in the which she abode in the sabbath days, and in her feast days, and pulled off the sackcloth which she had on, and put off the garments of her widowhood, and washed her body all over with water, and anointed herself with precious ointment, and braided the hair of her head, and put on a tire upon it, and put on her garments of gladness, wherewith she was clad during the life of Manasses her husband. And she took sandals upon her feet, and put about her her bracelets, and her chains, and her rings, and her earrings, and all her ornaments, and decked herself bravely, to allure the eyes of all men that should see her. Then she gave her maid a bottle of wine, and a cruse of oil, and filled a bag with parched corn, and lumps of figs, and with fine bread; so she folded all these things together, and laid them upon her.

Thus they went forth to the gate of the city of Bethulia, and found standing there Ozias, and the ancients of the city, Chabris and Charmis. And when they saw her, that her countenance was altered, and her apparel was changed, they wondered at her beauty very greatly, and said unto her, "The God, the God of our fathers, give thee favour, and accomplish thine enterprizes to the glory of the children of Israel, and to the exaltation of Jerusalem". Then they worshipped God. And she said unto them, "Command the gates of the city to be opened unto me, that I may go forth to accomplish the things whereof ye have spoken with me". So they commanded the young men to open unto her, as she had spoken.

And when they had done so, Judith went out, she, and her maid with her; and the men of the city looked after her, until she was gone down the mountain, and till she had passed the valley, and could see her no more. Thus they went straight forth in the valley: and the first watch of the Assyrians met her, and took her, and asked her,

"Of what people art thou? and whence comest thou? and whither goest thou?" And she said, "I am a woman of the Hebrews, and am fled from them: for they shall be given you to be consumed: and I am coming before Holofernes the chief captain of your army, to declare words of truth; and I will shew him a way, whereby he shall go, and win all the hill country, without losing the body or life of any one of his men". Now when the men heard her words, and beheld her countenance, they wondered greatly at her beauty, and said unto her, "Thou hast saved thy life, in that thou hast hasted to come down to the presence of our lord: now therefore come to his tent, and some of us shall conduct thee, until they have delivered thee to his hands. And when thou standest before him, be not afraid in thine heart, but shew unto him according to thy word; and he will entreat thee well." Then they chose out of them an hundred men to accompany her and her maid; and they brought her to the tent of Holofernes.

Then was there a concourse throughout all the camp: for her coming was noised among the tents, and they came about her, as she stood without the tent of Holofernes, till they told him of her. And they wondered at her beauty, and admired the children of Israel because of her, and every one said to his neighbour, "Who would despise this people, that have among them such women? surely it is not good that one man of them be left, who being let go might deceive the whole earth". And they that lay near Holofernes went out, and all his servants, and they brought her into the tent. Now Holofernes rested upon his bed under a canopy, which was woven with purple, and gold, and emeralds, and precious stones. So they shewed him of her; and he came out before his tent with silver lamps going before him. And when Judith was come before him and his servants, they all marvelled at the beauty of her countenance; and she fell down upon her face, and did reverence unto him: and his servants took her up.

[10:1–23]

And in the fourth day Holofernes made a feast to his own servants only, and called none of the officers to the banquet. Then said he to Bagoas the eunuch, who had charge over all that he had, "Go now, and persuade this Hebrew woman which is with thee, that she come unto us, and eat and drink with us. For, lo, it will be a shame for our person, if we shall let such a woman go, not having had her company; for if we draw her not unto us, she will laugh us to scorn." Then went Bagoas from the presence of Holofernes, and came to her, and he said, "Let not this fair damsel fear to come to my lord, and to be honoured in his presence, and drink wine, and be merry with us, and be made this day as one of the daughters of the Assyrians, which serve in the house of Nabuchodonosor". Then said Judith unto him, "Who am I now, that I should gainsay my lord? surely whatsoever pleaseth him I will do speedily, and it shall be my joy unto the day of my death". So she arose, and decked herself with her apparel and all her woman's attire, and her maid went and laid soft skins on the ground for her over against Holofernes, which she had received of Bagoas for her daily use, that she might sit and eat upon them. Now when Judith came in and sat down, Holofernes his heart was ravished with her, and his mind was moved, and he desired greatly her company; for he waited a time to deceive her, from the day that he had seen her. Then said Holofernes unto her, "Drink now, and be merry with us". So Judith said, "I will drink now, my lord, because my life is magnified in me this day more than all the days since I was born". Then she took and ate and drank before him what her maid had prepared. And Holofernes took great delight in her, and drank much more wine than he had drunk at any time in one day since he was born.

Now when the evening was come, his servants made haste to depart, and Bagoas shut his tent without, and dismissed the waiters from the presence of his lord; and they went to their beds: for they were all weary, because the feast had been long. And Judith was left alone in the tent, and Holofernes lying along upon his bed: for he was filled with wine. Now Judith had commanded her maid to stand without her bedchamber, and to wait for her coming forth, as she did daily: for she said she would go forth to her prayers, and she spake to Bagoas according to the same purpose. So all went forth, and none was left in the bed-chamber, neither little nor great. Then Judith, standing by his bed, said in her heart, "O Lord God of all power, look at this present upon the works of mine hands for the exaltation of Jerusalem. For now is the time to help thine inheritance, and to execute mine enterprizes to the destruction of the enemies which are risen against us." Then she came to the pillar of the bed, which was at Holofernes' head, and took down his fauchion from thence, and approached to his bed, and took hold of the hair of his head, and said, "Strengthen me, O Lord God of Israel, this day". And she smote twice upon his neck with all her might, and she took away his head from him, and tumbled his body down from the bed, and pulled down the canopy from the pillars; and anon after she went forth, and gave Holofernes his head to her maid; and she put it in her bag of meat: so they twain went together according to their custom unto prayer: and when they passed the camp, they compassed the valley, and went up the mountain of Bethulia, and came to the gates thereof.

Then said Judith afar off to the watchmen at the gate, "Open, open now the gate: God, even our God, is with us, to shew his power yet in Jerusalem, and his forces against the enemy, as he hath even done this day". Now when the men of her city heard her voice, they made haste to go down to the gate of their city, and they called the elders of the city. And then they ran all together, both small and great, for it was strange unto them that she was come: so they opened the gate, and received them, and made a fire for a light, and stood round about them.

Then she said to them with a loud voice, "Praise, praise God, praise God, I say, for he hath not taken away his mercy from the house of Israel, but hath destroyed our enemies by mine hands this night". So she took the head out of the bag, and shewed it, and said unto them, "Behold the head of Holofernes, the chief captain of the army of Assur, and behold the canopy, wherein he did lie in his drunkenness; and the Lord hath smitten him by the hand of a woman. As the Lord liveth, who hath kept me in my way that I went, my countenance hath deceived him to his destruction, and yet hath he not committed sin with me, to defile and shame me." Then all the people were wonderfully astonished, and bowed themselves, and worshipped God, and said with one accord, "Blessed be thou, O our God, which hast this day brought to nought the enemies of thy people". Then said Ozias unto her, "O daughter, blessed art thou of the Most High God above all the women upon the earth; and blessed be the Lord God, which hath created the heavens and the earth, which hath directed thee to the cutting off of the head of the chief of our enemies. For this thy confidence shall not depart from the heart of men, which remember the power of God for ever. And God turn these things to thee for a perpetual praise, to visit thee in good things, because thou hast not spared thy life for the affliction of our nation, but hast revenged our ruin, walking a straight way before our God." And all the people said, "So be it, so be it".

[12:10–20; 13:1–20]

And as soon as the morning arose, they hanged the head of Holofernes upon the wall, and every man took his weapons, and they went forth by bands unto the straits of the mountain. But when the Assyrians saw them, they sent to their leaders, which came to their captains and tribunes, and to every one of their rulers. So they came to Holofernes' tent, and said to him that had the charge of all his things, "Waken now our lord: for the slaves have been bold to come down against us to battle, that they may be utterly destroyed". Then went in Bagoas, and knocked at the door of the tent; for he thought that he had slept with Judith. But because none answered, he opened it, and went into the bedchamber, and found him cast upon the floor dead, and his head was taken from him. Therefore he cried with a loud voice, with weeping, and sighing, and a mighty cry, and rent his garments. After he went into the tent where Judith lodged: and when he found her not, he leaped out to the people, and cried, "These slaves have dealt treacherously; one woman of the Hebrews hath brought shame upon the house of king Nabuchodonosor: for, behold, Holofernes lieth upon the ground without a head". When the captains of the Assyrians' army heard these words, they rent their coats, and their minds were wonderfully troubled, and there was a cry and a very great noise throughout the camp.

And when they that were in the tents heard, they were astonished at the thing that was done. And fear and trembling fell upon them, so that there was no man that durst abide in the sight of his neighbour, but rushing out all together, they fled into every way of the plain, and of the hill country. They also that had camped in the mountains round about Bethulia fled away. Then the children of Israel, every one that was a warrior among them, rushed out upon them. Then sent Ozias to Betomasthem, and to Bebai, and Chobai, and Cola, and to all the coasts of Israel, such as should tell the things that were done, and that all should rush forth upon their enemies to destroy them. Now when the children of Israel heard it, they all fell upon them with one consent, and slew them unto Chobai: likewise also they that came from Jerusalem, and from all the hill country, (for men had told them what things were done in the camp of their enemies,) and they that were in Galaad, and in Galilee, chased them with a great slaughter, until they were past Damascus and the borders thereof. And the residue, that dwelt at Bethulia, fell upon the camp of Assur, and spoiled them, and were greatly enriched. And the children of Israel that returned from the slaughter had that which remained; and the villages and the cities, that were in the mountains and in the plain, gat many spoils: for the multitude was very great.

Then Joacim the high priest, and the ancients of the children of Israel that dwelt in Jerusalem, came to behold the good things that God had shewed to Israel, and to see Judith, and to salute her. And when they came unto her, they blessed her with one accord, and said unto her, "Thou art the exaltation of Jerusalem, thou art the great glory of Israel, thou art the great rejoicing of our nation: thou hast done all these things by thine hand: thou hast done much good to Israel, and God is pleased therewith: blessed be thou of the Almighty Lord for evermore". And all the people said, "So be it". And the people spoiled the camp the space of thirty days: and they gave unto Judith Holofernes his tent, and all his plate, and beds, and vessels, and all his stuff: and she took it, and laid it on her mule; and made ready her carts, and laid them thereon.

[14:11–19; 15:1–11]

Now as soon as they entered into Jerusalem, they worshipped the Lord; and as soon as the people were purified, they offered their burnt offerings, and their free offerings, and their gifts. Judith also dedicated all the stuff of Holofernes, which the people had given her, and gave the canopy, which she had taken out of his bedchamber, for a gift unto the Lord. So the people continued feasting in Jerusalem before the sanctuary for the space of three months, and Judith remained with them. After this time every one returned to his own inheritance, and Judith went to Bethulia, and remained in her own possession, and was in her time honourable in all the country. And many desired her, but none knew her all the days of her life, after that Manasses her husband was dead, and was gathered to his people. But she increased more and more in honour, and waxed old in her husband's house, being an hundred and five years old, and made her maid free; so she died in Bethulia: and they buried her in the cave of her husband Manasses. And the house of Israel lamented her seven days: and before she died, she did distribute her goods to all them that were nearest of kindred to Manasses her husband, and to them that were the nearest of her kindred. And there was none that made the children of Israel any more afraid in the days of Judith, nor a long time after her death. [16:18-25]

From ECCLESIASTICUS

OR

THE WISDOM OF JESUS THE SON OF SIRACH

Ecclesiasticus *is found only in the* Apocrypha.

He that toucheth pitch shall be defiled therewith;
And he that hath fellowship with a proud man shall
  be like unto him.
Burden not thyself above thy power while thou livest;
And have no fellowship with one that is mightier and
  richer than thyself:
For how agree the kettle and the earthen pot together?
For if the one be smitten against the other, it shall
  be broken.
The rich man hath done wrong, and yet he threateneth
  withal:
The poor is wronged, and he must intreat also.
If thou be for his profit, he will use thee:
But if thou have nothing, he will forsake thee.
If thou have any thing, he will live with thee;
Yea, he will make thee bare, and will not be sorry
  for it.
If he have need of thee, he will deceive thee,
And smile upon thee, and put thee in hope;
He will speak thee fair, and say, "What wantest
  thou?"
And he will shame thee by his meats,
Until he have drawn thee dry twice or thrice,
And at the last he will laugh thee to scorn:
Afterward, when he seeth thee, he will forsake thee,
And shake his head at thee.

Beware that thou be not deceived,
And brought down in thy jollity.
If thou be invited of a mighty man, withdraw thyself,
And so much the more will he invite thee.
Press thou not upon him, lest thou be put back;
Stand not far off, lest thou be forgotten.
Affect not to be made equal unto him in talk,
And believe not his many words:
For with much communication will he tempt thee,
And smiling upon thee will get out thy secrets:
But cruelly he will lay up thy words,
And will not spare to do thee hurt, and to put thee in
    prison.
Observe, and take good heed,
For thou walkest in peril of thy overthrowing:
When thou hearest these things, awake in thy sleep.
Love the Lord all thy life,
And call upon him for thy salvation.   [13:1–14]

He that loveth his son causeth him oft to feel the rod,
That he may have joy of him in the end.
He that chastiseth his son shall have joy in him,
And shall rejoice of him among his acquaintance.
He that teacheth his son grieveth the enemy:
And before his friends he shall rejoice of him.
Though his father die, yet he is as though he were not
    dead:
For he hath left one behind him that is like himself.
While he lived, he saw and rejoiced in him:
And when he died, he was not sorrowful.
He left behind him an avenger against his enemies,
And one that shall requite kindness to his friends.
He that maketh too much of his son shall bind up his
    wounds;
And his bowels will be troubled at every cry.
An horse not broken becometh headstrong:
And a child left to himself will be wilful.

Cocker thy child, and he shall make thee afraid:
Laugh not with him, lest thou have sorrow with him,
And lest thou gnash thy teeth in the end.
Give him no liberty in his youth,
And wink not at his follies.
Bow down his neck while he is young,
And beat him on the sides while he is a child,
Lest he wax stubborn, and be disobedient unto thee,
And so bring sorrow to thine heart.
Chastise thy son, and hold him to labour,
Lest his lewd behaviour be an offence unto thee.

Better is the poor, being sound and strong of
    constitution,
Than a rich man that is afflicted in his body.
Health and good estate of body are above all gold,
And a strong body above infinite wealth.
There is no riches above a sound body,
And no joy above the joy of the heart.
Death is better than a bitter life
Or continual sickness.
Delicates poured upon a mouth shut up
Are as messes of meat set upon a grave.
What good doeth the offering unto an idol?
For neither can it eat nor smell:
So is he that is persecuted of the Lord.
He seeth with his eyes and groaneth,
As an eunuch that embraceth a virgin and sigheth.

Give not over thy mind to heaviness,
And afflict not thyself in thine own counsel.
The gladness of the heart is the life of man,
And the joyfulness of a man prolongeth his days.
Love thine own soul,
And comfort thy heart,
Remove sorrow far from thee:
For sorrow hath killed many,
And there is no profit therein.

Envy and wrath shorten the life,
And carefulness bringeth age before the time.
A cheerful and good heart will have a care of his meat
    and diet.   [30:1–25]

The wisdom of a learned man cometh by opportunity
    of leisure:
And he that hath little business shall become wise.
How can he get wisdom that holdeth the plough,
And that glorieth in the goad,
That driveth oxen, and is occupied in their labours,
And whose talk is of bullocks?
He giveth his mind to make furrows;
And is diligent to give the kine fodder.
So every carpenter and workmaster,
That laboureth night and day:
And they that cut and grave seals,
And are diligent to make great variety,
And give themselves to counterfeit imagery,
And watch to finish a work:
The smith also sitting by the anvil,
And considering the iron work,
The vapour of the fire wasteth his flesh,
And he fighteth with the heat of the furnace:
The noise of the hammer and the anvil is ever in his
    ears,
And his eyes look still upon the pattern of the thing
    that he maketh;
He setteth his mind to finish his work,
And watcheth to polish it perfectly.
So doth the potter sitting at his work,
And turning the wheel about with his feet,
Who is alway carefully set at his work,
And maketh all his work by number;
He fashioneth the clay with his arm,
And boweth down his strength before his feet;

He applieth himself to lead it over;
And he is diligent to make clean the furnace:

All these trust to their hands:
And every one is wise in his work.
Without these cannot a city be inhabited:
And they shall not dwell where they will, nor go up
    and down:
They shall not be sought for in publick counsel,
Nor sit high in the congregation:
They shall not sit on the judges' seat,
Nor understand the sentence of judgment:
They cannot declare justice and judgment;
And they shall not be found where parables are
    spoken.
But they will maintain the state of the world,
And all their desire is in the work of their craft.

[38:24–34]

Let us now praise famous men,
And our fathers that begat us.
The Lord hath wrought great glory by them
Through his great power from the beginning.
Such as did bear rule in their kingdoms,
Men renowned for their power,
Giving counsel by their understanding,
And declaring prophecies:
Leaders of the people by their counsels,
And by their knowledge of learning meet for the
    people,
Wise and eloquent in their instructions:
Such as found out musical tunes,
And recited verses in writing:
Rich men furnished with ability,
Living peaceably in their habitations:
All these were honoured in their generations,
And were the glory of their times.

There be of them, that have left a name behind them,
That their praises might be reported.
And some there be, which have no memorial;
Who are perished, as though they had never been;
And are become as though they had never been born;
And their children after them.
But these were merciful men,
Whose righteousness hath not been forgotten.
With their seed shall continually remain a good in-
    heritance,
And their children are within the covenant.
Their seed standeth fast, and their children for their
    sakes.
Their seed shall remain for ever,
And their glory shall not be blotted out.
Their bodies are buried in peace;
But their name liveth for evermore.
The people will tell of their wisdom,
And the congregation will shew forth their praise.

[44:1–15]

The New Testament

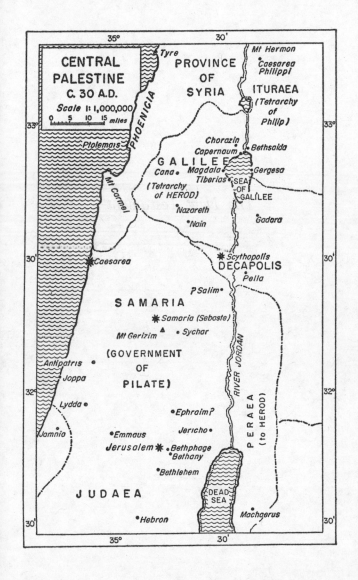

CENTRAL
PALESTINE
C. 30 A.D.

Scale 1: 1,000,000
0 . . . 5 . . 10 . . 15 miles

Tyre

PROVINCE
OF
SYRIA

Mt Hermon
Caesarea
Philippi

PHOENICIA

ITURAEA
(Tetrarchy
of Philip)

Ptolemais

Mt Carmel

Chorazin
Capernaum   Bethsaida

GALILEE

Cana   Magdala   Gergesa
(Tetrarchy   Tiberias   SEA
of HEROD)   OF
                      GALILEE

Nazareth   Gadara

Nain

Caesarea   Scythopolis
                  DECAPOLIS
                       Pella

P Salim

SAMARIA
        Samaria (Sebaste)

Mt Gerizim ▲   Sychar

(GOVERNMENT

Antipatris
        OF

Joppa
        PILATE)

Lydda   Ephraim?

Jamnia   Jericho

        Emmaus   Bethphage
Jerusalem ✴   Bethany

        Bethlehem

JUDAEA   DEAD
                         SEA

        Hebron   Machaerus

RIVER JORDAN

PERAEA
(to HEROD)

From THE GOSPEL ACCORDING TO MATTHEW

The Birth of Jesus. Now the birth of Jesus Christ was on this wise: When as his mother Mary was espoused to Joseph, before they came together, she was found with child of the Holy Ghost. Then Joseph her husband, being a just man, and not willing to make her a publick example, was minded to put her away privily. But while he thought on these things, behold, the angel of the Lord appeared unto him in a dream, saying, "Joseph, thou son of David, fear not to take unto thee Mary thy wife: for that which is conceived in her is of the Holy Ghost. And she shall bring forth a son, and thou shalt call his name JESUS: for he shall save his people from their sins." Now all this was done, that it might be fulfilled which was spoken of the Lord by the prophet, saying,

> "Behold, a virgin shall be with child, and shall bring
> forth a son,
> And they shall call his name Emmanuel."[1]

which being interpreted is, God with us. Then Joseph being raised from sleep did as the angel of the Lord had bidden him, and took unto him his wife: and knew her not till she had brought forth her firstborn son: and he called his name JESUS. [1:18–25]

The Wise Men from the East. Now when Jesus was born in Bethlehem of Judæa in the days of Herod[1] the king, behold, there came wise men from the east to Jerusalem, saying, "Where is he that is born King of the

1 See p. 302.
2 See Appendices 6 and 7.

Jews? for we have seen his star in the east, and are come to worship him". When Herod the king had heard these things, he was troubled, and all Jerusalem with him. And when he had gathered all the chief priests and scribes of the people together, he demanded of them where Christ should be born. And they said unto him, "In Bethlehem of Judæa: for thus it is written by the prophet,

> 'And thou Bethlehem, in the land of Juda,
>   Art not the least among the princes of Juda:
>   For out of thee shall come a Governor,
>   That shall rule my people Israel' ".

Then Herod, when he had privily called the wise men, enquired of them diligently what time the star appeared. And he sent them to Bethlehem, and said, "Go and search diligently for the young child; and when ye have found him, bring me word again, that I may come and worship him also". When they had heard the king, they departed; and, lo, the star, which they saw in the east, went before them, till it came and stood over where the young child was. When they saw the star, they rejoiced with exceeding great joy. And when they were come into the house, they saw the young child with Mary his mother, and fell down, and worshipped him: and when they had opened their treasures, they presented unto him gifts; gold, and frankincense, and myrrh. And being warned of God in a dream that they should not return to Herod, they departed into their own country another way.   [2:1–12]

The Flight into Egypt. And when they were departed, behold, the angel of the Lord appeareth to Joseph in a dream, saying, "Arise, and take the young child and his mother, and flee into Egypt, and be thou there until I bring thee word: for Herod will seek the young child to destroy him". When he arose, he took the young child and his mother by night, and departed into Egypt: and was there until the death of Herod: that it might be fulfilled which was spoken of the Lord by the prophet, saying,

"Out of Egypt have I called my son". Then Herod, when he saw that he was mocked of the wise men, was exceeding wroth, and sent forth, and slew all the children that were in Bethlehem, and in all the coasts thereof, from two years old and under, according to the time which he had diligently enquired of the wise men. Then was fulfilled that which was spoken by Jeremy the prophet, saying,

"In Rama was there a voice heard,
　Lamentation, and weeping, and great mourning,
　Rachel weeping for her children,
And would not be comforted, because they are not".

But when Herod was dead, behold, an angel of the Lord appeareth in a dream to Joseph in Egypt, saying, "Arise, and take the young child and his mother, and go into the land of Israel: for they are dead which sought the young child's life". And he arose, and took the young child and his mother, and came into the land of Israel. But when he heard that Archelaus did reign in Judæa in the room of his father Herod, he was afraid to go thither: notwith-standing, being warned of God in a dream, he turned aside into the parts of Galilee: and he came and dwelt in a city called Nazareth: that it might be fulfilled which was spoken by the prophets, "He shall be called a Nazarene".   [2:13–23]

The Preaching of John the Baptist. In those days came John the Baptist, preaching in the wilderness of Judæa, and saying, "Repent ye: for the kingdom of heaven is at hand". For this is he that was spoken of by the prophet Esaias,[3] saying,

"The voice of one crying in the wilderness,
'Prepare ye the way of the Lord,
　Make his paths straight' ".

And the same John had his raiment of camel's hair, and a leathern girdle about his loins; and his meat was locusts

[3] See p. 307. Esaias is the Greek form of Isaiah.

and wild honey. Then went out to him Jerusalem, and all Judæa, and all the region round about Jordan, and were baptized of him in Jordan, confessing their sins. But when he saw many of the Pharisees and Sadducees come to his baptism, he said unto them, "O generation of vipers, who hath warned you to flee from the wrath to come? Bring forth therefore fruits meet for repentance: and think not to say within yourselves, 'We have Abraham to our father': for I say unto you, that God is able of these stones to raise up children unto Abraham. And now also the axe is laid unto the root of the trees: therefore every tree which bringeth not forth good fruit is hewn down, and cast into the fire. I indeed baptize you with water unto repentance: but he that cometh after me is mightier than I, whose shoes I am not worthy to bear: he shall baptize you with the Holy Ghost, and with fire: whose fan is in his hand, and he will throughly purge his floor, and gather his wheat into the garner; but he will burn up the chaff with unquenchable fire." [3:1–12]

Jesus Baptized. Then cometh Jesus from Galilee to Jordan unto John, to be baptized of him. But John forbad him, saying, "I have need to be baptized of thee, and comest thou to me?" And Jesus answering said unto him, "Suffer it to be so now: for thus it becometh us to fulfil all righteousness". Then he suffered him. And Jesus, when he was baptized, went up straightway out of the water: and, lo, the heavens were opened unto him, and he saw the Spirit of God descending like a dove, and lighting upon him: and lo a voice from heaven, saying, "This is my beloved Son, in whom I am well pleased". [3:13–17]

The Temptation of Jesus. Then was Jesus led up of the Spirit into the wilderness to be tempted of the devil. And when he had fasted forty days and forty nights, he was afterward an hungred. And when the tempter came to him, he said, "If thou be the Son of God, command that these stones be made bread". But he answered and said, "It is written, 'Man shall not live by bread alone, but by every word that proceedeth out of the mouth of God'". Then the devil taketh him up into the holy city, and setteth him on a pinnacle of the temple, and saith unto him, "If thou be the Son of God, cast thyself down: for it is written,

'He shall give his angels charge concerning thee:
And in their hands they shall bear thee up,
Lest at any time thou dash thy foot against a stone'".

Jesus said unto him, "It is written again, 'Thou shalt not tempt the Lord thy God'". Again, the devil taketh him up into an exceeding high mountain, and sheweth him all the kingdoms of the world, and the glory of them; and saith unto him, "All these things will I give thee, if thou wilt fall down and worship me". Then saith Jesus unto him, "Get thee hence, Satan: for it is written. 'Thou shalt worship the Lord thy God, and him only shalt thou serve'". Then the devil leaveth him, and, behold, angels came and ministered unto him.

. . . . .

And Jesus, walking by the sea of Galilee, saw two brethren, Simon called Peter, and Andrew his brother, casting a net into the sea: for they were fishers. And he saith unto them, "Follow me, and I will make you fishers of men". And they straightway left their nets, and followed him. And going on from thence, he saw other two brethren, James the son of Zebedee, and John his brother, in a ship with Zebedee their father, mending their nets; and he called them. And they immediately left the ship and their father, and followed him.   [4:1–11, 18–22]

The Sermon on the Mount.   And seeing the multitudes, he went up into a mountain: and when he was set, his disciples came unto him: and he opened his mouth, and taught them, saying,

"Blessed are the poor in spirit: for theirs is the kingdom of heaven.

"Blessed are they that mourn: for they shall be comforted.

"Blessed are the meek: for they shall inherit the earth.

"Blessed are they which do hunger and thirst after righteousness: for they shall be filled.

"Blessed are the merciful: for they shall obtain mercy.

"Blessed are the pure in heart: for they shall see God.

"Blessed are the peacemakers: for they shall be called the children of God.

"Blessed are they which are persecuted for righteousness' sake: for theirs is the kingdom of heaven. Blessed are ye, when men shall revile you, and persecute you, and shall say all manner of evil against you falsely, for my sake. Rejoice, and be exceeding glad: for great is your reward in heaven: for so persecuted they the prophets which were before you.

"Ye are the salt of the earth: but if the salt have lost his savour, wherewith shall it be salted? it is thenceforth good for nothing, but to be cast out, and to be trodden under foot of men. Ye are the light of the world. A city that is set on an hill cannot be hid. Neither do men light a candle, and put it under a bushel, but on a candlestick; and it giveth light unto all that are in the house. Let your light so shine before men, that they may see your good works, and glorify your Father which is in heaven.

"Think not that I am come to destroy the law, or the prophets: I am not come to destroy, but to fulfil. For verily I say unto you, Till heaven and earth pass, one jot or one tittle[4] shall in no wise pass from the law, till all be fulfilled. Whosoever therefore shall break one of these least commandments, and shall teach men so, he shall be called the least in the kingdom of heaven: but whosoever shall do and teach them, the same shall be called great in the kingdom of heaven. For I say unto you, that except your righteousness shall exceed the righteousness of the scribes and Pharisees, ye shall in no case enter into the kingdom of heaven.

[4] I.e., smallest detail; "jot" and "tittle" are small marks or points used in writing.

"Ye have heard that it was said by them of old time, 'Thou shalt not kill; and whosoever shall kill shall be in danger of the judgment': but I say unto you, that whosoever is angry with his brother without a cause shall be in danger of the judgment: and whosoever shall say to his brother, 'Raca,' shall be in danger of the council: but whosoever shall say, 'Thou fool,' shall be in danger of hell fire. Therefore if thou bring thy gift to the altar, and there rememberest that thy brother hath aught against thee; leave there thy gift before the altar, and go thy way; first be reconciled to thy brother, and then come and offer thy gift. Agree with thine adversary quickly, whiles thou art in the way with him; lest at any time the adversary deliver thee to the judge, and the judge deliver thee to the officer, and thou be cast into prison. Verily I say unto thee, Thou shalt by no means come out thence, till thou hast paid the uttermost farthing.

"Ye have heard that it was said by them of old time, 'Thou shalt not commit adultery': but I say unto you, that whosoever looketh on a woman to lust after her hath committed adultery with her already in his heart. And if thy right eye offend thee, pluck it out, and cast it from thee: for it is profitable for thee that one of thy members should perish, and not that thy whole body should be cast into hell. And if thy right hand offend thee, cut it off, and cast it from thee: for it is profitable for thee that one of thy members should perish, and not that thy whole body should be cast into hell. It hath been said, 'Whosoever shall put away his wife, let him give her a writing of divorcement': but I say unto you, that whosoever shall put away his wife, saving for the cause of fornication, causeth her to commit adultery: and whosoever shall marry her that is divorced committeth adultery.

"Again, ye have heard that it hath been said by them of old time, 'Thou shalt not forswear thyself, but shalt perform unto the Lord thine oaths': but I say unto you, Swear not at all; neither by heaven; for it is God's throne:

nor by the earth; for it is his footstool: neither by Jerusalem; for it is the city of the great King. Neither shalt thou swear by thy head, because thou canst not make one hair white or black. But let your communication be, 'Yea, yea'; 'Nay, nay': for whatsoever is more than these cometh of evil.

"Ye have heard that it hath been said, 'An eye for an eye, and a tooth for a tooth': but I say unto you, that ye resist not evil: but whosoever shall smite thee on thy right cheek, turn to him the other also. And if any man will sue thee at the law, and take away thy coat, let him have thy cloke also. And whosoever shall compel thee to go a mile, go with him twain. Give to him that asketh thee, and from him that would borrow of thee turn not thou away.

"Ye have heard that it hath been said, 'Thou shalt love thy neighbour, and hate thine enemy'. But I say unto you, Love your enemies, bless them that curse you, do good to them that hate you, and pray for them which despitefully use you, and persecute you; that ye may be the children of your Father which is in heaven: for he maketh his sun to rise on the evil and on the good, and sendeth rain on the just and on the unjust. For if ye love them which love you, what reward have ye? do not even the publicans the same? And if ye salute your brethren only, what do ye more than others? do not even the publicans so? Be ye therefore perfect, even as your Father which is in heaven is perfect.

"Take heed that ye do not your alms before men, to be seen of them: otherwise ye have no reward of your Father which is in heaven.

"Therefore when thou doest thine alms, do not sound a trumpet before thee, as the hypocrites do in the synagogues and in the streets, that they may have glory of men. Verily I say unto you, They have their reward. But when thou doest alms, let not thy left hand know what thy right hand doeth: that thine alms may be in secret:

and thy Father which seeth in secret himself shall reward thee openly.

"And when thou prayest, thou shalt not be as the hypocrites are: for they love to pray standing in the synagogues and in the corners of the streets, that they may be seen of men. Verily I say unto you, They have their reward. But thou, when thou prayest, enter into thy closet, and when thou hast shut thy door, pray to thy Father which is in secret; and thy Father which seeth in secret shall reward thee openly. But when ye pray, use not vain repetitions, as the heathen do: for they think that they shall be heard for their much speaking. Be not ye therefore like unto them: for your Father knoweth what things ye have need of, before ye ask him. After this manner therefore pray ye: 'Our Father which art in heaven, Hallowed be thy name. Thy kingdom come. Thy will be done in earth, as it is in heaven. Give us this day our daily bread. And forgive us our debts, as we forgive our debtors. And lead us not into temptation, but deliver us from evil: For thine is the kingdom, and the power, and the glory, for ever. Amen.' For if ye forgive men their trespasses, your heavenly Father will also forgive you: but if ye forgive not men their trespasses, neither will your Father forgive your trespasses.

"Moreover when ye fast, be not, as the hypocrites, of a sad countenance: for they disfigure their faces, that they may appear unto men to fast. Verily I say unto you, They have their reward. But thou, when thou fastest, anoint thine head, and wash thy face; that thou appear not unto men to fast, but unto thy Father which is in secret: and thy Father, which seeth in secret, shall reward thee openly.

"Lay not up for yourselves treasures upon earth, where moth and rust doth corrupt, and where thieves break through and steal: but lay up for yourselves treasures in heaven, where neither moth nor rust doth corrupt, and where thieves do not break through nor steal: for where your treasure is, there will your heart be also. The light of the body is the eye: if therefore thine eye be single, thy whole body shall be full of light. But if thine eye be evil, thy whole body shall be full of darkness. If therefore the light that is in thee be darkness, how great is that darkness! No man can serve two masters: for either he will hate the one, and love the other; or else he will hold to the one, and despise the other. Ye cannot serve God and mammon.[5] Therefore I say unto you, Take no thought for your life, what ye shall eat, or what ye shall drink; nor yet for your body, what ye shall put on. Is not the life more than meat, and the body than raiment? Behold the fowls of the air: for they sow not, neither do they reap, nor gather into barns; yet your heavenly Father feedeth them. Are ye not much better than they? Which of you by taking thought can add one cubit unto his stature? And why take ye thought for raiment? Consider the lilies of the field, how they grow; they toil not, neither do they spin: and yet I say unto you, that even Solomon in all his glory was not arrayed like one of these. Wherefore, if God so clothe the grass of the field, which to day is, and to morrow is cast into the oven, shall he not much more clothe you, O ye of little faith? Therefore take no thought, saying, 'What shall we eat?' or, 'What shall we drink?' or, 'Wherewithal shall we be clothed?' (for after all these things do the Gentiles seek:) for your heavenly Father knoweth that ye have need of all these things. But seek ye first the kingdom of God, and his righteousness; and all these things shall be added unto you. Take therefore no thought for the morrow: for the morrow shall take thought for the things of itself. Sufficient unto the day is the evil thereof.

"Judge not, that ye be not judged. For with what judgment ye judge, ye shall be judged: and with what measure ye mete, it shall be measured to you again. And why beholdest thou the mote that is in thy brother's eye, but considerest not the beam that is in thine own eye? Or how

5 I.e., money.

wilt thou say to thy brother, 'Let me pull out the mote out of thine eye'; and, behold, a beam is in thine own eye? Thou hypocrite, first cast out the beam out of thine own eye; and then shalt thou see clearly to cast out the mote out of thy brother's eye.

"Give not that which is holy unto the dogs, neither cast ye your pearls before swine, lest they trample them under their feet, and turn again and rend you.

"Ask, and it shall be given you; seek, and ye shall find; knock, and it shall be opened unto you: for every one that asketh receiveth; and he that seeketh findeth; and to him that knocketh it shall be opened. Or what man is there of you, whom if his son ask bread, will he give him a stone? Or if he ask a fish, will he give him a serpent? If ye then, being evil, know how to give good gifts unto your children, how much more shall your Father which is in heaven give good things to them that ask him? Therefore all things whatsoever ye would that men should do to you, do ye even so to them: for this is the law and the prophets.

"Enter ye in at the strait gate: for wide is the gate, and broad is the way, that leadeth to destruction, and many there be which go in thereat: because strait is the gate, and narrow is the way, which leadeth unto life, and few there be that find it.

"Beware of false prophets, which come to you in sheep's clothing, but inwardly they are ravening wolves. Ye shall know them by their fruits. Do men gather grapes of thorns, or figs of thistles? Even so every good tree bringeth forth good fruit; but a corrupt tree bringeth forth evil fruit. A good tree cannot bring forth evil fruit, neither can a corrupt tree bring forth good fruit. Every tree that bringeth not forth good fruit is hewn down, and cast into the fire. Wherefore by their fruits ye shall know them. Not every one that saith unto me, 'Lord, Lord,' shall enter into the kingdom of heaven; but he that doeth the will of my Father which is in heaven. Many will say to me in that day, 'Lord, Lord, have we not prophesied in thy name? and in thy name have cast out devils? and in thy name done many wonderful works?' And then will I profess unto them, I never knew you: depart from me, ye that work iniquity. Therefore whosoever heareth these sayings of mine, and doeth them, I will liken him unto a wise man, which built his house upon a rock: and the rain descended, and the floods came, and the winds blew, and beat upon that house; and it fell not: for it was founded upon a rock. And every one that heareth these sayings of mine, and doeth them not, shall be likened unto a foolish man, which built his house upon the sand: and the rain descended, and the floods came, and the winds blew, and beat upon that house; and it fell: and great was the fall of it."

And it came to pass, when Jesus had ended these sayings, the people were astonished at his doctrine: for he taught them as one having authority, and not as the scribes.

[5:1–48; 6:1–34; 7:1–29]

The Call of Matthew. And as Jesus passed forth from thence, he saw a man, named Matthew, sitting at the receipt of custom: and he saith unto him, "Follow me". And he arose, and followed him.

And it came to pass, as Jesus sat at meat in the house, behold, many publicans and sinners came and sat down with him and his disciples. And when the Pharisees saw it, they said unto his disciples, "Why eateth your Master with publicans and sinners?"[6] But when Jesus heard that, he said unto them, "They that be whole need not a physician, but they that are sick. But go ye and learn what that meaneth, 'I will have mercy, and not sacrifice': for I am not come to call the righteous, but sinners to repentance."

Then came to him the disciples of John, saying, "Why do we and the Pharisees fast oft, but thy disciples fast not?" And Jesus said unto them, "Can the children of the bridechamber mourn, as long as the bridegroom is with them? but the days will come, when the bridegroom shall

[6] See Appendix 11.

be taken from them, and then shall they fast. No man putteth a piece of new cloth unto an old garment, for that which is put in to fill it up taketh from the garment, and the rent is made worse. Neither do men put new wine into old bottles:[7] else the bottles break, and the wine runneth out, and the bottles perish: but they put new wine into new bottles, and both are preserved."   [9:9–17]

The Mission of the Twelve. And when he had called unto him his twelve disciples, he gave them power against unclean spirits, to cast them out, and to heal all manner of sickness and all manner of disease.

Now the names of the twelve apostles are these; The first, Simon, who is called Peter, and Andrew his brother; James the son of Zebedee, and John his brother; Philip, and Bartholomew; Thomas, and Matthew the publican; James the son of Alphæus, and Lebbæus, whose surname was Thaddæus; Simon the Canaanite, and Judas Iscariot, who also betrayed him. These twelve Jesus sent forth, and commanded them, saying,

"Go not into the way of the Gentiles, and into any city of the Samaritans enter ye not: but go rather to the lost sheep of the house of Israel. And as ye go, preach, saying, 'The kingdom of heaven is at hand'. Heal the sick, cleanse the lepers, raise the dead, cast out devils: freely ye have received, freely give. Provide neither gold, nor silver, nor brass in your purses, nor scrip for your journey, neither two coats, neither shoes, nor yet staves: for the workman is worthy of his meat. And into whatsoever city or town ye shall enter, enquire who in it is worthy; and there abide till ye go thence. And when ye come into an house, salute it. And if the house be worthy, let your peace come upon it: but if it be not worthy, let your peace return to you. And whosoever shall not receive you, nor hear your words, when ye depart out of that house or city, shake off the dust of your feet. Verily I say unto you, It shall be more

[7] I.e., wineskins.

tolerable for the land of Sodom and Gomorrha in the day of judgment, than for that city.

"Behold, I send you forth as sheep in the midst of wolves: be ye therefore wise as serpents, and harmless as doves. But beware of men: for they will deliver you up to the councils, and they will scourge you in their synagogues; and ye shall be brought before governors and kings for my sake, for a testimony against them and the Gentiles. But when they deliver you up, take no thought how or what ye shall speak: for it shall be given you in that same hour what ye shall speak. For it is not ye that speak, but the Spirit of your Father which speaketh in you. And the brother shall deliver up the brother to death, and the father the child: and the children shall rise up against their parents, and cause them to be put to death. And ye shall be hated of all men for my name's sake: but he that endureth to the end shall be saved. But when they persecute you in this city, flee ye into another: for verily I say unto you, Ye shall not have gone over the cities of Israel, till the Son of man be come.

"The disciple is not above his master, nor the servant above his lord. It is enough for the disciple that he be as his master, and the servant as his lord. If they have called the master of the house Beelzebub, how much more shall they call them of his household? Fear them not therefore: for there is nothing covered, that shall not be revealed; and hid, that shall not be known. What I tell you in darkness, that speak ye in light: and what ye hear in the ear, that preach ye upon the housetops. And fear not them which kill the body, but are not able to kill the soul: but rather fear him which is able to destroy both soul and body in hell. Are not two sparrows sold for a farthing? and one of them shall not fall on the ground without your Father. But the very hairs of your head are all numbered. Fear ye not therefore, ye are of more value than many sparrows. Whosoever therefore shall confess me before men, him will I confess also before my Father which is in heaven.

But whosoever shall deny me before men, him will I also deny before my Father which is in heaven.

"Think not that I am come to send peace on earth: I came not to send peace, but a sword. For I am come to set a man at variance against his father, and the daughter against her mother, and the daughter in law against her mother in law. And a man's foes shall be they of his own household. He that loveth father or mother more than me is not worthy of me: and he that loveth son or daughter more than me is not worthy of me. And he that taketh not his cross, and followeth after me, is not worthy of me. He that findeth his life shall lose it: and he that loseth his life for my sake shall find it.

"He that receiveth you receiveth me, and he that receiveth me receiveth him that sent me. He that receiveth a prophet in the name of a prophet shall receive a prophet's reward; and he that receiveth a righteous man in the name of a righteous man shall receive a righteous man's reward. And whosoever shall give to drink unto one of these little ones a cup of cold water only in the name of a disciple, verily I say unto you, he shall in no wise lose his reward."

[10:1–42]

Jesus' Prayer. At that time Jesus answered and said, "I thank thee, O Father, Lord of heaven and earth, because thou hast hid these things from the wise and prudent, and hast revealed them unto babes. Even so, Father: for so it seemed good in thy sight. All things are delivered unto me of my Father: and no man knoweth the Son, but the Father; neither knoweth any man the Father, save the Son, and he to whomsoever the Son will reveal him. Come unto me, all ye that labour and are heavy laden, and I will give you rest. Take my yoke upon you, and learn of me; for I am meek and lowly in heart: and ye shall find rest unto your souls. For my yoke is easy, and my burden is light."

[11:25–30]

Blasphemy against the Holy Spirit. Then was brought unto him one possessed with a devil, blind, and dumb:

and he healed him, insomuch that the blind and dumb both spake and saw. And all the people were amazed, and said, "Is not this the Son of David?" But when the Pharisees heard it, they said, "This fellow doth not cast out devils, but by Beelzebub the prince of the devils". And Jesus knew their thoughts, and said unto them, "Every kingdom divided against itself is brought to desolation; and every city or house divided against itself shall not stand: and if Satan cast out Satan, he is divided against himself; how shall then his kingdom stand? And if I by Beelzebub cast out devils, by whom do your children cast them out? Therefore they shall be your judges. But if I cast out devils by the Spirit of God, then the kingdom of God is come unto you. Or else how can one enter into a strong man's house, and spoil his goods, except he first bind the strong man? and then he will spoil his house. He that is not with me is against me; and he that gathereth not with me scattereth abroad. Wherefore I say unto you, All manner of sin and blasphemy shall be forgiven unto men: but the blasphemy against the Holy Ghost shall not be forgiven unto men. And whosoever speaketh a word against the Son of man, it shall be forgiven him: but whosoever speaketh against the Holy Ghost, it shall not be forgiven him, neither in this world, neither in the world to come. Either make the tree good, and his fruit good; or else make the tree corrupt, and his fruit corrupt: for the tree is known by his fruit. O generation of vipers, how can ye, being evil, speak good things? for out of the abundance of the heart the mouth speaketh. A good man out of the good treasure of the heart bringeth forth good things: and an evil man out of the evil treasure bringeth forth evil things. But I say unto you, that every idle word that men shall speak, they shall give account thereof in the day of judgment. For by thy words thou shalt be justified, and by thy words thou shalt be condemned." [12:22–37]

A Sign Denied. Then certain of the scribes and of the Pharisees answered, saying, "Master, we would see a sign from thee". But he answered and said unto them, "An evil and adulterous generation seeketh after a sign; and there shall no sign be given to it, but the sign of the prophet Jonas: for as Jonas was three days and three nights in the whale's belly; so shall the Son of man be three days and three nights in the heart of the earth. The men of Nineveh shall rise in judgment with this generation, and shall condemn it: because they repented at the preaching of Jonas; and, behold, a greater than Jonas is here. The queen of the south shall rise up in the judgment with this generation, and shall condemn it: for she came from the uttermost parts of the earth to hear the wisdom of Solomon; and, behold, a greater than Solomon is here. When the unclean spirit is gone out of a man, he walketh through dry places, seeking rest, and findeth none. Then he saith, 'I will return into my house from whence I came out'; and when he is come, he findeth it empty, swept, and garnished. Then goeth he, and taketh with himself seven other spirits more wicked than himself, and they enter in and dwell there: and the last state of that man is worse than the first. Even so shall it be also unto this wicked generation."

[12:38–45]

Parables of the Kingdom. A. The Tares. Another parable put he forth unto them, saying, "The kingdom of heaven is likened unto a man which sowed good seed in his field: but while men slept, his enemy came and sowed tares among the wheat, and went his way. But when the blade was sprung up, and brought forth fruit, then appeared the tares also. So the servants of the householder came and said unto him, 'Sir, didst not thou sow good seed in thy field? from whence then hath it tares?' He said unto them, 'An enemy hath done this'. The servants said unto him, 'Wilt thou then that we go and gather them up?' But he said, 'Nay; lest while ye gather up the tares, ye root up also the wheat with them. Let both grow together until the harvest: and in the time of harvest I will say to the reapers, Gather ye together first the tares, and bind them in bundles to burn them: but gather the wheat into my barn.'"

B. The Grain of Mustard Seed. Another parable put he forth unto them, saying, "The kingdom of heaven is like to a grain of mustard seed, which a man took, and sowed in his field: which indeed is the least of all seeds: but when it is grown, it is the greatest among herbs, and becometh a tree, so that the birds of the air come and lodge in the branches thereof".

C. Leaven. Another parable spake he unto them; "The kingdom of heaven is like unto leaven, which a woman took, and hid in three measures of meal, till the whole was leavened".

All these things spake Jesus unto the multitude in parables; and without a parable spake he not unto them: that it might be fulfilled which was spoken by the prophet, saying,

> "I will open my mouth in parables;
> I will utter things which have been kept secret from
> the foundation of the world".

Then Jesus sent the multitude away, and went into the house: and his disciples came unto him, saying, "Declare unto us the parable of the tares of the field". He answered and said unto them, "He that soweth the good seed is the Son of man; the field is the world; the good seed are the children of the kingdom; but the tares are the children of the wicked one; the enemy that sowed them is the devil; the harvest is the end of the world; and the reapers are the angels. As therefore the tares are gathered and burned in the fire; so shall it be in the end of this world. The Son of man shall send forth his angels, and they shall gather out of his kingdom all things that offend, and them which do iniquity; and shall cast them into a furnace of fire: there shall be wailing and gnashing of teeth. Then shall the righteous shine forth as the sun in the kingdom of their Father. Who hath ears to hear, let him hear.

D. The Treasure. "Again, the kingdom of heaven is like unto treasure hid in a field; the which when a man hath found, he hideth, and for joy thereof goeth and selleth all that he hath, and buyeth that field.

E. The Pearl of Great Price. "Again, the kingdom of heaven is like unto a merchant man, seeking goodly pearls: who, when he had found one pearl of great price, went and sold all that he had, and bought it.

F. The Net. "Again, the kingdom of heaven is like unto a net, that was cast into the sea, and gathered of every kind: which, when it was full, they drew to shore, and sat down, and gathered the good into vessels, but cast the bad away. So shall it be at the end of the world: the angels shall come forth, and sever the wicked from among the just, and shall cast them into the furnace of fire: there shall be wailing and gnashing of teeth."

Jesus saith unto them, "Have ye understood all these things?" They say unto him, "Yea, Lord". Then said he unto them, "Therefore every scribe which is instructed unto the kingdom of heaven is like unto a man that is an householder, which bringeth forth out of his treasure things new and old".   [13:24–52]

Jesus Rejected by His Own People.   And it came to pass, that when Jesus had finished these parables, he departed thence. And when he was come into his own country, he taught them in their synagogue, insomuch that they were astonished, and said, "Whence hath this man this wisdom, and these mighty works? Is not this the carpenter's son? is not his mother called Mary? and his brethren, James, and Joses, and Simon, and Judas? And his sisters, are they not all with us? Whence then hath this man all these things?" And they were offended in him. But Jesus said unto them, "A prophet is not without honour, save in his own country, and in his own house". And he did not many mighty works there because of their unbelief.

[13:53–58]

Jesus and the Woman of Tyre. Then Jesus went thence, and departed into the coasts of Tyre and Sidon. And, behold, a woman of Canaan came out of the same coasts, and cried unto him, saying, "Have mercy on me, O Lord, thou Son of David; my daughter is grievously vexed with a devil". But he answered her not a word. And his disciples came and besought him, saying, "Send her away; for she crieth after us". But he answered and said, "I am not sent but unto the lost sheep of the house of Israel". Then came she and worshipped him, saying, "Lord, help me". But he answered and said, "It is not meet to take the children's bread, and to cast it to dogs". And she said, "Truth, Lord: yet the dogs eat of the crumbs which fall from their masters' table". Then Jesus answered and said unto her, "O woman, great is thy faith: be it unto thee even as thou wilt". And her daughter was made whole from that very hour.

And Jesus departed from thence, and came nigh unto the sea of Galilee; and went up into a mountain, and sat down there. And great multitudes came unto him, having with them those that were lame, blind, dumb, maimed, and many others, and cast them down at Jesus' feet; and he healed them: insomuch that the multitude wondered, when they saw the dumb to speak, the maimed to be whole, the lame to walk, and the blind to see: and they glorified the God of Israel. [15:21–31]

Jesus Feeds Four Thousand. Then Jesus called his disciples unto him, and said, "I have compassion on the multitude, because they continue with me now three days, and have nothing to eat: and I will not send them away fasting, lest they faint in the way". And his disciples say unto him, "Whence should we have so much bread in the wilderness, as to fill so great a multitude?" And Jesus saith unto them, "How many loaves have ye?" And they said, "Seven, and a few little fishes". And he commanded the multitude to sit down on the ground. And he took the seven loaves and the fishes, and gave thanks, and brake them, and gave to his disciples, and the disciples to the multitude. And they did all eat, and were filled: and they took up of the broken meat that was left seven baskets full. And they that did eat were four thousand men, beside women and children. And he sent away the multitude, and took ship, and came into the coasts of Magdala.

[15:32–39]

Peter's Confession. When Jesus came into the coasts of Cæsarea Philippi, he asked his disciples, saying, "Whom do men say that I the Son of man am?" And they said, "Some say that thou art John the Baptist: some, Elias; and others, Jeremias, or one of the prophets". He saith unto them, "But whom say ye that I am?" And Simon Peter answered and said, "Thou art the Christ, the Son of the living God". And Jesus answered and said unto him, "Blessed art thou, Simon Bar-jona: for flesh and blood hath not revealed it unto thee, but my Father which is in heaven. And I say also unto thee, that thou art Peter, and upon this rock I will build my church; and the gates of hell shall not prevail against it. And I will give unto thee the keys of the kingdom of heaven: and whatsoever thou shalt bind on earth shall be bound in heaven: and whatsoever thou shalt loose on earth shall be loosed in heaven." Then charged he his disciples that they should tell no man that he was Jesus the Christ. [16:13–20]

Peter Rebuked. From that time forth began Jesus to shew unto his disciples, how that he must go unto Jerusalem, and suffer many things of the elders and chief priests and scribes, and be killed, and be raised again the third day. Then Peter took him, and began to rebuke him, saying, "Be it far from thee, Lord: this shall not be unto thee". But he turned, and said unto Peter, "Get thee behind me, Satan: thou art an offence unto me: for thou savourest not the things that be of God, but those that be of men". Then said Jesus unto his disciples, "If any man will come after me, let him deny himself, and take up his cross, and follow me. For whosoever will save his life

shall lose it: and whosoever will lose his life for my sake
shall find it. For what is a man profited, if he shall gain
the whole world, and lose his own soul? or what shall a
man give in exchange for his soul? For the Son of man shall
come in the glory of his Father with his angels; and then
he shall reward every man according to his works. Verily
I say unto you, There be some standing here, which shall
not taste of death, till they see the Son of man coming in
his kingdom." [16:21–28]

Jesus and the Tribute. And when they were come to
Capernaum, they that received tribute money came to
Peter, and said, "Doth not your master pay tribute?" He
saith, "Yes". And when he was come into the house, Jesus
prevented him, saying, "What thinkest thou, Simon? of
whom do the kings of the earth take custom or tribute?
of their own children, or of strangers?" Peter saith unto
him, "Of strangers". Jesus saith unto him, "Then are the
children free. Notwithstanding, lest we should offend them,
go thou to the sea, and cast an hook, and take up the fish
that first cometh up; and when thou hast opened his mouth,
thou shalt find a piece of money: that take, and give unto
them for me and thee." [17:24–27]

Jesus and Little Children. At the same time came the
disciples unto Jesus, saying, "Who is the greatest in the
kingdom of heaven?" And Jesus called a little child unto
him, and set him in the midst of them, and said, "Verily I
say unto you, Except ye be converted, and become as little children, ye shall not enter into the kingdom of heaven.
Whosoever therefore shall humble himself as this little
child, the same is greatest in the kingdom of heaven. And
whoso shall receive one such little child in my name receiveth me. But whoso shall offend one of these little ones
which believe in me, it were better for him that a millstone
were hanged about his neck, and that he were drowned
in the depth of the sea. Woe unto the world because of
offences! for it must needs be that offences come; but
woe to that man by whom the offence cometh! Wherefore

if thy hand or thy foot offend thee, cut them off, and cast them from thee: it is better for thee to enter into life halt or maimed, rather than having two hands or two feet to be cast into everlasting fire. And if thine eye offend thee, pluck it out, and cast it from thee: it is better for thee to enter into life with one eye, rather than having two eyes to be cast into hell fire. Take heed that ye despise not one of these little ones; for I say unto you, that in heaven their angels do always behold the face of my Father which is in heaven. For the Son of man is come to save that which was lost. How think ye? if a man have an hundred sheep, and one of them be gone astray, doth he not leave the ninety and nine, and goeth into the mountains, and seeketh that which is gone astray? And if so be that he find it, verily I say unto you, he rejoiceth more of that sheep, than of the ninety and nine which went not astray. Even so it is not the will of your Father which is in heaven, that one of these little ones should perish.   [18:1–14]

Forgiveness. "Moreover if thy brother shall trespass against thee, go and tell him his fault between thee and him alone: if he shall hear thee, thou hast gained thy brother. But if he will not hear thee, then take with thee one or two more, that in the mouth of two or three witnesses every word may be established. And if he shall neglect to hear them, tell it unto the church: but if he neglect to hear the church, let him be unto thee as an heathen man and a publican. Verily I say unto you, Whatsoever ye shall bind on earth shall be bound in heaven: and whatsoever ye shall loose on earth shall be loosed in heaven. Again I say unto you, that if two of you shall agree on earth as touching any thing that they shall ask, it shall be done for them of my Father which is in heaven. For where two or three are gathered together in my name, there am I in the midst of them."   [18:15–20]

Parable of the Merciless Servant. Then came Peter to him, and said, "Lord, how oft shall my brother sin against me, and I forgive him? till seven times?" Jesus saith unto him, "I say not unto thee, Until seven times: but, Until seventy times seven. Therefore is the kingdom of heaven likened unto a certain king, which would take account of his servants. And when he had begun to reckon, one was brought unto him, which owed him ten thousand talents. But forasmuch as he had not to pay, his lord commanded him to be sold, and his wife, and children, and all that he had, and payment to be made. The servant therefore fell down, and worshipped him, saying, 'Lord, have patience with me, and I will pay thee all'. Then the lord of that servant was moved with compassion, and loosed him, and forgave him the debt. But the same servant went out, and found one of his fellowservants, which owed him an hundred pence: and he laid hands on him, and took him by the throat, saying, 'Pay me that thou owest'. And his fellowservant fell down at his feet, and besought him, saying, 'Have patience with me, and I will pay thee all'. And he would not: but went and cast him into prison, till he should pay the debt. So when his fellowservants saw what was done, they were very sorry, and came and told unto their lord all that was done. Then his lord, after that he had called him, said unto him, 'O thou wicked servant, I forgave thee all that debt, because thou desiredst me: shouldest not thou also have had compassion on thy fellowservant, even as I had pity on thee?' And his lord was wroth, and delivered him to the tormentors, till he should pay all that was due unto him. So likewise shall my heavenly Father do also unto you, if ye from your hearts forgive not every one his brother their trespasses."

[18:21–35]

The Parable of the Laborers in the Vineyard. "For the kingdom of heaven is like unto a man that is an householder, which went out early in the morning to hire labourers into his vineyard. And when he had agreed with the labourers for a penny a day, he sent them into his vineyard. And he went out about the third hour, and saw others standing idle in the marketplace, and said unto them; 'Go ye also into the vineyard, and whatsoever is right I will give you'. And they went their way. Again he went out about the sixth and ninth hour, and did likewise. And about the eleventh hour he went out, and found others standing idle, and saith unto them, 'Why stand ye here all the day idle?' They say unto him, 'Because no man hath hired us'. He saith unto them, 'Go ye also into the vineyard; and whatsoever is right, that shall ye receive'. So when even was come, the lord of the vineyard saith unto his steward, 'Call the labourers, and give them their hire, beginning from the last unto the first'. And when they came that were hired about the eleventh hour, they received every man a penny. But when the first came, they supposed that they should have received more; and they likewise received every man a penny. And when they had received it, they murmured against the goodman of the house, saying, 'These last have wrought but one hour, and thou hast made them equal unto us, which have borne the burden and heat of the day'. But he answered one of them, and said, 'Friend, I do thee no wrong: didst not thou agree with me for a penny? Take that thine is, and go thy way: I will give unto this last, even as unto thee. Is it not lawful for me to do what I will with mine own? Is thine eye evil, because I am good?' So the last shall be first, and the first last: for many be called, but few chosen."

And Jesus going up to Jerusalem took the twelve disciples apart in the way, and said unto them, "Behold, we go up to Jerusalem; and the Son of man shall be betrayed unto the chief priests and unto the scribes, and they shall condemn him to death, and shall deliver him to the Gentiles to mock, and to scourge, and to crucify him: and the third day he shall rise again".   [20:1–19]

The Request of the Mother of James and John. Then came to him the mother of Zebedee's children with her sons, worshipping him, and desiring a certain thing of him. And he said unto her, "What wilt thou?" She saith unto him, "Grant that these my two sons may sit, the one on thy right hand, and the other on the left, in thy kingdom". But Jesus answered and said, "Ye know not what ye ask. Are ye able to drink of the cup that I shall drink of, and to be baptized with the baptism that I am baptized with?" They say unto him, "We are able". And he saith unto them, "Ye shall drink indeed of my cup, and be baptized with the baptism that I am baptized with: but to sit on my right hand, and on my left, is not mine to give, but it shall be given to them for whom it is prepared of my Father". And when the ten heard it, they were moved with indignation against the two brethren. But Jesus called them unto him, and said, "Ye know that the princes of the Gentiles exercise dominion over them, and they that are great exercise authority upon them. But it shall not be so among you: but whosoever will be great among you, let him be your minister; and whosoever will be chief among you, let him be your servant: even as the Son of man came not to be ministered unto, but to minister, and to give his life a ransom for many."   [20:20–28]

Two Blind Men Healed. And as they departed from Jericho, a great multitude followed him. And, behold, two blind men sitting by the way side, when they heard that Jesus passed by, cried out, saying, "Have mercy on us, O Lord, thou Son of David". And the multitude rebuked them, because they should hold their peace: but they cried the more, saying, "Have mercy on us, O Lord, thou Son of David". And Jesus stood still, and called them, and said, "What will ye that I shall do unto you?" They say unto him, "Lord, that our eyes may be opened". So Jesus had compassion on them, and touched their eyes: and immediately their eyes received sight, and they followed him.   [20:29–34]

From THE GOSPEL ACCORDING TO MARK

The Parable of the Sower.   And he began again to teach by the sea side: and there was gathered unto him a great multitude, so that he entered into a ship, and sat in the sea; and the whole multitude was by the sea on the land. And he taught them many things by parables, and said unto them in his doctrine, "Hearken; Behold, there went out a sower to sow: and it came to pass, as he sowed, some fell by the way side, and the fowls of the air came and devoured it up. And some fell on stony ground, where it had not much earth; and immediately it sprang up, because it had no depth of earth: but when the sun was up, it was scorched; and because it had no root, it withered away. And some fell among thorns, and the thorns grew up, and choked it, and it yielded no fruit. And other fell on good ground, and did yield fruit that sprang up and increased; and brought forth, some thirty, and some sixty, and some an hundred." And he said unto them, "He that hath ears to hear, let him hear".

And when he was alone, they that were about him with the twelve asked of him the parable. And he said unto them, "Unto you it is given to know the mystery of the kingdom of God: but unto them that are without, all these things are done in parables: that seeing they may see, and not perceive; and hearing they may hear, and not understand; lest at any time they should be converted, and their sins should be forgiven them". And he said unto them, "Know ye not this parable? and how then will ye know all parables? The sower soweth the word. And these are they by the way side, where the word is sown; but when they have heard, Satan cometh immediately, and taketh away the word that was sown in their hearts. And these are they likewise which are sown on stony ground; who, when they have heard the word, immediately receive it with gladness; and have no root in themselves, and so endure but for a time: afterward, when affliction or persecution ariseth for the word's sake, immediately they are offended. And these are they which are sown among thorns; such as hear the word, and the cares of this world, and the deceitfulness of riches, and the lusts of other things entering in, choke the word, and it becometh unfruitful. And these are they which are sown on good ground; such as hear the word, and receive it, and bring forth fruit, some thirtyfold, some sixty, and some an hundred."   [4:1–20]

The Gadarene Demoniac. And they came over unto the other side of the sea, into the country of the Gadarenes. And when he was come out of the ship, immediately there met him out of the tombs a man with an unclean spirit, who had his dwelling among the tombs; and no man could bind him, no, not with chains: because that he had been often bound with fetters and chains, and the chains had been plucked asunder by him, and the fetters broken in pieces: neither could any man tame him. And always, night and day, he was in the mountains, and in the tombs, crying, and cutting himself with stones. But when he saw Jesus afar off, he ran and worshipped him, and cried with a loud voice, and said, "What have I to do with thee, Jesus, thou Son of the most high God? I adjure thee by God, that thou torment me not." For he said unto him, "Come out of the man, thou unclean spirit". And he asked him, "What is thy name?" And he answered, saying, "My name is Legion: for we are many". And he besought him much that he would not send them away out of the country. Now there was there nigh unto the mountains a great herd of swine feeding. And all the devils besought him, saying, "Send us into the swine, that we may enter into them".

And forthwith Jesus gave them leave. And the unclean spirits went out, and entered into the swine: and the herd ran violently down a steep place into the sea, (they were about two thousand;) and were choked in the sea. And they that fed the swine fled, and told it in the city, and in the country. And they went out to see what it was that was done. And they come to Jesus, and see him that was possessed with the devil, and had the legion, sitting, and clothed, and in his right mind: and they were afraid. And they that saw it told them how it befell to him that was possessed with the devil, and also concerning the swine. And they began to pray him to depart out of their coasts. And when he was come into the ship, he that had been possessed with the devil prayed him that he might be with him. Howbeit Jesus suffered him not, but saith unto him, "Go home to thy friends, and tell them how great things the Lord hath done for thee, and hath had compassion on thee". And he departed, and began to publish in Decapolis how great things Jesus had done for him: and all men did marvel.

And when Jesus was passed over again by ship unto the other side, much people gathered unto him: and he was nigh unto the sea. And, behold, there cometh one of the rulers of the synagogue, Jairus by name; and when he saw him, he fell at his feet, and besought him greatly, saying, "My little daughter lieth at the point of death: I pray thee, come and lay thy hands on her, that she may be healed; and she shall live". And Jesus went with him; and much people followed him, and thronged him.

[5:1–24]

A Woman with an Issue of Blood Healed. And a certain woman, which had an issue of blood twelve years, and had suffered many things of many physicians, and had spent all that she had, and was nothing bettered, but rather grew worse, when she had heard of Jesus, came in the press behind, and touched his garment. For she said,

"If I may touch but his clothes, I shall be whole". And straightway the fountain of her blood was dried up; and she felt in her body that she was healed of that plague. And Jesus, immediately knowing in himself that virtue had gone out of him, turned him about in the press, and said, "Who touched my clothes?" And his disciples said unto him, "Thou seest the multitude thronging thee, and sayest thou, 'Who touched me?'" And he looked round about to see her that had done this thing. But the woman fearing and trembling, knowing what was done in her, came and fell down before him, and told him all the truth. And he said unto her, "Daughter, thy faith hath made thee whole; go in peace, and be whole of thy plague".

[5:25–34]

Jairus' Daughter Restored to Life. While he yet spake, there came from the ruler of the synagogue's house certain which said, "Thy daughter is dead: why troublest thou the Master any further?" As soon as Jesus heard the word that was spoken, he saith unto the ruler of the synagogue, "Be not afraid, only believe". And he suffered no man to follow him, save Peter, and James, and John the brother of James. And he cometh to the house of the ruler of the synagogue, and seeth the tumult, and them that wept and wailed greatly. And when he was come in, he saith unto them, "Why make ye this ado, and weep? the damsel is not dead, but sleepeth". And they laughed him to scorn. But when he had put them all out, he taketh the father and the mother of the damsel, and them that were with him, and entereth in where the damsel was lying. And he took the damsel by the hand, and said unto her, "TALITHA CUMI"; which is, being interpreted, "Damsel, I say unto thee, arise". And straightway the damsel arose, and walked; for she was of the age of twelve years. And they were astonished with a great astonishment. And he charged them straitly that no man should know it; and commanded that something should be given her to eat.   [5:35–43]

Herod Kills John the Baptist. And king Herod[1] heard
of him; (for his name was spread abroad:) and he said,
that John the Baptist was risen from the dead, and therefore mighty works do shew forth themselves in him. Others
said, that it is Elias. And others said, that it is a prophet,
or as one of the prophets. But when Herod heard thereof,
he said, "It is John, whom I beheaded: he is risen from the
dead". For Herod himself had sent forth and laid hold
upon John, and bound him in prison for Herodias' sake,
his brother Philip's wife: for he had married her. For John
had said unto Herod, "It is not lawful for thee to have thy
brother's wife". Therefore Herodias had a quarrel against
him, and would have killed him; but she could not: for
Herod feared John, knowing that he was a just man and
an holy, and observed him; and when he heard him, he did
many things, and heard him gladly. And when a convenient
day was come, that Herod on his birthday made a supper
to his lords, high captains, and chief estates of Galilee;
and when the daughter[2] of the said Herodias came in, and
danced, and pleased Herod and them that sat with him, the
king said unto the damsel, "Ask of me whatsoever thou
wilt, and I will give it thee". And he sware unto her,
"Whatsoever thou shalt ask of me, I will give it thee, unto
the half of my kingdom". And she went forth, and said
unto her mother, "What shall I ask?" And she said, "The
head of John the Baptist". And she came in straightway
with haste unto the king, and asked, saying, "I will that
thou give me by and by in a charger the head of John the
Baptist". And the king was exceeding sorry; yet for his
oath's sake, and for their sakes which sat with him, he
would not reject her. And immediately the king sent an
executioner, and commanded his head to be brought: and
he went and beheaded him in the prison, and brought his
head in a charger, and gave it to the damsel: and the

[1] See Appendix 7.
[2] Josephus records that her name was Salome.

damsel gave it to her mother. And when his disciples heard
of it, they came and took up his corpse, and laid it in a
tomb.   [6:14-29]

Jesus Feeds Five Thousand. And the apostles gathered
themselves together unto Jesus, and told him all things,
both what they had done, and what they had taught. And
he said unto them, "Come ye yourselves apart into a desert place, and rest a while": for there were many coming
and going, and they had no leisure so much as to eat. And
they departed into a desert place by ship privately. And
the people saw them departing, and many knew him, and
ran afoot thither out of all cities, and outwent them, and
came together unto him. And Jesus, when he came out,
saw much people, and was moved with compassion toward
them, because they were as sheep not having a shepherd:
and he began to teach them many things. And when the
day was now far spent, his disciples came unto him, and
said, "This is a desert place, and now the time is far
passed: send them away, that they may go into the country
round about, and into the villages, and buy themselves
bread: for they have nothing to eat". He answered and
said unto them, "Give ye them to eat". And they say unto
him, "Shall we go and buy two hundred pennyworth of
bread, and give them to eat?" He saith unto them, "How
many loaves have ye? go and see". And when they knew,
they say, "Five, and two fishes". And he commanded them
to make all sit down by companies upon the green grass.
And they sat down in ranks, by hundreds, and by fifties.
And when he had taken the five loaves and the two fishes,
he looked up to heaven, and blessed, and brake the loaves,
and gave them to his disciples to set before them; and the
two fishes divided he among them all. And they did all
eat, and were filled. And they took up twelve baskets full
of the fragments, and of the fishes. And they that did eat of
the loaves were about five thousand men.   [6:30-44]

The Disciples Rebuked. Now the disciples had forgotten to take bread, neither had they in the ship with them

more than one loaf. And he charged them, saying, "Take heed, beware of the leaven of the Pharisees, and of the leaven of Herod". And they reasoned among themselves, saying, "It is because we have no bread". And when Jesus knew it, he saith unto them, "Why reason ye, because ye have no bread? perceive ye not yet, neither understand? have ye your heart yet hardened? Having eyes, see ye not? and having ears, hear ye not? and do ye not remember? When I brake the five loaves among five thousand, how many baskets full of fragments took ye up?" They say unto him, "Twelve". "And when the seven among four thousand, how many baskets full of fragments took ye up?" And they said, "Seven". And he said unto them, "How is it that ye do not understand?"

And he cometh to Bethsaida; and they bring a blind man unto him, and besought him to touch him. And he took the blind man by the hand, and led him out of the town; and when he had spit on his eyes, and put his hands upon him, he asked him if he saw aught. And he looked up, and said, "I see men as trees, walking". After that he put his hands again upon his eyes, and made him look up: and he was restored, and saw every man clearly. And he sent him away to his house, saying, "Neither go into the town, nor tell it to any in the town".   [8:14–26]

The Transfiguration of Jesus. And he said unto them, "Verily I say unto you, that there be some of them that stand here, which shall not taste of death, till they have seen the kingdom of God come with power".

And after six days Jesus taketh with him Peter, and James, and John, and leadeth them up into an high mountain apart by themselves: and he was transfigured before them. And his raiment became shining, exceeding white as snow; so as no fuller on earth can white them. And there appeared unto them Elias[3] with Moses: and they were talking with Jesus. And Peter answered and said to

[3] The Greek form of Elijah.

Jesus, "Master, it is good for us to be here: and let us make three tabernacles; one for thee, and one for Moses, and one for Elias". For he wist not what to say; for they were sore afraid. And there was a cloud that overshadowed them: and a voice came out of the cloud, saying, "This is my beloved Son: hear him". And suddenly, when they had looked round about, they saw no man any more, save Jesus only with themselves.

And as they came down from the mountain, he charged them that they should tell no man what things they had seen, till the Son of man were risen from the dead. And they kept that saying with themselves, questioning one with another what the rising from the dead should mean. And they asked him, saying, "Why say the scribes that Elias must first come?" And he answered and told them, "Elias verily cometh first, and restoreth all things; and how it is written of the Son of man, that he must suffer many things, and be set at nought. But I say unto you, that Elias is indeed come, and they have done unto him whatsoever they listed, as it is written of him."   [9:1–13]

The Boy with a Dumb Devil Healed. And when he came to his disciples, he saw a great multitude about them, and the scribes questioning with them. And straightway all the people, when they beheld him, were greatly amazed, and running to him saluted him. And he asked the scribes, "What question ye with them?" And one of the multitude answered and said, "Master, I have brought unto thee my son, which hath a dumb spirit; and wheresoever he taketh him, he teareth him: and he foameth, and gnasheth with his teeth, and pineth away: and I spake to thy disciples that they should cast him out; and they could not". He answereth him, and saith, "O faithless generation, how long shall I be with you? how long shall I suffer you? bring him unto me". And they brought him unto him: and when he saw him, straightway the spirit tare him; and he fell on the ground, and wallowed foaming. And he asked his father, "How long is it ago since this came unto him?" And he said, "Of a child. And ofttimes it hath cast him into the fire, and into the waters, to destroy him: but if thou canst do any thing, have compassion on us, and help us." Jesus said unto him, "If thou canst believe, all things are possible to him that believeth". And straightway the father of the child cried out, and said with tears, "Lord, I believe; help thou mine unbelief". When Jesus saw that the people came running together, he rebuked the foul spirit, saying unto him, "Thou dumb and deaf spirit, I charge thee, come out of him, and enter no more into him". And the spirit cried, and rent him sore, and came out of him: and he was as one dead; insomuch that many said, "He is dead". But Jesus took him by the hand, and lifted him up; and he arose. And when he was come into the house, his disciples asked him privately, "Why could not we cast him out?" And he said unto them, "This kind can come forth by nothing, but by prayer and fasting".

And they departed thence, and passed through Galilee; and he would not that any man should know it. For he taught his disciples, and said unto them, "The Son of man is delivered into the hands of men, and they shall kill him; and after that he is killed, he shall rise the third day". But they understood not that saying, and were afraid to ask him.   [9:14–32]

Jesus on Divorce. And he arose from thence, and cometh into the coasts of Judæa by the farther side of Jordan: and the people resort unto him again; and, as he was wont, he taught them again. And the Pharisees came to him, and asked him, "Is it lawful for a man to put away his wife?" tempting him. And he answered and said unto them, "What did Moses command you?" And they said, "Moses suffered to write a bill of divorcement, and to put her away".[4] And Jesus answered and said unto them, "For the hardness of your heart he wrote you this precept. But from the beginning of the creation God made

---

[4] See p. 96.

them male and female. For this cause shall a man leave his father and mother, and cleave to his wife; and they twain shall be one flesh: so then they are no more twain, but one flesh. What therefore God hath joined together, let not man put asunder." And in the house his disciples asked him again of the same matter. And he saith unto them, "Whosoever shall put away his wife, and marry another, committeth adultery against her. And if a woman shall put away her husband, and be married to another, she committeth adultery." [10:1–12]

Jesus and the Children. And they brought young children to him, that he should touch them: and his disciples rebuked those that brought them. But when Jesus saw it, he was much displeased, and said unto them, "Suffer the little children to come unto me, and forbid them not: for of such is the kingdom of God. Verily I say unto you, Whosoever shall not receive the kingdom of God as a little child, he shall not enter therein." And he took them up in his arms, put his hands upon them, and blessed them. [10:13–16]

Jesus on Riches. And when he was gone forth into the way, there came one running, and kneeled to him, and asked him, "Good Master, what shall I do that I may inherit eternal life?" And Jesus said unto him, "Why callest thou me good? there is none good but one, that is, God. Thou knowest the commandments, Do not commit adultery, Do not kill, Do not steal, Do not bear false witness, Defraud not, Honour thy father and mother." And he answered and said unto him, "Master, all these have I observed from my youth". Then Jesus beholding him loved him, and said unto him, "One thing thou lackest: go thy way, sell whatsoever thou hast, and give to the poor, and thou shalt have treasure in heaven: and come, take up the cross, and follow me". And he was sad at that saying, and went away grieved: for he had great possessions.

And Jesus looked round about, and saith unto his disciples, "How hardly shall they that have riches enter into the kingdom of God!" And the disciples were astonished at his words. But Jesus answereth again, and saith unto them, "Children, how hard is it for them that trust in riches to enter into the kingdom of God! It is easier for a camel to go through the eye of a needle, than for a rich man to enter into the kingdom of God." And they were astonished out of measure, saying among themselves, "Who then can be saved?" And Jesus looking upon them saith, "With men it is impossible, but not with God: for with God all things are possible". Then Peter began to say unto him, "Lo, we have left all, and have followed thee". And Jesus answered and said, "Verily I say unto you, There is no man that hath left house, or brethren, or sisters, or father, or mother, or wife, or children, or lands, for my sake, and the gospel's, but he shall receive an hundredfold now in this time, houses, and brethren, and sisters, and mothers, and children, and lands, with persecutions; and in the world to come eternal life. But many that are first shall be last; and the last first."   [10:17–31]

From THE GOSPEL ACCORDING TO LUKE

The Preface. Forasmuch as many have taken in hand to set forth in order a declaration of those things which are most surely believed among us, even as they delivered them unto us, which from the beginning were eyewitnesses, and ministers of the word; it seemed good to me also, having had perfect understanding of all things from the very first, to write unto thee in order, most excellent Theophilus, that thou mightest know the certainty of those things, wherein thou hast been instructed.   [1:1-4]

Zacharias and the Angel Gabriel. There was in the days of Herod,[1] the king of Judæa, a certain priest named Zacharias, of the course of Abia: and his wife was of the daughters of Aaron, and her name was Elisabeth. And they were both righteous before God, walking in all the commandments and ordinances of the Lord blameless. And they had no child, because that Elisabeth was barren, and they both were now well stricken in years.

And it came to pass, that while he executed the priest's office before God in the order of his course, according to the custom of the priest's office, his lot was to burn incense when he went into the temple of the Lord. And the whole multitude of the people were praying without at the time of incense. And there appeared unto him an angel of the Lord standing on the right side of the altar of incense. And when Zacharias saw him, he was troubled, and fear fell upon him. But the angel said unto him, "Fear not,

---

[1] I.e., Herod the Great; see Appendix 7.

Zacharias: for thy prayer is heard; and thy wife Elisabeth shall bear thee a son, and thou shalt call his name John. And thou shalt have joy and gladness; and many shall rejoice at his birth. For he shall be great in the sight of the Lord, and shall drink neither wine nor strong drink; and he shall be filled with the Holy Ghost, even from his mother's womb. And many of the children of Israel shall he turn to the Lord their God. And he shall go before him in the spirit and power of Elias, to turn the hearts of the fathers to the children, and the disobedient to the wisdom of the just; to make ready a people prepared for the Lord." And Zacharias said unto the angel, "Whereby shall I know this? for I am an old man, and my wife well stricken in years". And the angel answering said unto him, "I am Gabriel, that stand in the presence of God; and am sent to speak unto thee, and to shew thee these glad tidings. And, behold, thou shalt be dumb, and not able to speak, until the day that these things shall be performed, because thou believest not my words, which shall be fulfilled in their season." And the people waited for Zacharias, and marvelled that he tarried so long in the temple. And when he came out, he could not speak unto them: and they perceived that he had seen a vision in the temple: for he beckoned unto them, and remained speechless. And it came to pass, that, as soon as the days of his ministration were accomplished, he departed to his own house.

And after those days his wife Elisabeth conceived, and hid herself five months, saying, "Thus hath the Lord dealt with me in the days wherein he looked on me, to take away my reproach among men".   [1:5–25]

The Annunciation of the Angel Gabriel to Mary. And in the sixth month the angel Gabriel was sent from God unto a city of Galilee, named Nazareth, to a virgin espoused to a man whose name was Joseph, of the house of David; and the virgin's name was Mary. And the angel came in unto her, and said, "Hail, thou that art highly favoured, the Lord is with thee: blessed art thou among women". And when she saw him, she was troubled at his saying, and cast in her mind what manner of salutation this should be. And the angel said unto her, "Fear not, Mary: for thou hast found favour with God. And, behold, thou shalt conceive in thy womb, and bring forth a son, and shalt call his name JESUS. He shall be great, and shall be called the Son of the Highest: and the Lord God shall give unto him the throne of his father David: and he shall reign over the house of Jacob for ever; and of his kingdom there shall be no end." Then said Mary unto the angel, "How shall this be, seeing I know not a man?" And the angel answered and said unto her, "The Holy Ghost shall come upon thee, and the power of the Highest shall overshadow thee: therefore also that holy thing which shall be born of thee shall be called the Son of God. And, behold, thy cousin Elisabeth, she hath also conceived a son in her old age: and this is the sixth month with her, who was called barren. For with God nothing shall be impossible." And Mary said, "Behold the handmaid of the Lord; be it unto me according to thy word". And the angel departed from her. [1:26–38]

The Visitation of Elisabeth by Mary. And Mary arose in those days, and went into the hill country with haste, into a city of Juda; and entered into the house of Zacharias, and saluted Elisabeth. And it came to pass, that, when Elisabeth heard the salutation of Mary, the babe leaped in her womb; and Elisabeth was filled with the Holy Ghost: and she spake out with a loud voice, and said, "Blessed art thou among women, and blessed is the fruit of thy womb. And whence is this to me, that the mother of my Lord should come to me? For, lo, as soon as the voice of thy salutation sounded in mine ears, the babe leaped in my womb for joy. And blessed is she that believed: for there shall be a performance of those things which were told her from the Lord." [1:39–45]

The 'Magnificat'. And Mary said,

"My soul doth magnify the Lord,
And my spirit hath rejoiced in God my Saviour.
For he hath regarded the low estate of his hand-
    maiden:
For, behold, from henceforth all generations shall
    call me blessed.
For he that is mighty hath done to me great things;
And holy is his name.
And his mercy is on them that fear him
From generation to generation.
He hath shewed strength with his arm;
He hath scattered the proud in the imagination of
    their hearts.
He hath put down the mighty from their seats,
And exalted them of low degree.
He hath filled the hungry with good things;
And the rich he hath sent empty away.
He hath holpen his servant Israel,
In remembrance of his mercy;
As he spake to our fathers,
To Abraham, and to his seed for ever."

And Mary abode with her about three months, and returned to her own house.   [1:46–56]

The Birth of John.   Now Elisabeth's full time came that
she should be delivered; and she brought forth a son. And
her neighbours and her cousins heard how the Lord had
shewed great mercy upon her; and they rejoiced with her.
And it came to pass, that on the eighth day they came to
circumcise the child; and they called him Zacharias, after
the name of his father. And his mother answered and said,
"Not so; but he shall be called John". And they said unto
her, "There is none of thy kindred that is called by this
name". And they made signs to his father, how he would
have him called. And he asked for a writing table, and
wrote, saying, "His name is John". And they marvelled

all. And his mouth was opened immediately, and his tongue loosed, and he spake, and praised God. And fear came on all that dwelt round about them: and all these sayings were noised abroad throughout all the hill country of Judæa. And all they that heard them laid them up in their hearts, saying, "What manner of child shall this be!" And the hand of the Lord was with him.

And his father Zacharias was filled with the Holy Ghost, and prophesied, saying,

"Blessed be the Lord God of Israel;
For he hath visited and redeemed his people,
And hath raised up an horn of salvation for us
In the house of his servant David;
As he spake by the mouth of his holy prophets,
Which have been since the world began:
That we should be saved from our enemies,
And from the hand of all that hate us;
To perform the mercy promised to our fathers,
And to remember his holy covenant;
The oath which he sware to our father Abraham,
That he would grant unto us, that we being delivered
    out of the hand of our enemies
Might serve him without fear,
In holiness and righteousness before him,
All the days of our life.
And thou, child, shalt be called the prophet of the
    Highest:
For thou shalt go before the face of the Lord
To prepare his ways;
To give knowledge of salvation unto his people
By the remission of their sins,
Through the tender mercy of our God;
Whereby the dayspring from on high hath visited us,
To give light to them that sit in darkness and in the
    shadow of death,
To guide our feet into the way of peace."

And the child grew, and waxed strong in spirit, and was in the deserts till the day of his shewing unto Israel.

[1:57–80]

Jesus Born at Bethlehem.   And it came to pass in those days, that there went out a decree from Cæsar Augustus, that all the world should be taxed. (And this taxing was first made when Cyrenius was governor of Syria.) And all went to be taxed, every one into his own city. And Joseph also went up from Galilee, out of the city of Nazareth, into Judæa, unto the city of David, which is called Bethlehem; (because he was of the house and lineage of David:) to be taxed with Mary his espoused wife, being great with child. And so it was, that, while they were there, the days were accomplished that she should be delivered. And she brought forth her firstborn son, and wrapped him in swaddling clothes, and laid him in a manger; because there was no room for them in the inn.   [2:1–7]

The Shepherds of Bethlehem.   And there were in the same country shepherds abiding in the field, keeping watch over their flock by night. And, lo, the angel of the Lord came upon them, and the glory of the Lord shone round about them: and they were sore afraid. And the angel said unto them, "Fear not: for, behold, I bring you good tidings of great joy, which shall be to all people. For unto you is born this day in the city of David a Saviour, which is Christ the Lord. And this shall be a sign unto you; Ye shall find the babe wrapped in swaddling clothes, lying in a manger." And suddenly there was with the angel a multitude of the heavenly host praising God, and saying,

"Glory to God in the highest,
  And on earth peace,
  Good will toward men".

And it came to pass, as the angels were gone away from them into heaven, the shepherds said one to another, "Let us now go even unto Bethlehem, and see this thing which is come to pass, which the Lord hath made known unto us". And they came with haste, and found Mary, and Joseph, and the babe lying in a manger. And when they had seen it, they made known abroad the saying which was told them concerning this child. And all they that heard it wondered at those things which were told them by the shepherds. But Mary kept all these things, and pondered them in her heart. And the shepherds returned, glorifying and praising God for all the things that they had heard and seen, as it was told unto them.   [2:8-20]

The Naming of Jesus. And when eight days were accomplished for the circumcising of the child, his name was called JESUS, which was so named of the angel before he was conceived in the womb.   [2:21]

The Purification of Mary. And when the days of her purification according to the law of Moses were accomplished, they brought him to Jerusalem, to present him to the Lord; (as it is written in the law of the Lord,[2] "Every male that openeth the womb shall be called holy to the Lord";) and to offer a sacrifice according to that which is said in the law of the Lord, "A pair of turtledoves, or two young pigeons". And, behold, there was a man in Jerusalem, whose name was Simeon; and the same man was just and devout, waiting for the consolation of Israel: and the Holy Ghost was upon him. And it was revealed unto him by the Holy Ghost, that he should not see death, before he had seen the Lord's Christ. And he came by the Spirit into the temple: and when the parents brought in the child Jesus, to do for him after the custom of the law, then took he him up in his arms, and blessed God, and said,

"Lord, now lettest thou thy servant depart
   In peace, according to thy word:
For mine eyes have seen thy salvation,
   Which thou hast prepared before the face of all
      people;

2 See p. 82.

A light to lighten the Gentiles, and the glory of thy
people Israel".

And Joseph and his mother marvelled at those things
which were spoken of him. And Simeon blessed them, and
said unto Mary his mother, "Behold, this child is set for
the fall and rising again of many in Israel; and for a sign
which shall be spoken against; (yea, a sword shall pierce
through thy own soul also,) that the thoughts of many
hearts may be revealed". And there was one Anna, a
prophetess, the daughter of Phanuel, of the tribe of Aser:
she was of a great age, and had lived with an husband
seven years from her virginity; and she was a widow of
about fourscore and four years, which departed not from
the temple, but served God with fastings and prayers
night and day. And she coming in that instant gave thanks
likewise unto the Lord, and spake of him to all them that
looked for redemption in Jerusalem. And when they had
performed all things according to the law of the Lord,
they returned into Galilee, to their own city Nazareth.

And the child grew, and waxed strong in spirit, filled
with wisdom: and the grace of God was upon him.

[2:22–40]

The Boy Jesus in the Temple.   Now his parents went to
Jerusalem every year at the feast of the passover. And
when he was twelve years old, they went up to Jerusalem
after the custom of the feast. And when they had fulfilled
the days, as they returned, the child Jesus tarried behind
in Jerusalem; and Joseph and his mother knew not of it.
But they, supposing him to have been in the company,
went a day's journey; and they sought him among their
kinsfolk and acquaintance. And when they found him not,
they turned back again to Jerusalem, seeking him. And it
came to pass, that after three days they found him in the
temple, sitting in the midst of the doctors, both hearing
them, and asking them questions. And all that heard him
were astonished at his understanding and answers. And

when they saw him, they were amazed: and his mother said unto him, "Son, why hast thou thus dealt with us? behold, thy father and I have sought thee sorrowing". And he said unto them, "How is it that ye sought me? wist ye not that I must be about my Father's business?" And they understood not the saying which he spake unto them. And he went down with them, and came to Nazareth, and was subject unto them: but his mother kept all these sayings in her heart.

And Jesus increased in wisdom and stature, and in favour with God and man. [2:41–52]

The Preaching of John the Baptist. Now in the fifteenth year of the reign of Tiberius Cæsar, Pontius Pilate being governor of Judæa, and Herod being tetrarch of Galilee, and his brother Philip tetrarch of Ituræa and of the region of Trachonitis, and Lysanias the tetrarch of Abilene, Annas and Caiaphas being the high priests, the word of God came unto John the son of Zacharias in the wilderness. And he came into all the country about Jordan, preaching the baptism of repentance for the remission of sin; as it is written in the book of the words of Esaias the prophet,[3] saying,

> "The voice of one crying in the wilderness,
> 'Prepare ye the way of the Lord,
> Make his paths straight.
> Every valley shall be filled,
> And every mountain and hill shall be brought low;
> And the crooked shall be made straight,
> And the rough ways shall be made smooth;
> And all flesh shall see the salvation of God.'"

Then said he to the multitude that came forth to be baptized of him, "O generation of vipers, who hath warned you to flee from the wrath to come? Bring forth therefore fruits worthy of repentance, and begin not to say

[3] See pp. 307–8.

within yourselves, 'We have Abraham to our father': for I say unto you, that God is able of these stones to raise up children unto Abraham. And now also the axe is laid unto the root of the trees: every tree therefore which bringeth not forth good fruit is hewn down, and cast into the fire." And the people asked him, saying, "What shall we do then?" He answereth and saith unto them, "He that hath two coats, let him impart to him that hath none; and he that hath meat, let him do likewise". Then came also publicans to be baptized, and said unto him, "Master, what shall we do?" And he said unto them, "Exact no more than that which is appointed you". And the soldiers likewise demanded of him, saying, "And what shall we do?" And he said unto them, "Do violence to no man, neither accuse any falsely; and be content with your wages".

And as the people were in expectation, and all men mused in their hearts of John, whether he were the Christ, or not; John answered, saying unto them all, "I indeed baptize you with water; but one mightier than I cometh, the latchet of whose shoes I am not worthy to unloose: he shall baptize you with the Holy Ghost and with fire: whose fan is in his hand, and he will throughly purge his floor, and will gather the wheat into his garner; but the chaff he will burn with fire unquenchable".

And many other things in his exhortation preached he unto the people. But Herod the tetrarch, being reproved by him for Herodias his brother Philip's wife, and for all the evils which Herod had done, added yet this above all, that he shut up John in prison.   [3:1–20]

Jesus Baptized. Now when all the people were baptized, it came to pass, that Jesus also being baptized, and praying, the heaven was opened, and the Holy Ghost descended in a bodily shape like a dove upon him, and a voice came from heaven, which said, "Thou art my beloved Son; in thee I am well pleased".   [3:21–22]

Jesus Rejected at Nazareth. And he came to Nazareth, where he had been brought up: and, as his custom was, he went into the synagogue[4] on the sabbath day, and stood up for to read. And there was delivered unto him the book of the prophet Esaias. And when he had opened the book, he found the place where it was written,[5]

> "The Spirit of the Lord is upon me,
>> Because he hath anointed me to preach the gospel to the poor;
>
> He hath sent me to heal the brokenhearted,
>> To preach deliverance to the captives, and recovering of sight to the blind,
>
> To set at liberty them that are bruised,
> To preach the acceptable year of the Lord".

And he closed the book, and he gave it again to the minister, and sat down. And the eyes of all them that were in the synagogue were fastened on him. And he began to say unto them, "This day is this scripture fulfilled in your ears". And all bare him witness, and wondered at the gracious words which proceeded out of his mouth. And they said, "Is not this Joseph's son?" And he said unto them, "Ye will surely say unto me this proverb, 'Physician, heal thyself: whatsoever we have heard done in Capernaum, do also here in thy country'". And he said, "Verily I say unto you, No prophet is accepted in his own country. But I tell you of a truth, many widows were in Israel in the days of Elias, when the heaven was shut up three years and six months, when great famine was throughout all the land; but unto none of them was Elias sent, save unto Sarepta, a city of Sidon, unto a woman that was a widow. And many lepers were in Israel in the time of Eliseus the prophet; and none of them was cleansed, saving Naaman the Syrian." And all they in the synagogue, when they heard these things, were filled with wrath, and rose up, and thrust him out of the city, and led him unto the brow of the hill whereon their city was built, that they might

[4] See Appendix 10.
[5] See p. 312.

cast him down headlong. But he passing through the midst of them went his way, and came down to Capernaum, a city of Galilee, and taught them on the sabbath days. And they were astonished at his doctrine: for his word was with power. [4:16–32]

Jesus at Capernaum. And in the synagogue there was a man, which had a spirit of an unclean devil, and cried out with a loud voice, saying, "Let us alone; what have we to do with thee, thou Jesus of Nazareth? art thou come to destroy us? I know thee who thou art; the Holy One of God." And Jesus rebuked him, saying, "Hold thy peace, and come out of him". And when the devil had thrown him in the midst, he came out of him, and hurt him not. And they were all amazed, and spake among themselves, saying, "What a word is this! for with authority and power he commandeth the unclean spirits, and they come out". And the fame of him went out into every place of the country round about.

And he arose out of the synagogue, and entered into Simon's house. And Simon's wife's mother was taken with a great fever; and they besought him for her. And he stood over her, and rebuked the fever; and it left her: and immediately she arose and ministered unto them.

Now when the sun was setting, all they that had any sick with divers diseases brought them unto him; and he laid his hands on every one of them, and healed them. And devils also came out of many, crying out, and saying, "Thou art Christ the Son of God". And he rebuking them suffered them not to speak: for they knew that he was Christ.

And when it was day, he departed and went into a desert place: and the people sought him, and came unto him, and stayed him, that he should not depart from them. And he said unto them, "I must preach the kingdom of God to other cities also: for therefore am I sent".

And he preached in the synagogues of Galilee.

[4:33–44]

A Great Draught of Fishes. And it came to pass, that, as the people pressed upon him to hear the word of God, he stood by the lake of Gennesaret, and saw two ships standing by the lake: but the fishermen were gone out of them, and were washing their nets. And he entered into one of the ships, which was Simon's, and prayed him that he would thrust out a little from the land. And he sat down, and taught the people out of the ship. Now when he had left speaking, he said unto Simon, "Launch out into the deep, and let down your nets for a draught". And Simon answering said unto him, "Master, we have toiled all the night, and have taken nothing: nevertheless at thy word I will let down the net". And when they had this done, they inclosed a great multitude of fishes: and their net brake. And they beckoned unto their partners, which were in the other ship, that they should come and help them. And they came, and filled both the ships, so that they began to sink. When Simon Peter saw it, he fell down at Jesus' knees, saying, "Depart from me; for I am a sinful man, O Lord". For he was astonished, and all that were with him, at the draught of the fishes which they had taken: and so was also James, and John, the sons of Zebedee, which were partners with Simon. And Jesus said unto Simon, "Fear not; from henceforth thou shalt catch men". And when they had brought their ships to land, they forsook all, and followed him. [5:1–11]

A Leper Healed. And it came to pass, when he was in a certain city, behold a man full of leprosy: who seeing Jesus fell on his face, and besought him, saying, "Lord, if thou wilt, thou canst make me clean". And he put forth his hand, and touched him, saying, "I will: be thou clean". And immediately the leprosy departed from him. And he charged him to tell no man: "but go, and shew thyself to the priest, and offer for thy cleansing, according as Moses commanded, for a testimony unto them".[6] But so much

6 See p. 83.

the more went there a fame abroad of him: and great multitudes came together to hear, and to be healed by him of their infirmities. And he withdrew himself into the wilderness, and prayed.   [5:12–16]

A Paralytic Healed.   And it came to pass on a certain day, as he was teaching, that there were Pharisees and doctors of the law sitting by, which were come out of every town of Galilee, and Judæa, and Jerusalem: and the power of the Lord was present to heal them. And, behold, men brought in a bed a man which was taken with a palsy: and they sought means to bring him in, and to lay him before him. And when they could not find by what way they might bring him in because of the multitude, they went upon the housetop, and let him down through the tiling with his couch into the midst before Jesus. And when he saw their faith, he said unto him, "Man, thy sins are forgiven thee". And the scribes and the Pharisees began to reason, saying, "Who is this which speaketh blasphemies? Who can forgive sins, but God alone?" But when Jesus perceived their thoughts, he answering said unto them, "What reason ye in your hearts? Whether is easier, to say, 'Thy sins be forgiven thee'; or to say, 'Rise up and walk'? But that ye may know that the Son of man hath power upon earth to forgive sins," (he said unto the sick of the palsy,) "I say unto thee, Arise, and take up thy couch, and go into thine house." And immediately he rose up before them, and took up that whereon he lay, and departed to his own house, glorifying God. And they were all amazed, and they glorified God, and were filled with fear, saying, "We have seen strange things to day".

[5:17–26]

Jesus and the Sabbath.   And it came to pass on the second sabbath after the first, that he went through the corn fields; and his disciples plucked the ears of corn, and did eat, rubbing them in their hands. And certain of the Pharisees said unto them, "Why do ye that which is not lawful to do on the sabbath days?" And Jesus answering them said, "Have ye not read so much as this, what David did, when himself was an hungred, and they which were with him; how he went into the house of God, and did take and eat the shewbread, and gave also to them that were with him; which it is not lawful to eat but for the priests alone?" And he said unto them, that the Son of man is Lord also of the sabbath.

And it came to pass also on another sabbath, that he entered into the synagogue and taught: and there was a man whose right hand was withered. And the scribes and Pharisees watched him, whether he would heal on the sabbath day; that they might find an accusation against him. But he knew their thoughts, and said to the man which had the withered hand, "Rise up, and stand forth in the midst". And he arose and stood forth. Then said Jesus unto them, "I will ask you one thing; Is it lawful on the sabbath days to do good, or to do evil? to save life, or to destroy it?" And looking round about upon them all, he said unto the man, "Stretch forth thy hand". And he did so: and his hand was restored whole as the other. And they were filled with madness; and communed one with another what they might do to Jesus.   [6:1–11]

The Centurion and His Servant. Now when he had ended all his sayings in the audience of the people, he entered into Capernaum.

And a certain centurion's servant, who was dear unto him, was sick, and ready to die. And when he heard of Jesus, he sent unto him the elders of the Jews, beseeching him that he would come and heal his servant. And when they came to Jesus, they besought him instantly, saying, that he was worthy for whom he should do this: for he loveth our nation, and he hath built us a synagogue. Then Jesus went with them. And when he was now not far from the house, the centurion sent friends to him, saying unto him, "Lord, trouble not thyself: for I am not worthy that thou shouldest enter under my roof: wherefore neither thought I myself worthy to come unto thee: but say in a word, and my servant shall be healed. For I also am a man set under authority, having under me soldiers, and I say unto one, 'Go,' and he goeth; and to another, 'Come,' and he cometh; and to my servant, 'Do this,' and he doeth it." When Jesus heard these things, he marvelled at him, and turned him about, and said unto the people that followed him, "I say unto you, I have not found so great faith, no, not in Israel". And they that were sent, returning to the house, found the servant whole that had been sick. [7:1–10]

The Widow's Son at Nain Restored to Life. And it came to pass the day after, that he went into a city called Nain; and many of his disciples went with him, and much people. Now when he came nigh to the gate of the city, behold, there was a dead man carried out, the only son of his mother, and she was a widow: and much people of the city was with her. And when the Lord saw her, he had compassion on her, and said unto her, "Weep not". And he came and touched the bier: and they that bare him stood still. And he said, "Young man, I say unto thee, Arise". And he that was dead sat up, and began to speak. And he delivered him to his mother. And there came a fear on all: and they glorified God, saying, that a great prophet is risen up among us; and, that God hath visited his people. And this rumour of him went forth throughout all Judæa, and throughout all the region round about. [7:11–17]

John and Jesus. And the disciples of John shewed him of all these things. And John calling unto him two of his disciples sent them to Jesus, saying, "Art thou he that should come? or look we for another?" When the men were come unto him, they said, "John Baptist hath sent us unto thee, saying, 'Art thou he that should come? or look we for another?'" And in that same hour he cured many of their infirmities and plagues, and of evil spirits; and unto many that were blind he gave sight. Then Jesus answering said unto them, "Go your way, and tell John what things ye have seen and heard; how that the blind see, the lame walk, the lepers are cleansed, the deaf hear, the dead are raised, to the poor the gospel is preached. And blessed is he, whosoever shall not be offended in me."

And when the messengers of John were departed, he began to speak unto the people concerning John, "What went ye out into the wilderness for to see? A reed shaken with the wind? But what went ye out for to see? A man clothed in soft raiment? Behold, they which are gorgeously apparelled, and live delicately, are in kings' courts. But what went ye out for to see? A prophet? Yea, I say unto you, and much more than a prophet. This is he, of whom it is written,

'Behold, I send my messenger before thy face,
Which shall prepare thy way before thee'.

For I say unto you, Among those that are born of women there is not a greater prophet than John the Baptist: but he that is least in the kingdom of God is greater than he." And all the people that heard him, and the publicans, justified God, being baptized with the baptism of John. But the Pharisees and lawyers rejected the counsel of God against themselves, being not baptized of him. And the Lord said, "Whereunto then shall I liken the men of this generation? and to what are they like? They are like unto children sitting in the marketplace, and calling one to another, and saying, 'We have piped unto you, and ye have not danced; we have mourned to you, and ye have not wept'. For John the Baptist came neither eating bread nor drinking wine; and ye say, 'He hath a devil'. The Son of man is come eating and drinking; and ye say, 'Behold a gluttonous man, and a winebibber, a friend of publicans and sinners!' But wisdom is justified of all her children."

[7:18–35]

A Woman Washes the Feet of Jesus.[7]   And one of the Pharisees desired him that he would eat with him. And he went into the Pharisee's house, and sat down to meat. And, behold, a woman in the city, which was a sinner, when she knew that Jesus sat at meat in the Pharisee's house, brought an alabaster box of ointment, and stood at his feet behind him weeping, and began to wash his feet with tears, and did wipe them with the hairs of her head, and kissed his feet, and anointed them with the ointment. Now when the Pharisee which had bidden him saw it, he spake within himself, saying, "This man, if he were a prophet, would have known who and what manner of woman this is that toucheth him: for she is a sinner". And Jesus answering said unto him, "Simon, I have somewhat to say unto thee". And he saith, "Master, say on". "There was a certain creditor which had two debtors: the one owed five hundred pence, and the other fifty. And when they had nothing to pay, he frankly forgave them both. Tell me therefore, which of them will love him most?" Simon answered and said, "I suppose that he, to whom he forgave most". And he said unto him, "Thou hast rightly judged". And he turned to the woman, and said unto Simon, "Seest thou this woman? I entered into thine house, thou gavest me no water for my feet: but she hath washed my feet with tears, and wiped them with the hairs of her head. Thou gavest me no kiss: but this woman since the time I came in hath not ceased to kiss my feet. My head with oil thou didst not anoint: but this woman hath anointed my feet with ointment. Wherefore I say unto thee, Her sins, which are many, are forgiven; for she loved much: but to whom little is forgiven, the same loveth little". And he said unto her, "Thy sins are forgiven". And they that sat at meat with him began to say within themselves, "Who is this that forgiveth sins also?" And he said to the woman, "Thy faith hath saved thee; go in peace".

[7:36–50]

[7] See Appendix 12.

The Mission of the Seventy. After these things the Lord appointed other seventy also, and sent them two and two before his face into every city and place, whither he himself would come. Therefore said he unto them, "The harvest truly is great, but the labourers are few: pray ye therefore the Lord of the harvest, that he would send forth labourers into his harvest. Go your ways: behold, I send you forth as lambs among wolves. Carry neither purse, nor scrip, nor shoes: and salute no man by the way. And into whatsoever house ye enter, first say, 'Peace be to this house'. And if the son of peace be there, your peace shall rest upon it: if not, it shall turn to you again. And in the same house remain, eating and drinking such things as they give: for the labourer is worthy of his hire. Go not from house to house. And into whatsoever city ye enter, and they receive you, eat such things as are set before you: and heal the sick that are therein, and say unto them, 'The kingdom of God is come nigh unto you'. But into whatsoever city ye enter, and they receive you not, go your ways out into the streets of the same, and say, 'Even the very dust of your city, which cleaveth on us, we do wipe off against you: notwithstanding be ye sure of this, that the kingdom of God is come nigh unto you'. But I say unto you, that it shall be more tolerable in that day for Sodom, than for that city. Woe unto thee, Chorazin! woe unto thee, Bethsaida! for if the mighty works had been done in Tyre and Sidon, which have been done in you, they had a great while ago repented, sitting in sackcloth and ashes. But it shall be more tolerable for Tyre and Sidon at the judgment, than for you. And thou, Capernaum, which art exalted to heaven, shalt be thrust down to hell. He that heareth you heareth me; and he that despiseth you despiseth me; and he that despiseth me despiseth him that sent me."

And the seventy returned again with joy, saying, "Lord, even the devils are subject unto us through thy name". And he said unto them, "I beheld Satan as lightning fall from heaven. Behold, I give unto you power to tread on serpents and scorpions, and over all the power of the enemy: and nothing shall by any means hurt you. Notwithstanding in this rejoice not, that the spirits are subject unto you; but rather rejoice, because your names are written in heaven."

In that hour Jesus rejoiced in spirit, and said, "I thank thee, O Father, Lord of heaven and earth, that thou hast hid these things from the wise and prudent, and hast revealed them unto babes: even so, Father; for so it seemed good in thy sight. All things are delivered to me of my Father: and no man knoweth who the Son is, but the Father; and who the Father is, but the Son, and he to whom the Son will reveal him." And he turned him unto his disciples, and said privately, "Blessed are the eyes which see the things that ye see: for I tell you, that many prophets and kings have desired to see those things which ye see, and have not seen them; and to hear those things which ye hear, and have not heard them".   [10:1–24]

The Parable of the Good Samaritan.[8]   And, behold, a certain lawyer stood up, and tempted him, saying, "Master, what shall I do to inherit eternal life?" He said unto him, "What is written in the law? how readest thou?" And he answering said, "Thou shalt love the Lord thy God with all thy heart, and with all thy soul, and with all thy strength, and with all thy mind; and thy neighbour as thyself". And he said unto him, "Thou hast answered right: this do, and thou shalt live". But he, willing to justify himself, said unto Jesus, "And who is my neighbour?" And Jesus answering said, "A certain man went down from Jerusalem to Jericho, and fell among thieves, which stripped him of his raiment, and wounded him, and departed, leaving him half dead. And by chance there came down a certain priest that way: and when he saw him, he passed by on the other side. And likewise a Levite, when he was at the place, came and looked on him, and passed

[8] See Appendix 6.

by on the other side. But a certain Samaritan, as he journeyed, came where he was: and when he saw him, he had compassion on him, and went to him, and bound up his wounds, pouring in oil and wine, and set him on his own beast, and brought him to an inn, and took care of him. And on the morrow when he departed, he took out two pence, and gave them to the host, and said unto him, 'Take care of him; and whatsoever thou spendest more, when I come again, I will repay thee'. Which now of these three, thinkest thou, was neighbour unto him that fell among the thieves?" And he said, "He that shewed mercy on him". Then said Jesus unto him, "Go, and do thou likewise".

[10:25–37]

Martha and Mary. Now it came to pass, as they went, that he entered into a certain village: and a certain woman named Martha received him into her house. And she had a sister called Mary, which also sat at Jesus' feet, and heard his word. But Martha was cumbered about much serving, and came to him, and said, "Lord, dost thou not care that my sister hath left me to serve alone? bid her therefore that she help me". And Jesus answered and said unto her, "Martha, Martha, thou art careful and troubled about many things: but one thing is needful: and Mary hath chosen that good part, which shall not be taken away from her". [10:38–42]

The Lord's Prayer. And it came to pass, that, as he was praying in a certain place, when he ceased, one of his disciples said unto him, "Lord, teach us to pray, as John also taught his disciples". And he said unto them, "When ye pray, say, 'Our Father which art in heaven, Hallowed be thy name. Thy kingdom come. Thy will be done, as in heaven, so in earth. Give us day by day our daily bread. And forgive us our sins; for we also forgive every one that is indebted to us. And lead us not into temptation; but deliver us from evil.' "

And he said unto them, "Which of you shall have a

friend, and shall go unto him at midnight, and say unto him, 'Friend, lend me three loaves; for a friend of mine in his journey is come to me, and I have nothing to set before him'? And he from within shall answer and say, 'Trouble me not: the door is now shut, and my children are with me in bed; I cannot rise and give thee'. I say unto you, Though he will not rise and give him, because he is his friend, yet because of his importunity he will rise and give him as many as he needeth. And I say unto you, Ask, and it shall be given you; seek, and ye shall find; knock, and it shall be opened unto you. For every one that asketh receiveth; and he that seeketh findeth; and to him that knocketh it shall be opened. If a son shall ask bread of any of you that is a father, will he give him a stone? or if he ask a fish, will he for a fish give him a serpent? Or if he shall ask an egg, will he offer him a scorpion? If ye then, being evil, know how to give good gifts unto your children: how much more shall your heavenly Father give the Holy Spirit to them that ask him?" [11:1–13]

Pharisees[9] and Lawyers Rebuked. And as he spake, a certain Pharisee besought him to dine with him: and he went in, and sat down to meat. And when the Pharisee saw it, he marvelled that he had not first washed before dinner. And the Lord said unto him, "Now do ye Pharisees make clean the outside of the cup and the platter; but your inward part is full of ravening and wickedness. Ye fools, did not he that made that which is without make that which is within also? But rather give alms of such things as ye have; and, behold, all things are clean unto you.

"But woe unto you, Pharisees! for ye tithe mint and rue and all manner of herbs, and pass over judgment and the love of God: these ought ye to have done, and not to leave the other undone. Woe unto you, Pharisees! for ye love the uppermost seats in the synagogues, and greetings in the markets. Woe unto you, scribes and Pharisees,

9 See Appendix 9.

hypocrites! for ye are as graves which appear not, and the men that walk over them are not aware of them."

Then answered one of the lawyers, and said unto him, "Master, thus saying thou reproachest us also". And he said, "Woe unto you also, ye lawyers! for ye lade men with burdens grievous to be borne, and ye yourselves touch not the burdens with one of your fingers. Woe unto you! for ye build the sepulchres of the prophets, and your fathers killed them. Truly ye bear witness that ye allow the deeds of your fathers: for they indeed killed them, and ye build their sepulchres. Therefore also said the wisdom of God, 'I will send them prophets and apostles, and some of them they shall slay and persecute': that the blood of all the prophets, which was shed from the foundation of the world, may be required of this generation; from the blood of Abel unto the blood of Zacharias, which perished between the altar and the temple: verily I say unto you, It shall be required of this generation. Woe unto you, lawyers! for ye have taken away the key of knowledge: ye entered not in yourselves, and them that were entering in ye hindered."

And as he said these things unto them, the scribes and the Pharisees began to urge him vehemently, and to provoke him to speak of many things: laying wait for him, and seeking to catch something out of his mouth, that they might accuse him. [11:37–54]

Neglect of Material Things. And one of the company said unto him, "Master, speak to my brother, that he divide the inheritance with me". And he said unto him, "Man, who made me a judge or a divider over you?" And he said unto them, "Take heed, and beware of covetousness: for a man's life consisteth not in the abundance of the things which he possesseth". And he spake a parable unto them, saying, "The ground of a certain rich man brought forth plentifully: and he thought within himself, saying, 'What shall I do, because I have no room where to bestow my fruits?' And he said, 'This will I do: I will pull down my barns, and build greater; and there will I bestow all my fruits and my goods. And I will say to my soul, Soul, thou hast much goods laid up for many years; take thine ease, eat, drink, and be merry.' But God said unto him, 'Thou fool, this night thy soul shall be required of thee: then whose shall those things be, which thou hast provided?' So is he that layeth up treasure for himself, and is not rich toward God."

And he said unto his disciples, "Therefore I say unto you, Take no thought for your life, what ye shall eat; neither for the body, what ye shall put on. The life is more than meat, and the body is more than raiment. Consider the ravens: for they neither sow nor reap; which neither have storehouse nor barn; and God feedeth them: how much more are ye better than the fowls? And which of you with taking thought can add to his stature one cubit? If ye then be not able to do that thing which is least, why take ye thought for the rest? Consider the lilies how they grow: they toil not, they spin not; and yet I say unto you, that Solomon in all his glory was not arrayed like one of these. If then God so clothe the grass, which is to day in the field, and to morrow is cast into the oven; how much more will he clothe you, O ye of little faith? And seek not ye what ye shall eat, or what ye shall drink, neither be ye of doubtful mind. For all these things do the nations of the world seek after: and your Father knoweth that ye have need of these things. But rather seek ye the kingdom of God; and all these things shall be added unto you. Fear not, little flock; for it is your Father's good pleasure to give you the kingdom. Sell that ye have, and give alms; provide yourselves bags which wax not old, a treasure in the heavens that faileth not, where no thief approacheth, neither moth corrupteth. For where your treasure is, there will your heart be also.

"Let your loins be girded about, and your lights burning; and ye yourselves like unto men that wait for their lord, when he will return from the wedding; that when he cometh and knocketh, they may open unto him immediately. Blessed are those servants, whom the lord when he cometh shall find watching: verily I say unto you, that he shall gird himself, and make them to sit down to meat, and will come forth and serve them. And if he shall come in the second watch, or come in the third watch, and find them so, blessed are those servants. And this know, that if the goodman of the house had known what hour the thief would come, he would have watched, and not have suffered his house to be broken through. Be ye therefore ready also: for the Son of man cometh at an hour when ye think not."   [12:13–40]

Jesus and the Slain Galilæans. There were present at that season some that told him of the Galilæans, whose blood Pilate had mingled with their sacrifices. And Jesus answering said unto them, "Suppose ye that these Galilæans were sinners above all the Galilæans, because they suffered such things? I tell you, Nay: but, except ye repent, ye shall all likewise perish. Or those eighteen, upon whom the tower in Siloam fell, and slew them, think ye that they were sinners above all men that dwelt in Jerusalem? I tell you, Nay: but, except ye repent, ye shall all likewise perish."   [13:1–3]

The Parable of the Fig Tree. He spake also this parable; "A certain man had a fig tree planted in his vineyard; and he came and sought fruit thereon, and found none. Then said he unto the dresser of his vineyard, 'Behold, these three years I come seeking fruit on this fig tree, and find none: cut it down; why cumbereth it the ground?' And he answering said unto him, 'Lord, let it alone this year also, till I shall dig about it, and dung it: and if it bear fruit, well: and if not, then after that thou shalt cut it down'."
                                    [13:4–9]

A Woman Healed on the Sabbath. And he was teaching in one of the synagogues on the sabbath. And, behold, there was a woman which had a spirit of infirmity eighteen years, and was bowed together, and could in no wise lift up herself. And when Jesus saw her, he called her to him, and said unto her, "Woman, thou art loosed from thine infirmity". And he laid his hands on her: and immediately she was made straight, and glorified God. And the ruler of the synagogue answered with indignation, because that Jesus had healed on the sabbath day, and said unto the people, "There are six days in which men ought to work: in them therefore come and be healed, and not on the sabbath day". The Lord then answered him, and said, "Thou hypocrite, doth not each one of you on the sabbath loose his ox or his ass from the stall, and lead him away to watering? And ought not this woman, being a daughter of Abraham, whom Satan hath bound, lo, these eighteen years, be loosed from this bond on the sabbath day?" And when he had said these things, all his adversaries were ashamed: and all the people rejoiced for all the glorious things that were done by him.   [13:10–17]

Who Shall Be Saved?   And he went through the cities and villages, teaching, and journeying toward Jerusalem. Then said one unto him, "Lord, are there few that be saved?" And he said unto them, "Strive to enter in at the strait gate: for many, I say unto you, will seek to enter in, and shall not be able. When once the master of the house is risen up, and hath shut to the door, and ye begin to stand without, and to knock at the door, saying, 'Lord, Lord, open unto us'; and he shall answer and say unto you, 'I know you not whence ye are': then shall ye begin to say, 'We have eaten and drunk in thy presence, and thou hast taught in our streets'. But he shall say, 'I tell you, I know you not whence ye are; depart from me, all ye workers of iniquity'. There shall be weeping and gnashing of teeth, when ye shall see Abraham, and Isaac, and Jacob, and all the prophets, in the kingdom of God, and you yourselves thrust out. And they shall come from the east, and from the west, and from the north, and from the south, and shall sit down in the kingdom of God. And, behold,

there are last which shall be first, and there are first which
shall be last." [13:22–30]

Jesus Warned of Herod. The same day there came certain of the Pharisees, saying unto him, "Get thee out,
and depart hence: for Herod[10] will kill thee". And he said
unto them, "Go ye, and tell that fox, Behold, I cast out
devils, and I do cures to day and to morrow, and the third
day I shall be perfected. Nevertheless I must walk to day,
and to morrow, and the day following: for it cannot be
that a prophet perish out of Jerusalem. O Jerusalem,
Jerusalem, which killest the prophets, and stonest them
that are sent unto thee; how often would I have gathered
thy children together, as a hen doth gather her brood under her wings, and ye would not! Behold, your house is
left unto you desolate: and verily I say unto you, Ye shall
not see me, until the time come when ye shall say, 'Blessed
is he that cometh in the name of the Lord'." [13:31–35]

Healing on the Sabbath. And it came to pass, as he
went into the house of one of the chief Pharisees to eat
bread on the sabbath day, that they watched him. And,
behold, there was a certain man before him which had the
dropsy. And Jesus answering spake unto the lawyers and
Pharisees, saying, "Is it lawful to heal on the sabbath
day?" And they held their peace. And he took him, and
healed him, and let him go; and answered them, saying,
"Which of you shall have an ass or an ox fallen into a pit,
and will not straightway pull him out on the sabbath day?"
And they could not answer him again to these things.
[14:1–6]

Jesus on Humility. And he put forth a parable to those
which were bidden, when he marked how they chose out
the chief rooms; saying unto them, "When thou art bidden of any man to a wedding, sit not down in the highest
room; lest a more honourable man than thou be bidden
of him; and he that bade thee and him come and say to

[10] See Appendix 7.

thee, 'Give this man place'; and thou begin with shame to take the lowest room. But when thou art bidden, go and sit down in the lowest room; that when he that bade thee cometh, he may say unto thee, 'Friend, go up higher': then shalt thou have worship in the presence of them that sit at meat with thee. For whosoever exalteth himself shall be abased; and he that humbleth himself shall be exalted."

Then said he also to him that bade him, "When thou makest a dinner or a supper, call not thy friends, nor thy brethren, neither thy kinsmen, nor thy rich neighbours; lest they also bid thee again, and a recompence be made thee. But when thou makest a feast, call the poor, the maimed, the lame, the blind: and thou shalt be blessed; for they cannot recompense thee: for thou shalt be recompensed at the resurrection of the just."   [14:7–14]

The Parable of the Great Supper. And when one of them that sat at meat with him heard these things, he said unto him, "Blessed is he that shall eat bread in the kingdom of God". Then said he unto him, "A certain man made a great supper, and bade many: and sent his servant at supper time to say to them that were bidden, 'Come; for all things are now ready'. And they all with one consent began to make excuse. The first said unto him, 'I have bought a piece of ground, and I must needs go and see it: I pray thee have me excused'. And another said, 'I have bought five yoke of oxen, and I go to prove them: I pray thee have me excused'. And another said, 'I have married a wife, and therefore I cannot come'. So that servant came, and shewed his lord these things. Then the master of the house being angry said to his servant, 'Go out quickly into the streets and lanes of the city, and bring in hither the poor, and the maimed, and the halt, and the blind'. And the servant said, 'Lord, it is done as thou hast commanded, and yet there is room'. And the lord said unto the servant, 'Go out into the highways and hedges, and compel them to come in, that my house may be filled. For I say unto you, that none of those men which were bidden shall taste of my supper.'" [14:15–24]

The Cost of Following Jesus. And there went great multitudes with him: and he turned, and said unto them, "If any man come to me, and hate not his father, and mother, and wife, and children, and brethren, and sisters, yea, and his own life also, he cannot be my disciple. And whosoever doth not bear his cross, and come after me, cannot be my disciple. For which of you, intending to build a tower, sitteth not down first, and counteth the cost, whether he have sufficient to finish it? Lest haply, after he hath laid the foundation, and is not able to finish it, all that behold it begin to mock him, saying, 'This man began to build, and was not able to finish'. Or what king, going to make war against another king, sitteth not down first, and consulteth whether he be able with ten thousand to meet him that cometh against him with twenty thousand? Or else, while the other is yet a great way off, he sendeth an ambassage, and desireth conditions of peace. So likewise, whosoever he be of you that forsaketh not all that he hath, he cannot be my disciple. Salt is good: but if the salt have lost his savour, wherewith shall it be seasoned? It is neither fit for the land, nor yet for the dunghill; but men cast it out. He that hath ears to hear, let him hear."

Then drew near unto him all the publicans and sinners for to hear him. And the Pharisees and scribes murmured, saying, "This man receiveth sinners, and eateth with them". [14:25–35; 15:1–2]

Parable of the Lost Sheep. And he spake this parable unto them, saying, "What man of you, having an hundred sheep, if he lose one of them, doth not leave the ninety and nine in the wilderness, and go after that which is lost, until he find it? And when he hath found it, he layeth it on his shoulders, rejoicing. And when he cometh home, he calleth together his friends and neighbours, saying unto them, 'Rejoice with me; for I have found my sheep which was lost'. I say unto you, that likewise joy shall be in heaven over one sinner that repenteth, more than over ninety and nine just persons, which need no repentance.   [15:3–7]

Parable of the Lost Piece. "Either what woman having ten pieces of silver, if she lose one piece, doth not light a candle, and sweep the house, and seek diligently till she find it? And when she hath found it, she calleth her friends and her neighbours together, saying, 'Rejoice with me; for I have found the piece which I had lost'. Likewise, I say unto you, there is joy in the presence of the angels of God over one sinner that repenteth."   [15:8–10]

The Parable of the Prodigal Son. And he said, "A certain man had two sons: and the younger of them said to his father, 'Father, give me the portion of goods that falleth to me'. And he divided unto them his living. And not many days after the younger son gathered all together, and took his journey into a far country, and there wasted his substance with riotous living. And when he had spent all, there arose a mighty famine in that land; and he began to be in want. And he went and joined himself to a citizen of that country; and he sent him into his fields to feed swine. And he would fain have filled his belly with the husks that the swine did eat: and no man gave unto him. And when he came to himself, he said, 'How many hired servants of my father's have bread enough and to spare, and I perish with hunger! I will arise and go to my father, and will say unto him, Father, I have sinned against heaven, and before thee, and am no more worthy to be called thy son: make me as one of thy hired servants.' And he arose, and came to his father. But when he was yet a great way off, his father saw him, and had compassion, and ran, and fell on his neck, and kissed him. And the son said unto him, 'Father, I have sinned against heaven, and in thy sight, and am no more worthy to be called thy son'. But the father said to his servants, 'Bring forth the best robe, and put it on him; and put a ring on his hand, and shoes on his feet: and bring hither the fatted calf, and kill it; and let us eat, and be merry: for this my son was dead, and is alive again; he was lost, and is found'. And they began to be merry. Now his elder son was in the field: and as he came and drew nigh to the house, he heard musick and dancing. And he called one of the servants, and asked what these things meant. And he said unto him, 'Thy brother is come; and thy father hath killed the fatted calf, because he hath received him safe and sound'. And he was angry, and would not go in: therefore came his father out, and intreated him. And he answering said to his father, 'Lo, these many years do I serve thee, neither transgressed I at any time thy commandment: and yet thou never gavest me a kid, that I might make merry with my friends: but as soon as this thy son was come, which hath devoured thy living with harlots, thou hast killed for him the fatted calf'. And he said unto him, 'Son, thou art ever with me, and all that I have is thine. It was meet that we should make merry, and be glad: for this thy brother was dead, and is alive again; and was lost, and is found.'" [15:11–32]

The Parable of the Dishonest Steward. And he said also unto his disciples, "There was a certain rich man, which had a steward; and the same was accused unto him that he had wasted his goods. And he called him, and said unto him, 'How is it that I hear this of thee? give an account of thy stewardship; for thou mayest be no longer steward'. Then the steward said within himself, 'What shall I do? for my lord taketh away from me the stewardship: I cannot dig; to beg I am ashamed. I am resolved what to do, that, when I am put out of the stewardship, they may receive me into their houses.' So he called every one of his lord's debtors unto him, and said unto the first, 'How much owest thou unto my lord?' And he said, 'An hundred measures of oil'. And he said unto him, 'Take thy bill, and sit down quickly, and write fifty'. Then said he to another, 'And how much owest thou?' And he said, 'An hundred measures of wheat'. And he said unto him,

'Take thy bill, and write fourscore'. And the lord commended the unjust steward, because he had done wisely:
for the children of this world are in their generation wiser
than the children of light. And I say unto you, Make to
yourselves friends of the mammon of unrighteousness;
that, when ye fail, they may receive you into everlasting
habitations. He that is faithful in that which is least is
faithful also in much: and he that is unjust in the least is
unjust also in much. If therefore ye have not been faithful
in the unrighteous mammon, who will commit to your trust
the true riches? And if ye have not been faithful in that
which is another man's, who shall give you that which is
your own? No servant can serve two masters: for either he
will hate the one, and love the other; or else he will hold
to the one, and despise the other. Ye cannot serve God and
mammon."[11]   [16:1-13]

**The Parable of the Rich Man (Dives) and the Beggar
(Lazarus).** "There was a certain rich man, which was
clothed in purple and fine linen, and fared sumptuously
every day: and there was a certain beggar named Lazarus,
which was laid at his gate, full of sores, and desiring to be
fed with the crumbs which fell from the rich man's table:
moreover the dogs came and licked his sores. And it came
to pass, that the beggar died, and was carried by the angels
into Abraham's bosom: the rich man also died, and was
buried; and in hell he lift up his eyes, being in torments,
and seeth Abraham afar off, and Lazarus in his bosom.
And he cried and said, 'Father Abraham, have mercy on
me, and send Lazarus, that he may dip the tip of his finger
in water, and cool my tongue; for I am tormented in this
flame'. But Abraham said, 'Son, remember that thou in thy
lifetime receivedst thy good things, and likewise Lazarus
evil things: but now he is comforted, and thou art tormented. And beside all this, between us and you there is
a great gulf fixed: so that they which would pass from

11 "Mammon"—i.e., money.

hence to you cannot; neither can they pass to us, that would come from thence.' Then he said, 'I pray thee therefore, father, that thou wouldest send him to my father's house: for I have five brethren; that he may testify unto them, lest they also come into this place of torment'. Abraham saith unto him, 'They have Moses and the prophets; let them hear them'. And he said, 'Nay, father Abraham: but if one went unto them from the dead, they will repent'. And he said unto him, 'If they hear not Moses and the prophets, neither will they be persuaded, though one rose from the dead'." [16:19–31]

Forgiveness. Then said he unto the disciples, "It is impossible but that offences will come: but woe unto him, through whom they come! It were better for him that a millstone were hanged about his neck, and he cast into the sea, than that he should offend one of these little ones. Take heed to yourselves: If thy brother trespass against thee, rebuke him; and if he repent, forgive him. And if he trespass against thee seven times in a day, and seven times in a day turn again to thee, saying, 'I repent'; thou shalt forgive him." [17:1–4]

Faith. And the apostles said unto the Lord, "Increase our faith". And the Lord said, "If ye had faith as a grain of mustard seed, ye might say unto this sycamine tree, 'Be thou plucked up by the root, and be thou planted in the sea'; and it should obey you. But which of you, having a servant plowing or feeding cattle, will say unto him by and by, when he is come from the field, 'Go and sit down to meat?' And will not rather say unto him, 'Make ready wherewith I may sup, and gird thyself, and serve me, till I have eaten and drunken; and afterward thou shalt eat and drink'? Doth he thank that servant because he did the things that were commanded him? I trow not. So likewise ye, when ye shall have done all those things which are commanded you, say, 'We are unprofitable servants: we have done that which was our duty to do'." [17:5–10]

The Grateful Leper. And it came to pass, as he went to Jerusalem, that he passed through the midst of Samaria and Galilee. And as he entered into a certain village, there met him ten men that were lepers, which stood afar off: and they lifted up their voices, and said, "Jesus, Master, have mercy on us". And when he saw them, he said unto them, "Go shew yourselves unto the priests". And it came to pass, that, as they went, they were cleansed. And one of them, when he saw that he was healed, turned back, and with a loud voice glorified God, and fell down on his face at his feet, giving him thanks: and he was a Samaritan. And Jesus answering said, "Were there not ten cleansed? but where are the nine? There are not found that returned to give glory to God, save this stranger." And he said unto him, "Arise, go thy way: thy faith hath made thee whole".   [17:11–19]

The Kingdom of God. And when he was demanded of the Pharisees, when the kingdom of God should come, he answered them and said, "The kingdom of God cometh not with observation: neither shall they say, 'Lo here!' or, 'Lo there!' for, behold, the kingdom of God is within you".
                                                        [17:20–21]

Parable of the Importunate Widow. And he spake a parable unto them to this end, that men ought always to pray, and not to faint; saying, "There was in a city a judge, which feared not God, neither regarded man: and there was a widow in that city; and she came unto him, saying, 'Avenge me of mine adversary'. And he would not for a while: but afterward he said within himself, 'Though I fear not God, nor regard man; yet because this widow troubleth me, I will avenge her, lest by her continual coming she weary me'". And the Lord said, "Hear what the unjust judge saith. And shall not God avenge his own elect, which cry day and night unto him, though he bear long with them? I tell you that he will avenge them speedily. Nevertheless when the Son of man cometh, shall he find faith on the earth?"   [18:1–8]

Parable of the Pharisee and the Publican.[12] And he spake this parable unto certain which trusted in themselves that they were righteous, and despised others: "Two men went up into the temple to pray; the one a Pharisee, and the other a publican. The Pharisee stood and prayed thus with himself, 'God, I thank thee, that I am not as other men are, extortioners, unjust, adulterers, or even as this publican. I fast twice in the week, I give tithes of all that I possess.' And the publican, standing afar off, would not lift up so much as his eyes unto heaven, but smote upon his breast, saying, 'God be merciful to me a sinner'. I tell you, this man went down to his house justified rather than the other: for every one that exalteth himself shall be abased; and he that humbleth himself shall be exalted."

And they brought unto him also infants, that he would touch them: but when his disciples saw it, they rebuked them. But Jesus called them unto him, and said, "Suffer little children to come unto me, and forbid them not: for of such is the kingdom of God. Verily I say unto you, Whosoever shall not receive the kingdom of God as a little child shall in no wise enter therein."   [18:9–17]

Zacchæus. And Jesus entered and passed through Jericho. And, behold, there was a man named Zacchæus, which was the chief among the publicans, and he was rich. And he sought to see Jesus who he was; and could not for the press, because he was little of stature. And he ran before, and climbed up into a sycomore tree to see him: for he was to pass that way. And when Jesus came to the place, he looked up, and saw him, and said unto him, "Zacchæus, make haste, and come down; for to day I must abide at thy house". And he made haste, and came down, and received him joyfully. And when they saw it, they all murmured, saying, that he was gone to be guest with a man that is a sinner. And Zacchæus stood, and said unto the Lord; "Behold, Lord, the half of my goods

---

[12] See Appendices 9 and 11.

I give to the poor; and if I have taken any thing from any man by false accusation, I restore him fourfold". And Jesus said unto him, "This day is salvation come to this house, forsomuch as he also is a son of Abraham. For the Son of man is come to seek and to save that which was lost."

[19:1–10]

The Parable of the Pounds. And as they heard these things, he added and spake a parable, because he was nigh to Jerusalem, and because they thought that the kingdom of God should immediately appear. He said therefore, "A certain nobleman went into a far country to receive for himself a kingdom, and to return. And he called his ten servants, and delivered them ten pounds, and said unto them, 'Occupy till I come'. But his citizens hated him, and sent a message after him, saying, 'We will not have this man to reign over us'. And it came to pass, that when he was returned, having received the kingdom, then he commanded these servants to be called unto him, to whom he had given the money, that he might know how much every man had gained by trading. Then came the first, saying, 'Lord, thy pound hath gained ten pounds'. And he said unto him, 'Well, thou good servant: because thou hast been faithful in a very little, have thou authority over ten cities'. And the second came, saying, 'Lord, thy pound hath gained five pounds'. And he said likewise to him, 'Be thou also over five cities'. And another came, saying, 'Lord, behold, here is thy pound, which I have kept laid up in a napkin: for I feared thee, because thou art an austere man: thou takest up that thou layedst not down, and reapest that thou didst not sow'. And he saith unto him, 'Out of thine own mouth will I judge thee, thou wicked servant. Thou knewest that I was an austere man, taking up that I laid not down, and reaping that I did not sow: wherefore then gavest not thou my money into the bank, that at my coming I might have required mine own with usury?' And he said unto them that stood by, 'Take from him the pound, and give it to him that hath ten pounds'. (And they said unto him, 'Lord, he hath ten pounds'.) 'For I say unto you, that unto every one which hath shall be given; and from him that hath not, even that he hath shall be taken away from him. But those mine enemies, which would not that I should reign over them, bring hither, and slay them before me.'"

And when he had thus spoken, he went before, ascending up to Jerusalem. [19:11–28]

The Triumphant Entry into Jerusalem. And it came to pass, when he was come nigh to Bethphage and Bethany, at the mount called the mount of Olives, he sent two of his disciples, saying, "Go ye into the village over against you; in the which at your entering ye shall find a colt tied, whereon yet never man sat: loose him, and bring him hither. And if any man ask you, 'Why do ye loose him?' thus shall ye say unto him, 'Because the Lord hath need of him'." And they that were sent went their way, and found even as he had said unto them. And as they were loosing the colt, the owners thereof said unto them, "Why loose ye the colt?" And they said, "The Lord hath need of him". And they brought him to Jesus: and they cast their garments upon the colt, and they set Jesus thereon. And as he went, they spread their clothes in the way. And when he was come nigh, even now at the descent of the mount of Olives, the whole multitude of the disciples began to rejoice and praise God with a loud voice for all the mighty works that they had seen; saying, "Blessed be the King that cometh in the name of the Lord: peace in heaven, and glory in the highest". And some of the Pharisees from among the multitude said unto him, "Master, rebuke thy disciples". And he answered and said unto them, "I tell you that, if these should hold their peace, the stones would immediately cry out". [19:29–40]

Jesus Weeps over Jerusalem. And when he was come near, he beheld the city, and wept over it, saying, "If thou hadst known, even thou, at least in this thy day, the things which belong unto thy peace! but now they are hid from thine eyes. For the days shall come upon thee, that thine enemies shall cast a trench about thee, and compass thee round, and keep thee in on every side, and shall lay thee even with the ground, and thy children within thee; and they shall not leave in thee one stone upon another; because thou knewest not the time of thy visitation."

And he went into the temple, and began to cast out them that sold therein, and them that bought; saying unto them, "It is written, 'My house is the house of prayer': but ye have made it a den of thieves".

And he taught daily in the temple. But the chief priests and the scribes and the chief of the people sought to destroy him, and could not find what they might do: for all the people were very attentive to hear him.   [19:41–48]

Mark *adds:*

The Barren Fig Tree.   And Jesus entered into Jerusalem, and into the temple: and when he had looked round about upon all things, and now the eventide was come, he went out unto Bethany with the twelve.

And on the morrow, when they were come from Bethany, he was hungry: and seeing a fig tree afar off having leaves, he came, if haply he might find any thing thereon: and when he came to it, he found nothing but leaves; for the time of figs was not yet. And Jesus answered and said unto it, "No man eat fruit of thee hereafter for ever". And his disciples heard it.

And they come to Jerusalem: and Jesus went into the temple, and began to cast out them that sold and bought in the temple, and overthrew the tables of the moneychangers, and the seats of them that sold doves; and would not suffer that any man should carry any vessel through the temple. And he taught, saying unto them, "Is it not written, 'My house shall be called of all nations the house of prayer'? but ye have made it a den of thieves". And the scribes and chief priests heard it, and sought how they might destroy him: for they feared him, because all the people was astonished at his doctrine.

And when even was come, he went out of the city.

And in the morning, as they passed by, they saw the fig tree dried up from the roots. And Peter calling to remembrance saith unto him, "Master, behold, the fig tree which thou cursedst is withered away". And Jesus answering saith unto them, "Have faith in God. For verily I say unto you, that whosoever shall say unto this mountain, 'Be thou removed, and be thou cast into the sea'; and shall not doubt in his heart, but shall believe that those things which he saith shall come to pass; he shall have whatsoever he saith. Therefore I say unto you, What things soever ye desire, when ye pray, believe that ye receive them, and ye shall have them. And when ye stand praying, forgive, if ye have aught against any: that your Father also which is in heaven may forgive you your trespasses. But if ye do not forgive, neither will your Father which is in heaven forgive your trespasses."   [11:11–26]

Luke *resumes:*

The Pharisees' Challenge.   And it came to pass, that on one of those days, as he taught the people in the temple, and preached the gospel, the chief priests and the scribes came upon him with the elders, and spake unto him, saying, "Tell us, by what authority doest thou these things? or who is he that gave thee this authority?" And he answered and said unto them, "I will also ask you one thing; and answer me: The baptism of John, was it from heaven, or of men?" And they reasoned with themselves, saying, "If we shall say, 'From heaven'; he will say, 'Why then believed ye him not?' But and if we say, 'Of men'; all the people will stone us: for they be persuaded that John was a prophet." And they answered, that they could not tell whence it was. And Jesus said unto them, "Neither tell I you by what authority I do these things".   [20:1–8]

The Parable of the Vineyard. Then began he to speak to the people this parable; "A certain man planted a vineyard,[13] and let it forth to husbandmen, and went into a far country for a long time. And at the season he sent a servant to the husbandmen, that they should give him of the fruit of the vineyard: but the husbandmen beat him, and sent him away empty. And again he sent another servant: and they beat him also, and entreated him shamefully, and sent him away empty. And again he sent a third: and they wounded him also, and cast him out. Then said the lord of the vineyard, 'What shall I do? I will send my beloved son: it may be they will reverence him when they see him.' But when the husbandmen saw him, they reasoned among themselves, saying, 'This is the heir: come, let us kill him, that the inheritance may be ours'. So they cast him out of the vineyard, and killed him. What therefore shall the lord of the vineyard do unto them? He shall come and destroy these husbandmen, and shall give the vineyard to others." And when they heard it, they said, "God forbid". And he beheld them, and said, "What is this then that is written,

'The stone which the builders rejected,
The same is become the head of the corner'?

Whosoever shall fall upon that stone shall be broken; but on whomsoever it shall fall, it will grind him to powder."
[20:9–18]

The Pharisees' Question. And the chief priests and the scribes the same hour sought to lay hands on him; and they feared the people: for they perceived that he had spoken this parable against them. And they watched him, and sent forth spies, which should feign themselves just men, that they might take hold of his words, that so they might deliver him unto the power and authority of the governor. And they asked him, saying, "Master, we know that thou

[13] See p. 299–300.

sayest and teachest rightly, neither acceptest thou the person of any, but teachest the way of God truly: Is it lawful for us to give tribute unto Cæsar, or no?" But he perceived their craftiness, and said unto them, "Why tempt ye me? Shew me a penny. Whose image and superscription hath it?" They answered and said, "Cæsar's". And he said unto them, "Render therefore unto Cæsar the things which be Cæsar's, and unto God the things which be God's". And they could not take hold of his words before the people: and they marvelled at his answer, and held their peace.

[20:19–26]

The Sadducees' Question. Then came to him certain of the Sadducees, which deny that there is any resurrection; and they asked him, saying, "Master, Moses wrote unto us, 'If any man's brother die, having a wife, and he die without children, that his brother should take his wife, and raise up seed unto his brother'.[14] There were therefore seven brethren: and the first took a wife, and died without children. And the second took her to wife, and he died childless. And the third took her; and in like manner the seven also: and they left no children, and died. Last of all the woman died also. Therefore in the resurrection whose wife of them is she? for seven had her to wife." And Jesus answering said unto them, "The children of this world marry, and are given in marriage: but they which shall be accounted worthy to obtain that world, and the resurrection from the dead, neither marry, nor are given in marriage: neither can they die any more: for they are equal unto the angels; and are the children of God, being the children of the resurrection. Now that the dead are raised, even Moses shewed at the bush, when he calleth the Lord the God of Abraham, and the God of Isaac, and the God of Jacob. For he is not a God of the dead, but of the living: for all live unto him." Then certain of the scribes

14 See p. 97.

answering said, "Master, thou hast well said". And after that they durst not ask him any question at all.

[20:27–40]

Jesus' Question to the Pharisees. And he said unto them, "How say they that Christ is David's son? And David himself saith in the book of Psalms,[15]

> 'The LORD said unto my Lord,
> Sit thou on my right hand,
> Till I make thine enemies thy footstool'.

David therefore calleth him Lord, how is he then his son?"

Then in the audience of all the people he said unto his disciples, "Beware of the scribes, which desire to walk in long robes, and love greetings in the markets, and the highest seats in the synagogues, and the chief rooms at feasts; which devour widows' houses, and for a shew make long prayers: the same shall receive greater damnation".

[20:41–47]

The Widow's Mite. And he looked up, and saw the rich men casting their gifts into the treasury. And he saw also a certain poor widow casting in thither two mites. And he said, "Of a truth I say unto you, that this poor widow hath cast in more than they all: for all these have of their abundance cast in unto the offerings of God: but she of her penury hath cast in all the living that she had".

[21:1–4]

The End of Jerusalem and of the World. And as some spake of the temple, how it was adorned with goodly stones and gifts, he said, "As for these things which ye behold, the days will come, in the which there shall not be left one stone upon another, that shall not be thrown down". And they asked him, saying, "Master, but when shall these things be? and what sign will there be when these things shall come to pass?" And he said, "Take heed that ye be not deceived: for many shall come in my name, saying, 'I

15 See Psalm 110, p. 279.

am Christ'; and the time draweth near: go ye not therefore after them. But when ye shall hear of wars and commotions, be not terrified: for these things must first come to pass; but the end is not by and by."

Then said he unto them, "Nation shall rise against nation, and kingdom against kingdom: and great earthquakes shall be in divers places, and famines, and pestilences; and fearful sights and great signs shall there be from heaven. But before all these, they shall lay their hands on you, and persecute you, delivering you up to the synagogues, and into prisons, being brought before kings and rulers for my name's sake. And it shall turn to you for a testimony. Settle it therefore in your hearts, not to meditate before what ye shall answer: for I will give you a mouth and wisdom, which all your adversaries shall not be able to gainsay nor resist. And ye shall be betrayed both by parents, and brethren, and kinsfolks, and friends; and some of you shall they cause to be put to death. And ye shall be hated of all men for my name's sake. But there shall not an hair of your head perish. In your patience possess ye your souls.

"And when ye shall see Jerusalem compassed with armies, then know that the desolation thereof is nigh. Then let them which are in Judæa flee to the mountains; and let them which are in the midst of it depart out; and let not them that are in the countries enter thereinto. For these be the days of vengeance, that all things which are written may be fulfilled. But woe unto them that are with child, and to them that give suck, in those days! for there shall be great distress in the land, and wrath upon this people. And they shall fall by the edge of the sword, and shall be led away captive into all nations: and Jerusalem shall be trodden down of the Gentiles, until the times of the Gentiles be fulfilled. And there shall be signs in the sun, and in the moon, and in the stars; and upon the earth distress of nations, with perplexity; the sea and the waves roaring; men's hearts failing them for fear, and for looking after those things which are coming on the earth: for the powers of heaven shall be shaken. And then shall they see the Son of man coming in a cloud with power and great glory. And when these things begin to come to pass, then look up, and lift up your heads; for your redemption draweth nigh."

And he spake to them a parable; "Behold the fig tree, and all the trees; when they now shoot forth, ye see and know of your own selves that summer is now nigh at hand. So likewise ye, when ye see these things come to pass, know ye that the kingdom of God is nigh at hand. Verily I say unto you, This generation shall not pass away, till all be fulfilled. Heaven and earth shall pass away: but my words shall not pass away.

"And take heed to yourselves, lest at any time your hearts be overcharged with surfeiting, and drunkenness, and cares of this life, and so that day come upon you unawares. For as a snare shall it come on all them that dwell on the face of the whole earth. Watch ye therefore, and pray always, that ye may be accounted worthy to escape all these things that shall come to pass, and to stand before the Son of man."

And in the day time he was teaching in the temple; and at night he went out, and abode in the mount that is called the mount of Olives. And all the people came early in the morning to him in the temple, for to hear him.   [21:5–38]

Judas Betrays Jesus. Now the feast of unleavened bread drew nigh, which is called the Passover. And the chief priests and scribes sought how they might kill him; for they feared the people.

Then entered Satan into Judas surnamed Iscariot, being of the number of the twelve. And he went his way, and communed with the chief priests and captains, how he might betray him unto them. And they were glad, and covenanted to give him money. And he promised, and sought opportunity to betray him unto them in the absence of the multitude.   [22:1–6]

The Feast of the Passover. Then came the day of unleavened bread, when the passover must be killed. And he sent Peter and John, saying, "Go and prepare us the passover, that we may eat". And they said unto him, "Where wilt thou that we prepare?" And he said unto them, "Behold, when ye are entered into the city, there shall a man meet you, bearing a pitcher of water; follow him into the house where he entereth in. And ye shall say unto the goodman of the house, 'The Master saith unto thee, Where is the guestchamber, where I shall eat the passover with my disciples?' And he shall shew you a large upper room furnished: there make ready." And they went, and found as he had said unto them: and they made ready the passover. [22:7–13]

The Last Supper: the Eucharist Instituted. And when the hour was come, he sat down, and the twelve apostles with him. And he said unto them, "With desire I have desired to eat this passover with you before I suffer: for I say unto you, I will not any more eat thereof, until it be fulfilled in the kingdom of God". And he took the cup, and gave thanks, and said, "Take this, and divide it among yourselves: for I say unto you, I will not drink of the fruit of the vine, until the kingdom of God shall come". And he took bread, and gave thanks, and brake it, and gave unto them, saying, "This is my body which is given for you: this do in remembrance of me". Likewise also the cup after supper, saying, "This cup is the new testament in my blood, which is shed for you. But, behold, the hand of him that betrayeth me is with me on the table. And truly the Son of man goeth, as it was determined: but woe unto that man by whom he is betrayed!" And they began to enquire among themselves, which of them it was that should do this thing.

And there was also a strife among them, which of them should be accounted the greatest. And he said unto them, "The kings of the Gentiles exercise lordship over them; and they that exercise authority upon them are called

benefactors. But ye shall not be so: but he that is greatest
among you, let him be as the younger; and he that is chief,
as he that doth serve. For whether is greater, he that sitteth
at meat, or he that serveth? is not he that sitteth at meat?
but I am among you as he that serveth. Ye are they which
have continued with me in my temptations. And I appoint
unto you a kingdom, as my Father hath appointed unto
me; that ye may eat and drink at my table in my kingdom,
and sit on thrones judging the twelve tribes of Israel."

[22:14–30]

Peter Warned.   And the Lord said, "Simon, Simon, behold, Satan hath desired to have you, that he may sift you
as wheat: but I have prayed for thee, that thy faith fail
not: and when thou art converted, strengthen thy brethren". And he said unto him, "Lord, I am ready to go with
thee, both into prison, and to death". And he said, "I tell
thee, Peter, the cock shall not crow this day, before that
thou shalt thrice deny that thou knowest me".

And he said unto them, "When I sent you without purse,
and scrip, and shoes, lacked ye any thing?" And they said,
"Nothing". Then said he unto them, "But now, he that
hath a purse, let him take it, and likewise his scrip: and
he that hath no sword, let him sell his garment, and buy
one. For I say unto you, that this that is written must yet
be accomplished in me, 'And he was reckoned among the
transgressors': for the things concerning me have an end."
And they said, "Lord, behold, here are two swords". And
he said unto them, "It is enough".   [22:31–38]

The Agony in the Garden.   And he came out, and went,
as he was wont, to the mount of Olives; and his disciples
also followed him. And when he was at the place, he
said unto them, "Pray that ye enter not into temptation".
And he was withdrawn from them about a stone's cast,
and kneeled down, and prayed, saying, "Father, if thou be
willing, remove this cup from me: nevertheless not my
will, but thine, be done". And there appeared an angel
unto him from heaven, strengthening him. And being in an

agony he prayed more earnestly: and his sweat was as it
were great drops of blood falling down to the ground. And
when he rose up from prayer, and was come to his disciples, he found them sleeping for sorrow, and said unto
them, "Why sleep ye? rise and pray, lest ye enter into
temptation".   [22:39–46]

Jesus Arrested. And while he yet spake, behold a multitude, and he that was called Judas, one of the twelve,
went before them, and drew near unto Jesus to kiss him.
But Jesus said unto him, "Judas, betrayest thou the Son
of man with a kiss?" When they which were about him saw
what would follow, they said unto him, "Lord, shall we
smite with the sword?" And one of them smote the servant
of the high priest, and cut off his right ear. And Jesus answered and said, "Suffer ye thus far". And he touched his
ear, and healed him. Then Jesus said unto the chief
priests, and captains of the temple, and the elders, which
were come to him, "Be ye come out, as against a thief, with
swords and staves? When I was daily with you in the
temple, ye stretched forth no hands against me: but this
is your hour, and the power of darkness."   [22:47–53]

Mark *adds:*
And they all forsook him, and fled. And there followed him a certain young man, having a linen cloth cast
about his naked body; and the young men laid hold on
him: and he left the linen cloth, and fled from them naked.
                                                [14:50–52]

Luke *resumes:*
Peter's Denial. Then took they him, and led him, and
brought him into the high priest's house. And Peter followed afar off. And when they had kindled a fire in the
midst of the hall, and were set down together, Peter sat
down among them. But a certain maid beheld him as he
sat by the fire, and earnestly looked upon him, and said,
"This man was also with him". And he denied him, saying,

"Woman, I know him not". And after a little while another saw him, and said, "Thou art also of them". And Peter said, "Man, I am not". And about the space of one hour after another confidently affirmed, saying, "Of a truth this fellow also was with him: for he is a Galilæan". And Peter said, "Man, I know not what thou sayest". And immediately, while he yet spake, the cock crew. And the Lord turned, and looked upon Peter. And Peter remembered the word of the Lord, how he had said unto him, "Before the cock crow, thou shalt deny me thrice". And Peter went out, and wept bitterly. [22:54–62]

Jesus before the High Priest. And the men that held Jesus mocked him, and smote him. And when they had blindfolded him, they struck him on the face, and asked him, saying, "Prophesy, who is it that smote thee?" And many other things blasphemously spake they against him.

And as soon as it was day, the elders of the people and the chief priests and the scribes came together, and led him into their council, saying, "Art thou the Christ? tell us". And he said unto them, "If I tell you, ye will not believe: and if I also ask you, ye will not answer me, nor let me go. Hereafter shall the Son of man sit on the right hand of the power of God." Then said they all, "Art thou then the Son of God?" And he said unto them, "Ye say that I am". And they said, "What need we any further witness? for we ourselves have heard of his own mouth". [22:63–71]

Jesus before Pilate. And the whole multitude of them arose, and led him unto Pilate. And they began to accuse him, saying, "We found this fellow perverting the nation, and forbidding to give tribute to Cæsar, saying that he himself is Christ a King". And Pilate asked him, saying, "Art thou the King of the Jews?" And he answered him and said, "Thou sayest it". Then said Pilate to the chief priests and to the people, "I find no fault in this man". And they were the more fierce, saying, "He stirreth up the people, teaching throughout all Jewry, beginning from

Galilee to this place". When Pilate heard of Galilee, he asked whether the man were a Galilæan. And as soon as he knew that he belonged unto Herod's jurisdiction, he sent him to Herod,[16] who himself also was at Jerusalem at that time.   [23:1–7]

Jesus before Herod. And when Herod saw Jesus, he was exceeding glad: for he was desirous to see him of a long season, because he had heard many things of him; and he hoped to have seen some miracle done by him. Then he questioned with him in many words; but he answered him nothing. And the chief priests and scribes stood and vehemently accused him. And Herod with his men of war set him at nought, and mocked him, and arrayed him in a gorgeous robe, and sent him again to Pilate. And the same day Pilate and Herod were made friends together: for before they were at enmity between themselves.   [23:8–12]

Pilate Yields. And Pilate, when he had called together the chief priests and the rulers and the people, said unto them, "Ye have brought this man unto me, as one that perverteth the people: and, behold, I, having examined him before you, have found no fault in this man touching those things whereof ye accuse him: no, nor yet Herod: for I sent you to him; and, lo, nothing worthy of death is done unto him. I will therefore chastise him, and release him." (For of necessity he must release one unto them at the feast.) And they cried out all at once, saying, "Away with this man, and release unto us Barabbas": (who for a certain sedition made in the city, and for murder, was cast into prison.) Pilate therefore, willing to release Jesus, spake again to them. But they cried, saying, "Crucify him, crucify him". And he said unto them the third time, "Why, what evil hath he done? I have found no cause of death in him: I will therefore chastise him, and let him go." And they were instant with loud voices,

16 See Appendix 7.

requiring that he might be crucified. And the voices of
them and of the chief priests prevailed. And Pilate gave
sentence that it should be as they required. And he released unto them him that for sedition and murder was
cast into prison, whom they had desired; but he delivered
Jesus to their will.

Matthew *adds:*

When Pilate saw that he could prevail nothing, but that
rather a tumult was made, he took water, and washed
his hands before the multitude, saying, "I am innocent of
the blood of this just person: see ye to it". Then answered
all the people, and said, "His blood be on us, and on our
children". Then released he Barabbas unto them: and
when he had scourged Jesus, he delivered him to be
crucified.   [27:24–25]

Luke *resumes:*

And as they led him away, they laid hold upon one
Simon, a Cyrenian, coming out of the country, and on him
they laid the cross, that he might bear it after Jesus.

And there followed him a great company of people, and
of women, which also bewailed and lamented him. But
Jesus turning unto them said, "Daughters of Jerusalem,
weep not for me, but weep for yourselves, and for your
children. For, behold, the days are coming, in the which
they shall say, 'Blessed are the barren, and the wombs
that never bare, and the paps which never gave suck'.
Then shall they begin to say to the mountains, 'Fall on
us'; and to the hills, 'Cover us'. For if they do these things
in a green tree, what shall be done in the dry?"

And there were also two other, malefactors, led with
him to be put to death.   [23:13–32]

Jesus Crucified. And when they were come to the
place, which is called Calvary, there they crucified him,
and the malefactors, one on the right hand, and the other
on the left. Then said Jesus, "Father, forgive them; for

they know not what they do". And they parted his raiment, and cast lots. And the people stood beholding. And the rulers also with them derided him, saying, "He saved others; let him save himself, if he be Christ, the chosen of God". And the soldiers also mocked him, coming to him, and offering him vinegar, and saying, "If thou be the king of the Jews, save thyself". And a superscription also was written over him in letters of Greek, and Latin, and Hebrew, THIS IS THE KING OF THE JEWS.

[23:33–38]

The Penitent Thief. And one of the malefactors which were hanged railed on him, saying, "If thou be Christ, save thyself and us". But the other answering rebuked him, saying, "Dost not thou fear God, seeing thou art in the same condemnation? And we indeed justly; for we receive the due reward of our deeds: but this man hath done nothing amiss." And he said unto Jesus, "Lord, remember me when thou comest into thy kingdom". And Jesus said unto him, "Verily I say unto thee, To day shalt thou be with me in paradise".

And it was about the sixth hour, and there was a darkness over all the earth until the ninth hour. And the sun was darkened, and the veil of the temple was rent in the midst. [23:39–45]

Matthew *records:*

And about the ninth hour Jesus cried with a loud voice, saying, "ELI, ELI, LAMA SABACHTHANI?" that is to say, "My God, my God, why hast thou forsaken me?"[17] Some of them that stood there, when they heard that, said, "This man calleth for Elias". And straightway one of them ran, and took a spunge, and filled it with vinegar, and put it on a reed, and gave him to drink. The rest said, "Let be, let us see whether Elias will come to save him".

[27:46–49]

[17] See Psalm 22, p. 263.

Luke *resumes:*

Jesus Dies on the Cross.   And when Jesus had cried
with a loud voice, he said, "Father, into thy hands I com-
mend my spirit": and having said thus, he gave up the
ghost. Now when the centurion saw what was done, he
glorified God, saying, "Certainly this was a righteous man".
And all the people that came together to that sight, beholding the things which were done, smote their breasts, and
returned. And all his acquaintance, and the women that
followed him from Galilee, stood afar off, beholding these
things.   [23:46–49]

Jesus' Body Entombed.   And, behold, there was a man
named Joseph, a counsellor; and he was a good man, and
a just: (the same had not consented to the counsel and
deed of them;) he was of Arimathæa, a city of the Jews:
who also himself waited for the kingdom of God. This
man went unto Pilate, and begged the body of Jesus. And
he took it down, and wrapped it in linen, and laid it in a
sepulchre that was hewn in stone, wherein never man before was laid. And that day was the preparation, and the
sabbath drew on. And the women also, which came with
him from Galilee, followed after, and beheld the sepulchre,
and how his body was laid. And they returned, and prepared spices and ointments; and rested the sabbath day
according to the commandment.   [23:50–56]

The Resurrection of Jesus.   Now upon the first day of
the week, very early in the morning, they came unto the
sepulchre, bringing the spices which they had prepared,
and certain others with them. And they found the stone
rolled away from the sepulchre. And they entered in, and
found not the body of the Lord Jesus. And it came to
pass, as they were much perplexed thereabout, behold,
two men stood by them in shining garments: and as they
were afraid, and bowed down their faces to the earth,
they said unto them, "Why seek ye the living among the
dead? He is not here, but is risen: remember how he

spake unto you when he was yet in Galilee, saying, 'The Son of man must be delivered into the hands of sinful men, and be crucified, and the third day rise again'." And they remembered his words, and returned from the sepulchre, and told all these things unto the eleven, and to all the rest. It was Mary Magdalene, and Joanna, and Mary the mother of James, and other women that were with them, which told these things unto the apostles. And their words seemed to them as idle tales, and they believed them not. Then arose Peter, and ran unto the sepulchre; and stooping down, he beheld the linen clothes laid by themselves, and departed, wondering in himself at that which was come to pass. [24:1–12]

Jesus Appears to Two Disciples. And, behold, two of them went that same day to a village called Emmaus, which was from Jerusalem about threescore furlongs. And they talked together of all these things which had happened. And it came to pass, that, while they communed together and reasoned, Jesus himself drew near, and went with them. But their eyes were holden that they should not know him. And he said unto them, "What manner of communications are these that ye have one to another, as ye walk, and are sad?" And the one of them, whose name was Cleopas, answering said unto him, "Art thou only a stranger in Jerusalem, and hast not known the things which are come to pass there in these days?" And he said unto them, "What things?" And they said unto him, "Concerning Jesus of Nazareth, which was a prophet mighty in deed and word before God and all the people: and how the chief priests and our rulers delivered him to be condemned to death, and have crucified him. But we trusted that it had been he which should have redeemed Israel: and beside all this, to day is the third day since these things were done. Yea, and certain women also of our company made us astonished, which were early at the sepulchre; and when they found not his body, they came, saying, that they had also seen a vision of angels, which said that he was alive.

And certain of them which were with us went to the sepulchre, and found it even so as the women had said: but him they saw not." Then he said unto them, "O fools, and slow of heart to believe all that the prophets have spoken: ought not Christ to have suffered these things, and to enter into his glory?" And beginning at Moses and all the prophets, he expounded unto them in all the scriptures the things concerning himself. And they drew nigh unto the village, whither they went: and he made as though he would have gone further. But they constrained him, saying, "Abide with us: for it is toward evening, and the day is far spent". And he went in to tarry with them. And it came to pass, as he sat at meat with them, he took bread, and blessed it, and brake, and gave to them. And their eyes were opened, and they knew him; and he vanished out of their sight. And they said one to another, "Did not our heart burn within us, while he talked with us by the way, and while he opened to us the scriptures?" And they rose up the same hour, and returned to Jerusalem, and found the eleven gathered together, and them that were with them, saying, "The Lord is risen indeed, and hath appeared to Simon". And they told what things were done in the way, and how he was known of them in breaking of bread.   [24:13–35]

Jesus Appears to His Apostles. And as they thus spake, Jesus himself stood in the midst of them, and saith unto them, "Peace be unto you". But they were terrified and affrighted, and supposed that they had seen a spirit. And he said unto them, "Why are ye troubled? and why do thoughts arise in your hearts? Behold my hands and my feet, that it is I myself: handle me, and see; for a spirit hath not flesh and bones, as ye see me have." And when he had thus spoken, he shewed them his hands and his feet. And while they yet believed not for joy, and wondered, he said unto them, "Have ye here any meat?" And they gave him a piece of a broiled fish, and of an honeycomb. And he took it, and did eat before them.

And he said unto them, "These are the words which I spake unto you, while I was yet with you, that all things must be fulfilled, which were written in the law of Moses, and in the prophets, and in the psalms, concerning me". Then opened he their understanding, that they might understand the scriptures, and said unto them, "Thus it is written, and thus it behoved Christ to suffer, and to rise from the dead the third day: and that repentance and remission of sins should be preached in his name among all nations, beginning at Jerusalem. And ye are witnesses of these things. And, behold, I send the promise of my Father upon you: but tarry ye in the city of Jerusalem, until ye be endued with power from on high."

And he led them out as far as to Bethany, and he lifted up his hands, and blessed them. And it came to pass, while he blessed them, he was parted from them, and carried up into heaven. And they worshipped him, and returned to Jerusalem with great joy: and were continually in the temple, praising and blessing God. Amen.   [24:36–53]

From THE GOSPEL ACCORDING TO JOHN

The Preface: the Divine Word. In the beginning was the Word, and the Word was with God, and the Word was God. The same was in the beginning with God. All things were made by him; and without him was not any thing made that was made. In him was life; and the life was the light of men. And the light shineth in darkness; and the darkness comprehended it not. There was a man sent from God, whose name was John. The same came for a witness, to bear witness of the Light, that all men through him might believe. He was not that Light, but was sent to bear witness of that Light. That was the true Light, which lighteth every man that cometh into the world. He was in the world, and the world was made by him, and the world knew him not. He came unto his own, and his own received him not. But as many as received him, to them gave he power to become the sons of God, even to them that believe on his name: which were born, not of blood, nor of the will of the flesh, nor of the will of man, but of God. And the Word was made flesh, and dwelt among us, (and we beheld his glory, the glory as of the only begotten of the Father,) full of grace and truth. John bare witness of him, and cried, saying, "This was he of whom I spake, He that cometh after me is preferred before me: for he was before me". And of his fulness have all we received, and grace for grace. For the law was given by Moses, but grace and truth came by Jesus Christ. No man hath seen God at any time; the only begotten Son, which is in the bosom of the Father, he hath declared him. [1:1–18]

The Testimony of John the Baptist. And this is the record of John, when the Jews sent priests and Levites from Jerusalem to ask him, "Who art thou?" And he confessed, and denied not; but confessed, "I am not the Christ". And they asked him, "What then? Art thou Elias?" And he saith, "I am not". "Art thou that prophet?" And he answered, "No". Then said they unto him, "Who art thou? that we may give an answer to them that sent us. What sayest thou of thyself?" He said, "I am the voice of one crying in the wilderness, 'Make straight the way of the Lord,' as said the prophet Esaias". And they which were sent were of the Pharisees. And they asked him, and said unto him, "Why baptizest thou then, if thou be not that Christ, nor Elias, neither that prophet?" John answered them, saying, "I baptize with water: but there standeth one among you, whom ye know not; he it is, who coming after me is preferred before me, whose shoe's latchet I am not worthy to unloose". These things were done in Bethabara beyond Jordan, where John was baptizing.

The next day John seeth Jesus coming unto him, and saith, "Behold the Lamb of God, which taketh away the sin of the world. This is he of whom I said, After me cometh a man which is preferred before me: for he was before me. And I knew him not: but that he should be made manifest to Israel, therefore am I come baptizing with water." And John bare record, saying, "I saw the Spirit descending from heaven like a dove, and it abode upon him. And I knew him not: but he that sent me to baptize with water, the same said unto me, 'Upon whom thou shalt see the Spirit descending, and remaining on him, the same is he which baptizeth with the Holy Ghost'. And I saw, and bare record that this is the Son of God."

Again the next day after John stood, and two of his disciples; and looking upon Jesus as he walked, he saith, "Behold the Lamb of God!" And the two disciples heard him speak, and they followed Jesus. Then Jesus turned, and saw them following, and saith unto them, "What seek ye?"

They said unto him, "Rabbi," (which is to say, being interpreted, "Master,") "where dwellest thou?" He saith unto
them, "Come and see". They came and saw where he
dwelt, and abode with him that day: for it was about the
tenth hour. One of the two which heard John speak, and
followed him, was Andrew, Simon Peter's brother. He first
findeth his own brother Simon, and saith unto him, "We
have found the Messias," which is, being interpreted, "the
Christ". And he brought him to Jesus. And when Jesus
beheld him, he said, "Thou art Simon the son of Jona:
thou shalt be called Cephas," which is by interpretation,
"A stone".   [1:19–42]

Philip and Nathanael. The day following Jesus would
go forth into Galilee, and findeth Philip, and saith unto
him, "Follow me". Now Philip was of Bethsaida, the city
of Andrew and Peter. Philip findeth Nathanael, and saith
unto him, "We have found him, of whom Moses in the
law, and the prophets, did write, Jesus of Nazareth, the
son of Joseph". And Nathanael said unto him, "Can there
any good thing come out of Nazareth?" Philip saith unto
him, "Come and see". Jesus saw Nathanael coming to him,
and saith of him, "Behold an Israelite indeed, in whom is
no guile!" Nathanael saith unto him, "Whence knowest
thou me?" Jesus answered and said unto him, "Before that
Philip called thee, when thou wast under the fig tree, I saw
thee". Nathanael answered and saith unto him, "Rabbi,
thou art the Son of God; thou art the King of Israel".
Jesus answered and said unto him, "Because I said unto
thee, I saw thee under the fig tree, believest thou? thou
shalt see greater things than these". And he saith unto
him, "Verily, verily, I say unto you, Hereafter ye shall see
heaven open, and the angels of God ascending and descending upon the Son of man".   [1:43–51]

The Marriage at Cana. And the third day there was a
marriage in Cana of Galilee; and the mother of Jesus was
there: and both Jesus was called, and his disciples, to the
marriage. And when they wanted wine, the mother of

Jesus saith unto him, "They have no wine". Jesus saith unto her, "Woman, what have I to do with thee?[1] mine hour is not yet come". His mother saith unto the servants, "Whatsoever he saith unto you, do it". And there were set there six waterpots of stone, after the manner of the purifying of the Jews, containing two or three firkins apiecé. Jesus saith unto them, "Fill the waterpots with water". And they filled them up to the brim. And he saith unto them, "Draw out now, and bear unto the governor of the feast". And they bare it. When the ruler of the feast had tasted the water that was made wine, and knew not whence it was: (but the servants which drew the water knew;) the governor of the feast called the bridegroom, and saith unto him, "Every man at the beginning doth set forth good wine; and when men have well drunk, then that which is worse: but thou hast kept the good wine until now". This beginning of miracles did Jesus in Cana of Galilee, and manifested forth his glory; and his disciples believed on him. [2:1–11]

Nicodemus Comes to Jesus. There was a man of the Pharisees, named Nicodemus, a ruler of the Jews: the same came to Jesus by night, and said unto him, "Rabbi, we know that thou art a teacher come from God: for no man can do these miracles that thou doest, except God be with him". Jesus answered and said unto him, "Verily, verily, I say unto thee, Except a man be born again, he cannot see the kingdom of God". Nicodemus saith unto him, "How can a man be born when he is old? can he enter the second time into his mother's womb, and be born?" Jesus answered, "Verily, verily, I say unto thee, Except a man be born of water and of the Spirit, he cannot enter into the kingdom of God. That which is born of the flesh is flesh; and that which is born of the Spirit is spirit. Marvel not that I said unto thee, Ye must be born again. The wind bloweth where it listeth, and thou hearest the sound

[1] A better translation is, "Lady, what concern is this of yours?"

thereof, but canst not tell whence it cometh, and whither it goeth: so is every one that is born of the Spirit." Nicodemus answered and said unto him, "How can these things be?" Jesus answered and said unto him, "Art thou a master of Israel, and knowest not these things? Verily, verily, I say unto thee, We speak that we do know, and testify that we have seen; and ye receive not our witness. If I have told you earthly things, and ye believe not, how shall ye believe, if I tell you of heavenly things? And no man hath ascended up to heaven, but he that came down from heaven, even the Son of man which is in heaven. And as Moses lifted up the serpent in the wilderness, even so must the Son of man be lifted up: that whosoever believeth in him should not perish, but have eternal life."

For God so loved the world, that he gave his only begotten Son, that whosoever believeth in him should not perish, but have everlasting life. For God sent not his Son into the world to condemn the world; but that the world through him might be saved. He that believeth on him is not condemned: but he that believeth not is condemned already, because he hath not believed in the name of the only begotten Son of God. And this is the condemnation, that light is come into the world, and men loved darkness rather than light, because their deeds were evil. For every one that doeth evil hateth the light, neither cometh to the light, lest his deeds should be reproved. But he that doeth truth cometh to the light, that his deeds may be made manifest, that they are wrought in God.   [3:1–21]

Jesus and the Woman of Samaria.[2] When therefore the Lord knew how the Pharisees had heard that Jesus made and baptized more disciples than John, (though Jesus himself baptized not, but his disciples,) he left Judæa, and departed again into Galilee. And he must needs go through Samaria. Then cometh he to a city of Samaria, which is called Sychar, near to the parcel of

[2] See Appendix 8.

ground that Jacob gave to his son Joseph. Now Jacob's well was there. Jesus therefore, being wearied with his journey, sat thus on the well: and it was about the sixth hour. There cometh a woman of Samaria to draw water: Jesus saith unto her, "Give me to drink". (For his disciples were gone away unto the city to buy meat.) Then saith the woman of Samaria unto him, "How is it that thou, being a Jew, askest drink of me, which am a woman of Samaria?" for the Jews have no dealings with the Samaritans. Jesus answered and said unto her, "If thou knewest the gift of God, and who it is that saith to thee, Give me to drink; thou wouldest have asked of him, and he would have given the living water". The woman saith unto him, "Sir, thou hast nothing to draw with, and the well is deep: from whence then hast thou that living water? Art thou greater than our father Jacob, which gave us the well, and drank thereof himself, and his children, and his cattle?" Jesus answered and said unto her, "Whosoever drinketh of this water shall thirst again: but whosoever drinketh of the water that I shall give him shall never thirst; but the water that I shall give him shall be in him a well of water springing up into everlasting life". The woman saith unto him, "Sir, give me this water, that I thirst not, neither come hither to draw". Jesus saith unto her, "Go, call thy husband, and come hither". The woman answered and said, "I have no husband". Jesus said unto her, "Thou hast well said, 'I have no husband': for thou hast had five husbands; and he whom thou now hast is not thy husband: in that saidst thou truly". The woman saith unto him, "Sir, I perceive that thou art a prophet. Our fathers worshipped in this mountain; and ye say, that in Jerusalem is the place where men ought to worship." Jesus saith unto her, "Woman, believe me, the hour cometh, when ye shall neither in this mountain, nor yet at Jerusalem, worship the Father. Ye worship ye know not what: we know what we worship: for salvation is of the Jews. But the hour cometh, and now is, when the true worshippers shall worship the

Father in spirit and in truth: for the Father seeketh such to worship him. God is a Spirit: and they that worship him must worship him in spirit and in truth." The woman saith unto him, "I know that Messias cometh, which is called Christ: when he is come, he will tell us all things". Jesus saith unto her, "I that speak unto thee am he".

And upon this came his disciples, and marvelled that he talked with the woman: yet no man said, "What seekest thou?" or, "Why talkest thou with her?" The woman then left her waterpot, and went her way into the city, and saith to the men, "Come, see a man, which told me all things that ever I did: is not this the Christ?" Then they went out of the city, and came unto him. In the mean while his disciples prayed him, saying, "Master, eat". But he said unto them, "I have meat to eat that ye know not of". Therefore said the disciples one to another, "Hath any man brought him aught to eat?" Jesus saith unto them, "My meat is to do the will of him that sent me, and to finish his work. Say not ye, 'There are yet four months, and then cometh harvest'? behold, I say unto you, Lift up your eyes, and look on the fields; for they are white already to harvest. And he that reapeth receiveth wages, and gathereth fruit unto life eternal: that both he that soweth and he that reapeth may rejoice together. And herein is that saying true, 'One soweth, and another reapeth'. I sent you to reap that whereon ye bestowed no labour: other men laboured, and ye are entered into their labours."

And many of the Samaritans of that city believed on him for the saying of the woman, which testified, "He told me all that ever I did". So when the Samaritans were come unto him, they besought him that he would tarry with them: and he abode there two days. And many more believed because of his own word; and said unto the woman, "Now we believe, not because of thy saying: for we have heard him ourselves, and know that this is indeed the Christ, the Saviour of the world".   [4:1-42]

Jesus Feeds Five Thousand.[3] After these things Jesus went over the sea of Galilee, which is the sea of Tiberias. And a great multitude followed him, because they saw his miracles which he did on them that were diseased. And Jesus went up into a mountain, and there he sat with his disciples. And the passover, a feast of the Jews, was nigh. When Jesus then lifted up his eyes, and saw a great company come unto him, he saith unto Philip, "Whence shall we buy bread, that these may eat?" And this he said to prove him: for he himself knew what he would do. Philip answered him, "Two hundred pennyworth of bread is not sufficient for them, that every one of them may take a little". One of his disciples, Andrew, Simon Peter's brother, saith unto him, "There is a lad here, which hath five barley loaves, and two small fishes: but what are they among so many?" And Jesus said, "Make the men sit down". Now there was much grass in the place. So the men sat down, in number about five thousand. And Jesus took the loaves; and when he had given thanks, he distributed to the disciples, and the disciples to them that were set down; and likewise of the fishes as much as they would. When they were filled, he said unto his disciples, "Gather up the fragments that remain, that nothing be lost". Therefore they gathered them together, and filled twelve baskets with the fragments of the five barley loaves, which remained over and above unto them that had eaten. Then those men, when they had seen the miracle that Jesus did, said, "This is of a truth that prophet that should come into the world".

When Jesus therefore perceived that they would come and take him by force, to make him a king, he departed again into a mountain himself alone.   [6:1–15]

Jesus Walks on the Sea. And when even was now come, his disciples went down unto the sea, and entered into a ship, and went over the sea toward Capernaum. And it was now dark, and Jesus was not come to them.

---

[3] For Mark's account of this miracle, see p. 384.

And the sea arose by reason of a great wind that blew. So when they had rowed about five and twenty or thirty furlongs, they see Jesus walking on the sea, and drawing nigh unto the ship: and they were afraid. But he saith unto them, "It is I; be not afraid". Then they willingly received him into the ship: and immediately the ship was at the land whither they went. [6:16–21]

Jesus' Teaching on the Heavenly Bread. The day following, when the people which stood on the other side of the sea saw that there was none other boat there, save that one whereinto his disciples were entered, and that Jesus went not with his disciples into the boat, but that his disciples were gone away alone; (howbeit there came other boats from Tiberias nigh unto the place where they did eat bread, after that the Lord had given thanks:) when the people therefore saw that Jesus was not there, neither his disciples, they also took shipping, and came to Capernaum, seeking for Jesus. And when they had found him on the other side of the sea, they said unto him, "Rabbi, when camest thou hither?" Jesus answered them and said, "Verily, verily, I say unto you, Ye seek me, not because ye saw the miracles, but because ye did eat of the loaves, and were filled. Labour not for the meat which perisheth, but for that meat which endureth unto everlasting life, which the Son of man shall give unto you: for him hath God the Father sealed." Then said they unto him, "What shall we do, that we might work the works of God?" Jesus answered and said unto them, "This is the work of God, that ye believe on him whom he hath sent". They said therefore unto him, "What sign shewest thou then, that we may see, and believe thee? what dost thou work? Our fathers did eat manna in the desert; as it is written, 'He gave them bread from heaven to eat'." Then Jesus said unto them, "Verily, verily, I say unto you, Moses gave you not that bread from heaven; but my Father giveth you the true bread from heaven. For the bread of God is he which cometh down from heaven, and giveth life unto the world."

Then said they unto him, "Lord, evermore give us this bread". And Jesus said unto them, "I am the bread of life: he that cometh to me shall never hunger; and he that believeth on me shall never thirst. But I said unto you, that ye also have seen me, and believe not. All that the Father giveth me shall come to me; and him that cometh to me I will in no wise cast out. For I came down from heaven, not to do mine own will, but the will of him that sent me. And this is the Father's will which hath sent me, that of all which he hath given me I should lose nothing, but should raise it up again at the last day. And this is the will of him that sent me, that every one which seeth the Son, and believeth on him, may have everlasting life: and I will raise him up at the last day."

The Jews then murmured at him, because he said, "I am the bread which came down from heaven". And they said, "Is not this Jesus, the son of Joseph, whose father and mother we know? how is it then that he saith, 'I came down from heaven'?" Jesus therefore answered and said unto them, "Murmur not among yourselves. No man can come to me, except the Father which hath sent me draw him: and I will raise him up at the last day. It is written in the prophets, 'And they shall be all taught of God'. Every man therefore that hath heard, and hath learned of the Father, cometh unto me. Not that any man hath seen the Father, save he which is of God, he hath seen the Father. Verily, verily, I say unto you, He that believeth on me hath everlasting life. I am that bread of life. Your fathers did eat manna in the wilderness, and are dead. This is the bread which cometh down from heaven, that a man may eat thereof, and not die. I am the living bread which came down from heaven: if any man eat of this bread, he shall live for ever: and the bread that I will give is my flesh, which I will give for the life of the world."

The Jews therefore strove among themselves, saying, "How can this man give us his flesh to eat?" Then Jesus said unto them, "Verily, verily, I say unto you, Except ye eat the flesh of the Son of man, and drink his blood, ye have no life in you. Whoso eateth my flesh, and drinketh my blood, hath eternal life; and I will raise him up at the last day. For my flesh is meat indeed, and my blood is drink indeed. He that eateth my flesh, and drinketh my blood, dwelleth in me, and I in him. As the living Father hath sent me, and I live by the Father: so he that eateth me, even he shall live by me. This is that bread which came down from heaven: not as your fathers did eat manna, and are dead: he that eateth of this bread shall live for ever." These things said he in the synagogue, as he taught in Capernaum.   [6:22–59]

Some Disciples Offended. Many therefore of his disciples, when they had heard this, said, "This is an hard saying; who can hear it?" When Jesus knew in himself that his disciples murmured at it, he said unto them, "Doth this offend you? What and if ye shall see the Son of man ascend up where he was before? It is the spirit that quickeneth; the flesh profiteth nothing: the words that I speak unto you, they are spirit, and they are life. But there are some of you that believe not." For Jesus knew from the beginning who they were that believed not, and who should betray him. And he said, "Therefore said I unto you, that no man can come unto me, except it were given unto him of my Father".

From that time many of his disciples went back, and walked no more with him. Then said Jesus unto the twelve, "Will ye also go away?" Then Simon Peter answered him, "Lord, to whom shall we go? thou hast the words of eternal life. And we believe and are sure that thou art that Christ, the Son of the living God." Jesus answered them, "Have not I chosen you twelve, and one of you is a devil?" He spake of Judas Iscariot the son of Simon: for he it was that should betray him, being one of the twelve.   [6:60–71]

The Woman Taken in Adultery. Jesus went unto the mount of Olives. And early in the morning he came again into the temple, and all the people came unto him; and he sat down, and taught them. And the scribes and Pharisees brought unto him a woman taken in adultery; and when they had set her in the midst, they say unto him, "Master, this woman was taken in adultery, in the very act. Now Moses in the law commanded us, that such should be stoned: but what sayest thou?" This they said, tempting him, that they might have to accuse him. But Jesus stooped down, and with his finger wrote on the ground, as though he heard them not. So when they continued asking him, he lifted up himself, and said unto them, "He that is without sin among you, let him first cast a stone at her". And again he stooped down, and wrote on the ground. And they which heard it, being convicted by their own conscience, went out one by one, beginning at the eldest, even unto the last: and Jesus was left alone, and the woman standing in the midst. When Jesus had lifted up himself, and saw none but the woman, he said unto her, "Woman, where are those thine accusers? hath no man condemned thee?" She said, "No man, Lord". And Jesus said unto her, "Neither do I condemn thee: go, and sin no more".

[8:1–11]

Jesus and the Pharisees. Then spake Jesus again unto them, saying, "I am the light of the world: he that followeth me shall not walk in darkness, but shall have the light of life". The Pharisees therefore said unto him, "Thou bearest record of thyself; thy record is not true". Jesus answered and said unto them, "Though I bear record of myself, yet my record is true: for I know whence I came, and whither I go; but ye cannot tell whence I come, and whither I go. Ye judge after the flesh; I judge no man. And yet if I judge, my judgment is true: for I am not alone, but I and the Father that sent me. It is also written in your law, that the testimony of two men is true. I am one that bear witness of myself, and the Father that sent me beareth witness of me". Then said they unto him, "Where is thy Father?" Jesus answered, "Ye neither know me, nor my Father: if ye had known me, ye should have known my Father also". These words spake Jesus in the treasury, as he taught in the temple: and no man laid hands on him; for his hour was not yet come.

Then said Jesus again unto them, "I go my way, and ye shall seek me, and shall die in your sins: whither I go, ye cannot come". Then said the Jews, "Will he kill himself? because he saith, 'Whither I go, ye cannot come'". And he said unto them, "Ye are from beneath; I am from above: ye are of this world; I am not of this world. I said therefore unto you, that ye shall die in your sins: for if ye believe not that I am he, ye shall die in your sins." Then said they unto him, "Who art thou?" And Jesus saith unto them, "Even the same that I said unto you from the beginning. I have many things to say and to judge of you: but he that sent me is true; and I speak to the world those things which I have heard of him." They understood not that he spake to them of the Father. Then said Jesus unto them, "When ye have lifted up the Son of man, then shall ye know that I am he, and that I do nothing of myself; but as my Father hath taught me, I speak these things. And he that sent me is with me: the Father hath not left me alone; for I do always those things that please him." As he spake these words, many believed on him.

Then said Jesus to those Jews which believed on him, "If ye continue in my word, then are ye my disciples indeed; and ye shall know the truth, and the truth shall make you free". They answered him, "We be Abraham's seed, and were never in bondage to any man: how sayest thou, 'Ye shall be made free'?" Jesus answered them, "Verily, verily, I say unto you, Whosoever committeth sin is the servant of sin. And the servant abideth not in the house for ever: but the Son abideth ever. If the Son therefore shall make you free, ye shall be free indeed. I know that ye are Abraham's seed; but ye seek to kill me, because my word hath no place in you. I speak that which I have seen with my Father: and ye do that which ye have seen with your father." They answered and said unto him, "Abraham is our father". Jesus saith unto them, "If ye were Abraham's children, ye would do the works of Abraham. But now ye seek to kill me, a man that hath told you the truth, which I have heard of God: this did not Abraham. Ye do the deeds of your father." Then said they to him, "We be not born of fornication; we have one Father, even God". Jesus said unto them, "If God were your Father, ye would love me: for I proceeded forth and came from God; neither came I of myself, but he sent me. Why do ye not understand my speech? even because ye cannot hear my word. Ye are of your father the devil, and the lusts of your father ye will do. He was a murderer from the beginning, and abode not in the truth, because there is no truth in him. When he speaketh a lie, he speaketh of his own: for he is a liar, and the father of it. And because I tell you the truth, ye believe me not. Which of you convinceth me of sin? And if I say the truth, why do ye not believe me? He that is of God heareth God's words: ye therefore hear them not, because ye are not of God." Then answered the Jews, and said unto him, "Say we not well that thou art a Samaritan, and hast a devil?" Jesus answered, "I have not a devil; but I honour my Father, and ye do dishonour me. And I seek not mine own glory: there is one that seeketh and judgeth. Verily, verily, I say unto you, If a man keep my saying, he shall never see death." Then said the Jews unto him, "Now we know that thou hast a devil. Abraham is dead, and the prophets; and thou sayest, 'If a man keep my saying, he shall never taste of death'. Art thou greater than our father Abraham, which is dead? and the prophets are dead: whom makest thou thyself?" Jesus answered, "If I honour myself, my honour is nothing: it is my Father that honoureth me; of whom ye say, that he is your God: yet ye have not known him; but I know him: and if I should say, I know him not, I shall be a liar like unto you: but I know him, and keep his saying. Your father Abraham rejoiced to see my day: and he saw it, and was glad." Then said the Jews unto him, "Thou art not yet fifty years old, and hast thou seen Abraham?" Jesus said unto them, "Verily, verily, I say unto you, Before Abraham was, I am". Then took they up stones to cast at him: but Jesus hid himself, and went out of the temple, going through the midst of them, and so passed by. [8:12–59]

Jesus Heals a Blind Man. And as Jesus passed by, he saw a man which was blind from his birth. And his disciples asked him, saying, "Master, who did sin, this man, or his parents, that he was born blind?" Jesus answered, "Neither hath this man sinned, nor his parents: but that the works of God should be made manifest in him. I must work the works of him that sent me, while it is day: the night cometh, when no man can work. As long as I am in the world, I am the light of the world." When he had thus spoken, he spat on the ground, and made clay of the spittle, and he anointed the eyes of the blind man with the clay, and said unto him, "Go, wash in the pool of Siloam," (which is by interpretation, "Sent".) He went his way therefore, and washed, and came seeing. The neighbours therefore, and they which before had seen him that he was blind, said, "Is not this he that sat and begged?" Some said, "This is he": others said, "He is like him": but he said, "I am he". Therefore said they unto him, "How were thine eyes opened?" He answered and said, "A man that is called Jesus made clay, and anointed mine eyes, and said unto me, 'Go to the pool of Siloam, and wash': and I went and washed, and I received sight". Then said they unto him, "Where is he?" He said, "I know not". [9:1–12]

The Pharisees and the Blind Man. They brought to the Pharisees him that aforetime was blind. And it was the sabbath day when Jesus made the clay, and opened his eyes. Then again the Pharisees also asked him how he had received his sight. He said unto them, "He put clay upon mine eyes, and I washed, and do see". Therefore said some of the Pharisees, "This man is not of God, because he keepeth not the sabbath day". Others said, "How can a man that is a sinner do such miracles?" And there was a division among them. They say unto the blind man again, "What sayest thou of him, that he hath opened thine eyes?" He said, "He is a prophet". But the Jews did not believe concerning him, that he had been blind, and received his sight, until they called the parents of him that had received his sight. And they asked them, saying, "Is this your son, who ye say was born blind? how then doth he now see?" His parents answered them and said, "We know that this is our son, and that he was born blind: but by what means he now seeth, we know not; or who hath opened his eyes, we know not: he is of age; ask him: he shall speak for himself". These words spake his parents, because they feared the Jews: for the Jews had agreed already, that if any man did confess that he was Christ, he should be put out of the synagogue. Therefore said his parents, "He is of age; ask him".

Then again called they the man that was blind, and said unto him, "Give God the praise: we know that this man is a sinner". He answered and said, "Whether he be a sinner or no, I know not: one thing I know, that, whereas I was blind, now I see". Then said they to him again, "What did he to thee? how opened he thine eyes?" He answered them, "I have told you already, and ye did not hear: wherefore would ye hear it again? will ye also be his disciples?" Then they reviled him, and said, "Thou art his disciple; but we are Moses' disciples. We know that God spake unto Moses: as for this fellow, we know not from whence he is." The man answered and said unto them, "Why herein is a marvellous thing, that ye know not from whence he is, and yet he hath opened mine eyes. Now we know that God heareth not sinners: but if any man be a worshipper of God, and doeth his will, him he heareth. Since the world began was it not heard that any man opened the eyes of one that was born blind. If this man were not of God, he could do nothing." They answered and said unto him, "Thou wast altogether born in sins, and dost thou teach us?" And they cast him out.

Jesus heard that they had cast him out; and when he had found him, he said unto him, "Dost thou believe on the Son of God?" He answered and said, "Who is he, Lord, that I might believe on him?" And Jesus said unto him, "Thou hast both seen him, and it is he that talketh with thee". And he said, "Lord, I believe". And he worshipped him. And Jesus said, "For judgment I am come into this world, that they which see not might see; and that they which see might be made blind". And some of the Pharisees which were with him heard these words, and said unto him, "Are we blind also?" Jesus said unto them, "If ye were blind, ye should have no sin: but now ye say, 'We see'; therefore your sin remaineth".   [9:13–41]

"The Good Shepherd." "Verily, verily, I say unto you, He that entereth not by the door into the sheepfold, but climbeth up some other way, the same is a thief and a robber. But he that entereth in by the door is the shepherd of the sheep. To him the porter openeth; and the sheep hear his voice: and he calleth his own sheep by name, and leadeth them out. And when he putteth forth his own sheep, he goeth before them, and the sheep follow him: for they know his voice. And a stranger will they not follow, but will flee from him: for they know not the voice of strangers." This parable spake Jesus unto them: but they understood not what things they were which he spake unto them.

Then said Jesus unto them again, "Verily, verily, I say unto you, I am the door of the sheep. All that ever came before me are thieves and robbers: but the sheep did not hear them. I am the door: by me if any man enter in, he shall be saved, and shall go in and out, and find pasture. The thief cometh not, but for to steal, and to kill, and to destroy: I am come that they might have life, and that they might have it more abundantly. I am the good shepherd: the good shepherd giveth his life for the sheep. But he that is an hireling, and not the shepherd, whose own the sheep are not, seeth the wolf coming, and leaveth the sheep, and fleeth: and the wolf catcheth them, and scattereth the sheep. The hireling fleeth, because he is an hireling, and careth not for the sheep. I am the good shepherd, and know my sheep, and am known of mine. As the Father knoweth me, even so know I the Father: and I lay down my life for the sheep. And other sheep I have, which are not of this fold: them also I must bring, and they shall hear my voice; and there shall be one fold, and one shepherd. Therefore doth my Father love me, because I lay down my life, that I might take it again. No man taketh it from me, but I lay it down of myself. I have power to lay it down, and I have power to take it again. This commandment have I received of my Father." [10:1-18]

Lazarus Restored to Life. Now a certain man was sick, named Lazarus, of Bethany, the town of Mary and her sister Martha. (It was that Mary which anointed the Lord with ointment, and wiped his feet with her hair, whose brother Lazarus was sick.) Therefore his sisters sent unto him, saying, "Lord, behold, he whom thou lovest is sick". When Jesus heard that, he said, "This sickness is not unto death, but for the glory of God, that the Son of God might be glorified thereby". Now Jesus loved Martha, and her sister, and Lazarus. When he had heard therefore that he was sick, he abode two days still in the same place where he was. Then after that saith he to his disciples, "Let us go into Judæa again". His disciples say unto him, "Master, the Jews of late sought to stone thee; and goest thou thither again?" Jesus answered, "Are there not twelve hours in the day? If any man walk in the day, he stumbleth not, because he seeth the light of this world. But if a man walk in the night, he stumbleth, because there is no light in him." These things said he: and after that he saith unto them, "Our friend Lazarus sleepeth; but I go, that I may awake him out of sleep". Then said his disciples, "Lord, if he sleep, he shall do well". Howbeit Jesus spake of his death: but they thought that he had spoken of taking of rest in sleep. Then said Jesus unto them plainly, "Lazarus is dead. And I am glad for your sakes that I was not there, to the intent ye may believe; nevertheless let us go unto him." Then said Thomas, which is called Didymus, unto his fellowdisciples, "Let us also go, that we may die with him".

Then when Jesus came, he found that he had lain in the grave four days already. Now Bethany was nigh unto Jerusalem, about fifteen furlongs off: and many of the Jews came to Martha and Mary, to comfort them concerning their brother. Then Martha, as soon as she heard that Jesus was coming, went and met him: but Mary sat still in the house. Then said Martha unto Jesus, "Lord, if thou hadst been here, my brother had not died. But I know, that even now, whatsoever thou wilt ask of God, God will give it thee." Jesus saith unto her, "Thy brother shall rise again". Martha saith unto him, "I know that he shall rise again in the resurrection at the last day". Jesus said unto her, "I am the resurrection, and the life: he that believeth in me, though he were dead, yet shall he live: and whosoever liveth and believeth in me shall never die. Believest thou this?" She saith unto him, "Yea, Lord: I believe that thou art the Christ, the Son of God, which should come into the world". And when she had so said, she went her way, and called Mary her sister secretly, saying, "The Master is come, and calleth for thee". As soon as she heard that, she arose quickly, and came unto him.

Now Jesus was not yet come into the town, but was in that place where Martha met him. The Jews then which were with her in the house, and comforted her, when they saw Mary, that she rose up hastily and went out, followed her, saying, "She goeth unto the grave to weep there". Then when Mary was come where Jesus was, and saw him, she fell down at his feet, saying unto him, "Lord, if thou hadst been here, my brother had not died". When Jesus therefore saw her weeping, and the Jews also weeping which came with her, he groaned in the spirit, and was troubled, and said, "Where have ye laid him?" They said unto him, "Lord, come and see". Jesus wept. Then said the Jews, "Behold how he loved him!" And some of them said, "Could not this man, which opened the eyes of the blind, have caused that even this man should not have died?" Jesus therefore again groaning in himself cometh to the grave. It was a cave, and a stone lay upon it. Jesus said, "Take ye away the stone". Martha, the sister of him that was dead, saith unto him, "Lord, by this time he stinketh: for he hath been dead four days". Jesus saith unto her, "Said I not unto thee, that, if thou wouldest believe, thou shouldest see the glory of God?" Then they took away the stone from the place where the dead was laid. And Jesus lifted up his eyes, and said, "Father, I thank thee that thou hast heard me. And I knew that thou hearest me always: but because of the people which stand by I said it, that they may believe that thou hast sent me." And when he thus had spoken, he cried with a loud voice, "Lazarus, come forth". And he that was dead came forth, bound hand and foot with graveclothes: and his face was bound about with a napkin. Jesus saith unto them, "Loose him, and let him go".

Then many of the Jews which came to Mary, and had seen the things which Jesus did, believed on him. But some of them went their ways to the Pharisees, and told them what things Jesus had done. [11:1–46]

Mary Anoints the Feet of Jesus.[4]   Then Jesus six days before the passover came to Bethany, where Lazarus was which had been dead, whom he raised from the dead. There they made him a supper; and Martha served: but Lazarus was one of them that sat at the table with him. Then took Mary a pound of ointment of spikenard, very costly, and anointed the feet of Jesus, and wiped his feet

4 See Appendix 12.

with her hair: and the house was filled with the odour of the ointment. Then saith one of his disciples, Judas Iscariot, Simon's son, which should betray him, "Why was not this ointment sold for three hundred pence, and given to the poor?" This he said, not that he cared for the poor; but because he was a thief, and had the bag, and bare what was put therein. Then said Jesus, "Let her alone: against the day of my burying hath she kept this. For the poor always ye have with you; but me ye have not always."

Much people of the Jews therefore knew that he was there: and they came not for Jesus' sake only, but that they might see Lazarus also, whom he had raised from the dead. But the chief priests consulted that they might put Lazarus also to death; because that by reason of him many of the Jews went away, and believed on Jesus.

On the next day much people that were come to the feast, when they heard that Jesus was coming to Jerusalem, took branches of palm trees, and went forth to meet him, and cried, "Hosanna: Blessed is the King of Israel that cometh in the name of the Lord". And Jesus, when he had found a young ass, sat thereon; as it is written, "Fear not, daughter of Sion: behold, thy King cometh, sitting on an ass's colt". These things understood not his disciples at the first: but when Jesus was glorified, then remembered they that these things were written of him, and that they had done these things unto him. The people therefore that was with him when he called Lazarus out of his grave, and raised him from the dead, bare record. For this cause the people also met him, for that they heard that he had done this miracle. The Pharisees therefore said among themselves, "Perceive ye how ye prevail nothing? behold, the world is gone after him".   [12:1–19]

Jesus in Jerusalem. And there were certain Greeks among them that came up to worship at the feast: the same came therefore to Philip, which was of Bethsaida of

Galilee, and desired him, saying, "Sir, we would see Jesus".
Philip cometh and telleth Andrew: and again Andrew
and Philip tell Jesus. And Jesus answered them, saying,
"The hour is come, that the Son of man should be glorified. Verily, verily, I say unto you, Except a corn of wheat
fall into the ground and die, it abideth alone: but if it die,
it bringeth forth much fruit. He that loveth his life shall
lose it; and he that hateth his life in this world shall keep
it unto life eternal. If any man serve me, let him follow
me; and where I am, there shall also my servant be: if any
man serve me, him will my Father honour. Now is my
soul troubled; and what shall I say? Father, save me from
this hour: but for this cause came I unto this hour. Father,
glorify thy name." Then came there a voice from heaven,
saying, "I have both glorified it, and will glorify it again".
The people therefore, that stood by, and heard it, said that
it thundered: others said, "An angel spake to him". Jesus
answered and said, "This voice came not because of me,
but for your sakes. Now is the judgment of this world: now
shall the prince of this world be cast out. And I, if I be
lifted up[5] from the earth, will draw all men unto me."
This he said, signifying what death he should die. The people answered him, "We have heard out of the law that
Christ abideth for ever: and how sayest thou, 'The Son of
man must be lifted up'? who is this Son of man?" Then
Jesus said unto them, "Yet a little while is the light with
you. Walk while ye have the light, lest darkness come
upon you: for he that walketh in darkness knoweth not
whither he goeth. While ye have light, believe in the light,
that ye may be the children of light."

These things spake Jesus, and departed, and did hide
himself from them. But though he had done so many miracles before them, yet they believed not on him: that the
saying of Esaias the prophet might be fulfilled, which he
spake,

[5] "Lifted up," i.e., crucified.

"Lord, who hath believed our report?
And to whom hath the arm of the Lord been revealed?"

Therefore they could not believe, because that Esaias said again,

"He hath blinded their eyes, and hardened their heart;
That they should not see with their eyes, nor understand with their heart,
And be converted,
And I should heal them".

These things said Esaias, when he saw his glory, and spake of him. Nevertheless among the chief rulers also many believed on him; but because of the Pharisees they did not confess him, lest they should be put out of the synagogue: for they loved the praise of men more than the praise of God.

Jesus cried and said, "He that believeth on me, believeth not on me, but on him that sent me. And he that seeth me seeth him that sent me. I am come a light into the world, that whosoever believeth on me should not abide in darkness. And if any man hear my words, and believe not, I judge him not: for I came not to judge the world, but to save the world. He that rejecteth me, and receiveth not my words, hath one that judgeth him: the word that I have spoken, the same shall judge him in the last day. For I have not spoken of myself; but the Father which sent me, he gave me a commandment, what I should say, and what I should speak. And I know that his commandment is life everlasting: whatsoever I speak therefore, even as the Father said unto me, so I speak."   [12:20–50]

The Last Supper: Jesus Washes the Feet of His Disciples.
Now before the feast of the passover, when Jesus knew that his hour was come that he should depart out of this world unto the Father, having loved his own which were in the world, he loved them unto the end. And supper

being ended, the devil having now put into the heart of Judas Iscariot, Simon's son, to betray him; Jesus knowing that the Father had given all things into his hands, and that he was come from God, and went to God; he riseth from supper, and laid aside his garments; and took a towel, and girded himself. After that he poureth water into a bason, and began to wash the disciples' feet, and to wipe them with the towel wherewith he was girded. Then cometh he to Simon Peter: and Peter saith unto him, "Lord, dost thou wash my feet?" Jesus answered and said unto him, "What I do thou knowest not now; but thou shalt know hereafter". Peter saith unto him, "Thou shalt never wash my feet". Jesus answered him, "If I wash thee not, thou hast no part with me". Simon Peter saith unto him, "Lord, not my feet only, but also my hands and my head". Jesus saith to him, "He that is washed needeth not save to wash his feet, but is clean every whit: and ye are clean, but not all". For he knew who should betray him; therefore said he, "Ye are not all clean".

So after he had washed their feet, and had taken his garments, and was set down again, he said unto them, "Know ye what I have done to you? Ye call me Master and Lord: and ye say well; for so I am. If I then, your Lord and Master, have washed your feet; ye also ought to wash one another's feet. For I have given you an example, that ye should do as I have done to you. Verily, verily, I say unto you, The servant is not greater than his lord; neither he that is sent greater than he that sent him. If ye know these things, happy are ye if ye do them. I speak not of you all: I know whom I have chosen: but that the scripture may be fulfilled, 'He that eateth bread with me hath lifted up his heel against me'. Now I tell you before it come, that, when it is come to pass, ye may believe that I am he. Verily, verily, I say unto you, He that receiveth whomsoever I send receiveth me; and he that receiveth me receiveth him that sent me." [13:1–20]

Judas the Traitor. When Jesus had thus said, he was troubled in spirit, and testified, and said, "Verily, verily, I say unto you, that one of you shall betray me". Then the disciples looked one on another, doubting of whom he spake. Now there was leaning on Jesus' bosom one of his disciples, whom Jesus loved. Simon Peter therefore beckoned to him, that he should ask who it should be of whom he spake. He then lying on Jesus' breast saith unto him, "Lord, who is it?" Jesus answered, "He it is, to whom I shall give a sop, when I have dipped it". And when he had dipped the sop, he gave it to Judas Iscariot, the son of Simon. And after the sop Satan entered into him. Then said Jesus unto him, "That thou doest, do quickly". Now no man at the table knew for what intent he spake this unto him. For some of them thought, because Judas had the bag, that Jesus had said unto him, "Buy those things that we have need of against the feast"; or, that he should give something to the poor. He then having received the sop went immediately out: and it was night.

Therefore, when he was gone out, Jesus said, "Now is the Son of man glorified, and God is glorified in him. If God be glorified in him, God shall also glorify him in himself, and shall straightway glorify him. Little children, yet a little while I am with you. Ye shall seek me: and as I said unto the Jews, Whither I go, ye cannot come; so now I say to you. A new commandment I give unto you, that ye love one another; as I have loved you, that ye also love one another. By this shall all men know that ye are my disciples, if ye have love one to another."

Simon Peter said unto him, "Lord, whither goest thou?" Jesus answered him, "Whither I go, thou canst not follow me now; but thou shalt follow me afterwards". Peter said unto him, "Lord, why cannot I follow thee now? I will lay down my life for thy sake." Jesus answered him, "Wilt thou lay down thy life for my sake? Verily, verily, I say unto thee, The cock shall not crow, till thou hast denied me thrice."   [13:21–38]

Jesus' Words at the Last Supper. "Let not your heart
be troubled: ye believe in God, believe also in me. In my
Father's house are many mansions: if it were not so, I
would have told you. I go to prepare a place for you. And
if I go and prepare a place for you, I will come again, and
receive you unto myself; that where I am, there ye may
be also. And whither I go ye know, and the way ye
know." Thomas saith unto him, "Lord, we know not
whither thou goest; and how can we know the way?" Jesus
saith unto him, "I am the way, the truth, and the life: no
man cometh unto the Father, but by me. If ye had known
me, ye should have known my Father also: and from
henceforth ye know him, and have seen him." Philip saith
unto him, "Lord, shew us the Father, and it sufficeth us".
Jesus saith unto him, "Have I been so long time with
you, and yet hast thou not known me, Philip? he that hath
seen me hath seen the Father; and how sayest thou then,
'Shew us the Father'? Believest thou not that I am in the
Father, and the Father in me? the words that I speak unto
you I speak not of myself: but the Father that dwelleth in
me, he doeth the works. Believe me that I am in the Father, and the Father in me: or else believe me for the very
works' sake. Verily, verily, I say unto you, He that believeth on me, the works that I do shall he do also; and
greater works than these shall he do; because I go unto my
Father. And whatsoever ye shall ask in my name, that will
I do, that the Father may be glorified in the Son. If ye
shall ask any thing in my name, I will do it. If ye love
me, keep my commandments. And I will pray the Father,
and he shall give you another Comforter, that he may
abide with you for ever; even the Spirit of truth; whom
the world cannot receive, because it seeth him not, neither
knoweth him: but ye know him; for he dwelleth with you,
and shall be in you. I will not leave you comfortless: I
will come to you. Yet a little while, and the world seeth
me no more; but ye see me: because I live, ye shall live
also. At that day ye shall know that I am in my Father,

and ye in me, and I in you. He that hath my commandments, and keepeth them, he it is that loveth me: and he
that loveth me shall be loved of my Father, and I will
love him, and will manifest myself to him." Judas saith
unto him, not Iscariot, "Lord, how is it that thou wilt
manifest thyself unto us, and not unto the world?" Jesus
answered and said unto him, "If a man love me, he will
keep my words: and my Father will love him, and we will
come unto him, and make our abode with him. He that
loveth me not keepeth not my sayings: and the word
which ye hear is not mine, but the Father's which sent me.

"These things have I spoken unto you, being yet present
with you. But the Comforter, which is the Holy Ghost,
whom the Father will send in my name, he shall teach you
all things, and bring all things to your remembrance, whatsoever I have said unto you. Peace I leave with you, my
peace I give unto you: not as the world giveth, give I unto
you. Let not your heart be troubled, neither let it be afraid.
Ye have heard how I said unto you, I go away, and come
again unto you. If ye loved me, ye would rejoice, because
I said, I go unto the Father: for my Father is greater than
I. And now I have told you before it come to pass, that,
when it is come to pass, ye might believe. Hereafter I will
not talk much with you: for the prince of this world
cometh, and hath nothing in me. But that the world may
know that I love the Father; and as the Father gave me
commandment, even so I do. Arise, let us go hence."

[14:1–31]

"The True Vine." "I am the true vine, and my Father
is the husbandman. Every branch in me that beareth not
fruit he taketh away: and every branch that beareth fruit,
he purgeth it, that it may bring forth more fruit. Now ye
are clean through the word which I have spoken unto you.
Abide in me, and I in you. As the branch cannot bear
fruit of itself, except it abide in the vine; no more can ye,
except ye abide in me. I am the vine, ye are the branches:
He that abideth in me, and I in him, the same bringeth

forth much fruit: for without me ye can do nothing. If a man abide not in me, he is cast forth as a branch, and is withered; and men gather them, and cast them into the fire, and they are burned. If ye abide in me, and my words abide in you, ye shall ask what ye will, and it shall be done unto you. Herein is my Father glorified, that ye bear much fruit; so shall ye be my disciples. As the Father hath loved me, so have I loved you: continue ye in my love. If ye keep my commandments, ye shall abide in my love; even as I have kept my Father's commandments, and abide in his love. These things have I spoken unto you, that my joy might remain in you, and that your joy might be full. This is my commandment, that ye love one another, as I have loved you. Greater love hath no man than this, that a man lay down his life for his friends. Ye are my friends, if ye do whatsoever I command you. Henceforth I call you not servants; for the servant knoweth not what his lord doeth: but I have called you friends; for all things that I have heard of my Father I have made known unto you. Ye have not chosen me, but I have chosen you, and ordained you, that ye should go and bring forth fruit, and that your fruit should remain: that whatsoever ye shall ask of the Father in my name, he may give it you. These things I command you, that ye love one another. If the world hate you, ye know that it hated me before it hated you. If ye were of the world, the world would love his own: but because ye are not of the world, but I have chosen you out of the world, therefore the world hateth you. Remember the word that I said unto you, The servant is not greater than his lord. If they have persecuted me, they will also persecute you; if they have kept my saying, they will keep yours also. But all these things will they do unto you for my name's sake, because they know not him that sent me. If I had not come and spoken unto them, they had not had sin: but now they have no cloke for their sin. He that hateth me hateth my Father also. If I had not done among them the works which none other man did, they had not had sin: but now have they both seen and hated both me and my Father. But this cometh to pass, that the word might be fulfilled that is written in their law, 'They hated me without a cause'. But when the Comforter is come, whom I will send unto you from the Father, even the Spirit of truth, which proceedeth from the Father, he shall testify of me: and ye also shall bear witness, because ye have been with me from the beginning."

"These things have I spoken unto you, that ye should not be offended. They shall put you out of the synagogues: yea, the time cometh, that whosoever killeth you will think that he doeth God service. And these things will they do unto you, because they have not known the Father, nor me. But these things have I told you, that when the time shall come, ye may remember that I told you of them. And these things I said not unto you at the beginning, because I was with you. But now I go my way to him that sent me; and none of you asketh me, 'Whither goest thou?' But because I have said these things unto you, sorrow hath filled your heart. Nevertheless I tell you the truth; It is expedient for you that I go away: for if I go not away, the Comforter will not come unto you; but if I depart, I will send him unto you. And when he is come, he will reprove the world of sin, and of righteousness, and of judgment: of sin, because they believe not on me; of righteousness, because I go to my Father, and ye see me no more; of judgment, because the prince of this world is judged. I have yet many things to say unto you, but ye cannot bear them now. Howbeit when he, the Spirit of truth, is come, he will guide you into all truth: for he shall not speak of himself; but whatsoever he shall hear, that shall he speak: and he will shew you things to come. He shall glorify me: for he shall receive of mine, and shall shew it unto you. All things that the Father hath are mine: therefore said I, that he shall take of mine, and shall shew it unto you. A little while, and ye shall not see me:

and again, a little while, and ye shall see me, because I go to the Father."

Then said some of his disciples among themselves, "What is this that he saith unto us, 'A little while, and ye shall not see me: and again, a little while, and ye shall see me': and, 'Because I go to the Father'?" They said therefore, "What is this that he saith, 'A little while'? we cannot tell what he saith". Now Jesus knew that they were desirous to ask him, and said unto them, "Do ye enquire among yourselves of that I said, A little while, and ye shall not see me: and again, a little while, and ye shall see me? Verily, verily, I say unto you, that ye shall weep and lament, but the world shall rejoice: and ye shall be sorrowful, but your sorrow shall be turned into joy. A woman when she is in travail hath sorrow, because her hour is come: but as soon as she is delivered of the child, she remembereth no more the anguish, for joy that a man is born into the world. And ye now therefore have sorrow: but I will see you again, and your heart shall rejoice, and your joy no man taketh from you. And in that day ye shall ask me nothing. Verily, verily, I say unto you, Whatsoever ye shall ask the Father in my name, he will give it you. Hitherto have ye asked nothing in my name: ask, and ye shall receive, that your joy may be full.

"These things have I spoken unto you in proverbs: but the time cometh, when I shall no more speak unto you in proverbs, but I shall shew you plainly of the Father. At that day ye shall ask in my name: and I say not unto you, that I will pray the Father for you: for the Father himself loveth you, because ye have loved me, and have believed that I came out from God. I came forth from the Father, and am come into the world: again, I leave the world, and go to the Father." His disciples said unto him, "Lo, now speakest thou plainly, and speakest no proverb. Now are we sure that thou knowest all things, and needest not that any man should ask thee: by this we believe that thou camest forth from God." Jesus answered them, "Do ye now believe? Behold, the hour cometh, yea, is now come, that ye shall be scattered, every man to his own, and shall leave me alone: and yet I am not alone, because the Father is with me. These things I have spoken unto you, that in me ye might have peace. In the world ye shall have tribulation: but be of good cheer; I have overcome the world." [15:1–27; 16:1–33]

Jesus' Prayer. These words spake Jesus, and lifted up his eyes to heaven, and said, "Father, the hour is come; glorify thy Son, that thy Son also may glorify thee: as thou hast given him power over all flesh, that he should give eternal life to as many as thou hast given him. And this is life eternal, that they might know thee the only true God, and Jesus Christ, whom thou hast sent. I have glorified thee on the earth: I have finished the work which thou gavest me to do. And now, O Father, glorify thou me with thine own self with the glory which I had with thee before the world was. I have manifested thy name unto the men which thou gavest me out of the world: thine they were, and thou gavest them me; and they have kept thy word. Now they have known that all things whatsoever thou hast given me are of thee. For I have given unto them the words which thou gavest me; and they have received them, and have known surely that I came out from thee, and they have believed that thou didst send me. I pray for them: I pray not for the world, but for them which thou hast given me; for they are thine. And all mine are thine, and thine are mine; and I am glorified in them. And now I am no more in the world, but these are in the world, and I come to thee. Holy Father, keep through thine own name those whom thou hast given me, that they may be one, as we are. While I was with them in the world, I kept them in thy name: those that thou gavest me I have kept, and none of them is lost, but the son of perdition; that the scripture might be fulfilled. And now come I to thee; and these things I speak in the world, that they might have my joy fulfilled in themselves. I have given them thy word; and the world hath hated them, because they are not of the world, even as I am not of the world. I pray not that thou shouldest take them out of the world, but that thou shouldest keep them from the evil. They are not of the world, even as I am not of the world. Sanctify them through thy truth: thy word is truth. As thou hast sent me into the world, even so have I also sent them into the world. And for their sakes I sanctify myself, that they also might be sanctified through the truth. Neither pray I for these alone, but for them also which shall believe on me through their word; that they all may be one; as thou, Father, art in me, and I in thee, that they also may be one in us: that the world may believe that thou hast sent me. And the glory which thou gavest me I have given them; that they may be one, even as we are one: I in them, and thou in me, that they may be made perfect in one; and that the world may know that thou hast sent me, and hast loved them, as thou hast loved me. Father, I will that they also, whom thou hast given me, be with me where I am; that they may behold my glory, which thou hast given me: for thou lovedst me before the foundation of the world. O righteous Father, the world hath not known thee: but I have known thee, and these have known that thou hast sent me. And I have declared unto them thy name, and will declare it: that the love wherewith thou hast loved me may be in them, and I in them." [17:1–26]

Jesus Arrested. When Jesus had spoken these words, he went forth with his disciples over the brook Cedron, where was a garden, into the which he entered, and his disciples. And Judas also, which betrayed him, knew the place: for Jesus ofttimes resorted thither with his disciples. Judas then, having received a band of men and officers from the chief priests and Pharisees, cometh thither with lanterns and torches and weapons. Jesus therefore, knowing all things that should come upon him, went forth, and said unto them, "Whom seek ye?" They an-

swered him, "Jesus of Nazareth". Jesus saith unto them,
"I am he". And Judas also, which betrayed him, stood
with them. As soon then as he had said unto them, "I am
he", they went backward, and fell to the ground. Then
asked he them again, "Whom seek ye?" And they said,
"Jesus of Nazareth". Jesus answered, "I have told you
that I am he: if therefore ye seek me, let these go their
way": that the saying might be fulfilled, which he spake,
"Of them which thou gavest me have I lost none". Then
Simon Peter having a sword drew it, and smote the high
priest's servant, and cut off his right ear. The servant's
name was Malchus. Then said Jesus unto Peter, "Put up
thy sword into the sheath: the cup which my Father hath
given me, shall I not drink it?"

Then the band and the captain and officers of the Jews
took Jesus, and bound him, and led him away to Annas
first; for he was father in law to Caiaphas, which was the
high priest that same year. Now Caiaphas was he, which
gave counsel to the Jews, that it was expedient that one
man should die for the people.

And Simon Peter followed Jesus, and so did another
disciple: that disciple was known unto the high priest, and
went in with Jesus into the palace of the high priest. But
Peter stood at the door without. Then went out that other
disciple, which was known unto the high priest, and spake
unto her that kept the door, and brought in Peter. Then
saith the damsel that kept the door unto Peter, "Art not
thou also one of this man's disciples?" He saith, "I am
not". And the servants and officers stood there, who had
made a fire of coals; for it was cold: and they warmed
themselves: and Peter stood with them, and warmed himself.

The high priest then asked Jesus of his disciples, and of
his doctrine. Jesus answered him, "I spake openly to the
world; I ever taught in the synagogue, and in the temple,
whither the Jews always resort; and in secret have I said
nothing. Why askest thou me? ask them which heard me,

what I have said unto them: behold, they know what I said." And when he had thus spoken, one of the officers which stood by struck Jesus with the palm of his hand, saying, "Answerest thou the high priest so?" Jesus answered him, "If I have spoken evil, bear witness of the evil: but if well, why smitest thou me?" Now Annas had sent him bound unto Caiaphas the high priest.

And Simon Peter stood and warmed himself. They said therefore unto him, "Art not thou also one of his disciples?" He denied it, and said, "I am not". One of the servants of the high priest, being his kinsman whose ear Peter cut off, saith, "Did not I see thee in the garden with him?" Peter then denied again: and immediately the cock crew. [18:1–27]

Jesus before Pilate. Then led they Jesus from Caiaphas unto the hall of judgment: and it was early; and they themselves went not into the judgment hall, lest they should be defiled; but that they might eat the passover. Pilate then went out unto them, and said, "What accusation bring ye against this man?" They answered and said unto him, "If he were not a malefactor, we would not have delivered him up unto thee". Then said Pilate unto them, "Take ye him, and judge him according to your law". The Jews therefore said unto him, "It is not lawful for us to put any man to death": that the saying of Jesus might be fulfilled, which he spake, signifying what death he should die.

Then Pilate entered into the judgment hall again, and called Jesus, and said unto him, "Art thou the King of the Jews?" Jesus answered him, "Sayest thou this thing of thyself, or did others tell it thee of me?" Pilate answered, "Am I a Jew? Thine own nation and the chief priests have delivered thee unto me: what hast thou done?" Jesus answered, "My kingdom is not of this world: if my kingdom were of this world, then would my servants fight, that I should not be delivered to the Jews: but now is my kingdom not from hence". Pilate therefore said unto him, "Art thou a king then?" Jesus answered, "Thou sayest that

I am a king. To this end was I born, and for this cause
came I into the world, that I should bear witness unto the
truth. Every one that is of the truth heareth my voice."
Pilate saith unto him, "What is truth?"

And when he had said this, he went out again unto the
Jews, and saith unto them, "I find in him no fault at all.
But ye have a custom, that I should release unto you one
at the passover: will ye therefore that I release unto you
the King of the Jews?" Then cried they all again, saying,
"Not this man, but Barabbas". Now Barabbas was a
robber.   [18:28–40]

Jesus Scourged. Then Pilate therefore took Jesus, and
scourged him. And the soldiers platted a crown of thorns,
and put it on his head, and they put on him a purple robe,
and said, "Hail, King of the Jews!" and they smote him
with their hands. Pilate therefore went forth again, and
saith unto them, "Behold, I bring him forth to you, that
ye may know that I find no fault in him". Then came Jesus
forth, wearing the crown of thorns, and the purple robe.
And Pilate saith unto them, "Behold the man!" When the
chief priests therefore and officers saw him, they cried out,
saying, "Crucify him, crucify him". Pilate saith unto them,
"Take ye him, and crucify him: for I find no fault in him".
The Jews answered him, "We have a law, and by our law
he ought to die, because he made himself the Son of God".
When Pilate therefore heard that saying, he was the more
afraid; and went again into the judgment hall, and saith
unto Jesus, "Whence art thou?" But Jesus gave him no
answer. Then saith Pilate unto him, "Speakest thou not
unto me? knowest thou not that I have power to crucify
thee, and have power to release thee?" Jesus answered,
"Thou couldest have no power at all against me, except it
were given thee from above: therefore he that delivered
me unto thee hath the greater sin". And from thenceforth
Pilate sought to release him: but the Jews cried out, saying, "If thou let this man go, thou art not Cæsar's friend:
whosoever maketh himself a king speaketh against Cæ-

sar". When Pilate therefore heard that saying, he brought Jesus forth, and sat down in the judgment seat in a place that is called the Pavement, but in the Hebrew, Gabbatha. And it was the preparation of the passover, and about the sixth hour: and he saith unto the Jews, "Behold your King!" But they cried out, "Away with him, away with him, crucify him". Pilate saith unto them, "Shall I crucify your King?" The chief priests answered, "We have no king but Cæsar". Then delivered he him therefore unto them to be crucified. [19:1–16]

Jesus Crucified. And they took Jesus, and led him away. And he bearing his cross went forth into a place called the place of a skull, which is called in the Hebrew Golgotha: where they crucified him, and two other with him, on either side one, and Jesus in the midst. And Pilate wrote a title, and put it on the cross. And the writing was, JESUS OF NAZARETH THE KING OF THE JEWS. This title then read many of the Jews: for the place where Jesus was crucified was nigh to the city: and it was written in Hebrew, and Greek, and Latin. Then said the chief priests of the Jews to Pilate, "Write not, 'The King of the Jews'; but that he said, 'I am King of the Jews'". Pilate answered, "What I have written I have written".

Then the soldiers, when they had crucified Jesus, took his garments, and made four parts, to every soldier a part; and also his coat: now the coat was without seam, woven from the top throughout. They said therefore among themselves, "Let us not rend it, but cast lots for it, whose it shall be": that the scripture might be fulfilled, which saith,

"They parted my raiment among them,
    And for my vesture they did cast lots".

These things therefore the soldiers did. [19:16–24]

Jesus and His Mother. Now there stood by the cross of Jesus his mother, and his mother's sister, Mary the wife of Cleophas, and Mary Magdalene.[6] When Jesus therefore saw his mother, and the disciple standing by, whom he loved, he saith unto his mother, "Woman, behold thy son!" Then saith he to the disciple, "Behold thy mother!" And from that hour that disciple took her unto his own home. [19:25–27]

The Death of Jesus. After this, Jesus knowing that all things were now accomplished, that the scripture might be fulfilled, saith, "I thirst". Now there was set a vessel full of vinegar: and they filled a spunge with vinegar, and put it upon hyssop, and put it to his mouth. When Jesus therefore had received the vinegar, he said, "It is finished": and he bowed his head, and gave up the ghost. [19:28–30]

Jesus' Body Entombed. The Jews therefore, because it was the preparation, that the bodies should not remain upon the cross on the sabbath day, (for that sabbath day was an high day,) besought Pilate that their legs might be broken, and that they might be taken away. Then came the soldiers, and brake the legs of the first, and of the other which was crucified with him. But when they came to Jesus, and saw that he was dead already, they brake not his legs: but one of the soldiers with a spear pierced his side, and forthwith came there out blood and water. And he that saw it bare record, and his record is true: and he knoweth that he saith true, that ye might believe. For these things were done, that the scripture should be fulfilled, "A bone of him shall not be broken". And again another scripture saith, "They shall look on him whom they pierced".

And after this Joseph of Arimathæa, being a disciple of Jesus, but secretly for fear of the Jews, besought Pilate that he might take away the body of Jesus: and Pilate gave him leave. He came therefore, and took the body of Jesus. And there came also Nicodemus, which at the first came to Jesus by night, and brought a mixture of myrrh

[6] See Appendix 12.

and aloes, about an hundred pound weight. Then took they the body of Jesus, and wound it in linen clothes with the spices, as the manner of the Jews is to bury. Now in the place where he was crucified there was a garden; and in the garden a new sepulchre, wherein was never man yet laid. There laid they Jesus therefore because of the Jews' preparation day; for the sepulchre was nigh at hand.

[19:31–42]

The Resurrection of Jesus. The first day of the week cometh Mary Magdalene early, when it was yet dark, unto the sepulchre, and seeth the stone taken away from the sepulchre. Then she runneth, and cometh to Simon Peter, and to the other disciple, whom Jesus loved, and saith unto them, "They have taken away the Lord out of the sepulchre, and we know not where they have laid him". Peter therefore went forth, and that other disciple, and came to the sepulchre. So they ran both together: and the other disciple did outrun Peter, and came first to the sepulchre. And he stooping down, and looking in, saw the linen clothes lying; yet went he not in. Then cometh Simon Peter following him, and went into the sepulchre, and seeth the linen clothes lie, and the napkin, that was about his head, not lying with the linen clothes, but wrapped together in a place by itself. Then went in also that other disciple, which came first to the sepulchre, and he saw, and believed. For as yet they knew not the scripture, that he must rise again from the dead. Then the disciples went away again unto their own home. [20:1–10]

Jesus and Mary. But Mary stood without at the sepulchre weeping: and as she wept, she stooped down, and looked into the sepulchre, and seeth two angels in white sitting, the one at the head, and the other at the feet, where the body of Jesus had lain. And they say unto her, "Woman, why weepest thou?" She saith unto them, "Because they have taken away my Lord, and I know not where they have laid him". And when she had thus said, she turned herself back, and saw Jesus standing, and knew not that it was Jesus. Jesus saith unto her, "Woman, why weepest thou? whom seekest thou?" She, supposing him to be the gardener, saith unto him, "Sir, if thou have borne him hence, tell me where thou hast laid him, and I will take him away". Jesus saith unto her, "Mary". She turned herself, and saith unto him, "Rabboni"; which is to say, "Master". Jesus saith unto her, "Touch me not; for I am not yet ascended to my Father: but go to my brethren, and say unto them, I ascend unto my Father, and your Father; and to my God, and your God". Mary Magdalene came and told the disciples that she had seen the Lord, and that he had spoken these things unto her.[20:11–18]

Jesus Appears to His Disciples.   Then the same day at evening, being the first day of the week, when the doors were shut where the disciples were assembled for fear of the Jews, came Jesus and stood in the midst, and saith unto them, "Peace be unto you". And when he had so said, he shewed unto them his hands and his side. Then were the disciples glad, when they saw the Lord. Then said Jesus to them again, "Peace be unto you: as my Father hath sent me, even so send I you". And when he had said this, he breathed on them, and saith unto them, "Receive ye the Holy Ghost: whose soever sins ye remit, they are remitted unto them; and whose soever sins ye retain, they are retained".   [20:19–23]

Thomas Doubts.   But Thomas, one of the twelve, called Didymus, was not with them when Jesus came. The other disciples therefore said unto him, "We have seen the Lord". But he said unto them, "Except I shall see in his hands the print of the nails, and put my finger into the print of the nails, and thrust my hand into his side, I will not believe".

And after eight days again his disciples were within, and Thomas with them: then came Jesus, the doors being shut, and stood in the midst, and said, "Peace be unto you". Then saith he to Thomas, "Reach hither thy finger, and behold my hands; and reach hither thy hand, and thrust it into my side: and be not faithless, but believing". And Thomas answered and said unto him, "My Lord and my God". Jesus saith unto him, "Thomas, because thou hast seen me, thou hast believed: blessed are they that have not seen, and yet have believed". [20:24–29]

Jesus Appears by the Sea of Tiberias. After these things Jesus shewed himself again to the disciples at the sea of Tiberias; and on this wise shewed he himself. There were together Simon Peter, and Thomas called Didymus, and Nathanael of Cana in Galilee, and the sons of Zebedee, and two other of his disciples. Simon Peter saith unto them, "I go a fishing". They say unto him, "We also go with thee". They went forth, and entered into a ship immediately; and that night they caught nothing. But when the morning was now come, Jesus stood on the shore: but the disciples knew not that it was Jesus. Then Jesus saith unto them, "Children, have ye any meat?" They answered him, "No". And he said unto them, "Cast the net on the right side of the ship, and ye shall find". They cast therefore, and now they were not able to draw it for the multitude of fishes. Therefore that disciple whom Jesus loved saith unto Peter, "It is the Lord". Now when Simon Peter heard that it was the Lord, he girt his fisher's coat unto him, (for he was naked,) and did cast himself into the sea. And the other disciples came in a little ship; (for they were not far from land, but as it were two hundred cubits,) dragging the net with fishes. As soon then as they were come to land, they saw a fire of coals there, and fish laid thereon, and bread. Jesus saith unto them, "Bring of the fish which ye have now caught". Simon Peter went up, and drew the net to land full of great fishes, an hundred and fifty and three: and for all there were so many, yet was not the net broken. Jesus saith unto them, "Come and dine". And none of the disciples durst ask him, "Who art thou?" knowing that it was the Lord. Jesus then cometh, and taketh bread, and giveth them, and fish likewise. This is now the third time that Jesus shewed himself to his disciples, after that he was risen from the dead.

So when they had dined, Jesus saith to Simon Peter, "Simon, son of Jonas, lovest thou me more than these?" He saith unto him, "Yea, Lord; thou knowest that I love thee". He saith unto him, "Feed my lambs". He saith to him again the second time, "Simon, son of Jonas, lovest thou me?" He saith unto him, "Yea, Lord; thou knowest that I love thee". He saith unto him, "Feed my sheep". He saith unto him the third time, "Simon, son of Jonas, lovest thou me?" Peter was grieved because he said unto him the third time, "Lovest thou me?" And he said unto him, "Lord, thou knowest all things; thou knowest that I love thee". Jesus saith unto him, "Feed my sheep. Verily, verily, I say unto thee, When thou wast young, thou girdedst thyself, and walkedst whither thou wouldest: but when thou shalt be old, thou shalt stretch forth thy hands, and another shall gird thee, and carry thee whither thou wouldest not." This spake he, signifying by what death he should glorify God. And when he had spoken this, he saith unto him, "Follow me". Then Peter, turning about, seeth the disciple whom Jesus loved following; which also leaned on his breast at supper, and said, "Lord, which is he that betrayeth thee?" Peter seeing him saith to Jesus, "Lord, and what shall this man do?" Jesus saith unto him, "If I will that he tarry till I come, what is that to thee? follow thou me". Then went this saying abroad among the brethren, that that disciple should not die: yet Jesus said not unto him, "He shall not die"; but, "If I will that he tarry till I come, what is that to thee?"   [21:1–23]

End of Fourth Gospel. This is the disciple which testifieth of these things, and wrote these things: and we know that his testimony is true. And there are also many other things which Jesus did, the which, if they should be written every one, I suppose that even the world itself could not contain the books that should be written. Amen.

[21:24–25]

THE EASTERN
MEDITERRANEAN
in New Testament Times

Legend
&
SCALE

Roman Provinces, thus: **ASIA**
Cities containing Christians according to
the evidence of the New Testament, thus: ✳
1:8,000,000   0   100   200 miles

BITHYNIA & PONTUS

KINGDOM
OF
POLEMON

40°

MYSIA

ASIA

GALATIA

CAPPADOCIA

Pergamos

Thyatira

PHRYGIA

Antioch

Sardis

Mytilene

Smyrna

Philadelphia

Iconium

PISIDIA

Lystra

Ephesus

Colossae

LYCAONIA

Derbe

Tarsus

Laodicea

Miletus

PAMPHYLIA

KINGDOM OF ANTIOCHUS

CILICIA

Patmos

LYCIA

Perga

Cos

Attalia

&

Cnidus

RHODES

Myra

Patara

Antioch

Seleucia

SYRIA

35°

Salamis

CYPRUS

Paphos

Damascus

Sidon

Tyre

KINGDOM

Ptolemais

OF AGRIPPA

Caesarea

Joppa

Samaria

Lydda

Jerusalem

Ascalon

Gaza

Alexandria

30°

ARABIA

EGYPT

SINAI

30°   35°

From THE ACTS OF THE APOSTLES

The Preface. The former treatise have I made, O Theophilus, of all that Jesus began both to do and teach, until the day in which he was taken up, after that he through the Holy Ghost had given commandments unto the apostles whom he had chosen: to whom also he shewed himself alive after his passion by many infallible proofs, being seen of them forty days, and speaking of the things pertaining to the kingdom of God: and, being assembled together with them, commanded them that they should not depart from Jerusalem, but wait for the promise of the Father, "which," saith he, "ye have heard of me. For John truly baptized with water; but ye shall be baptized with the Holy Ghost not many days hence."   [1:1–5]

Jesus Ascends into Heaven. When they therefore were come together, they asked of him, saying, "Lord, wilt thou at this time restore again the kingdom to Israel?" And he said unto them, "It is not for you to know the times or the seasons, which the Father hath put in his own power. But ye shall receive power, after that the Holy Ghost is come upon you: and ye shall be witnesses unto me both in Jerusalem, and in all Judæa, and in Samaria, and unto the uttermost part of the earth." And when he had spoken these things, while they beheld, he was taken up; and a cloud received him out of their sight. And while they looked stedfastly toward heaven as he went up, behold, two men stood by them in white apparel; which also said, "Ye men of Galilee, why stand ye gazing up into heaven? this same Jesus, which is taken up from you into heaven, shall so come in like manner as ye have seen him go into heaven". [1:6–11]

A Successor Chosen to Judas. Then returned they unto Jerusalem from the mount called Olivet, which is from Jerusalem a sabbath day's journey. And when they were come in, they went up into an upper room, where abode both Peter, and James, and John, and Andrew, Philip, and Thomas, Bartholomew, and Matthew, James the son of Alphæus, and Simon Zelotes, and Judas the brother of James. These all continued with one accord in prayer and supplication, with the women, and Mary the mother of Jesus, and with his brethren.

And in those days Peter stood up in the midst of the disciples, and said, (the number of names together were about an hundred and twenty,) "Men and brethren, this scripture must needs have been fulfilled, which the Holy Ghost by the mouth of David spake before concerning Judas, which was guide to them that took Jesus. For he was numbered with us, and had obtained part of this ministry." Now this man purchased a field with the reward of iniquity; and falling headlong, he burst asunder in the midst, and all his bowels gushed out. And it was known unto all the dwellers at Jerusalem; insomuch as that field is called in their proper tongue, Aceldama, that is to say, The field of blood. "For it is written in the book of Psalms,

'Let his habitation be desolate,
    And let no man dwell therein':

and

'His bishoprick let another take'.

Wherefore of these men which have companied with us all the time that the Lord Jesus went in and out among us, beginning from the baptism of John, unto that same day that he was taken up from us, must one be ordained to be a witness with us of his resurrection." And they appointed two, Joseph called Barsabas, who was surnamed

Justus, and Matthias. And they prayed, and said, "Thou, Lord, which knowest the hearts of all men, shew whether of these two thou hast chosen, that he may take part of this ministry and apostleship, from which Judas by transgression fell, that he might go to his own place". And they gave forth their lots; and the lot fell upon Matthias; and he was numbered with the eleven apostles.   [1:12–26]

The Descent of the Holy Spirit. And when the day of Pentecost was fully come, they were all with one accord in one place. And suddenly there came a sound from heaven as of a rushing mighty wind, and it filled all the house where they were sitting. And there appeared unto them cloven tongues like as of fire, and it sat upon each of them. And they were all filled with the Holy Ghost, and began to speak with other tongues, as the Spirit gave them utterance.

And there were dwelling at Jerusalem Jews, devout men, out of every nation under heaven. Now when this was noised abroad, the multitude came together, and were confounded, because that every man heard them speak in his own language. And they were all amazed and marvelled, saying one to another, "Behold, are not all these which speak Galilæans? And how hear we every man in our own tongue, wherein we were born? Parthians, and Medes, and Elamites, and the dwellers in Mesopotamia, and in Judæa, and Cappadocia, in Pontus, and Asia, Phrygia, and Pamphylia, in Egypt, and in the parts of Libya about Cyrene, and strangers of Rome, Jews and proselytes, Cretes and Arabians, we do hear them speak in our tongues the wonderful works of God". And they were all amazed, and were in doubt, saying one to another, "What meaneth this?" Others mocking said, "These men are full of new wine".   [2:1–13]

[Peter spoke to the multitude, declaring that Jesus whom they had crucified]

". . . hath God raised up, whereof we all are witnesses.

Therefore being by the right hand of God exalted, and having received of the Father the promise of the Holy Ghost, he hath shed forth this, which ye now see and hear. For David is not ascended into the heavens: but he saith himself,

> 'The LORD said unto my Lord, Sit thou on my right hand,
> Until I make thy foes thy footstool'.

Therefore let all the house of Israel know assuredly, that God hath made that same Jesus, whom ye have crucified, both Lord and Christ."

Now when they heard this, they were pricked in their heart, and said unto Peter and to the rest of the apostles, "Men and brethren, what shall we do?" Then Peter said unto them, "Repent, and be baptized every one of you in the name of Jesus Christ for the remission of sins, and ye shall receive the gift of the Holy Ghost. For the promise is unto you, and to your children, and to all that are afar off, even as many as the Lord our God shall call." And with many other words did he testify and exhort, saying, "Save yourselves from this untoward generation". Then they that gladly received his word were baptized: and the same day there were added unto them about three thousand souls. And they continued stedfastly in the apostles' doctrine and fellowship, and in breaking of bread, and in prayers.

And fear came upon every soul: and many wonders and signs were done by the apostles. And all that believed were together, and had all things common; and sold their possessions and goods, and parted them to all men, as every man had need. And they, continuing daily with one accord in the temple, and breaking bread from house to house, did eat their meat with gladness and singleness of heart, praising God, and having favour with all the people. And the Lord added to the church daily such as should be saved.   [2:32–47]

A Lame Man Healed. Now Peter and John went up together into the temple at the hour of prayer, being the ninth hour. And a certain man lame from his mother's womb was carried, whom they laid daily at the gate of the temple which is called Beautiful, to ask alms of them that entered into the temple; who seeing Peter and John about to go into the temple asked an alms. And Peter, fastening his eyes upon him with John, said, "Look on us". And he gave heed unto them, expecting to receive something of them. Then Peter said, "Silver and gold have I none; but such as I have give I thee: In the name of Jesus Christ of Nazareth rise up and walk". And he took him by the right hand, and lifted him up: and immediately his feet and ankle bones received strength. And he leaping up stood, and walked, and entered with them into the temple, walking, and leaping, and praising God. And all the people saw him walking and praising God: and they knew that it was he which sat for alms at the Beautiful gate of the temple: and they were filled with wonder and amazement at that which had happened unto him.

And as the lame man which was healed held Peter and John, all the people ran together unto them in the porch that is called Solomon's, greatly wondering.   [3:1-11]

Community of Goods. And the multitude of them that believed were of one heart and of one soul: neither said any of them that aught of the things which he possessed was his own; but they had all things common. And with great power gave the apostles witness of the resurrection of the Lord Jesus: and great grace was upon them all. Neither was there any among them that lacked: for as many as were possessors of lands or houses sold them, and brought the prices of the things that were sold, and laid them down at the apostles' feet: and distribution was made unto every man according as he had need.

And Joses, who by the apostles was surnamed Barnabas, (which is, being interpreted, The son of consolation,) a

Levite, and of the country of Cyprus, having land, sold it, and brought the money, and laid it at the apostles' feet.

[4:32–37]

Ananias and Sapphira. But a certain man named Ananias, with Sapphira his wife, sold a possession, and kept back part of the price, his wife also being privy to it, and brought a certain part, and laid it at the apostles' feet. But Peter said, "Ananias, why hath Satan filled thine heart to lie to the Holy Ghost, and to keep back part of the price of the land? Whiles it remained, was it not thine own? and after it was sold, was it not in thine own power? why hast thou conceived this thing in thine heart? thou hast not lied unto men, but unto God." And Ananias hearing these words fell down, and gave up the ghost: and great fear came on all them that heard these things. And the young men arose, wound him up, and carried him out, and buried him.

And it was about the space of three hours after, when his wife, not knowing what was done, came in. And Peter answered unto her, "Tell me whether ye sold the land for so much?" And she said, "Yea, for so much". Then Peter said unto her, "How is it that ye have agreed together to tempt the Spirit of the Lord? behold, the feet of them which have buried thy husband are at the door, and shall carry thee out". Then fell she down straightway at his feet, and yielded up the ghost: and the young men came in, and found her dead, and, carrying her forth, buried her by her husband. And great fear came upon all the church, and upon as many as heard these things.   [5:1–11]

The Sick Healed. And by the hands of the apostles were many signs and wonders wrought among the people; (and they were all with one accord in Solomon's porch. And of the rest durst no man join himself to them: but the people magnified them. And believers were the more added to the Lord, multitudes both of men and women.) Insomuch that they brought forth the sick into the streets, and laid them on beds and couches, that at the least the shadow of Peter passing by might overshadow some of them. There came also a multitude out of the cities round about unto Jerusalem, bringing sick folks, and them which were vexed with unclean spirits: and they were healed every one.   [5:12–16]

The Apostles Imprisoned.   Then the high priest rose up, and all they that were with him, (which is the sect of the Sadducees,) and were filled with indignation, and laid their hands on the apostles, and put them in the common prison. But the angel of the Lord by night opened the prison doors, and brought them forth, and said, "Go, stand and speak in the temple to the people all the words of this life". And when they heard that, they entered into the temple early in the morning, and taught. But the high priest came, and they that were with him, and called the council together, and all the senate of the children of Israel, and sent to the prison to have them brought. But when the officers came, and found them not in the prison, they returned, and told, saying, "The prison truly found we shut with all safety, and the keepers standing without before the doors: but when we had opened, we found no man within". Now when the high priest and the captain of the temple and the chief priests heard these things, they doubted of them whereunto this would grow. Then came one and told them, saying, "Behold, the men whom ye put in prison are standing in the temple, and teaching the people". Then went the captain with the officers, and brought them without violence: for they feared the people, lest they should have been stoned.   [5:17–26]

Peter before the Council.   And when they had brought them, they set them before the council: and the high priest asked them, saying, "Did not we straitly command you that ye should not teach in this name? and, behold, ye have filled Jerusalem with your doctrine, and intend to bring this man's blood upon us". Then Peter and the other apostles answered and said, "We ought to obey God rather than men. The God of our fathers raised up Jesus, whom ye slew and hanged on a tree. Him hath God exalted with his right hand to be a Prince and a Saviour, for to give repentance to Israel, and forgiveness of sins. And we are his witnesses of these things; and so is also the Holy Ghost, whom God hath given to them that obey him."

[5:27–32]

Gamaliel's Advice. When they heard that, they were cut to the heart, and took counsel to slay them. Then stood there up one in the council, a Pharisee, named Gamaliel, a doctor of the law, had in reputation among all the people, and commanded to put the apostles forth a little space; and said unto them, "Ye men of Israel, take heed to yourselves what ye intend to do as touching these men. For before these days rose up Theudas, boasting himself to be somebody; to whom a number of men, about four hundred, joined themselves: who was slain; and all, as many as obeyed him, were scattered, and brought to nought. After this man rose up Judas of Galilee in the days of the taxing, and drew away much people after him: he also perished; and all, even as many as obeyed him, were dispersed. And now I say unto you, Refrain from these men, and let them alone: for if this counsel or this work be of men, it will come to nought: but if it be of God, ye cannot overthrow it; lest haply ye be found even to fight against God." And to him they agreed: and when they had called the apostles, and beaten them, they commanded that they should not speak in the name of Jesus, and let them go. And they departed from the presence of the council, rejoicing that they were counted worthy to suffer shame for his name. And daily in the temple, and in every house, they ceased not to teach and preach Jesus Christ.

[5:33–42]

Deacons Appointed. And in those days, when the number of the disciples was multiplied, there arose a murmuring of the Grecians against the Hebrews, because their widows were neglected in the daily ministration. Then the twelve called the multitude of the disciples unto them, and said, "It is not reason that we should leave the word of God, and serve tables. Wherefore, brethren, look ye out among you seven men of honest report, full of the Holy Ghost and wisdom, whom we may appoint over this business. But we will give ourselves continually to prayer, and to the ministry of the word." And the saying pleased the whole multitude: and they chose Stephen, a man full of faith and of the Holy Ghost, and Philip, and Prochorus, and Nicanor, and Timon, and Parmenas, and Nicolas a proselyte of Antioch: whom they set before the apostles: and when they had prayed, they laid their hands on them.

And the word of God increased; and the number of the disciples multiplied in Jerusalem greatly; and a great company of the priests were obedient to the faith.   [6:1–7]

Stephen before the Council. And Stephen, full of faith and power, did great wonders and miracles among the people. Then there arose certain of the synagogue, which is called the synagogue of the Libertines, and Cyrenians, and Alexandrians, and of them of Cilicia and of Asia, disputing with Stephen. And they were not able to resist the wisdom and the spirit by which he spake. Then they suborned men, which said, "We have heard him speak blasphemous words against Moses, and against God". And they stirred up the people, and the elders, and the scribes, and came upon him, and caught him, and brought him to the council, and set up false witnesses, which said, "This man ceaseth not to speak blasphemous words against this holy place, and the law: for we have heard him say, that this Jesus of Nazareth shall destroy this place, and shall change the customs which Moses delivered us". And all that sat in the council, looking stedfastly on him, saw his face as it had been the face of an angel.   [6:8–15]

[Then said the high priest, "Are these things so?" Stephen replied by declaring that their fathers had rejected Moses who was sent to deliver them.]

"Ye stiffnecked and uncircumcised in heart and ears, ye do always resist the Holy Ghost: as your fathers did, so do ye. Which of the prophets have not your fathers persecuted? and they have slain them which shewed before of the coming of the Just One; of whom ye have been now the betrayers and murderers: who have received the law by the disposition of angels, and have not kept it."

Stephen Stoned. When they heard these things, they were cut to the heart, and they gnashed on him with their teeth. But he, being full of the Holy Ghost, looked up stedfastly into heaven, and saw the glory of God, and Jesus standing on the right hand of God, and said, "Behold, I see the heavens opened, and the Son of man standing on the right hand of God". Then they cried out with a loud voice, and stopped their ears, and ran upon him with one accord, and cast him out of the city, and stoned him: and the witnesses laid down their clothes at a young man's feet, whose name was Saul. And they stoned Stephen, calling upon God, and saying, "Lord Jesus, receive my spirit". And he kneeled down, and cried with a loud voice, "Lord, lay not this sin to their charge". And when he had said this, he fell asleep.   [7:51–60]

The Church Persecuted. And Saul was consenting unto his death. And at that time there was a great persecution against the church which was at Jerusalem; and they were all scattered abroad throughout the regions of Judæa and Samaria, except the apostles. And devout men carried Stephen to his burial, and made great lamentation over him. As for Saul, he made havock of the church, entering into every house, and haling men and women committed them to prison.

Therefore they that were scattered abroad went every where preaching the word. Then Philip went down to the city of Samaria, and preached Christ unto them. And the people with one accord gave heed unto those things which Philip spake, hearing and seeing the miracles which he did. For unclean spirits, crying with loud voice, came out of many that were possessed with them: and many taken

with palsies, and that were lame, were healed. And there
was great joy in that city. [8:1–8]

Simon the Sorcerer. But there was a certain man,
called Simon, which beforetime in the same city used sor-
cery, and bewitched the people of Samaria, giving out that
himself was some great one: to whom they all gave heed,
from the least to the greatest, saying, "This man is the
great power of God". And to him they had regard, because
that of long time he had bewitched them with sorceries.
But when they believed Philip preaching the things concerning the kingdom of God, and the name of Jesus
Christ, they were baptized, both men and women. Then
Simon himself believed also: and when he was baptized,
he continued with Philip, and wondered, beholding the
miracles and signs which were done.

Now when the apostles which were at Jerusalem heard
that Samaria had received the word of God, they sent unto
them Peter and John: who, when they were come down,
prayed for them, that they might receive the Holy Ghost:
(for as yet he was fallen upon none of them: only they
were baptized in the name of the Lord Jesus.) Then laid
they their hands on them, and they received the Holy
Ghost. And when Simon saw that through laying on of the
apostles' hands the Holy Ghost was given, he offered them
money, saying, "Give me also this power, that on whomsoever I lay hands, he may receive the Holy Ghost". But
Peter said unto him, "Thy money perish with thee, because
thou hast thought that the gift of God may be purchased
with money. Thou hast neither part nor lot in this matter:
for thy heart is not right in the sight of God. Repent therefore of this thy wickedness, and pray God, if perhaps the
thought of thine heart may be forgiven thee. For I perceive
that thou art in the gall of bitterness, and in the bond of
iniquity." Then answered Simon, and said, "Pray ye to
the Lord for me, that none of these things which ye have
spoken come upon me".

And they, when they had testified and preached the word of the Lord, returned to Jerusalem, and preached the gospel in many villages of the Samaritans.   [8:9–25]

Philip and the Ethiopian. And the angel of the Lord spake unto Philip, saying, "Arise, and go toward the south unto the way that goeth down from Jerusalem unto Gaza, which is desert". And he arose and went: and, behold, a man of Ethiopia, an eunuch of great authority under Candace queen of the Ethiopians, who had the charge of all her treasure, and had come to Jerusalem for to worship, was returning, and sitting in his chariot read Esaias the prophet. Then the Spirit said unto Philip, "Go near, and join thyself to this chariot". And Philip ran thither to him, and heard him read the prophet Esaias, and said, "Understandest thou what thou readest?" And he said, "How can I, except some man should guide me?" And he desired Philip that he would come up and sit with him. The place of the scripture which he read was this,[1]

> "He was led as a sheep to the slaughter;
> And like a lamb dumb before his shearer,
> So opened he not his mouth:
> In his humiliation his judgment was taken away:
> And who shall declare his generation?
> For his life is taken from the earth".

And the eunuch answered Philip, and said, "I pray thee, of whom speaketh the prophet this? of himself, or of some other man?" Then Philip opened his mouth, and began at the same scripture, and preached unto him Jesus. And as they went on their way, they came unto a certain water: and the eunuch said, "See, here is water; what doth hinder me to be baptized?" And Philip said, "If thou believest with all thine heart, thou mayest". And he answered and said, "I believe that Jesus Christ is the Son of God". And he commanded the chariot to stand still: and they went

[1] See p. 309–10.

down both into the water, both Philip and the eunuch; and he baptized him. And when they were come up out of the water, the Spirit of the LORD caught away Philip, that the eunuch saw him no more: and he went on his way rejoicing. But Philip was found at Azotus: and passing through he preached in all the cities, till he came to Cæsarea.

[8:26–40]

The Conversion of Saul (Paul). And Saul, yet breathing out threatenings and slaughter against the disciples of the Lord, went unto the high priest, and desired of him letters to Damascus to the synagogues, that if he found any of this way, whether they were men or women, he might bring them bound unto Jerusalem. And as he journeyed, he came near Damascus: and suddenly there shined round about him a light from heaven: and he fell to the earth, and heard a voice saying unto him, "Saul, Saul, why persecutest thou me?" And he said, "Who art thou, Lord?" And the Lord said, "I am Jesus whom thou persecutest: it is hard for thee to kick against the pricks". And he trembling and astonished said, "Lord, what wilt thou have me to do?" And the Lord said unto him, "Arise, and go into the city, and it shall be told thee what thou must do". And the men which journeyed with him stood speechless, hearing a voice, but seeing no man. And Saul arose from the earth; and when his eyes were opened, he saw no man: but they led him by the hand, and brought him into Damascus. And he was three days without sight, and neither did eat nor drink.

And there was a certain disciple at Damascus, named Ananias; and to him said the Lord in a vision, "Ananias". And he said, "Behold, I am here, Lord". And the Lord said unto him, "Arise, and go into the street which is called Straight, and enquire in the house of Judas for one called Saul, of Tarsus: for, behold, he prayeth, and hath seen in a vision a man named Ananias coming in, and putting his hand on him, that he might receive his sight". Then Ananias answered, "Lord, I have heard by many of this man, how much evil he hath done to thy saints at Jerusalem: and here he hath authority from the chief priests to bind all that call on thy name". But the Lord said unto him, "Go thy way: for he is a chosen vessel unto me, to bear my name before the Gentiles, and kings, and the children of Israel: for I will shew him how great things he must suffer for my name's sake". And Ananias went his way, and entered into the house; and putting his hands on him said, "Brother Saul, the Lord, even Jesus, that appeared unto thee in the way as thou camest, hath sent me, that thou mightest receive thy sight, and be filled with the Holy Ghost". And immediately there fell from his eyes as it had been scales: and he received sight forthwith, and arose, and was baptized. And when he had received meat, he was strengthened.

Then was Saul certain days with the disciples which were at Damascus. And straightway he preached Christ in the synagogues, that he is the Son of God. But all that heard him were amazed, and said; "Is not this he that destroyed them which called on this name in Jerusalem, and came hither for that intent, that he might bring them bound unto the chief priests?" But Saul increased the more in strength, and confounded the Jews which dwelt at Damascus, proving that this is very Christ.

And after that many days were fulfilled, the Jews took counsel to kill him: but their laying await was known of Saul. And they watched the gates day and night to kill him. Then the disciples took him by night, and let him down by the wall in a basket.

And when Saul was come to Jerusalem, he assayed to join himself to the disciples: but they were all afraid of him, and believed not that he was a disciple. But Barnabas took him, and brought him to the apostles, and declared unto them how he had seen the Lord in the way, and that he had spoken to him, and how he had preached boldly at Damascus in the name of Jesus. And he was with them coming in and going out at Jerusalem. And he spake boldly in the name of the Lord Jesus, and disputed against the Grecians: but they went about to slay him. Which when the brethren knew, they brought him down to Cæsarea, and sent him forth to Tarsus.

Then had the churches rest throughout all Judæa and Galilee and Samaria, and were edified; and walking in the fear of the Lord, and in the comfort of the Holy Ghost, were multiplied. [9:1–31]

Miracles of Peter. And it came to pass, as Peter passed throughout all quarters, he came down also to the saints which dwelt at Lydda. And there he found a certain man named Æneas, which had kept his bed eight years, and was sick of the palsy. And Peter said unto him, "Æneas, Jesus Christ maketh thee whole: arise, and make thy bed". And he arose immediately. And all that dwelt at Lydda and Saron saw him, and turned to the Lord.

Now there was at Joppa a certain disciple named Tabitha, which by interpretation is called Dorcas: this woman was full of good works and almsdeeds which she did. And it came to pass in those days, that she was sick, and died: whom when they had washed, they laid her in an upper chamber. And forasmuch as Lydda was nigh to Joppa, and the disciples had heard that Peter was there, they sent unto him two men, desiring him that he would not delay to come to them. Then Peter arose and went with them. When he was come, they brought him into the upper chamber: and all the widows stood by him weeping, and shewing the coats and garments which Dorcas made, while she was with them. But Peter put them all forth, and kneeled down, and prayed; and turning him to the body said, "Tabitha, arise". And she opened her eyes: and when she saw Peter, she sat up. And he gave her his hand, and lifted her up, and when he had called the saints and widows, presented her alive. And it was known throughout all Joppa; and many believed in the Lord. And it came to pass, that he tarried many days in Joppa with one Simon a tanner. [9:32–43]

Cornelius the Centurion. There was a certain man in Cæsarea called Cornelius, a centurion of the band called the Italian band, a devout man, and one that feared God with all his house, which gave much alms to the people, and prayed to God alway. He saw in a vision evidently about the ninth hour of the day an angel of God coming in to him, and saying unto him, "Cornelius". And when he looked on him, he was afraid, and said, "What is it, Lord?" And he said unto him, "Thy prayers and thine alms are come up for a memorial before God. And now send men to Joppa, and call for one Simon, whose surname is Peter: he lodgeth with one Simon a tanner, whose house is by the sea side: he shall tell thee what thou oughtest to do." And when the angel which spake unto Cornelius was departed, he called two of his household servants, and a devout soldier of them that waited on him continually; and when he had declared all these things unto them, he sent them to Joppa. [10:1–8]

Peter's Vision. On the morrow, as they went on their journey, and drew nigh unto the city, Peter went up upon the housetop to pray, about the sixth hour: and he became very hungry, and would have eaten: but while they made ready, he fell into a trance, and saw heaven opened, and a certain vessel descending unto him, as it had been a great sheet knit at the four corners, and let down to the earth: wherein were all manner of fourfooted beasts of the earth, and wild beasts, and creeping things, and fowls of the air. And there came a voice to him, "Rise, Peter; kill, and eat". But Peter said, "Not so, Lord; for I have never eaten any thing that is common or unclean".[2] And the voice spake unto him again the second time, "What God hath cleansed, that call not thou common". This was done thrice: and the vessel was received up again into heaven.

Now while Peter doubted in himself what this vision which he had seen should mean, behold, the men which

[2] See p. 95.

were sent from Cornelius had made enquiry for Simon's house, and stood before the gate, and called, and asked whether Simon, which was surnamed Peter, were lodged there. While Peter thought on the vision, the Spirit said unto him, "Behold, three men seek thee. Arise therefore, and get thee down, and go with them, doubting nothing: for I have sent them." Then Peter went down to the men which were sent unto him from Cornelius; and said, "Behold, I am he whom ye seek: what is the cause wherefore ye are come?" And they said, "Cornelius the centurion, a just man, and one that feareth God, and of good report among all the nation of the Jews, was warned from God by an holy angel to send for thee into his house, and to hear words of thee". Then called he them in, and lodged them.

[Peter therefore went to Cornelius and talked with him although it was unlawful for a Jew to keep company with one of another nation; but when Cornelius told him of his vision, Peter understood that his own vision meant that the Gentiles also were to receive the word of God. And while he was still speaking, the Holy Ghost fell upon all who heard. Peter therefore caused them to be baptized. When Peter returned to the apostles and brethren who were at Jerusalem, they rebuked him for eating with men who were uncircumcised; but he told them of his vision and how the Holy Ghost had fallen upon them.]

"Forasmuch then as God gave them the like gift as he did unto us, who believed on the Lord Jesus Christ; what was I, that I could withstand God?" When they heard these things, they held their peace, and glorified God, saying, "Then hath God also to the Gentiles granted repentance unto life".   [10:9–23; 11:17–18]

Peter Imprisoned by Herod.[3] Now about that time Herod the king stretched forth his hands to vex certain of the church. And he killed James the brother of John with the sword. And because he saw it pleased the Jews, he

---

[3] See Appendix 7.

proceeded further to take Peter also. (Then were the days of unleavened bread.) And when he had apprehended him, he put him in prison, and delivered him to four quaternions of soldiers to keep him; intending after Easter to bring him forth to the people. Peter therefore was kept in prison: but prayer was made without ceasing of the church unto God for him. And when Herod would have brought him forth, the same night Peter was sleeping between two soldiers, bound with two chains: and the keepers before the door kept the prison. And, behold, the angel of the Lord came upon him, and a light shined in the prison: and he smote Peter on the side, and raised him up, saying, "Arise up quickly". And his chains fell off from his hands. And the angel said unto him, "Gird thyself, and bind on thy sandals". And so he did. And he saith unto him, "Cast thy garment about thee, and follow me". And he went out, and followed him; and wist not that it was true which was done by the angel; but thought he saw a vision. When they were past the first and the second ward, they came unto the iron gate that leadeth unto the city; which opened to them of his own accord: and they went out, and passed on through one street; and forthwith the angel departed from him. And when Peter was come to himself, he said, "Now I know of a surety, that the Lord hath sent his angel, and hath delivered me out of the hand of Herod, and from all the expectation of the people of the Jews". And when he had considered the thing, he came to the house of Mary the mother of John, whose surname was Mark; where many were gathered together praying. And as Peter knocked at the door of the gate, a damsel came to hearken, named Rhoda. And when she knew Peter's voice, she opened not the gate for gladness, but ran in, and told how Peter stood before the gate. And they said unto her, "Thou art mad". But she constantly affirmed that it was even so. Then said they, "It is his angel". But Peter continued knocking: and when they had opened the door, and saw him, they were astonished. But he, beckoning unto

them with the hand to hold their peace, declared unto them
how the Lord had brought him out of the prison. And
he said, "Go shew these things unto James, and to the
brethren". And he departed, and went into another place.
Now as soon as it was day, there was no small stir among
the soldiers, what was become of Peter. And when Herod
had sought for him, and found him not, he examined the
keepers, and commanded that they should be put to death.
And he went down from Judæa to Cæsarea, and there
abode.   [12:1–19]

The Death of Herod.   And Herod was highly displeased
with them of Tyre and Sidon: but they came with one
accord to him, and, having made Blastus the king's cham-
berlain their friend, desired peace; because their country
was nourished by the king's country. And upon a set day
Herod, arrayed in royal apparel, sat upon his throne, and
made an oration unto them. And the people gave a shout,
saying, "It is the voice of a god, and not of a man". And
immediately the angel of the Lord smote him, because he
gave not God the glory: and he was eaten of worms, and
gave up the ghost.

But the word of God grew and multiplied.

And Barnabas and Saul returned from Jerusalem, when
they had fulfilled their ministry, and took with them John,
whose surname was Mark.   [12:20–25]

[Paul and Barnabas set out on a missionary journey
from Antioch to Cyprus, and thence to Pamphylia in
southern Asia Minor. They met with great opposition from
the Jews settled in those parts, though some believed their
message. They came to Lystra, a city in Lycaonia.]

Paul at Lystra.   And there sat a certain man at Lystra,
impotent in his feet, being a cripple from his mother's
womb, who never had walked: the same heard Paul
speak: who stedfastly beholding him, and perceiving that
he had faith to be healed, said with a loud voice, "Stand
upright on thy feet". And he leaped and walked. And
when the people saw what Paul had done, they lifted up

their voices, saying in the speech of Lycaonia, "The gods are come down to us in the likeness of men". And they called Barnabas, Jupiter; and Paul, Mercurius, because he was the chief speaker. Then the priest of Jupiter, which was before their city, brought oxen and garlands unto the gates, and would have done sacrifice with the people. Which when the apostles, Barnabas and Paul, heard of, they rent their clothes, and ran in among the people, crying out, and saying, "Sirs, why do ye these things? We also are men of like passions with you, and preach unto you that ye should turn from these vanities unto the living God, which made heaven, and earth, and the sea, and all things that are therein: who in times past suffered all nations to walk in their own ways. Nevertheless he left not himself without witness, in that he did good, and gave us rain from heaven, and fruitful seasons, filling our hearts with food and gladness." And with these sayings scarce restrained they the people, that they had not done sacrifice unto them.

And there came thither certain Jews from Antioch and Iconium, who persuaded the people, and, having stoned Paul, drew him out of the city, supposing he had been dead. Howbeit, as the disciples stood round about him, he rose up, and came into the city: and the next day he departed with Barnabas to Derbe. And when they had preached the gospel to that city, and had taught many, they returned again to Lystra, and to Iconium, and Antioch, confirming the souls of the disciples, and exhorting them to continue in the faith, and that we must through much tribulation enter into the kingdom of God. And when they had ordained them elders in every church, and had prayed with fasting, they commended them to the Lord, on whom they believed. And after they had passed throughout Pisidia, they came to Pamphylia. And when they had preached the word in Perga, they went down into Attalia: and thence sailed to Antioch, from whence they had been recommended to the grace of God for the work which they fulfilled. And when they were come, and had gathered the church together, they rehearsed all that God had done with them, and how he had opened the door of faith unto the Gentiles. And there they abode long time with the disciples.   [14:8–28]

The Great Debate over Circumcision. And certain men which came down from Judæa taught the brethren, and said, "Except ye be circumcised after the manner of Moses, ye cannot be saved". When therefore Paul and Barnabas had no small dissension and disputation with them, they determined that Paul and Barnabas, and certain other of them, should go up to Jerusalem unto the apostles and elders about this question. And being brought on their way by the church, they passed through Phenice and Samaria, declaring the conversion of the Gentiles: and they caused great joy unto all the brethren. And when they were come to Jerusalem, they were received of the church, and of the apostles and elders, and they declared all things that God had done with them. But there rose up certain of the sect of the Pharisees which believed, saying, that it was needful to circumcise them, and to command them to keep the law of Moses.

And the apostles and elders came together for to consider of this matter. And when there had been much disputing, Peter rose up, and said unto them,

"Men and brethren, ye know how that a good while ago God made choice among us, that the Gentiles by my mouth should hear the word of the gospel, and believe. And God, which knoweth the hearts, bare them witness, giving them the Holy Ghost, even as he did unto us; and put no difference between us and them, purifying their hearts by faith. Now therefore why tempt ye God, to put a yoke upon the neck of the disciples, which neither our fathers nor we were able to bear? But we believe that through the grace of the Lord Jesus Christ we shall be saved, even as they."

Then all the multitude kept silence, and gave audience to Barnabas and Paul, declaring what miracles and wonders God had wrought among the Gentiles by them. And after they had held their peace, James answered, saying,

"Men and brethren, hearken unto me: Simeon hath declared how God at the first did visit the Gentiles, to take out of them a people for his name. And to this agree the words of the prophets; as it is written,

'After this I will return,
And will build again the tabernacle of David, which
   is fallen down;
And I will build again the ruins thereof,
And I will set it up:
That the residue of men might seek after the Lord,
And all the Gentiles, upon whom my name is called,
Saith the Lord, who doeth all these things.
Known unto God are all his works from the beginning of the world.'

Wherefore my sentence is, that we trouble not them, which from among the Gentiles are turned to God: but that we write unto them, that they abstain from pollutions of idols, and from fornication, and from things strangled, and from blood. For Moses of old time hath in every city them that preach him, being read in the synagogues every sabbath day."   [15:1–21]

The Decision over Circumcision. Then pleased it the apostles and elders, with the whole church, to send chosen men of their own company to Antioch with Paul and Barnabas; namely, Judas surnamed Barsabas, and Silas, chief men among the brethren: and they wrote letters by them after this manner; "The apostles and elders and brethren send greeting unto the brethren which are of the Gentiles in Antioch and Syria and Cilicia: Forasmuch as we have heard, that certain which went out from us have troubled you with words, subverting your souls, saying, 'Ye must be circumcised, and keep the law': to whom we gave no such commandment: it seemed good unto us, being assembled with one accord, to send chosen men unto you with our beloved Barnabas and Paul, men that have hazarded their lives for the name of our Lord Jesus Christ. We have sent therefore Judas and Silas, who shall also tell you the same things by mouth. For it seemed good to the Holy Ghost, and to us, to lay upon you no greater burden than these necessary things; that ye abstain from meats offered to idols, and from blood, and from things strangled, and from fornication: from which if ye keep yourselves, ye shall do well. Fare ye well." [15:22–29]

[On the second journey, Paul and Silas passed through western Asia Minor and crossed the Aegean Sea to Philippi in Macedonia, where their enemies rose and brought them before the magistrates who commanded them to be beaten and imprisoned.]

Paul's Roman Citizenship. And when it was day, the magistrates sent the serjeants, saying, "Let those men go". And the keeper of the prison told this saying to Paul, "The magistrates have sent to let you go: now therefore depart, and go in peace". But Paul said unto them, "They have beaten us openly uncondemned, being Romans, and have cast us into prison; and now do they thrust us out privily? nay verily; but let them come themselves and fetch us out". And the serjeants told these words unto the magistrates: and they feared, when they heard that they were Romans. And they came and besought them, and brought them out, and desired them to depart out of the city. And they went out of the prison, and entered into the house of Lydia: and when they had seen the brethren, they comforted them, and departed. [16:35–40]

[Thence they came to Thessalonica, where hostile Jews stirred up "certain lewd fellows of the baser sort and gathered a company and set all the city in an uproar." Paul next visited Athens.]

Paul at Athens. Now while Paul waited for them at Athens, his spirit was stirred in him, when he saw the city wholly given to idolatry. Therefore disputed he in the synagogue with the Jews, and with the devout persons, and in the market daily with them that met with him. Then certain philosophers of the Epicureans, and of the Stoicks, encountered him. And some said, "What will this babbler say?" other some, "He seemeth to be a setter forth of strange gods": because he preached unto them Jesus, and the resurrection. And they took him, and brought him unto Areopagus, saying, "May we know what this new doctrine, whereof thou speakest, is? For thou bringest certain strange things to our ears: we would know therefore what these things mean." (For all the Athenians and strangers which were there spent their time in nothing else, but either to tell, or to hear some new thing.) Then Paul stood in the midst of Mars' hill, and said,

"Ye men of Athens, I perceive that in all things ye are too superstitious. For as I passed by, and beheld your devotions, I found an altar with this inscription, TO THE UNKNOWN GOD. Whom therefore ye ignorantly worship, him declare I unto you. God that made the world and all things therein, seeing that he is Lord of heaven and earth, dwelleth not in temples made with hands; neither is worshipped with men's hands, as though he needed any thing, seeing he giveth to all life, and breath, and all things; and hath made of one blood all nations of men for to dwell on all the face of the earth, and hath determined the times before appointed, and the bounds of their habitation; that they should seek the Lord, if haply they might feel after him, and find him, though he be not far from every one of us: for in him we live, and move, and have our being; as certain also of your own poets have said, 'For we are also his offspring'. Forasmuch then as we are the offspring of God, we ought not to think that the Godhead is like unto gold, or silver, or stone, graven by art and man's device. And the times of this ignorance God winked at; but now commandeth all men every where to repent: because he hath appointed a day, in the which he will judge the world in righteousness by that man whom he hath ordained; whereof he hath given assurance unto all men, in that he hath raised him from the dead."

And when they heard of the resurrection of the dead, some mocked: and others said, "We will hear thee again of this matter". So Paul departed from among them. Howbeit certain men clave unto him, and believed: among the which was Dionysius the Areopagite, and a woman named Damaris, and others with them. [17:16–34]

Paul at Corinth. After these things Paul departed from Athens, and came to Corinth; and found a certain Jew named Aquila, born in Pontus, lately come from Italy, with his wife Priscilla; (because that Claudius had commanded all Jews to depart from Rome:) and came unto them. And because he was of the same craft, he abode with them, and wrought: for by their occupation they were tentmakers. And he reasoned in the synagogue every sabbath, and persuaded the Jews and the Greeks.

And when Silas and Timotheus were come from Macedonia, Paul was pressed in the spirit, and testified to the Jews that Jesus was Christ. And when they opposed themselves, and blasphemed, he shook his raiment, and said unto them, "Your blood be upon your own heads; I am clean: from henceforth I will go unto the Gentiles". And he departed thence, and entered into a certain man's house, named Justus, one that worshipped God, whose house joined hard to the synagogue. And Crispus, the chief ruler of the synagogue, believed on the Lord with all his house; and many of the Corinthians hearing believed, and were baptized. Then spake the Lord to Paul in the night by a vision, "Be not afraid, but speak, and hold not thy peace: for I am with thee, and no man shall set on thee to hurt thee: for I have much people in this city". And he continued there a year and six months, teaching the word of God among them. [18:1–11]

Paul before Gallio. And when Gallio was the deputy of Achaia, the Jews made insurrection with one accord against Paul, and brought him to the judgment seat, saying, "This fellow persuadeth men to worship God contrary to the law". And when Paul was now about to open his mouth, Gallio said unto the Jews, "If it were a matter of wrong or wicked lewdness, O ye Jews, reason would that I should bear with you: but if it be a question of words and names, and of your law, look ye to it; for I will be no judge of such matters". And he drave them from the judgment seat. Then all the Greeks took Sosthenes, the chief ruler of the synagogue, and beat him before the judgment seat. And Gallio cared for none of those things.

[18:12–17]

[From Corinth Paul went to Ephesus, where he stayed a short while and then returned to Jerusalem. He went to Antioch before setting out on a third journey to revisit the disciples in Galatia and Phrygia.]

Paul at Ephesus. And it came to pass, that, while Apollos was at Corinth, Paul having passed through the upper coasts came to Ephesus: and finding certain disciples, he said unto them, "Have ye received the Holy Ghost since ye believed?" And they said unto him, "We have not so much as heard whether there be any Holy Ghost". And he said unto them, "Unto what then were ye baptized?" And they said, "Unto John's baptism". Then said Paul, "John verily baptized with the baptism of repentance, saying unto the people, that they should believe on him which should come after him, that is, on Christ Jesus". When they heard this, they were baptized in the name of the Lord Jesus. And when Paul had laid his hands upon them, the Holy Ghost came on them; and they spake with tongues, and prophesied. And all the men were about twelve.

And he went into the synagogue, and spake boldly for the space of three months, disputing and persuading the things concerning the kingdom of God. But when divers were hardened, and believed not, but spake evil of that way before the multitude, he departed from them, and separated the disciples, disputing daily in the school of one

Tyrannus. And this continued by the space of two years; so that all they which dwelt in Asia heard the word of the Lord Jesus, both Jews and Greeks. And God wrought special miracles by the hands of Paul: so that from his body were brought unto the sick handkerchiefs or aprons, and the diseases departed from them, and the evil spirits went out of them. Then certain of the vagabond Jews, exorcists, took upon them to call over them which had evil spirits the name of the Lord Jesus, saying, "We adjure you by Jesus whom Paul preacheth". And there were seven sons of one Sceva, a Jew, and chief of the priests, which did so. And the evil spirit answered and said, "Jesus I know, and Paul I know; but who are ye?" And the man in whom the evil spirit was leaped on them, and overcame them, and prevailed against them, so that they fled out of that house naked and wounded. And this was known to all the Jews and Greeks also dwelling at Ephesus and fear fell on them all, and the name of the Lord Jesus was magnified. And many that believed came, and confessed, and shewed their deeds. Many of them also which used curious arts brought their books together, and burned them before all men: and they counted the price of them, and found it fifty thousand pieces of silver. So mightily grew the word of God and prevailed.

After these things were ended, Paul purposed in the spirit, when he had passed through Macedonia and Achaia, to go to Jerusalem, saying, "After I have been there, I must also see Rome". So he sent into Macedonia two of them that ministered unto him, Timotheus and Erastus; but he himself stayed in Asia for a season. [19:1–22]

A Riot at Ephesus. And the same time there arose no small stir about that way. For a certain man named Demetrius, a silversmith, which made silver shrines for Diana, brought no small gain unto the craftsmen; whom he called together with the workmen of like occupation, and said, "Sirs, ye know that by this craft we have our wealth. Moreover ye see and hear, that not alone at Ephesus, but almost throughout all Asia, this Paul hath persuaded and turned away much people, saying that they be no gods, which are made with hands: so that not only this our craft is in danger to be set at nought; but also that the temple of the great goddess Diana should be despised, and her magnificence should be destroyed, whom all Asia and the world worshippeth." And when they heard these sayings, they were full of wrath, and cried out, saying, "Great is Diana of the Ephesians". And the whole city was filled with confusion: and having caught Gaius and Aristarchus, men of Macedonia, Paul's companions in travel, they rushed with one accord into the theatre. And when Paul would have entered in unto the people, the disciples suffered him not. And certain of the chief of Asia, which were his friends, sent unto him, desiring him that he would not adventure himself into the theatre. Some therefore cried one thing, and some another: for the assembly was confused; and the more part knew not wherefore they were come together. And they drew Alexander out of the multitude, the Jews putting him forward. And Alexander beckoned with the hand, and would have made his defence unto the people. But when they knew that he was a Jew, all with one voice about the space of two hours cried out, "Great is Diana of the Ephesians". And when the townclerk had appeased the people, he said, "Ye men of Ephesus, what man is there that knoweth not how that the city of the Ephesians is a worshipper of the great goddess Diana, and of the image which fell down from Jupiter? Seeing then that these things cannot be spoken against, ye ought to be quiet, and to do nothing rashly. For ye have brought hither these men, which are neither robbers of churches, nor yet blasphemers of your goddess. Wherefore if Demetrius, and the craftsmen which are with him, have a matter against any man, the law is open, and there are deputies: let them implead one another. But if ye enquire any thing concerning other matters, it shall be determined in a lawful assembly. For we are in danger to be called in question for this day's uproar, there being no cause whereby we may give an account of this concourse." And when he had thus spoken, he dismissed the assembly.

[19:23–41]

[After the uproar had ceased, Paul went into Macedonia to Philippi; and then returned to Jerusalem for the feast of Pentecost.]

Paul Returns to Jerusalem. And when we were come to Jerusalem, the brethren received us gladly. And the day following Paul went in with us unto James; and all the elders were present. And when he had saluted them, he declared particularly what things God had wrought among the Gentiles by his ministry. And when they heard it, they glorified the Lord, and said unto him, "Thou seest, brother, how many thousands of Jews there are which believe; and they are all zealous of the law: and they are informed of thee, that thou teachest all the Jews which are among the Gentiles to forsake Moses, saying that they ought not to circumcise their children, neither to walk after the customs. What is it therefore? the multitude must needs come together: for they will hear that thou art come. Do therefore this that we say to thee: We have four men which have a vow on them; them take, and purify thyself with them, and be at charges with them, that they may shave their heads: and all may know that those things, whereof they were informed concerning thee, are nothing; but that thou thyself also walkest orderly, and keepest the law. As touching the Gentiles which believe, we have written and concluded that they observe no such thing, save only that they keep themselves from things offered to idols, and from blood, and from strangled, and from fornication." Then Paul took the men, and the next day purifying himself with them entered into the temple, to signify the accomplishment of the days of purification, until that an offering should be offered for every one of them.

[21:17–26]

A Riot against Paul in the Temple. And when the seven days were almost ended, the Jews which were of Asia, when they saw him in the temple, stirred up all the people, and laid hands on him, crying out, "Men of Israel, help: This is the man, that teacheth all men every where against the people, and the law, and this place: and further brought Greeks also into the temple, and hath polluted this holy place". (For they had seen before with him in the city Trophimus an Ephesian, whom they supposed that Paul had brought into the temple.) And all the city was moved, and the people ran together: and they took Paul, and drew him out of the temple: and forthwith the doors were shut. And as they went about to kill him, tidings came unto the chief captain of the band, that all Jerusalem was in an uproar. Who immediately took soldiers and centurions, and ran down unto them: and when they saw the chief captain and the soldiers, they left beating of Paul. Then the chief captain came near, and took him, and commanded him to be bound with two chains; and demanded who he was, and what he had done. And some cried one thing, some another, among the multitude: and when he could not know the certainty for the tumult, he commanded him to be carried into the castle. And when he came upon the stairs, so it was, that he was borne of the soldiers for the violence of the people. For the multitude of the people followed after, crying, "Away with him".

And as Paul was to be led into the castle, he said unto the chief captain, "May I speak unto thee?" Who said, "Canst thou speak Greek? Art not thou that Egyptian, which before these days madest an uproar, and leddest out into the wilderness four thousand men that were murderers?" But Paul said, "I am a man which am a Jew of Tarsus, a city in Cilicia, a citizen of no mean city: and, I beseech thee, suffer me to speak unto the people". And when he had given him licence, Paul stood on the stairs, and beckoned with the hand unto the people. And when there was made a great silence, he spake unto them in the Hebrew tongue.   [21:27–40]

[Paul told them of his conversion and of his mission to the Gentiles.]

Paul Rescued. And they gave him audience unto this word, and then lifted up their voices, and said, "Away with such a fellow from the earth: for it is not fit that he should live". And as they cried out, and cast off their clothes, and threw dust into the air, the chief captain commanded him to be brought into the castle, and bade that he should be examined by scourging; that he might know wherefore they cried so against him. And as they bound him with thongs, Paul said unto the centurion that stood by, "Is it lawful for you to scourge a man that is a Roman, and uncondemned?" When the centurion heard that, he went and told the chief captain, saying, "Take heed what thou doest: for this man is a Roman". Then the chief captain came, and said unto him, "Tell me, art thou a Roman?" He said, "Yea". And the chief captain answered, "With a great sum obtained I this freedom". And Paul said, "But I was free born". Then straightway they departed from him which should have examined him: and the chief captain also was afraid, after he knew that he was a Roman, and because he had bound him.

On the morrow, because he would have known the certainty wherefore he was accused of the Jews, he loosed him from his bands, and commanded the chief priests and all their council to appear, and brought Paul down, and set him before them.   [22:22–30]

Paul before the Council. And Paul, earnestly beholding the council, said, "Men and brethren, I have lived in all good conscience before God until this day". And the high priest Ananias commanded them that stood by him to smite him on the mouth. Then said Paul unto him, "God shall smite thee, thou whited wall: for sittest thou to judge me after the law, and commandest me to be smitten contrary to the law?" And they that stood by said, "Revilest thou God's high priest?" Then said Paul, "I wist not, brethren, that he was the high priest: for it is written, 'Thou shalt not speak evil of the ruler of thy people'". But when Paul perceived that the one part were Sadducees, and the other Pharisees, he cried out in the council, "Men and brethren, I am a Pharisee, the son of a Pharisee: of the hope and resurrection of the dead I am called in question". And when he had so said, there arose a dissension between the Pharisees and the Sadducees: and the multitude was divided. For the Sadducees say that there is no resurrection, neither angel, nor spirit: but the Pharisees confess both. And there arose a great cry: and the scribes that were of the Pharisees' part arose, and strove, saying, "We find no evil in this man: but if a spirit or an angel hath spoken to him, let us not fight against God". And when there arose a great dissension, the chief captain, fearing lest Paul should have been pulled in pieces of them, commanded the soldiers to go down, and to take him by force from among them, and to bring him into the castle.   [23:1–10]

[Paul learned that certain Jews had bound themselves under a curse that they would neither eat nor drink till they had killed him. This was told to the chief captain of the Roman garrison, who sent Paul with a large guard to Felix the governor at Cæsarea where Paul remained a prisoner.

Felix was succeeded as governor by Festus.]

Paul and Festus the Governor.   Now when Festus was come into the province, after three days he ascended from Cæsarea to Jerusalem. Then the high priest and the chief of the Jews informed him against Paul, and besought him, and desired favour against him, that he would send for him to Jerusalem, laying wait in the way to kill him. But Festus answered, that Paul should be kept at Cæsarea, and that he himself would depart shortly thither. "Let them therefore," said he, "which among you are able, go down with me, and accuse this man, if there be any wickedness in him."

And when he had tarried among them more than ten days, he went down unto Cæsarea; and the next day sitting on the judgment seat commanded Paul to be brought. And when he was come, the Jews which came down from Jerusalem stood round about, and laid many and grievous complaints against Paul, which they could not prove. While he answered for himself, "Neither against the law of the Jews, neither against the temple, nor yet against Cæsar, have I offended any thing at all". But Festus, willing to do the Jews a pleasure, answered Paul, and said, "Wilt thou go up to Jerusalem, and there be judged of these things before me?" Then said Paul, "I stand at Cæsar's judgment seat, where I ought to be judged: to the Jews have I done no wrong, as thou very well knowest. For if I be an offender, or have committed any thing worthy of death, I refuse not to die: but if there be none of these things whereof these accuse me, no man may deliver me unto them. I appeal unto Cæsar." Then Festus, when he had conferred with the council, answered, "Hast thou appealed unto Cæsar? unto Cæsar shalt thou go".

[25:1–12]

Paul before Agrippa. And after certain days king Agrippa[4] and Bernice came unto Cæsarea to salute Festus. And when they had been there many days, Festus declared Paul's cause unto the king, saying, "There is a certain man left in bonds by Felix: about whom, when I was at Jerusalem, the chief priests and the elders of the Jews informed me, desiring to have judgment against him. To whom I answered, It is not the manner of the Romans to deliver any man to die, before that he which is accused have the accusers face to face, and have licence to answer for himself concerning the crime laid against him. Therefore, when they were come hither, without any delay on the morrow I sat on the judgment seat, and commanded the man to be brought forth. Against whom when the accusers

[4] See Appendix 7.

stood up, they brought none accusation of such things as I supposed: but had certain questions against him of their own superstition, and of one Jesus, which was dead, whom Paul affirmed to be alive. And because I doubted of such manner of questions, I asked him whether he would go to Jerusalem, and there be judged of these matters. But when Paul had appealed to be reserved unto the hearing of Augustus, I commanded him to be kept till I might send him to Cæsar." Then Agrippa said unto Festus, "I would also hear the man myself". "To morrow", said he, "thou shalt hear him."

And on the morrow, when Agrippa was come, and Bernice, with great pomp, and was entered into the place of hearing, with the chief captains, and principal men of the city, at Festus' commandment Paul was brought forth. And Festus said, "King Agrippa, and all men which are here present with us, ye see this man, about whom all the multitude of the Jews have dealt with me, both at Jerusalem, and also here, crying that he ought not to live any longer. But when I found that he had committed nothing worthy of death, and that he himself hath appealed to Augustus, I have determined to send him. Of whom I have no certain thing to write unto my lord. Wherefore I have brought him forth before you, and specially before thee, O king Agrippa, that, after examination had, I might have somewhat to write. For it seemeth to me unreasonable to send a prisoner, and not withal to signify the crimes laid against him."

Then Agrippa said unto Paul, "Thou art permitted to speak for thyself".   [25:13-27; 26:1]

[Paul told of his conversion and of his mission to the Gentiles, and also of the resurrection of Christ.]

Paul Appeals to Cæsar. And as he thus spake for himself, Festus said with a loud voice, "Paul, thou art beside thyself; much learning doth make thee mad". But he said, "I am not mad, most noble Festus; but speak forth the words of truth and soberness. For the king knoweth of these things, before whom also I speak freely: for I am persuaded that none of these things are hidden from him; for this thing was not done in a corner. King Agrippa, believest thou the prophets? I know that thou believest." Then Agrippa said unto Paul, "Almost thou persuadest me to be a Christian". And Paul said, "I would to God, that not only thou, but also all that hear me this day, were both almost, and altogether such as I am, except these bonds".

And when he had thus spoken, the king rose up, and the governor, and Bernice, and they that sat with them: and when they were gone aside, they talked between themselves, saying, "This man doeth nothing worthy of death or of bonds". Then said Agrippa unto Festus, "This man might have been set at liberty, if he had not appealed unto Cæsar". [26:24-32]

Paul's Voyage to Rome. And when it was determined that we should sail into Italy, they delivered Paul and certain other prisoners unto one named Julius, a centurion of Augustus' band. And entering into a ship of Adramyttium, we launched, meaning to sail by the coasts of Asia; one Aristarchus, a Macedonian of Thessalonica, being with us. And the next day we touched at Sidon. And Julius courteously entreated Paul, and gave him liberty to go unto his friends to refresh himself. And when we had launched from thence, we sailed under Cyprus, because the winds were contrary. And when we had sailed over the sea of Cilicia and Pamphylia, we came to Myra, a city of Lycia. And there the centurion found a ship of Alexandria sailing into Italy; and he put us therein. And when we had sailed slowly many days, and scarce were come over against Cnidus, the wind not suffering us, we sailed under Crete, over against Salmone; and, hardly passing it, came unto a place which is called The fair havens; nigh whereunto was the city of Lasea.

Now when much time was spent, and when sailing was now dangerous, because the fast was now already past,

Paul admonished them, and said unto them, "Sirs, I perceive that this voyage will be with hurt and much damage, not only of the lading and ship, but also of our lives". Nevertheless the centurion believed the master and the owner of the ship, more than those things which were spoken by Paul. And because the haven was not commodious to winter in, the more part advised to depart thence also, if by any means they might attain to Phenice, and there to winter; which is an haven of Crete, and lieth toward the south west and north west. And when the south wind blew softly, supposing that they had obtained their purpose, loosing thence, they sailed close by Crete. But not long after there arose against it a tempestuous wind, called Euroclydon. And when the ship was caught, and could not bear up into the wind, we let her drive. And running under a certain island which is called Clauda, we had much work to come by the boat: which when they had taken up, they used helps, undergirding the ship; and, fearing lest they should fall into the quicksands, strake sail, and so were driven. And we being exceedingly tossed with a tempest, the next day they lightened the ship; and the third day we cast out with our own hands the tackling of the ship. And when neither sun nor stars in many days appeared, and no small tempest lay on us, all hope that we should be saved was then taken away. But after long abstinence Paul stood forth in the midst of them, and said, "Sirs, ye should have hearkened unto me, and not have loosed from Crete, and to have gained this harm and loss. And now I exhort you to be of good cheer: for there shall be no loss of any man's life among you, but of the ship. For there stood by me this night the angel of God, whose I am, and whom I serve, saying, 'Fear not, Paul; thou must be brought before Cæsar: and, lo, God hath given thee all them that sail with thee'. Wherefore, sirs, be of good cheer: for I believe God, that it shall be even as it was told me. Howbeit we must be cast upon a certain island." [27:1–26]

Paul's Ship Wrecked. But when the fourteenth night was come, as we were driven up and down in Adria, about midnight the shipmen deemed that they drew near to some country; and sounded, and found it twenty fathoms: and when they had gone a little further, they sounded again, and found it fifteen fathoms. Then fearing lest we should have fallen upon rocks, they cast four anchors out of the stern, and wished for the day. And as the shipmen were about to flee out of the ship, when they had let down the boat into the sea, under colour as though they would have cast anchors out of the foreship, Paul said to the centurion and to the soldiers, "Except these abide in the ship, ye cannot be saved". Then the soldiers cut off the ropes of the boat, and let her fall off. And while the day was coming on, Paul besought them all to take meat, saying, "This day is the fourteenth day that ye have tarried and continued fasting, having taken nothing. Wherefore I pray you to take some meat: for this is for your health: for there shall not an hair fall from the head of any of you." And when he had thus spoken, he took bread, and gave thanks to God in presence of them all: and when he had broken it, he began to eat. Then were they all of good cheer, and they also took some meat. And we were in all in the ship two hundred threescore and sixteen souls. And when they had eaten enough, they lightened the ship, and cast out the wheat into the sea. And when it was day, they knew not the land: but they discovered a certain creek with a shore, into the which they were minded, if it were possible, to thrust in the ship. And when they had taken up the anchors, they committed themselves unto the sea, and loosed the rudder bands, and hoised up the mainsail to the wind, and made toward shore. And falling into a place where two seas met, they ran the ship aground; and the forepart stuck fast, and remained unmoveable, but the hinder part was broken with the violence of the waves. And the soldiers' counsel was to kill the prisoners, lest any of them should swim out, and escape. But the centurion, willing to save Paul, kept them from their purpose; and commanded that they which could swim should cast themselves first into the sea, and get to land: and the rest, some on boards, and some on broken pieces of the ship. And so it came to pass, that they escaped all safe to land.

[27:27–44]

Paul Saved on Malta. And when they were escaped, then they knew that the island was called Melita. And the barbarous people shewed us no little kindness: for they kindled a fire, and received us every one, because of the present rain, and because of the cold. And when Paul had gathered a bundle of sticks, and laid them on the fire, there came a viper out of the heat, and fastened on his hand. And when the barbarians saw the venomous beast hang on his hand, they said among themselves, "No doubt this man is a murderer, whom, though he hath escaped the sea, yet vengeance suffereth not to live". And he shook off the beast into the fire, and felt no harm. Howbeit they looked when he should have swollen, or fallen down dead suddenly: but after they had looked a great while, and saw no harm come to him, they changed their minds, and said that he was a god.

In the same quarters were possessions of the chief man of the island, whose name was Publius; who received us, and lodged us three days courteously. And it came to pass, that the father of Publius lay sick of a fever and of a bloody flux: to whom Paul entered in, and prayed, and laid his hands on him, and healed him. So when this was done, others also, which had diseases in the island, came, and were healed: who also honoured us with many honours; and when we departed, they laded us with such things as were necessary.

[28:1–10]

Paul Comes to Rome. And after three months we departed in a ship of Alexandria, which had wintered in the isle, whose sign was Castor and Pollux. And landing at Syracuse, we tarried there three days. And from thence we fetched a compass, and came to Rhegium: and after one day the south wind blew, and we came the next day to Puteoli: where we found brethren, and were desired to tarry with them seven days: and so we went toward Rome. And from thence, when the brethren heard of us, they came to meet us as far as Appii forum, and The three taverns: whom when Paul saw, he thanked God, and took courage.

And when we came to Rome, the centurion delivered the prisoners to the captain of the guard: but Paul was suffered to dwell by himself with a soldier that kept him.

. . . .

And Paul dwelt two whole years in his own hired house, and received all that came in unto him, preaching the kingdom of God, and teaching those things which concern the Lord Jesus Christ, with all confidence, no man forbidding him.   [28:11–16, 30–31]

From THE EPISTLE TO THE ROMANS

Justification by Faith. Now we know that what things soever the law saith, it saith to them who are under the law: that every mouth may be stopped, and all the world may become guilty before God. Therefore by the deeds of the law there shall no flesh be justified in his sight: for by the law is the knowledge of sin. But now the righteousness of God without the law is manifested, being witnessed by the law and the prophets; even the righteousness of God which is by faith of Jesus Christ unto all and upon all them that believe: for there is no difference: for all have sinned, and come short of the glory of God; being justified freely by his grace through the redemption that is in Christ Jesus: whom God hath set forth to be a propitiation through faith in his blood, to declare his righteousness for the remission of sins that are past, through the forbearance of God; to declare, I say, at this time his righteousness: that he might be just, and the justifier of him which believeth in Jesus. Where is boasting then? It is excluded. By what law? of works? Nay: but by the law of faith. Therefore we conclude that a man is justified by faith without the deeds of the law. Is he the God of the Jews only? is he not also of the Gentiles? Yes, of the Gentiles also: seeing it is one God, which shall justify the circumcision by faith, and uncircumcision through faith. Do we then make void the law through faith? God forbid: yea, we establish the law.

. . . .

Therefore being justified by faith, we have peace with God through our Lord Jesus Christ: by whom also we have access by faith into this grace wherein we stand, and rejoice in hope of the glory of God. And not only so, but we glory in tribulations also: knowing that tribulation worketh patience; and patience, experience; and experience, hope: and hope maketh not ashamed; because the love of God is shed abroad in our hearts by the Holy Ghost which is given unto us. For when we were yet without strength, in due time Christ died for the ungodly. For scarcely for a righteous man will one die: yet peradventure for a good man some would even dare to die. But God commendeth his love toward us, in that, while we were yet sinners, Christ died for us. Much more then, being now justified by his blood, we shall be saved from wrath through him. For if, when we were enemies, we were reconciled to God by the death of his Son, much more, being reconciled, we shall be saved by his life. And not only so, but we also joy in God through our Lord Jesus Christ, by whom we have now received the atonement.

[3:19–31; 5:1–11]

Obedience to Authority. Let every soul be subject unto the higher powers. For there is no power but of God: the powers that be are ordained of God. Whosoever therefore resisteth the power, resisteth the ordinance of God: and they that resist shall receive to themselves damnation. For rulers are not a terror to good works, but to the evil. Wilt thou then not be afraid of the power? do that which is good, and thou shalt have praise of the same: for he is the minister of God to thee for good. But if thou do that which is evil, be afraid; for he beareth not the sword in vain: for he is the minister of God, a revenger to execute wrath upon him that doeth evil. Wherefore ye must needs be subject, not only for wrath, but also for conscience sake. For for this cause pay ye tribute also: for they are God's ministers, attending continually upon this very thing. Render therefore to all their dues: tribute to whom tribute is due; custom to whom custom; fear to whom fear; honour to whom honour.

Owe no man any thing, but to love one another: for he that loveth another hath fulfilled the law. For this, "Thou shalt not commit adultery, Thou shalt not kill, Thou shalt not steal, Thou shalt not bear false witness, Thou shalt not covet"; and if there be any other commandment, it is briefly comprehended in this saying, namely, "Thou shalt love thy neighbour as thyself". Love worketh no ill to his neighbour: therefore love is the fulfilling of the law.

And that, knowing the time, that now it is high time to awake out of sleep: for now is our salvation nearer than when we believed. The night is far spent, the day is at hand: let us therefore cast off the works of darkness, and let us put on the armour of light. Let us walk honestly, as in the day; not in rioting and drunkenness, not in chambering and wantonness, not in strife and envying. But put ye on the Lord Jesus Christ, and make not provision for the flesh, to fulfil the lusts thereof.   [13:1–14]

From THE FIRST EPISTLE TO THE CORINTHIANS

The Duty of Man and Woman. Be ye followers of me, even as I also am of Christ. Now I praise you, brethren, that ye remember me in all things, and keep the ordinances, as I delivered them to you. But I would have you know, that the head of every man is Christ; and the head of the woman is the man; and the head of Christ is God. Every man praying or prophesying, having his head covered, dishonoureth his head. But every woman that prayeth or prophesieth with her head uncovered dishonoureth her head: for that is even all one as if she were shaven. For if the woman be not covered, let her also be shorn: but if it be a shame for a woman to be shorn or shaven, let her be covered. For a man indeed ought not to cover his head, forasmuch as he is the image and glory of God: but the woman is the glory of the man. For the man is not of the woman; but the woman of the man. Neither was the man created for the woman; but the woman for the man. For this cause ought the woman to have power on her head because of the angels. Nevertheless neither is the man without the woman, neither the woman without the man, in the Lord. For as the woman is of the man, even so is the man also by the woman; but all things of God. Judge in yourselves: is it comely that a woman pray unto God uncovered? Doth not even nature itself teach you, that, if a man have long hair, it is a shame unto him? But if a woman have long hair, it is a glory to her: for her hair is given her for a covering. But if any man seem to be contentious,

we have no such custom, neither the churches of God.
[11:1–16]

The Supper of the Lord. Now in this that I declare unto
you I praise you not, that ye come together not for the
better, but for the worse. For first of all, when ye come
together in the church, I hear that there be divisions among
you; and I partly believe it. For there must be also heresies
among you, that they which are approved may be made
manifest among you. When ye come together therefore
into one place, this is not to eat the Lord's supper. For
in eating every one taketh before other his own supper:
and one is hungry, and another is drunken. What? have ye
not houses to eat and to drink in? or despise ye the church
of God, and shame them that have not? What shall I say
to you? shall I praise you in this? I praise you not. For I
have received of the Lord that which also I delivered unto
you, that the Lord Jesus the same night in which he was
betrayed took bread: and when he had given thanks, he
brake it, and said, "Take, eat: this is my body, which is
broken for you: this do in remembrance of me". After
the same manner also he took the cup, when he had
supped, saying, "This cup is the new testament in my
blood: this do ye, as oft as ye drink it, in remembrance
of me". For as often as ye eat this bread, and drink this
cup, ye do shew the Lord's death till he come. Wherefore
whosoever shall eat this bread, and drink this cup of the
Lord, unworthily, shall be guilty of the body and blood
of the Lord. But let a man examine himself, and so let
him eat of that bread, and drink of that cup. For he that
eateth and drinketh unworthily, eateth and drinketh damnation to himself, not discerning the Lord's body. For this
cause many are weak and sickly among you, and many
sleep. For if we would judge ourselves, we should not be
judged. But when we are judged, we are chastened of the
Lord, that we should not be condemned with the world.
Wherefore, my brethren, when ye come together to eat,
tarry one for another. And if any man hunger, let him

eat at home; that ye come not together unto condemnation. And the rest will I set in order when I come.

[11:17–34]

Charity. Though I speak with the tongues of men and of angels, and have not charity, I am become as sounding brass, or a tinkling cymbal. And though I have the gift of prophecy, and understand all mysteries, and all knowledge; and though I have all faith, so that I could remove mountains, and have not charity, I am nothing. And though I bestow all my goods to feed the poor, and though I give my body to be burned, and have not charity, it profiteth me nothing. Charity suffereth long, and is kind; charity envieth not; charity vaunteth not itself, is not puffed up, doth not behave itself unseemly, seeketh not her own, is not easily provoked, thinketh no evil; rejoiceth not in iniquity, but rejoiceth in the truth; beareth all things, believeth all things, hopeth all things, endureth all things. Charity never faileth: but whether there be prophecies, they shall fail; whether there be tongues, they shall cease; whether there be knowledge, it shall vanish away. For we know in part, and we prophesy in part. But when that which is perfect is come, then that which is in part shall be done away. When I was a child, I spake as a child, I understood as a child, I thought as a child: but when I became a man, I put away childish things. For now we see through a glass, darkly; but then face to face: now I know in part; but then shall I know even as also I am known. And now abideth faith, hope, charity, these three; but the greatest of these is charity.   [13:1–13]

The Resurrection of the Dead. Moreover, brethren, I declare unto you the gospel which I preached unto you, which also ye have received, and wherein ye stand; by which also ye are saved, if ye keep in memory what I preached unto you, unless ye have believed in vain. For I delivered unto you first of all that which I also received, how that Christ died for our sins according to the scriptures; and that he was buried, and that he rose again the third day according to the scriptures: and that he was seen of Cephas, then of the twelve: after that, he was seen of above five hundred brethren at once; of whom the greater part remain unto this present, but some are fallen asleep. After that, he was seen of James; then of all the apostles. And last of all he was seen of me also, as of one born out of due time. For I am the least of the apostles, that am not meet to be called an apostle, because I persecuted the church of God. But by the grace of God I am what I am: and his grace which was bestowed upon me was not in vain; but I laboured more abundantly than they all: yet not I, but the grace of God which was with me. Therefore whether it were I or they, so we preach, and so ye believed.

Now if Christ be preached that he rose from the dead, how say some among you that there is no resurrection of the dead? But if there be no resurrection of the dead, then is Christ not risen: and if Christ be not risen, then is our preaching vain, and your faith is also vain. Yea, and we are found false witnesses of God; because we have testified of God that he raised up Christ: whom he raised not up, if so be that the dead rise not. For if the dead rise not, then is not Christ raised: and if Christ be not raised, your faith is vain; ye are yet in your sins. Then they also which are fallen asleep in Christ are perished. If in this life only we have hope in Christ, we are of all men most miserable.

But now is Christ risen from the dead, and become the firstfruits of them that slept. For since by man came death, by man came also the resurrection of the dead. For as in Adam all die, even so in Christ shall all be made alive. But every man in his own order: Christ the firstfruits; afterward they that are Christ's at his coming. Then cometh the end, when he shall have delivered up the kingdom to God, even the Father; when he shall have put down all rule and all authority and power. For he must reign, till he hath put all enemies under his feet. The last enemy that shall be destroyed is death. For he hath put all things un-

der his feet. But when he saith all things are put under
him, it is manifest that he is excepted, which did put all
things under him. And when all things shall be subdued
unto him, then shall the Son also himself be subject unto
him that put all things under him, that God may be all in
all.

. . . .

But some man will say, "How are the dead raised up?
and with what body do they come?" Thou fool, that which
thou sowest is not quickened, except it die: and that which
thou sowest, thou sowest not that body that shall be, but
bare grain, it may chance of wheat, or of some other
grain: but God giveth it a body as it hath pleased him,
and to every seed his own body. All flesh is not the same
flesh: but there is one kind of flesh of men, another flesh
of beasts, another of fishes, and another of birds. There
are also celestial bodies, and bodies terrestrial: but the
glory of the celestial is one, and the glory of the terrestrial
is another. There is one glory of the sun, and another
glory of the moon, and another glory of the stars: for one
star differeth from another star in glory. So also is the
resurrection of the dead. It is sown in corruption; it is
raised in incorruption: it is sown in dishonour; it is raised
in glory: it is sown in weakness; it is raised in power: it is
sown a natural body; it is raised a spiritual body. There is
a natural body, and there is a spiritual body. And so it is
written, "The first man Adam was made a living soul; the
last Adam was made a quickening spirit". Howbeit that
was not first which is spiritual, but that which is natural;
and afterward that which is spiritual. The first man is of
the earth, earthy: the second man is the Lord from
heaven. As is the earthy, such are they also that are
earthy: and as is the heavenly, such are they also that are
heavenly. And as we have borne the image of the earthy,
we shall also bear the image of the heavenly.
Now this I say, brethren, that flesh and blood cannot

inherit the kingdom of God; neither doth corruption inherit incorruption. Behold, I shew you a mystery; We shall not all sleep, but we shall all be changed, in a moment, in the twinkling of an eye, at the last trump: for the trumpet shall sound, and the dead shall be raised incorruptible, and we shall be changed. For this corruptible must put on incorruption, and this mortal must put on immortality. So when this corruptible shall have put on incorruption, and this mortal shall have put on immortality, then shall be brought to pass the saying that is written, "Death is swallowed up in victory". O death, where is thy sting? O grave, where is thy victory? The sting of death is sin; and the strength of sin is the law. But thanks be to God, which giveth us the victory through our Lord Jesus Christ. Therefore, my beloved brethren, be ye stedfast, unmoveable, always abounding in the work of the Lord, forasmuch as ye know that your labour is not in vain in the Lord.   [13:1–28, 35–58]

From THE SECOND EPISTLE TO TIMOTHY

Paul's Farewell Charge to Timothy. I charge thee therefore before God, and the Lord Jesus Christ, who shall judge the quick and the dead at his appearing and his kingdom; preach the word; be instant in season, out of season; reprove, rebuke, exhort with all longsuffering and doctrine. For the time will come when they will not endure sound doctrine; but after their own lusts shall they heap to themselves teachers, having itching ears; and they shall turn away their ears from the truth, and shall be turned unto fables. But watch thou in all things, endure afflictions, do the work of an evangelist, make full proof of thy ministry. For I am now ready to be offered, and the time of my departure is at hand. I have fought a good fight, I have finished my course, I have kept the faith: henceforth there is laid up for me a crown of righteousness, which the Lord, the righteous judge, shall give me at that day: and not to me only, but unto all them also that love his appearing. [4:1–8]

From THE EPISTLE TO THE HEBREWS

The Power of Faith. Now faith is the substance of things hoped for, the evidence of things not seen. For by it the elders obtained a good report. Through faith we understand that the worlds were framed by the word of God, so that things which are seen were not made of things which do appear. By faith Abel offered unto God a more excellent sacrifice than Cain, by which he obtained witness that he was righteous, God testifying of his gifts: and by it he being dead yet speaketh. By faith Enoch was translated that he should not see death; and was not found, because God had translated him: for before his translation he had this testimony, that he pleased God. But without faith it is impossible to please him: for he that cometh to God must believe that he is, and that he is a rewarder of them that diligently seek him. By faith Noah, being warned of God of things not seen as yet, moved with fear, prepared an ark to the saving of his house; by the which he condemned the world, and became heir of the righteousness which is by faith. By faith Abraham, when he was called to go out into a place which he should after receive for an inheritance, obeyed; and he went out, not knowing whither he went. By faith he sojourned in the land of promise, as in a strange country, dwelling in tabernacles with Isaac and Jacob, the heirs with him of the same promise: for he looked for a city which hath foundations, whose builder and maker is God. Through faith also Sara herself received strength to conceive seed, and was delivered of a child when she was past age, because she judged him faithful who had promised. Therefore sprang there even of one, and him as good as dead, so many as the stars of the sky in multitude, and as the sand which is by the sea shore innumerable.

These all died in faith, not having received the promises, but having seen them afar off, and were persuaded of them, and embraced them, and confessed that they were strangers and pilgrims on the earth. For they that say such things declare plainly that they seek a country. And truly, if they had been mindful of that country from whence they came out, they might have had opportunity to have returned. But now they desire a better country, that is, an heavenly: wherefore God is not ashamed to be called their God: for he hath prepared for them a city.

By faith Abraham, when he was tried, offered up Isaac: and he that had received the promises offered up his only begotten son, of whom it was said, "That in Isaac shall thy seed be called": accounting that God was able to raise him up, even from the dead; from whence also he received him in a figure. By faith Isaac blessed Jacob and Esau concerning things to come. By faith Jacob, when he was a dying, blessed both the sons of Joseph; and worshipped, leaning upon the top of his staff. By faith Joseph, when he died, made mention of the departing of the children of Israel; and gave commandment concerning his bones.

By faith Moses, when he was born, was hid three months of his parents, because they saw he was a proper child; and they were not afraid of the king's commandment. By faith Moses, when he was come to years, refused to be called the son of Pharaoh's daughter; choosing rather to suffer affliction with the people of God, than to enjoy the pleasures of sin for a season; esteeming the reproach of Christ greater riches than the treasures in Egypt: for he had respect unto the recompence of the reward. By faith he forsook Egypt, not fearing the wrath of the king: for he endured, as seeing him who is invisible. Through faith he kept the passover, and the sprinkling of blood, lest he that destroyed the firstborn should touch them. By faith they passed through the Red sea as by dry land: which the Egyptians assaying to do were drowned. By faith the walls of Jericho fell down, after they were compassed about seven days. By faith the harlot Rahab perished not with them that believed not, when she had received the spies with peace. And what shall I more say? for the time would fail me to tell of Gedeon, and of Barak, and of Samson, and of Jephthae; of David also, and of Samuel, and of the prophets: who through faith subdued kingdoms, wrought righteousness, obtained promises, stopped the mouths of lions, quenched the violence of fire, escaped the edge of the sword, out of weakness were made strong, waxed valiant in fight, turned to flight the armies of the aliens. Women received their dead raised to life again: and others were tortured, not accepting deliverance; that they might obtain a better resurrection: and others had trial of cruel mockings and scourgings, yea, moreover of bonds and imprisonment: they were stoned, they were sawn asunder, were tempted, were slain with the sword: they wandered about in sheepskins and goatskins; being destitute, afflicted, tormented; (of whom the world was not worthy:) they wandered in deserts, and in mountains, and in dens and caves of the earth. And these all, having obtained a good report through faith, received not the promise: God having provided some better thing for us, that they without us should not be made perfect. [11:1-40]

From THE EPISTLE OF JAMES

Faith and Works. What doth it profit, my brethren, though a man say he hath faith, and have not works? can faith save him? If a brother or sister be naked, and destitute of daily food, and one of you say unto them, "Depart in peace, be ye warmed and filled"; notwithstanding ye give them not those things which are needful to the body; what doth it profit? Even so faith, if it hath not works, is dead, being alone. Yea, a man may say, "Thou hast faith, and I have works": shew me thy faith without thy works, and I will shew thee my faith by my works. Thou believest that there is one God; thou doest well: the devils also believe, and tremble. But wilt thou know, O vain man, that faith without works is dead? Was not Abraham our father justified by works, when he had offered Isaac his son upon the altar? Seest thou how faith wrought with his works, and by works was faith made perfect? And the scripture was fulfilled which saith, "Abraham believed God, and it was imputed unto him for righteousness: and he was called the Friend of God". Ye see then how that by works a man is justified, and not by faith only. Likewise also was not Rahab the harlot justified by works, when she had received the messengers, and had sent them out another way? For as the body without the spirit is dead, so faith without works is dead also.   [2:14–26]

From THE REVELATION OF JOHN
THE DIVINE

John's Vision. John to the seven churches which are in Asia: Grace be unto you, and peace, from him which is, and which was, and which is to come; and from the seven Spirits which are before his throne; and from Jesus Christ, who is the faithful witness, and the first begotten of the dead, and the prince of the kings of the earth. Unto him that loved us, and washed us from our sins in his own blood, and hath made us kings and priests unto God and his Father; to him be glory and dominion for ever and ever. Amen. Behold, he cometh with clouds; and every eye shall see him, and they also which pierced him: and all kindreds of the earth shall wail because of him. Even so, Amen.

"I am Alpha and Omega, the beginning and the ending," saith the Lord, which is, and which was, and which is to come, the Almighty.

I John, who also am your brother, and companion in tribulation, and in the kingdom and patience of Jesus Christ, was in the isle that is called Patmos, for the word of God, and for the testimony of Jesus Christ. I was in the Spirit on the Lord's day, and heard behind me a great voice, as of a trumpet, saying, "I am Alpha and Omega, the first and the last": and, "What thou seest, write in a book, and send it unto the seven churches which are in Asia; unto Ephesus, and unto Smyrna, and unto Pergamos, and unto Thyatira, and unto Sardis, and unto Philadelphia, and unto Laodicea". And I turned to see the voice that spake with me. And being turned, I saw seven golden candlesticks; and in the midst of the seven candlesticks one like unto the Son of man, clothed with a garment down to the foot, and girt about the paps with a golden girdle. His head and his hairs were white like wool, as white as snow; and his eyes were as a flame of fire; and his feet like unto fine brass, as if they burned in a furnace; and his voice as the sound of many waters. And he had in his right hand seven stars: and out of his mouth went a sharp twoedged sword: and his countenance was as the sun shineth in his strength. And when I saw him, I fell at his feet as dead. And he laid his right hand upon me, saying unto me, "Fear not; I am the first and the last: I am he that liveth, and was dead; and, behold, I am alive for evermore, Amen; and have the keys of hell and of death. Write the things which thou hast seen, and the things which are, and the things which shall be hereafter; the mystery of the seven stars which thou sawest in my right hand, and the seven golden candlesticks. The seven stars are the angels of the seven churches: and the seven candlesticks which thou sawest are the seven churches."

[1:4–20]

The Four Angels of the Apocalypse. And after these things I saw four angels standing on the four corners of the earth, holding the four winds of the earth, that the wind should not blow on the earth, nor on the sea, nor on any tree. And I saw another angel ascending from the east, having the seal of the living God: and he cried with a loud voice to the four angels, to whom it was given to hurt the earth and the sea, saying, "Hurt not the earth, neither the sea, nor the trees, till we have sealed the servants of our God in their foreheads". And I heard the number of them which were sealed: and there were sealed an hundred and forty and four thousand of all the tribes of the children of Israel.

. . . . .

After this I beheld, and, lo, a great multitude, which no man could number, of all nations, and kindreds, and people, and tongues, stood before the throne, and before the Lamb, clothed with white robes, and palms in their hands; and cried with a loud voice, saying, "Salvation to our God which sitteth upon the throne, and unto the Lamb". And all the angels stood round about the throne, and about the elders and the four beasts, and fell before the throne on their faces, and worshipped God, saying, "Amen: Blessing, and glory, and wisdom, and thanksgiving, and honour, and power, and might, be unto our God for ever and ever. Amen." And one of the elders answered, saying unto me, "What are these which are arrayed in white robes? and whence came they?" And I said unto him, "Sir, thou knowest". And he said to me, "These are they which came out of great tribulation, and have washed their robes, and made them white in the blood of the Lamb. Therefore are they before the throne of God, and serve him day and night in his temple: and he that sitteth on the throne shall dwell among them. They shall hunger no more, neither thirst any more; neither shall the sun light on them, nor any heat. For the Lamb which is in the midst of the throne shall feed them, and shall lead them unto living fountains of waters: and God shall wipe away all tears from their eyes."

[7:1–4, 9–17]

The Woman Clothed with the Sun. And there appeared a great wonder in heaven; a woman clothed with the sun, and the moon under her feet, and upon her head a crown of twelve stars: and she being with child cried, travailing in birth, and pained to be delivered. And there appeared another wonder in heaven; and behold a great red dragon, having seven heads and ten horns, and seven crowns upon his heads. And his tail drew the third part of the stars of heaven, and did cast them to the earth: and the dragon stood before the woman which was ready to be delivered, for to devour her child as soon as it was born. And she brought forth a man child, who was to rule all nations with a rod of iron: and her child was caught up unto God, and to his throne. And the woman fled into the wilderness, where she hath a place prepared of God, that they should feed her there a thousand two hundred and threescore days.

And there was war in heaven: Michael and his angels fought against the dragon; and the dragon fought and his angels, and prevailed not; neither was their place found any more in heaven. And the great dragon was cast out, that old serpent, called the Devil, and Satan, which deceiveth the whole world: he was cast out into the earth, and his angels were cast out with him. And I heard a loud voice saying in heaven, "Now is come salvation, and strength, and the kingdom of our God, and the power of his Christ: for the accuser of our brethren is cast down, which accused them before our God day and night. And they overcame him by the blood of the Lamb, and by the word of their testimony; and they loved not their lives unto the death. Therefore rejoice, ye heavens, and ye that dwell in them. Woe to the inhabiters of the earth and of the sea! for the devil is come down unto you, having great wrath, because he knoweth that he hath but a short time."

And when the dragon saw that he was cast unto the earth, he persecuted the woman which brought forth the man child. And to the woman were given two wings of a great eagle, that she might fly into the wilderness, into her place, where she is nourished for a time, and times, and half a time, from the face of the serpent. And the serpent cast out of his mouth water as a flood after the woman, that he might cause her to be carried away of the flood. And the earth helped the woman, and the earth opened her mouth, and swallowed up the flood which the dragon cast out of his mouth. And the dragon was wroth with the woman, and went to make war with the remnant of her seed, which keep the commandments of God, and have the testimony of Jesus Christ.   [12:1–17]

The Scarlet Woman and the Beast with Seven Heads. And there came one of the seven angels which had the seven vials, and talked with me, saying unto me, "Come hither; I will shew unto thee the judgment of the great whore that sitteth upon many waters: with whom the kings of the earth have committed fornication, and the inhabitants of the earth have been made drunk with the wine of her fornication". So he carried me away in the spirit into the wilderness: and I saw a woman sit upon a scarlet coloured beast, full of names of blasphemy, having seven heads and ten horns. And the woman was arrayed in purple and scarlet colour, and decked with gold and precious stones and pearls, having a golden cup in her hand full of abominations and filthiness of her fornication: and upon her forehead was a name written, MYSTERY, BABYLON THE GREAT, THE MOTHER OF HARLOTS AND ABOMINATIONS OF THE EARTH. And I saw the woman drunken with the blood of the saints, and with the blood of the martyrs of Jesus: and when I saw her, I wondered with great admiration.

And the angel said unto me, "Wherefore didst thou marvel? I will tell thee the mystery of the woman, and of the beast that carrieth her, which hath the seven heads and ten horns. The beast that thou sawest was, and is not; and shall ascend out of the bottomless pit, and go into perdition: and they that dwell on the earth shall wonder, whose names were not written in the book of life from the foundation of the world, when they behold the beast that was, and is not, and yet is. And here is the mind which hath wisdom. The seven heads are seven mountains, on which the woman sitteth. And there are seven kings: five are fallen, and one is, and the other is not yet come; and when he cometh, he must continue a short space. And the beast that was, and is not, even he is the eighth, and is of the seven, and goeth into perdition. And the ten horns which thou sawest are ten kings, which have received no kingdom as yet; but receive power as kings one hour with the beast. These have one mind, and shall give their power and strength unto the beast. These shall make war with the Lamb, and the Lamb shall overcome them: for he is Lord of lords, and King of kings: and they that are with him are called, and chosen, and faithful."

And he saith unto me, "The waters which thou sawest, where the whore sitteth, are peoples, and multitudes, and nations, and tongues. And the ten horns which thou sawest upon the beast, these shall hate the whore, and shall make her desolate and naked, and shall eat her flesh, and burn her with fire. For God hath put in their hearts to fulfil his will, and to agree, and give their kingdom unto the beast, until the words of God shall be fulfilled. And the woman which thou sawest is that great city, which reigneth over the kings of the earth." [17:1-18]

The New Jerusalem. And I saw a new heaven and a new earth: for the first heaven and the first earth were passed away; and there was no more sea. And I John saw the holy city, new Jerusalem, coming down from God out of heaven, prepared as a bride adorned for her husband. And I heard a great voice out of heaven saying, "Behold, the tabernacle of God is with men, and he will dwell with them, and they shall be his people, and God himself shall be with them, and be their God. And God shall wipe away all tears from their eyes; and there shall be no more death, neither sorrow, nor crying, neither shall there be any more pain: for the former things are passed away." And he that sat upon the throne said, "Behold, I make all things new". And he said unto me, "Write: for these words are true and faithful". And he said unto me, "It is done. I am Alpha and Omega, the beginning and the end. I will give unto him that is athirst of the fountain of the water of life freely. He that overcometh shall inherit all things; and I will be his God, and he shall be my son. But the fearful, and unbelieving, and the abominable, and murderers, and whoremongers, and sorcerers, and idolaters, and all liars, shall have their part in the lake which burneth with fire and brimstone: which is the second death."

And there came unto me one of the seven angels which had the seven vials full of the seven last plagues, and talked with me, saying, "Come hither, I will shew thee the bride, the Lamb's wife". And he carried me away in the spirit to a great and high mountain, and shewed me that great city, the holy Jerusalem, descending out of heaven from God, having the glory of God: and her light was like unto a stone most precious, even like a jasper stone, clear as crystal; and had a wall great and high, and had twelve gates, and at the gates twelve angels, and names written thereon, which are the names of the twelve tribes of the children of Israel: on the east three gates; on the north three gates; on the south three gates; and on the west three gates. And the wall of the city had twelve foundations, and in them the names of the twelve apostles of the Lamb.

And he that talked with me had a golden reed to measure the city, and the gates thereof, and the wall thereof. And the city lieth foursquare, and the length is as large as the breadth: and he measured the city with the reed, twelve thousand furlongs. The length and the breadth and the height of it are equal. And he measured the wall thereof, an hundred and forty and four cubits, according to the measure of a man, that is, of the angel. And the building of the wall of it was of jasper: and the city was pure gold, like unto clear glass. And the foundations of the wall of the city were garnished with all manner of precious stones. The first foundation was jasper; the second, sapphire; the third, a chalcedony; the fourth, an emerald; the fifth, sardonyx; the sixth, sardius; the seventh, chrysolite; the eighth, beryl; the ninth, a topaz; the tenth, a chrysoprasus; the eleventh, a jacinth; the twelfth, an amethyst. And the twelve gates were twelve pearls; every several gate was of one pearl: and the street of the city was pure gold, as it were transparent glass. And I saw no temple therein: for the Lord God Almighty and the Lamb are the temple of it. And the city had no need of the sun, neither of the moon, to shine in it: for the glory of God did lighten it, and the Lamb is the light thereof. And the nations of them which are saved shall walk in the light of it: and the kings of the earth do bring their glory and honour into it. And the gates of it shall not be shut at all by day: for there shall be no night there. And they shall bring the glory and honour of the nations into it. And there shall in no wise enter into it any thing that defileth, neither whatsoever worketh abomination, or maketh a lie: but they which are written in the Lamb's book of life.

[21:1–27]

APPENDICES

1. The Christian Era

Events in the Roman world were dated from the Founding of the City (*Ab Urbe Condita*), which by our modern reckoning was 754 B.C. The reckoning that Jesus was born in the year 754 A.U.C. was first made in the sixth century by a Scythian monk known as Dionysius the Little, so that thereafter 754 A.U.C. coincided with A.D. 1. Dionysius was, however, some years out in his calculation. It is clear from the narrative in Matthew that Jesus was born some time before the death of Herod the Great, which happened in 750 A.U.C. / 4 B.C. Modern scholars usually assign the birth of Jesus to 8 or 6 B.C.

2. Jehovah

Modern scholars more accurately render the name Yahweh (Jahveh). In Hebrew writing only consonants were written down; and *j* and *v* are equivalent to *y* and *w*. The word means *He is*. The English rendering "Jehovah" was apparently first used by Tyndale in his translation. The Hebrews had such veneration for Yahweh that they avoided the use of the Sacred Name, substituting "the Lord" whenever they had to speak of the Almighty.

3. The Tabernacle and the Ark

The making of the tabernacle, the sacred vessels, and the priestly vestments is described in considerable detail in Exodus 36–39. This tabernacle was a movable shrine, made of boards which could be fitted together and taken apart. It was covered with an outer covering of rams' skins dyed red, a second covering of goats' hair, and an inner covering of embroidered work. The tabernacle was divided into two chambers. The outer chamber was 20 cubits (30 feet) in length, 10 cubits wide, and 10 cubits high; it was known as the Holy Place and contained the seven-branched candlestick, the table of offering, and the altar of incense. The inner chamber, called the Holy of Holies, was 10 cubits long, 10 cubits wide, and 10 cubits high. Only the priests of the family of Aaron were allowed to enter the Holy Place, but the Holy of Holies was entered only by the High Priest once a year. All the sacred vessels were fitted with poles for carrying.

The ark was a chest of wood, overlaid with gold, 2½ cubits long and 1½ cubits wide and 1½ cubits high. At either end of the covering, known as the Mercy Seat, was a cherub of beaten gold, facing inward, with wings spread over the Mercy Seat. Within the ark rested the two tables of stone placed there by Moses. The ark was regarded as the actual resting place of Yahweh, and was thus the holiest of all sacred emblems.

In Joshua's attack on Jericho, the ark was carried by the priests before the people (p. 103). In Eli's time it was captured by the Philistines, but they soon sent it back (p. 137–39). Later, David with great ceremony brought the ark to Jerusalem (p. 162–64), where it rested in the tabernacle until, on the completion of Solomon's Temple, it was carried into the new Holy of Holies as the final ceremony in the solemn dedication; and there it was still standing at the time when I Kings was written. There is no mention of its final loss or destruction in the Old Testament. It is thus uncertain whether the ark was carried off on an occasion when the Temple treasures were plundered by some invader, or whether before the final sack of Jerusalem (p. 225–26) it was hidden away and still remains to be unearthed.

4. The Temple

The Temple at Jerusalem was first built by King Solomon (p. 185); it was destroyed by the Babylonians in 587 B.C. (p. 225–26). The Temple was rebuilt by the Jews who returned from Babylon in 515 B.C. This second Temple was replaced between 20 B.C. and A.D. 62 by a magnificent new building, begun by Herod the Great and only finally completed a few years before Jerusalem was destroyed by the Romans in A.D. 70. Jesus taught in the Temple of Herod.

5. Hebrew Poetry

Hebrew poetry had rhythm produced by stressed and unstressed syllables, but unlike European poetry, it was not controlled by any formal patterns of syllables, stresses, or rhymes. Instead, the poet wrote a series of balanced lines in which a thought expressed in one line is paralleled, contrasted, or augmented in the following. It is very rich in stirring metaphors, similes, often hyperbolical, with an imagery taken from nature and common experience. For an example:

> Be not far from me; for trouble is near;
> For there is none to help.
> Many bulls have compassed me;
> Strong bulls of Bashan have beset me round.
> They gaped upon me with their mouths,
> As a ravening and a roaring lion.
> I am poured out like water,
> And all my bones are out of joint:
> My heart is like wax;
> It is melted in the midst of my bowels.
> My strength is dried up like a potsherd,

And my tongue cleaveth to my jaws;
And thou hast brought me into the dust of death.

[Psalm 22:11–15]

Although the Book of Psalms is the principal collection of poetry, poems of all kinds are scattered through the Old Testament, and some of the prophetic books are also written in poetry.

6. The Magi

According to legend, the Wise Men (Magi) were three kings of the East, named Melchior, Gaspar, and Balthasar, of whom one was a Negro. Their gifts were symbolic: gold was for a king, incense for a god, and myrrh (an aromatic used in burials) foretold the death and burial of Jesus.

7. Herod

Several kings of the Jews named Herod are mentioned in the New Testament. Herod the Great (who reigned from 37–4 B.C.) was the son of Antipater, who had risen to power by his timely support of Julius Caesar. Antipater was lowborn and not even a Jew. Herod was a bloody-minded tyrant who murdered several of his relatives, including some of his own sons, but he maintained his power by always backing the victorious side in the civil wars of the Romans which followed the assassination of Julius Caesar. Herod the Great was a grandiose builder. His most famous building was the Temple of Jerusalem, but he also built pagan temples at Samaria and Cæsarea and elsewhere. Herod the Great was king when Jesus was born, and he ordered the slaughter of the Innocents (p. 355). When Herod the Great died, his kingdom was divided among his sons Archelaus, Antipas, and Philip II. After some years, Archelaus was deposed by the Roman Emperor Augustus. Herod Antipas was more successful. In A.D. 28 he went to Rome to visit the Emperor Tiberius and there fell in love with Herodias, the wife of his half brother Philip I, who lived in Rome as a private citizen. Herodias was a most ambitious woman, and when Antipas returned to Palestine she followed him with her daughter Salome. Antipas divorced his own wife and married Herodias, for which he was denounced by John the Baptist (p. 383). At Herodias' instigation, John was beheaded. Herod Antipas was also the Herod by whom Jesus was mocked (p. 438). Ultimately Antipas was deposed by the Emperor Caligula in A.D. 39; he was succeeded by Herod Agrippa I, who persecuted the early Christians (p. 505). He died in A.D. 44 (p. 507); and was succeeded by his son, Herod Agrippa II, before whom Paul was tried (p. 521).

8. The Samaritans

In the New Testament there is frequent mention of the bitter enmity between the Jews and the Samaritans. The Samaritans were descendants of the foreign settlers established by the Assyrians around the old capital of the Kingdom of Israel (p. 223–25). By the time of Jesus, they had developed a form of Judaism with a temple on Mount Gerizim which they regarded as the center of the true worship of Yahweh (p. 450). As Samaritan territory, bounded on the east by the Jordan, lay between Galilee on the north and Judæa on the south, anyone journeying from Galilee to Jerusalem had either to pass through Samaritan territory or make a considerable detour.

9. Pharisees, Scribes, and Sadducees

Among educated Jews two parties were conspicuous—the Pharisees and the Sadducees. The Pharisees (or "the Separated") were those who accepted the principle of rabbinical interpretation of the Written Law; the Sadducees insisted rather on a literal observance of the Written Law.

Jewish scholars reject the charge that the Pharisees were rigid legalists in their observation of the many oral traditions arising out of the Law, especially the observance of the Sabbath rest and the intricate laws concerning worship and ritual purity. The scribes (lawyers) were men who had received a long training in the Mosaic Law and its traditions; but they were not professional lawyers (as the word is now understood) and many of them worked also at some manual trade. Students and interpreters of the Law were honored by the title of "Rabbi." Both Pharisees and scribes were highly regarded by the common people, who were hostile to all foreign domination and influence.

The Sadducees were laxer in their practices, and were found particularly among the governing classes. They had less reluctance to mixing with non-Jews and many of them were well-disposed to Greek and Roman culture. The High Priest and his circle were Sadducees.

10. The Synagogue

The synagogue in the time of Jesus (as today) was a building set apart for prayer and instruction wherever a congregation of Jews had been established. It contained an ark (or chest) wherein scrolls of the Scriptures were kept and a pulpit. The Jews gathered in their synagogue every Sabbath for the recitation of prayers and the reading of the Scriptures, which was followed by an instruction. There were no regularly appointed clergy, but each synagogue was under the charge of a ruler of the synagogue who might call upon anyone whom he considered capable of giving instruction.

11. The Roman Governor, Publicans, and Sinners

In the time of Jesus, Palestine was a Roman Province, governed by a procurator or governor sent out from Rome. The procurator at the time of the crucifixion was Pontius

Pilate, who was notorious for his dislike of the Jews and for his cruelty. The Romans collected taxes through *publicani*—contractors who paid a fixed sum to the procurator; they reimbursed themselves by gathering the taxes directly from Jewish citizens. Publicans were regarded by their fellow Jews as contemptible. Jews regarded all who in any way broke the Mosaic laws as "sinners"; the term applied not only to lax Jews but also to all Gentiles, i.e., non-Jews. In the gospels "gentiles" are usually the Romans. Orthodox Jews refused to eat with "sinners," publicans, or Gentiles.

12. Mary Magdalene

Luke (7:37–50) records that a woman who was a "sinner" (which does not necessarily mean a harlot) anointed the feet of Jesus when he was at supper with Simon the Pharisee (p. 407). In 8:2–3, Luke notes that certain women ministered to Jesus, among them "Mary called Magdalene, out of whom went seven devils"; and in 10:41–42, Luke also records the reply of Jesus when Martha complained that her sister Mary left her to serve the guests alone (p. 410). Matthew, Mark, and John note that Mary Magdalene was one of the women who stood by the cross when Jesus was crucified. John records that Mary, the sister of Martha and Lazarus of Bethany, was present when Lazarus was raised from the dead (p. 462–64); that shortly afterward she anointed the feet of Jesus while he was at supper with Simon the leper (p. 464). After the resurrection Mary Magdalene was the first to whom Jesus appeared (p. 482–83). In popular tradition Mary Magdalene, Mary the sister of Martha, and the unnamed sinner were all the same person; but many authorities, ancient and modern, have questioned this identity. In older English, the name Magdalene was often spelled Maudlyn and was so pronounced (as still in the colleges of that name at Oxford and Cambridge).

INDEX

Biblical Subjects Most Popular with Artists

Many sacred pictures are based not only on the Bible narratives but on non-canonical books and stories which were not included in the New Testament, especially pictures dealing with incidents in the life of Our Lady. References are to pages in this book.